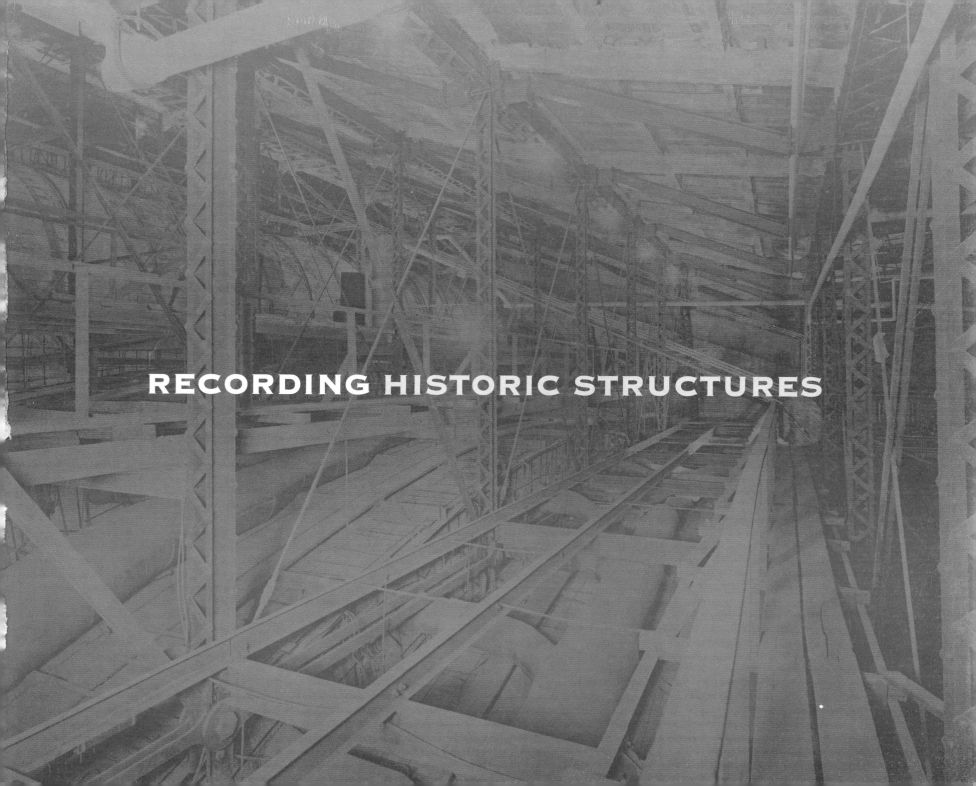

RECORDING HISTORIC STRUCTURES

RECORDING HISTORIC STRUCTURES

SECOND EDITION

Edited by John A. Burns
and the Staff of the Historic American Buildings Survey,
Historic American Engineering Record,
and Historic American Landscapes Survey

National Park Service
U.S. Department of the Interior
in cooperation with
The American Institute of Architects

WILEY

JOHN WILEY & SONS, INC.

Library of Congress Cataloging-in-Publication Data:
Recording historic structures / edited by John A. Burns and the staff of the Historic American Buildings
Survey, Historic American Engineering Record, and Historic American Landscapes Survey, National Park
Service, U.S. Department of the Interior.—2nd ed.
    p.   cm.
Includes bibliographical references and index.
  ISBN 0-471-27380-5 (alk. paper)
  1. Historic preservation—United States. 2. Historic buildings—Conservation and restoration—United
States. I. Burns, John A. II. Historic American Buildings Survey/Historic American Engineering
Record. III. Historic American Landscapes Survey.
  E159 .R425 2004
  363 .6'9'0973—dc21

Printed in the United States of America

10 9 8 7 6 5 4 3 2 1

This book is dedicated to

the continuum of talented

and committed individuals

who, over seven decades, have

developed the standards and

guidelines of the Historic

American Buildings Survey,

the Historic American

Engineering Record, and

the Historic American

Landscapes Survey.

CONTENTS

FOREWORD

In his foreword to the 1989 edition of *Recording Historic Structures,* Charles Peterson, then a mere 82 years old, reflected on the inception and the history of the Historic American Buildings Survey (HABS). He noted its development from a 1930s unemployment relief program to the current combination of National Park Service projects and summer academic programs.

He referenced the charter for HABS and the role of the American Institute of Architects, which, together with the Library of Congress, continues to guide this critical work.

My own connection with measured drawings of existing buildings began at the University of Manchester, where the examination and delineation of existing buildings was used to teach hand and mechanical drawing, a knowledge of historical styles, an understanding of building details, and an appreciation of craftsmanship. At the time, Professor Reginald Cordingley, a master draftsman of the old school, was leading a national movement to awaken an interest in vernacular architecture. Therefore, the range of buildings we scrutinized extended beyond the great works of the classical tradition to include farmhouses, barns, and other buildings whose forms were generated by utility.

More than 25 years ago, I decided that my students in a professional degree program in architecture would find as much enjoyment as I had found in learning from real buildings instead of just imagining new ones. A retrospective exhibit in April 2002 gave me the chance to ask the ultimate question of these former students, and their responses were positive and overwhelming. Many of them echoed Wes Good, AIA, senior vice president of Kirksey Architects in Houston, Texas, who said, "Measuring Grimes County Courthouse in 1989 was one of the most memorable times in my college career. Beyond the re-creation of a beautiful building on paper, I learned the importance of detail, scale, and proportion in architecture."

The Grimes County Courthouse documentation was also important, since the team achieved first place in the competition for the Charles E. Peterson Prize that year. This national competition has attracted an increasing number of programs across the United States to participate in summer documentation projects. While the gain for the Library of Congress collection is obvious, the gain in learning from our architectural heritage has been of immeasurable benefit to the professions, and to society at large.

As more and more professional work focuses on existing building stock, the HABS graduate plays a critical role in guiding the wise use of these historic resources. Indeed, the recent interest by our engineering colleagues and the development of the Historic American Engineering Record (HAER) and the Historic American Landscape Survey (HALS) suggest that future preservation teams will have the benefit of a rich lode of talent.

Too often, education focuses on individual accomplishment, as evidenced by the ever-increasing use of the standardized test or the evaluation of the studio design project. Yet successful practice has always required a team approach, based on individual ability in a given field, but open to respectful dialogue with others.

Here again, the production of measured drawings, whether the subject is a simple house or a major institutional structure, relies on the ability of individuals to work together. Sylvia LaPoint, now in practice in Dallas, Texas, noted, "Very seldom does a student work with a group on a design project. The HABS course was not only rewarding for the skills learned, but also for the opportunity to work with a team. The sharing of ideas, solving difficult situations, finding new ways to measure and record, working with a team as professionals, all responsible for the final product. What a great experience; after all, it is teamwork that makes our professional life as architects successful."

The 25-year celebration of the relationship between Texas A&M and HABS in 2002 gave me the opportunity to gather many statements such as this, and to note that many of the friendships formed through HABS projects have endured over many years—one has actually blossomed into marriage. While the latter may have been an extreme example, it perhaps embodies the depth of commitment inherent in a true love of place and the high level of respect we have for those with whom we work.

As the technology of documentation develops, and equipment becomes more sophisticated, I find that an analogy to medicine becomes even more apt. We happily talk about diagnostics and testing, and technology enables us to get information through laser-based tools and remote sensing. However, knowledge remains our primary stock-in-trade and is applied only though understanding honed by experience. A proper diagnosis must be built on facts, but treatment can be prescribed only from a strong foundation of experience.

This new edition of *Recording Historic Structures* continues to teach methods of learning by doing, and I am delighted to commend it to the next generation as the basis for an exploration that will change them forever. May the disciplined approach, careful measure, respect for the team, and delight in developing your own understanding of the subject be as rewarding for you as they have been for generations of your predecessors.

DAVID G. WOODCOCK, FAIA
Department of Architecture
Texas A&M University

FOREWORD TO THE 1989 EDITION

I am glad to have the opportunity to tell you readers a bit about the history of HABS, which I helped found. It all began with a long, detailed memorandum dated November 13, 1933, which served as the charter for the Historic American Buildings Survey. HABS, as it became known, was quickly implemented by the National Park Service and first staffed by architects Thomas T. Waterman, called back from a study visit to Britain, and John P. O'Neil, an architectural graduate of Notre Dame University with some archaeological experience in Latin America. Work proceeded with such speed that within weeks it was possible to have a showing of fine measured drawings from across the country at the National Museum in Washington.

Waterman was mainly responsible for the architectural standards of the recording work. He had a solid background, having made field records of the Cathedral at Palma in the Balearics for Ralph Adams Cram. While working with Perry, Shaw and Hepburn in Williamsburg, he had published (John A. Barrows) a landmark volume, *The Domestic Colonial Architecture of Tidewater Virginia* (New York and London, 1932), which featured measured drawings with exquisite attention to details of work in brick and wood.

Quite apart from whatever value measured drawings may have as a historical record, the process of measuring and drawing careful records to scale is the most effective way to gain an understanding of a building's fabric. Someone has aptly called it "graphic analysis."

In schools of architecture today, students are taught to "talk architecture" and even make pretty pictures or models of things which could—or could not—be built. But there is no way to appreciate an existing, working structure—its virtues and its failures—like making a careful drawing of it. The man who doesn't get his hands dirty on the job will never know enough.

The high quality of architectural delineation in HABS work of the 1930s was due to the skill of the draftsmen recruited with the help of the HABS National Advisory Board and the American Institute of Architects. The early employees were all architects. There wasn't a building full of people; the administrative staff was small, and the architects had the historical training necessary to do the work. Standards of presentation were achieved by circulating memoranda to field parties. These were compiled in the haste and battle smoke of the emergency campaign to relieve professional unemployment—the overriding problem of the period.

World War II understandably closed down HABS (though Waterman continued to make drawings surreptitiously in a Bureau of Yards and Docks drafting room). When the war ended, the Park Service resumed making HABS records of its own historic buildings while preparing for restoration plans. But new questions arose when substantial funds under the Park Service Mission 66 Program became available with the mandate to record structures outside of government management. The innovation of summer programs employing architectural students brought new problems in directing field parties of beginners, often in remote places.

At this time, we started using the 1930s instructions to guide the work. But the need for an overall handy reference volume became apparent and it was decided to produce one. Who had the field experience—working under Park Service rules and regulations—to tackle the job?

Among the outstanding leaders I had recruited to run the teams in the East was Professor Harley J. McKee of Syracuse University. I had met him during the first Society of Architectural Historians summer field trip, which toured Nantucket Island and Martha's Vineyard in August 1951. McKee had a sharp eye, a clear, discriminating mind, and a long-term interest in American buildings. He had run student teams through several successful seasons, the last one being at Charleston, South Carolina. McKee was the man for the job.

Professor McKee spent two entire summers in our Philadelphia office compiling a set of instructions to the field. The only complete set of circulars from the WPA days was a collection lately inherited from Earl H. Reed, FAIA, of Chicago, one of the original HABS district officers, who had later served as national advisor to the program. I worked very closely with McKee, and it was a pleasure. As the various parts of the new book were drafted, they were mimeographed and sent to the field for comment and recommendations. At the end of the 1961 recording season we had a measured drawings manual of 109 pages, which seemed to serve the purpose.

In 1970 architect James C. Massey, originally a student recruited from the University of Pennsylvania who eventually served as national head of HABS in Washington, directed a handsome production of McKee's work, *Recording Historic Buildings,* through the U.S. Government Printing Office. For that he deserves great credit.

We are now to have a new version for a new generation of readers and users. I wish you well.

CHARLES E. PETERSON, FAIA
Former Supervising Architect for Historic Structures
Eastern Office of Design and Construction
National Park Service
Philadelphia
June 1988

PREFACE

The second edition of *Recording Historic Structures* is the third formal publication the National Park Service has authored on documenting the historic built environment, preceded by the 1989 first edition and the 1970 book *Recording Historic Buildings*. More than 70 new illustrations enhance this edition, and new case studies reflect growing interest in vernacular architecture, historic bridges, and historic landscapes, as well as the stewardship of memorials and monuments in the national parks. The Secretary of the Interior's *Guidelines for Architectural and Engineering Documentation*, which appears in the appendix, has been revised to include the Historic American Landscapes Survey program, E-size drawings, and large-format color transparencies. In addition, Level IV documentation has been dropped from the current version of the Secretary's *Guidelines*. Paralleling this, the inventory chapter from the first edition was not included in this edition of *Recording Historic Structures*.

The most significant difference between this edition and the last, however, is the inclusion of digital technologies, both in recording historic structures and sites and in making the documentation accessible to the public. Discussed are computer-aided drafting, digital convergent photogrammetry, laser scanning, digital photography, and Internet research and access. The effect of these technologies on HABS, HAER, and HALS is most visible to the public in the Library of Congress's *Built in America* Web site, which makes digital copies of the drawings, photographs, and histories in the programs' collections readily accessible to anyone with Internet access.

The National Park Service looks forward to continuing its partnership with the Library of Congress and affiliated professional organizations that support the work of HABS, HAER, and now HALS. This new edition of *Recording Historic Structures* will serve as a guide for private preservation professionals and college students who participate in documentation efforts in the twenty-first century.

PREFACE TO THE 1989 EDITION

America has a long, rich architectural and engineering heritage, as evidenced by our built environment. The study of historic structures provides insight into the ways in which earlier generations lived and worked. Through the techniques discussed in *Recording Historic Structures,* that heritage is being documented so that many future generations can understand and appreciate their rich heritage.

Recording Historic Structures will assist individuals in preparing documentation (usually measured drawings, large-format photographs, and histories) for inclusion in the Historic American Buildings Survey/Historic American Engineering Record (HABS/HAER) collections maintained by the Library of Congress. *Recording Historic Structures* is the principal handbook, the bible, so to speak, of the HABS/HAER programs for those who are interested in America's historic architecture, engineering, and industry and who wish to see that heritage documented for subsequent generations. The book is thus indispensable for the student architect, photographer, or historian working on a HABS/HAER summer recording team, as well as for the professional who has been hired to document, to HABS/HAER standards, historic structures that are about to be demolished or substantially altered as a result of federal action.

The book is also intended for another group of individuals: those interested in the general principles of architectural, engineering, and industrial documentation used to prepare drawings, photographs, and data pages to archival standards, and in the general requirements of documenting historic structures. *Recording Historic Structures* is not only a handbook directed specifically to the preparation of HABS/HAER documentation; it also covers the broader principles applicable to the field.

The gestation of the book began after the "Secretary of the Interior's Standards and Guidelines for Architectural and Engineering Documentation" were published in 1983. Harley J. McKee's predecessor to this volume, *Recording Historic Buildings,* had gone out of print. Diane Maddex of Preservation Press had approached HABS/HAER about reprinting McKee's book as a classic work in preservation literature, prompting discussions within HABS/HAER over whether to reprint, revise, or replace *Recording Historic Buildings,* a text which had over the previous decade and a half become a familiar sight on the bookshelves of persons interested in preserving and documenting historic structures. A committee of HABS/HAER staff members, chaired by Deputy Chief Sally Kress Tompkins, was formed to discuss the options. Ultimately a consensus emerged from the committee that a new handbook was needed. It was decided that senior staff members would author chapters in their areas of expertise.

I selected John Burns to be the overall editor based on his knowledge of the HABS/HAER recording process, his knowledge of architecture and photography, and his excellent writing ability. Sometimes John and I would meet daily for weeks on end to iron out problems. In the end, it was John who made this book work.

At one time or another, virtually the entire staff of HABS/HAER has worked on the preparation of the manuscript, whether researching, writing, typing, gathering illustrations, or providing peer review. Their years of accumulated field experience plus thousands of measured drawings, photographs, and pages of historical and descriptive data are synthesized in the pages of this volume.

Since the founding of HABS in 1933, more than 3,000 men and women have worked with the Historic American Buildings Survey/ Historic American Engineering Record to "preserve" approximately 22,000 historic structures throughout the United States, using documentation processes described in this book. At least one-third of these structures have been lost to us forever. But the historical documentation sits safely in the Library of Congress.

Through written studies, measured drawings, and photographs stored in the Library of Congress collections, a permanent record now exists that is accessible to the public. In fact, these records represent the most widely used of all the special collections of the library. This architectural and engineering documentation will continue to provide future generations with information on our precious built heritage long after the structures themselves have disappeared.

We hope that the methods explained here and the structures already documented will inspire students, professionals, and others interested in architecture, engineering, history, photography, and landscape to continue this important quest.

ROBERT J. KAPSCH, CHIEF
Historic American Buildings Survey/
Historic American Engineering Record

ACKNOWLEDGMENTS

Recording Historic Structures draws heavily on the accumulated knowledge and writings of former HABS and HAER employees who produced the early "Bulletins," "Circulars," and "Specifications," and the more recent "Field Instructions" and "Procedures Manuals." It also owes a special debt to the National Park Service people involved with *Recording Historic Buildings,* the predecessor to this book. Charles E. Peterson, then supervising architect for historic structures, identified the need for a handbook students could use and hired the late Harley J. McKee to produce the text. McKee, working under Peterson's supervision and with the assistance of HABS architect James C. Massey, wrote the "Manual of the Historic American Buildings Survey" in several parts and it was issued starting in 1961. In 1968, under Massey's supervision as chief of HABS, parts were first published collectively under the title "Recording Historic Buildings." That offset edition of 1968 was further refined and ultimately became the book *Recording Historic Buildings* in 1970. The first edition of *Recording Historic Structures* was published in 1989.

The second edition of *Recording Historic Structures* owes its existence to a collaborative effort among a large number of people. The other authors and I would like to acknowledge and thank these people for their contributions. Chief of HABS/HAER/HALS Blaine Cliver supported and allowed staff the time to work on the second edition. Many of the program's professional staff provided suggestions for additions and improvements based on more than a decade of field experience with the first edition, including Lisa Davidson, Gigi Price, Tom Behrens, Christopher Marston, Richard O'Connor, and Justin Spivey.

Todd Croteau updated the maritime case study with recent recording technologies. Martin Perschler updated the guidelines for HABS/HAER/HALS Standards to include HALS, E-size drawing sheets, and color transparencies. Jennifer Baldwin expanded and updated the bibliography. Kelly Young was responsible for assembling more than 250 high-resolution digital images of the illustrations and their associated captions and credits.

Robert Score, AIA, helped expand the case study on structural and mechanical systems to include the laser-scanned documentation of the Auditorium Building's hydraulic stage equipment. Kit Peterson provided technical guidance on the Library of Congress' *Built in America* Web site. Dr. Dario Gasparini, Dr. Tom Boothby, Stephen Buonopane, Dr. Benjamin Schafer, and Justin Spivey helped HAER pioneer its bridge engineering analysis program. Cari Goetcheus and Tim Davis provided valuable input and insight for the landscape architecture case study.

Joseph Demkin, AIA, and Pamela James Blumgart at the American Institute of Architects, and Amanda Miller from John Wiley and Sons, oversaw the conversion of raw manuscript text and illustrations into the completed book. The vast majority of the illustrations were printed from high-resolution digital scans downloaded from the Library of Congress' *Built in America* Web site. Scans of documentation not yet transmitted to the Library of Congress were produced by Kelly Young and James Lewin.

JOHN A. BURNS, FAIA
Deputy Chief and Principal Architect, HABS/HAER/HALS

The methodologies and technologies used by the Historic American Buildings Survey, Historic American Engineering Record, and Historic American Landscapes Survey are discussed in Part 1, beginning with the history and evolution of the programs since HABS was founded in 1933. The formal documentation, hard copy measured and interpretive drawings, large-format photographs, and written historical and descriptive data appear to have changed little in the intervening seven decades.

On the other hand, new technologies have become integral tools in the production of HABS, HAER, and HALS documentation. The Internet facilitates access to remote archives and collections, extending the breadth and reach of contemporary historical research. The large-format view camera has long dominated documentary photography. However, digital photography is making gains in resolution and archival stability and may some day supplant traditional continuous-tone films. The tools used to produce the drawings have evolved from hand measurements and drawings made with T-square, triangle, and ruling pens to computer-generated drawings produced from laser scans. The methodology and technologies used to develop each type of formal documentation are described in the following chapters.

PART 1

RECORDING

METHODS

CHAPTER 1

OVERVIEW
John A. Burns

*R*ecording Historic Structures *is the basic guide for creating architectural, engineering, and landscape documentation to the standards of the Historic American Buildings Survey (HABS), the Historic American Engineering Record (HAER), and the Historic American Landscapes Survey (HALS) of the National Park Service. While the book primarily focuses on production of documentation for the archival collections of HABS, HAER, and HALS, the methods and techniques described can be used to examine and record structures for other purposes as well.*

To simplify the language in the book, the word structure *will be used to refer to any building, site, structure, or object, with no distinction made between architecture (HABS), engineering (HAER), or landscapes (HALS).*

What Is Architectural, Engineering, and Landscape Documentation?

With the help of architectural, engineering, and landscape documentation, we should be able to study a structure without visiting it. This type of documentation combines both graphic and written records to explain and illustrate the significant characteristics of a historic structure. Graphic records most commonly are photographs and drawings. Photographic records can include contemporary and historic photographs and photographic copies of historic documents or illustrations. Drawings may be historic drawings, measured drawings, or interpretive drawings. Measured drawings are produced from measurements taken from the structure being documented. Interpretive drawings can be measured but may be schematic, illustrating process or function. Written records are both historical and descriptive. Written historical records are based on research to determine the chronology and context of the structure being documented. Descriptive records are based on inspection of the physical fabric of the structure.

Background of HABS, HAER, and HALS

HABS, HAER, and HALS records are a particular form of architectural, engineering, and landscape documentation that has evolved since the founding of HABS in 1933. Charles E. Peterson proposed the establishment of HABS to his National Park Service superiors in a memorandum that also determined the survey's initial direction:

> The plan I propose is to enlist a qualified group of architects and draftsmen to study, measure and draw up the plans, elevations and details of the important antique buildings of the United States. Our architectural heritage of buildings

from the last four centuries diminishes daily at an alarming rate. The ravages of fire and the natural elements together with the demolition and alterations caused by real estate "improvements" form an inexorable tide of destruction destined to wipe out the great majority of the buildings which knew the beginning and first flourish of the nation. The comparatively few structures which can be saved by extraordinary effort and presented as exhibition houses and museums or altered and used for residences or minor commercial uses comprise only a minor percentage of the interesting and important architectural specimens which remain from the old days. It is the responsibility of the American people that if the great number of our antique buildings must disappear through economic causes, they should not pass into unrecorded oblivion. . . .

The list of building types . . . should include public buildings, churches, residences, bridges, forts, barns, mills, shops, rural outbuildings, and any other kind of structure of which there are good specimens extant. . . . Other structures which would not engage the especial interest of an architectural connoisseur are the great number of plain structures which by fate or accident are identified with historic events.

Peterson's memorandum included a recommendation that the survey should not document structures built after 1860. A logical end point, the date determined the type and style of buildings that would dominate the early recording efforts of HABS. The recommendation

implied that buildings should be at least seventy-three years old to be considered historic, and it eliminated from consideration the huge number of buildings constructed in the last part of the nineteenth century.

Given these limitations, the body of buildings to be studied was relatively small and included a limited number of building types and materials of construction. Before 1860, brick, stone, and wood were the predominant construction materials. The format designed for the documentation was correspondingly simple and straightforward. The drawing sheet size accommodated structures of roughly 60′ × 80′ at the common scale of ¼″ = 1′0″, which allowed most pre-1860 buildings to fit on a single sheet. The drawing format was horizontal; the need to document tall buildings was outside the scope of early HABS work.

Another factor that influenced early recordings was the fact that HABS was designed as relief employment for unemployed architects. The funds were targeted for salaries, not materials or equipment, and the labor-intensive measured drawings were the dominant means of recording. At the time, these drawings defined HABS. The program is still known primarily as a measured drawings collection (see fig. 1.1). By contrast, the accompanying early photographs and histories seem inadequate by current standards.

Interestingly, despite its emphasis on buildings and its staff primarily made up of architects, HABS recorded a broad range of the built environment, including vernacular architecture, bridges, canals, mills, street furniture, gardens, and what we would today call cultural landscapes.

Seventy years later, the circumstances have changed. The labor-intensive nature of hand measuring and drafting, ideal for relief employment, is expensive. Students have been substi-

tuted for the professionals employed in the early days. Following National Register of Historic Places criteria, buildings come of age historically in just fifty years, which means that HABS increasingly is documenting buildings younger than itself (see fig. 1.2).

After 1860, manufactured building materials began to dominate construction. Structural systems changed as well, from simple bearing wall or post-and-beam construction to balloon and platform frame, steel skeleton, and reinforced concrete (see fig. 1.3). Composite materials and systems became common. Building systems—including heating, plumbing, gas, electrical, and vertical movement—developed as an integral part of almost every building.

Paralleling these developments in the building industry were even broader changes in engineering and industry. By the 1960s interest in America's technological heritage was growing. Gail Hathaway, past president of the American Society of Civil Engineers (ASCE) and chairman of ASCE's History and Heritage Committee, approached the National Park Service with the idea of setting up a companion program to HABS that would record historic engineering and industrial sites. The Historic American Engineering Record (HAER) was established in 1969, and HABS managed the first recording efforts of the fledgling program until congressional funding could be secured. In 2000 the National Park Service founded the Historic American Landscapes Survey (HALS), in cooperation with the American Society of Landscape Architects and the Library of Congress. As were HAER's, the first HALS projects are being managed by HABS until congressional funding is obtained.

The founding of HAER and HALS reflected the growing interest in all aspects of the built environment as well as the changing scope and emphasis of documentary recording (see figs. 1.4, 1.5, and 1.6). Changes such as these have

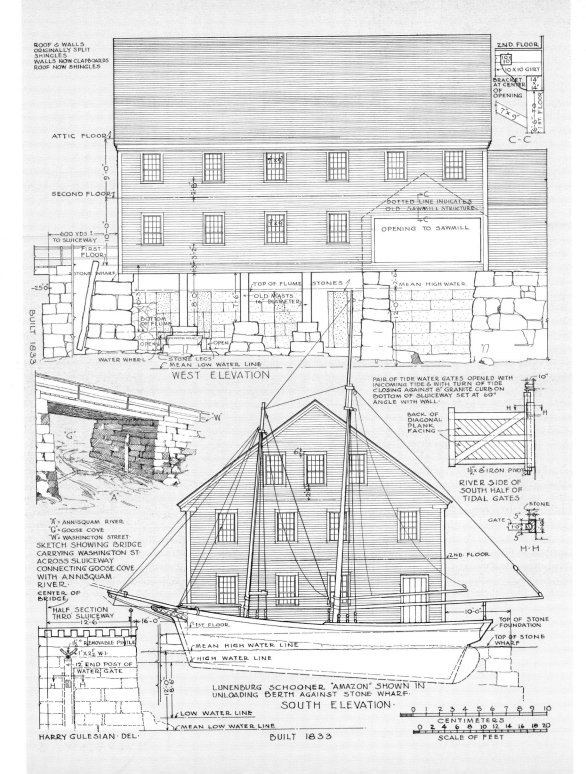

forced reassessment and adjustment in the HABS/HAER/HALS methodology and will continue to do so. In the future, such changes will be governed by (1) the resources available to produce documentation, (2) the actual structures considered historic and significant, and (3) the research materials available on those structures.

HAER recording expanded the scope of the collections to include large and technologically complex structures, linear resources such as roads and railroads, and industrial processes (*see fig. 1.7*). Interpretive and process drawings and narrative histories had to be added to explain engineering and industrial sites. The HALS program brings different challenges, from seasonal and temporal changes to the need to document movement through the landscape.

Given the greatly increased universe of structures that HABS, HAER, and HALS are mandated to survey and the limited resources available, the three programs will, of necessity, become more selective about which structures they record.

HABS/HAER/HALS Standards

Throughout their history, HABS and HAER have had consistent standards concerning the size, format, and reproducibility of documentation. The resulting uniformity in format and reproducibility set these collections apart from most other collections of architectural, engineering,

Figure 1.1
Early in the HABS program, architecture, industry, and a sailing vessel were recorded on one densely composed sheet. Close inspection reveals a framing detail, three details of a tidal gate, and a sketch of an adjacent bridge.

Figure 1.2
HABS is recording buildings younger than itself, in this case the Walter Gropius house of 1937 in Lincoln, Massachusetts.

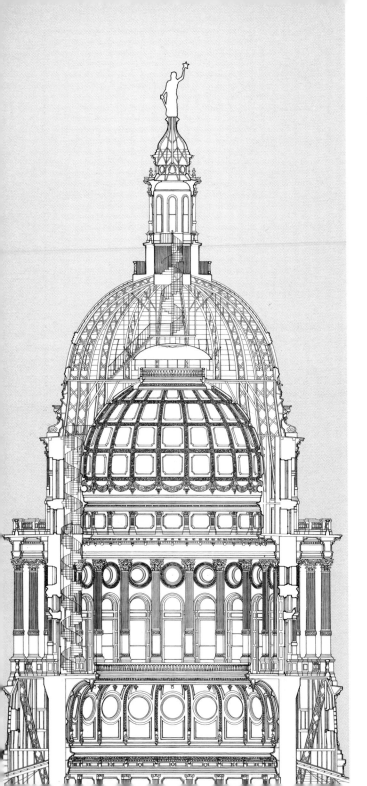

Figure 1.3
A HABS initiative to record state capitols resulted in this CAD section drawing through the sheet-metal dome of the Texas Capitol in Austin. Compare it with a hand-delineated drawing of the Maryland State House in Annapolis (see fig. 4.42).

and landscape documentation and make them easily accessible to users.

The National Historic Preservation Act, as amended in 1980, directed the secretary of the interior to develop "a uniform process and standards for documenting historic properties by public agencies and private parties for purposes of incorporation into, or complementing, the national historical architectural and engineering records within the Library of Congress." These standards derived from HABS and HAER standards. "The Secretary of the Interior's Standards and Guidelines for Architectural and Engineering Documentation" were published in 1983 as part of "Archeology and Historic Preservation, Secretary of the Interior's Standards and Guidelines" (*Federal Register*, September 29, 1983). The 1983 guidelines were updated in 2003 to add E-size drawings (34″ × 44″) and large-format color transparencies, to drop Level IV documentation, and to incorporate the HALS program. The four standards remain unchanged. The standards and guidelines are hereafter referred to as HABS/HAER/HALS standards (see Appendix A).

HABS/HAER/HALS Standard I covers content, requiring documentation to adequately explain and illustrate what is significant or valuable about the structure being recorded. Standard II addresses quality, requiring accurate preparation of documentation from reliable sources and stating clear limitations to permit independent verification of information. Standard III requires use of readily reproducible, durable, standard-size materials for preparation of documentation. Standard IV specifies that documentation must be produced clearly and concisely.

Why Document?

Architectural, engineering, and landscape documentation broadens our experience of U.S. history. The historic built environment is frequently the only tangible evidence of history, and historic structures can open new doors to understanding the past. They can be significant for their characteristics and features as well as for their association with people and events. As artifacts, they can provide insights into past cultures and activities, events, and people.

If a structure is significant—whether for its history, design, sentiment, or some other criterion—some means of preservation can usually be found. Continued use is the most common and best form of preservation, ideal for structures that have not lost their functional usefulness (see fig. 1.8). Other historic structures have been adapted to new uses or turned into museums (see fig. 1.9). A major problem with preserving historic structures is their size. The vast majority of historic structures, being too large to move, must be preserved in place (see fig. 1.10).

One important purpose for architectural, engineering, and landscape documentation is academic study. The records can provide a way to investigate artifacts from the past that may otherwise be too scattered or too difficult to visit or that have subsequently disappeared. Some artifacts whose physical remains are gone may exist only in documentation.

Architectural, engineering, and landscape documentation can be used to record historic

Figure 1.4
A shaft of light illuminates the work area as molten metal is poured from a furnace into molds at the American Brass Company in Buffalo. Industrial photography presents challenges to the photographer, who must explain and interpret a production process, often under difficult lighting conditions.

Figure 1.5
HAER's long-standing interest in documenting iron and steel industry structures was realized in a series of congressionally mandated projects in Pennsylvania and Alabama. The 12,000-ton hydraulic forging press shown here is the only surviving example of heavy steel forging from the turn of the twentieth century. Built for the U.S. Steel Corporation's Homestead Works by the Bethlehem Steel Corporation in 1903, the press was designed to shape steel into armor plate by exerting 12,000 tons of pressure on large, heated steel ingots. The U.S. Navy used armor produced by the Homestead Works to construct battleships such as the USS Missouri *from the Spanish-American War era to World War II.*

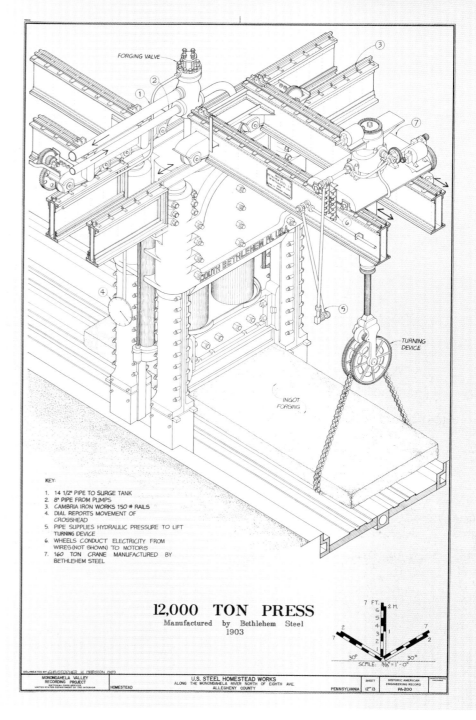

KEY:
1. 14 1/2" PIPE TO SURGE TANK
2. 8" PIPE FROM PUMPS
3. CAMBRIA IRON WORKS 150 # RAILS
4. DIAL REPORTS MOVEMENT OF CROSSHEAD
5. PIPE SUPPLIES HYDRAULIC PRESSURE TO LIFT TURNING DEVICE
6. WHEELS CONDUCT ELECTRICITY FROM WIRES (NOT SHOWN) TO MOTORS
7. 160 TON CRANE MANUFACTURED BY BETHLEHEM STEEL

12,000 TON PRESS
Manufactured by Bethlehem Steel
1903

SCALE: 3/8" = 1'-0"

MONONGAHELA VALLEY RECORDING PROJECT
NATIONAL PARK SERVICE
UNITED STATES DEPARTMENT OF THE INTERIOR

HOMESTEAD

U.S. STEEL HOMESTEAD WORKS
ALONG THE MONONGAHELA RIVER NORTH OF EIGHTH AVE,
ALLEGHENY COUNTY

PENNSYLVANIA

SHEET 12 13

HISTORIC AMERICAN ENGINEERING RECORD
PA-200

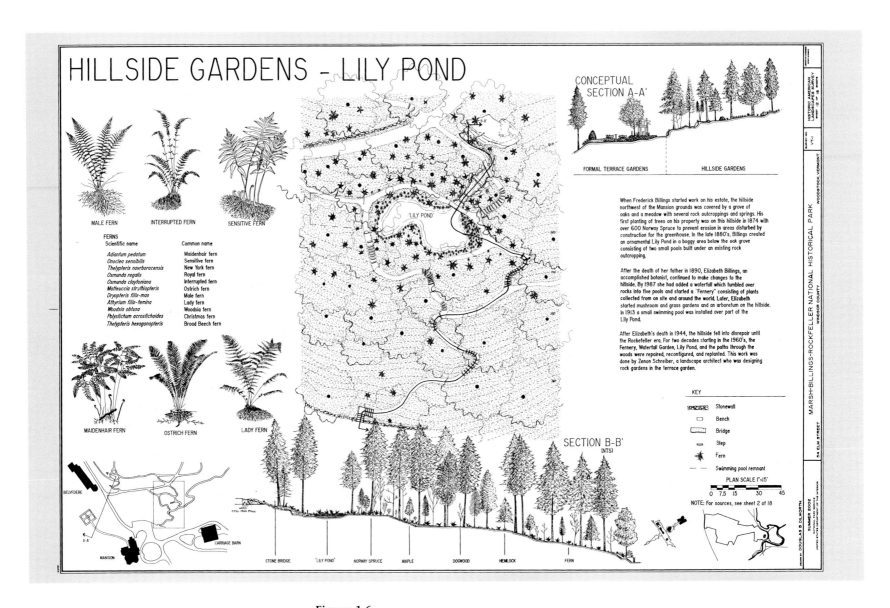

Figure 1.6

The first HALS project was conducted at Marsh-Billings-Rockefeller National Historical Park in Vermont, the only national park to focus on conservation history and the evolving nature of land stewardship in America. This drawing records landscape features dating from the 1880s and includes a plan with topographic lines; several sections, one of which follows a meandering path in the hillside garden; and details of the understory plant materials.

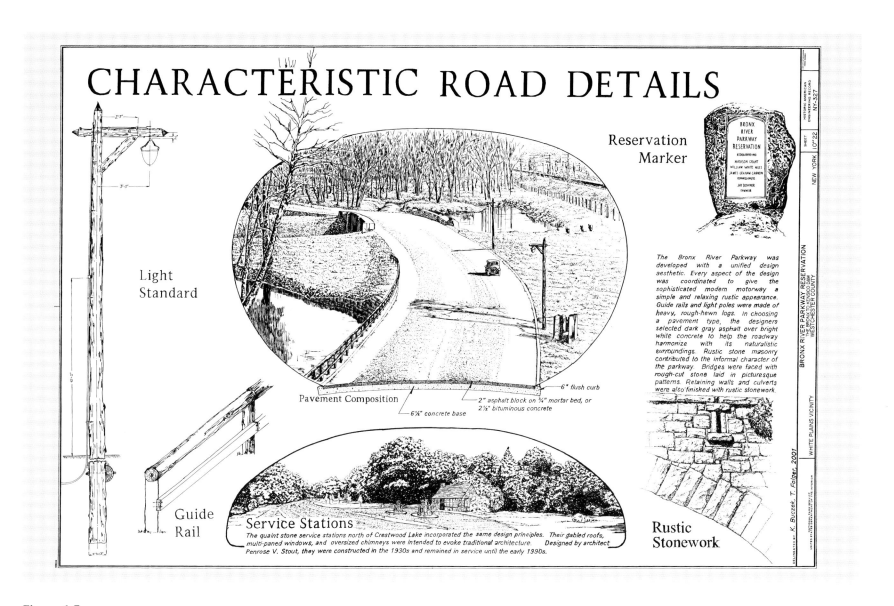

CHARACTERISTIC ROAD DETAILS

Light Standard

Reservation Marker

BRONX RIVER PARKWAY RESERVATION

Pavement Composition

6" flush curb

2" asphalt block on ¾" mortar bed, or 2½" bituminous concrete

6¼" concrete base

Guide Rail

The Bronx River Parkway was developed with a unified design aesthetic. Every aspect of the design was coordinated to give the sophisticated modern motorway a simple and relaxing rustic appearance. Guide rails and light poles were made of heavy, rough-hewn logs. In choosing a pavement type, the designers selected dark gray asphalt over bright white concrete to help the roadway harmonize with its naturalistic surroundings. Rustic stone masonry contributed to the informal character of the parkway. Bridges were faced with rough-cut stone laid in picturesque patterns. Retaining walls and culverts were also finished with rustic stonework.

Service Stations
The quaint stone service stations north of Crestwood Lake incorporated the same design principles. Their gabled roofs, multi-paned windows, and oversized chimneys were intended to evoke traditional architecture. Designed by architect Penrose V. Stout, they were constructed in the 1930s and remained in service until the early 1990s.

Rustic Stonework

BRONX RIVER PARKWAY RESERVATION THE BRONX AND YONKERS WESTCHESTER COUNTY

WHITE PLAINS VICINITY

HISTORIC AMERICAN ENGINEERING RECORD

NEW YORK NY-327

SHEET 10 of 22

DELINEATED BY K. Buczek, T. Folger, 2001

Figure 1.7

HAER studied highways as part of the landscape in a series of projects documenting park roads and parkways. This drawing of the Bronx River Parkway utilizes both mea-sured drawings and sketches to depict characteristic road details and the thoughtful integration of the roadway with surrounding landscape features.

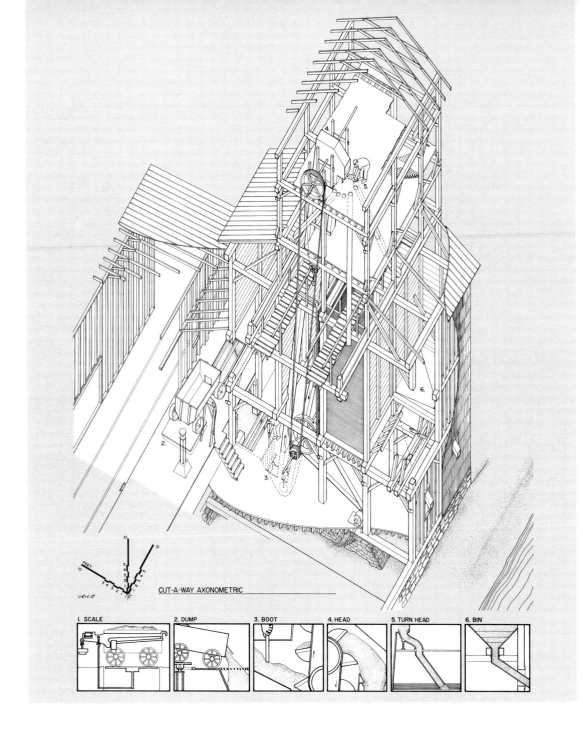

CUT-A-WAY AXONOMETRIC

1/4"=1'-0"

FEET

| 1. SCALE | 2. DUMP | 3. BOOT | 4. HEAD | 5. TURN HEAD | 6. BIN |

structures that cannot be saved or are too big for exhibition in museums. Structures are destroyed in many ways and for many reasons: new development, technical or functional obsolescence, neglect, fire, natural disaster, and war. Some of the causes can be mitigated, and precautions can be taken against others. In the event a structure does not survive, documentation can present it to future generations. Documentation can also serve as a form of insurance for a significant structure, making it possible to reconstruct it in case of a catastrophic loss (*see fig. 1.11*).

A fundamental principle of architectural, engineering, and landscape documentation is that words alone cannot adequately record and explain historic structures. The graphic content is integral to the process of recording the history of the built environment (*see figs. 1.12 and 1.13*).

The advantages of HABS/HAER/HALS as a repository of historical information are quality of documentation, standardized methodology, durability of archival materials, reliability of archival storage methods, and accessibility to the public. Unlike preservation agencies that lose interest in historical documentation once a building has been demolished, HABS, HAER, and HALS retain all material that is accessioned into their collections. The HABS and HAER collections are in the public domain and are avail-

Figure 1.8
This 1861 grain elevator in Illinois is still used to store grain, although the method of transport has changed from horse-drawn wagons and canal boats to railroad cars to trucks. For this drawing, a portion of the elevator was cut away graphically to depict the movement and storage of the grain and to reveal the structural system of the bins.

Figure 1.9
The location of this richly detailed longitudinal section drawing of the home of a wealthy Pennsylvania industrialist was chosen to illustrate the relationship between the original three-story house and the flanking additions. This drawing also allows a comparative analysis of the interior decorative details that define the public, private, and utilitarian functions of the house, now a museum.

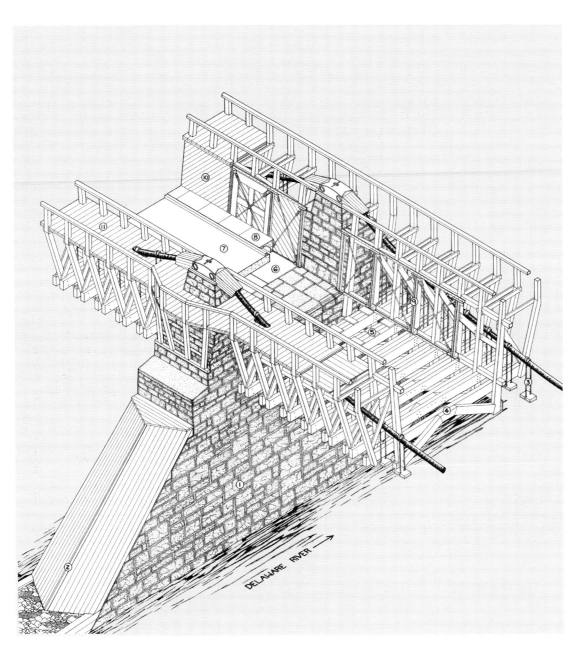

able at the Library of Congress and through the library's American Memory Web site.

The collections make the written material permanent not only through its retention but also by keeping it, typed or photocopied xerographically, on archival paper. The permanency of the HABS, HAER, and HALS collections also provides an advantage for primary material that may be unprotected. Rare documents can be photocopied xerographically onto archival paper and included with the historical reports. Unprotected graphic material can similarly be photographed or photocopied for the collections, barring copyright problems for either.

The permanence and accessibility of the photographs are ensured by careful archival processing of the negatives and prints and careful handling and storage. The original large-format negatives are retained and used for making prints, so there is no degradation of the image from the original. The Library of Congress first accepted large-format color transparencies in 1996, but the relative instability of color photographic materials has required special precautions. The original transparencies are kept in cold storage, and user copies are made from duplicate originals.

Reproducible copies of the measured drawings are made so that additional copies can be produced without damage to the originals. The original drawings are currently prepared with archival ink on polyester sheets or are plotted

Figure 1.10
After the Delaware Aqueduct was converted to an interpretive structure demonstrating its use as a canal aqueduct and as a modern highway bridge, HAER returned to supplement drawings done by the program 19 years earlier (see also fig. 4.28).

with laser or electrostatic plotters on polyester sheets for archival permanence.

Written material is filed along with the large-format photographs and measured drawings, all of which constitute the formal HABS/HAER/HALS documentation. The important relationship between the written information and the graphic material is fostered by the careful guardianship they are afforded. The compiled package, in a permanent and accessible repository, makes an important addition to our store of historical knowledge.

How HABS/HAER/HALS Documentation Is Produced

Most HABS/HAER/HALS documentation is produced during the summer by undergraduate and graduate students who work in teams under a professional supervisor, usually a professor with credentials in the subject area being studied. Architecture and landscape architecture students do the measuring and drafting. A historian, again with credentials in the area being studied, provides the historical research. Teams are tailored to the needs of each project, taking into account the nature and significance of the site, existing records, site conditions, and the ultimate purpose of the documentation. A team works in the field for approximately twelve

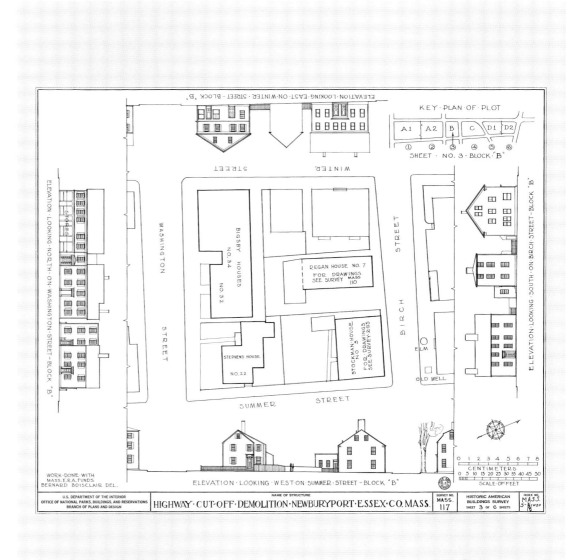

Figure 1.11
The HABS program has long emphasized the importance of producing graphic and written records of threatened structures for future generations. All of the city block recorded in this 1934 drawing was demolished to make way for a highway overpass. Many of the buildings in the affected four-block area were also individually recorded.

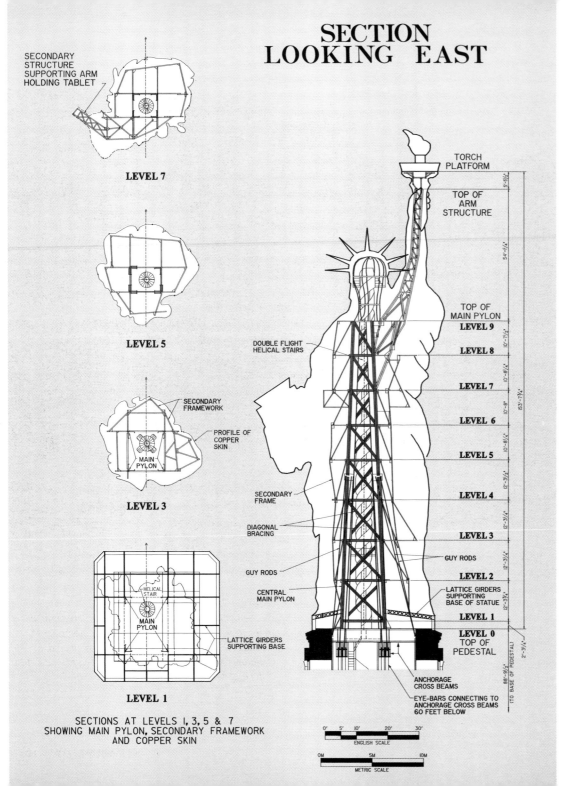

SECTION LOOKING EAST

SECONDARY STRUCTURE SUPPORTING ARM HOLDING TABLET

LEVEL 7

LEVEL 5

SECONDARY FRAMEWORK

PROFILE OF COPPER SKIN

MAIN PYLON

LEVEL 3

HELICAL STAIR

MAIN PYLON

LATTICE GIRDERS SUPPORTING BASE

LEVEL 1

SECTIONS AT LEVELS 1, 3, 5 & 7
SHOWING MAIN PYLON, SECONDARY FRAMEWORK
AND COPPER SKIN

TORCH PLATFORM

TOP OF ARM STRUCTURE

DOUBLE FLIGHT HELICAL STAIRS

TOP OF MAIN PYLON

LEVEL 9

LEVEL 8

LEVEL 7

LEVEL 6

SECONDARY FRAME

LEVEL 5

LEVEL 4

DIAGONAL BRACING

LEVEL 3

GUY RODS

GUY RODS

LEVEL 2

CENTRAL MAIN PYLON

LATTICE GIRDERS SUPPORTING BASE OF STATUE

LEVEL 1

LEVEL 0
TOP OF PEDESTAL

ANCHORAGE CROSS BEAMS

EYE-BARS CONNECTING TO ANCHORAGE CROSS BEAMS 60 FEET BELOW

0' 5' 10'   20'   30'
ENGLISH SCALE

0M   5M   10M
METRIC SCALE

weeks, completing the measured drawings and the written historical and descriptive data. A HABS/HAER/HALS photographer usually takes the formal photographs.

Priority has always been given to recording structures threatened with destruction. Although the federal government has taken steps to ensure that its activities do not adversely affect historic structures, when there is no reasonable alternative to demolition or substantial alteration HABS/HAER/HALS documentation can mitigate the loss by providing permanent graphic and written records (*see figs. 1.14 and 15*).

The National Historic Preservation Act, as amended in 1980, stipulates that "each Federal agency shall initiate measures to assure that where, as a result of Federal action or assistance carried out by such agency, an historic property is to be substantially altered or demolished, timely steps are taken to make or have made appropriate records, and that such records then be deposited . . . in the Library of Congress . . . for future use and reference."

The documentation produced in compliance with this law adds hundreds of structures a year to the collections (*see fig. 1.16*). Several states and local jurisdictions have laws that produce similar results. New Jersey, for instance,

Figure 1.12
This diagrammatic drawing was produced on a computer to show the armature for the Statue of Liberty. The drawing, one of a set produced for the restoration of the statue in 1983, was among the first computer-generated HAER drawings. In 2001 HABS began a laser-scanning project to document the statue's copper skin, which was not recorded at the time of the restoration (see also fig. 9.20).

has a law protecting its coastal areas that extends some protection to historic structures along the shoreline. Several historic hotels have been documented under this law.

Architecture schools have been using HABS documentation as part of their curricula for decades. Producing documentation provides training in research, inspection, analysis, measuring, and drafting and yields invaluable records of historic structures, not to mention drawings for the students' portfolios. Faculty and students who work with HABS material in their courses are an important source of summer employees. Engineering and landscape architecture schools are also showing increased interest in documentation as a teaching tool.

The Charles E. Peterson Prize, established by HABS and endowed by a private fund of the Athenaeum of Philadelphia, is an annual cash award that recognizes the best sets of measured drawings of a historic structure produced by students and donated to HABS (*see figs. 1.17 and 18*). The prize honors Charles E. Peterson, FAIA, founder of the HABS program, and is intended to increase awareness and knowledge of historic buildings throughout the United States. Students who participate in the competition learn about historic construction materials and techniques while gaining hands-on experience in measuring and producing measured drawings of a historic structure. HABS, in turn, gains hundreds of measured drawings for its collection.

From the beginning, HABS, HAER, and HALS have relied on the generosity of organizations and individuals as a major source of documentation. Donated records continue to be a significant part of the collections, and preservation professionals who work with historic structures are another good source for measured drawings and historical research. Architects, engineers, landscape architects, historians, photographers, and others who work with historic

Figure 1.13
This 1962 photograph was one of a series illustrating life on the farm taken to supplement HABS photographs of structures on the Walker Family Farm in Great Smoky Mountains National Park. These two women are daughters of the original builder of the house.

Figure 1.14
A private developer produced HABS documentation of the City of Paris Dry Goods Company building in San Francisco before it was demolished. The rotunda, with the stained-glass skylight shown here, was dismantled and reconstructed in a new department store on the same site.

Figure 1.15
HABS extensively photographed Baltimore's Memorial Stadium in 2001 as its demolition was commencing. While the 1947 structure was not considered historic, it was nevertheless a significant presence in the neighborhood and in the hearts of Baltimore sports fans. Many photographs exist of games and events, but the HABS photographs are the only record of the architecture and structure of the stadium.

Figure 1.16
This photograph of an 1875 cast-iron commercial building in Connecticut was made for HABS by a local redevelopment agency. Agencies receiving federal funding for a project are required to document historic structures to HABS/HAER standards before demolishing them.

Documenting Historic Structures in the National Parks

Randall J. Biallas
Chief Historical Architect, National Park Service

The Historic American Buildings Survey and Historic American Engineering Record (HABS/HAER) programs have long played a vital role in the cultural resource stewardship efforts of the National Park Service (NPS). Conceived by NPS employee Charles E. Peterson, FAIA, and nurtured by a series of historically minded architects, landscape architects, and administrators, HABS continues to stand at the forefront of Park Service preservation efforts. From the 1930s to today, HABS/HAER drawings have recorded park structures and helped guide their maintenance, rehabilitation, and restoration.

While HABS initially focused on structures outside the National Park System, a number of structures documented during the survey's first decade either were or eventually became part of national monuments, memorials, or historical parks. Among the prominent structures recorded by early HABS teams were Fort Marion, later Castillo de San Marcos National Monument, in Florida; the Old Saint Louis Court House, later part of the Jefferson National Expansion Memorial, Missouri; Fort Winfield Scott, later part of Golden Gate National Recreation Area, California; Longfellow House and Garden, later Longfellow National Historic Site, Massachusetts; the Old United States Sub-Treasury Building, later Federal Hall National Memorial, New York; Mission San José de Tumacácori, Tumacácori National Historical Park, Arizona; canal structures at the Chesapeake and Ohio Canal National Historical Park, Maryland; and Independence Hall, later part of Independence National Historical Park, Pennsylvania.

Since the Historic American Engineering Record was formed in 1969, HAER teams have set about documenting industrial resources in parks as diverse as Kennecott Mines in Wrangell-St. Elias National Park, Alaska; power canals and mills in Lowell National Historical Park, Massachusetts; the saltpetre works at Mammoth Cave National Park, Kentucky; bathhouses in Hot Springs National Park, Arkansas; 20-mule-team borax wagons in Death Valley National Park, California; and a Minuteman missile silo in one of the most recent national park areas, Minuteman Missile National Historic Site, South Dakota. From 1988 to 2002, HAER conducted the NPS Park Roads and Bridges Recording Program, creating an outstanding corpus of documentation on those essential park resources. The authorization of the Historic American Landscapes Survey (HALS) in 2001 promises to expand the documentation of park resources to address additional dimensions of great interest to natural and cultural resource managers alike.

The value of HABS, HAER, and HALS to the Park Service extends beyond the compilation of data for traditional preservation and management purposes, however. The historical narratives; high-quality, large-format photographs; and measured and interpretive drawings provide a wealth of material to enrich Park Service education and interpretation efforts. Individual parks and Service-wide programs have benefited greatly from the compelling graphics and detailed historical research prepared by HABS/HAER, as these resources have been employed in a wide range of exhibits, publications, and public programs.

The role of HABS/HAER in training preservation professionals has also been of incalculable value to NPS cultural resource programs. The intensive summer fieldwork sessions have prepared generations of young people for careers in cultural resource management, providing a thorough grounding in technical skills while instilling an ethic of preservation and commitment to public service that has profoundly benefited the National Park Service and preservation efforts worldwide.

structures are encouraged to produce their documentation to HABS/HAER/HALS standards for inclusion in the collections (*see figs. 1.19, 2.14, and 11.19*).

Copies of documentation can be donated to HABS, HAER, and HALS for safekeeping. Unlike records stored in office files, the program collections are stored under conditions in which temperature and humidity are controlled to ensure longevity. Furthermore, having a structure documented in the HABS, HAER, or HALS collections adds to its prestige and makes it accessible to a wide variety of scholars, researchers, professors and teachers, primary and secondary students, and the general public.

The Administrative Organization of HABS/HAER/HALS

HABS/HAER/HALS is part of the National Park Service of the Department of the Interior. All three programs operate under congressional authorization from the Historic Sites Act of 1935. The records are housed and made available to the public through the Library of Congress Prints and Photographs Division and online through Built in America, part of the library's American Memory digital library.

The National Park Service operates HABS under a tripartite agreement with the Library of Congress and the American Institute of Architects (AIA). The AIA provides technical advice and assistance through its Committee on Historic Resources and general membership.

HAER was founded in 1969 under another tripartite agreement among the National Park Service, the Library of Congress, and the American Society of Civil Engineers (ASCE). ASCE provides technical advice and assistance through its History and Heritage Committee and general

membership. A protocol signed in 1987 adds the support of other engineering societies—the American Society of Mechanical Engineers, the Institute of Electrical and Electronics Engineers, the American Institute of Chemical Engineers, and the American Institute of Mining, Metallurgical, and Petroleum Engineers.

HALS was established in 2000 and operates under a tripartite agreement among the National Park Service, the American Society of Landscape Architects (ASLA), and the Library of Congress. ASLA provides advice and technical assistance through its Historic Preservation Professional Interest Group and general membership.

About This Book

In the history chapter of *Recording Historic Structures,* Alison K. Hoagland and Gray Fitzsimons describe how historical research provides context, chronology, description, interpretation, and assessment for architectural and engineering documentation. Research forms the basis for identifying significant structures, the initial step in the documentation process. Historians investigate and assemble information on selected structures, analyze the structure and the historical data, and distill the information into a cogent history and description. The authors describe a methodology for research, discuss what questions should be asked, and offer guidelines for describing architectural and technological sites. The chapter concludes with a section on the various reporting formats used by the programs.

In the photography chapter, William L. Lebovich describes techniques for producing photographs that record, reveal, and interpret historic structures. Photography is a universally

accepted medium for conveying graphic information. Documentary photography is specialized and demands more of the photographer than merely technical ability and artistic skill. For a photograph to convey the necessary information, the photographer must understand the subject matter. The best documentary photographs do more than record and interpret; they also exhibit attributes such as lighting and composition more familiar in high-quality photography. The suggestions in this chapter can help those photographing historic structures improve both the technical quality and informational content of their documentary photography. All but the most specialized techniques are usable in any format.

In the measured drawings chapter, John A. Burns explains what measured drawings are and how to plan and execute them. Measured drawings can vary from simple line drawings that show room relationships or the arrangement of machine tools in a shop to elaborately detailed drawings of a pin connection in a bridge or moldings in a mantelpiece. The chapter discusses what to draw, how to obtain the measurements, levels of accuracy, types of drawings, and appropriate scales, as well as the special characteristics of HABS, HAER, and HALS measured drawings.

The second part presents case studies of HABS, HAER, and HALS documentation projects. Each study shows how the nature of a resource dictates the manner in which it should be documented. The Auditorium Building, for instance, is significant for many reasons and, therefore, required multiple recording techniques. Picatinny Arsenal was the site of the U.S. Army's first smokeless powder production line, so recording the industrial process was a major focus of the documentation. Two of the case studies describe methodologies for identify-

Digital Documentation Technologies

Over the past decade, computers have become an increasingly important tool for the documentation of historic structures, simultaneously facilitating and complicating the documentation process. Computers are such a ubiquitous part of professional life in the twenty-first century that little attention is paid to how they work, that is, how they acquire, input, store, and process data, and how they report data back. Society is comfortable, perhaps too comfortable, with the speed and convenience of computers. Nonetheless, the digital revolution is not without risk because it relies on complex hardware and software to store and retrieve data.

Rapidly evolving computer technologies speed the obsolescence of hardware and software faster than critical data can be migrated or archived. Furthermore, the ease of replication and manipulation of digital files raises many questions about rights and provenance. Archival stability and migration are significant problems that are only beginning to be addressed. By contrast, paper documents need only the viewer's eyes and a light source to read, and procedures for curation and conservation are well established.

The HABS/HAER/HALS programs are by definition archival. All the materials are produced with the goal of achieving a 500-year service life. That means approaching new technologies with caution until it is certain they can meet the programs' standards for accuracy, verifiability, ease of reproduction, and archival stability. HABS/HAER/HALS has performance standards, and the products, or formal documentation, are hand-inked or laser-plotted measured drawings; large-format film negatives and prints; and typescript histories. Digital technologies are used as a tool to produce documentation, but not as a final product.

Word processing automated the mechanical process of typing, making it vastly easier to manipulate, review, edit, and print textual materials. Other software automated financial and database management, drafting, publishing, and a myriad of other formerly manual tasks. The computer simply reports back in different formats what was entered. Once entered, data can be manipulated almost infinitely. The prudent user of computer-generated products is careful to consider the original source material, including the conventions used in its production, its reliability and accuracy, and its relevance to the task at hand. Unfortunately, most people are far too trusting of computer-generated products.

They are confident that what was entered into a computer is accurate when it comes back out, as if the computer somehow certifies or enhances the original. However, nothing could be further from the truth. The problem of faulty data has been defined with the simple acronym GIGO, for "garbage in, garbage out." Computer data is no better or worse than any other historical data. It is still important to be somewhat skeptical of a source until it has been proven accurate.

Computer-aided drafting (CAD) mechanized the task of drafting. Designed for creating drawings for new construction, it assumes great precision, with all measurements exact, all alignments perfect, all floors level, and all walls plumb. Lines are points and vectors of known length, which works best for rigidly orthographic forms. Historic structures, which seldom exhibit these characteristics, are thus difficult to document using CAD. It is not possible to measure around the perimeter of a historic structure and have the floor plan close with ¹⁄₆₄" accuracy. Tolerances in the construction industry are simply not that precise.

HABS/HAER first invested in CAD in the mid-1980s. At that time, however, CAD programs were slow and not sophisticated enough to meet our graphic standards. In addition, archival plots required technical pen plotters, which had limited capabilities. CAD could not mach the quality of hand drafting, and the system got little use. Nonetheless, several early decisions facilitated the programs' eventual entry into the CAD environment. One was to proceed cautiously because of the archival nature of the program. Another was to buy readily available, off-the-shelf products. Today HABS/HAER and now HALS use the NPS standard, AutoCAD, but also have several seats of MicroStation. These and other contemporary CAD programs are capable of meeting graphic standards, and contemporary laser and electrostatic plotters meet our archival standards.

Scanning historic drawings and converting them into CAD drawings seems at first glance as simple as operating a photocopier. Like a photocopy, the first product of a scanner is a raster image, a series of dots located in a grid to replicate the original image. A scanner can be too faithful to the original, since watermarks, stray marks, blemishes, creases, and other defects in the original become part of the computer image. If the original document changed shape, the scanned image would be of the distorted original. Another consideration is the reliability of the original drawing, as its original purpose, drafting conventions, and accuracy would be represented in the derivative scanned image. Independent verification of the accuracy and suitability of the scanned image for the task at hand is an essential step before historic drawings can be used as the basis for modern work. A further complication is the need to use raster-to-vector software, which produces lines with single attributes, all in a single layer. A frequently preferable option is to trace a historic drawing to produce a new CAD original, either on a digitizing table or from a scanned image in a separate layer within the new CAD drawing.

Using a sequence of convergent photographs, CAD/photogrammetry merges the science of measuring with computer-aided drafting and reports the results as CAD vector files. This major advance made photogrammetry available to nonphotogrammetrists by using the computational power of a desktop computer to provide the geometric rigidity inherent in traditional glass-plate stereophotogrammetry. While most of the software works similarly and with great precision, the data must be gathered and entered with care to avoid impairing the accuracy of the results. An operator must have a firm grasp of geometry, understand optics and photographic techniques and technologies, and possess a working knowledge of computer-aided drafting.

In the late 1980s, digital convergent photogrammetric software was developed that could be run on a desktop computer using photographs taken with a semi-metric camera. The new technology made photogrammetry feasible for HABS/HAER, and the program leased a camera and software system in 1989. The new equipment was used to document wildfire-threatened National Historic Landmarks in Yellowstone National Park and historic structures damaged during the Loma Prieta earthquake in California. Pleased with the results, we decided to invest in a convergent photogrammetry system and purchased a Leica Metrika 45 camera because it produced large-format negatives ($4'' \times 5''$) and PhotoCAD software that operated as a pull-down menu within AutoCAD.

The documentation of the Lincoln and Thomas Jefferson Memorials, followed by the Washington Monument, was the first project for which CAD/photogrammetry was used. The resulting drawings served as the basis for the treatment drawings used in the restoration of the three structures. (See the case study on recording monuments for more details.)

ing significant structure types—bridges and Quaker meetinghouses—and how to document them. The schooner *Wawona* was HAER's first documented historic ship, and this case study features specialized traditional and recently developed techniques required to record a historic vessel. Documenting landscapes presents unique challenges, such as seasonal changes, which are explored in the case study on recording historic landscapes.

The following chapters will guide those interested in the production of architectural, engineering, and landscape documentation for any purpose, although ideally for inclusion in the HABS, HAER, or HALS collections. Regardless of the changing focus and form of recording, these National Park Service programs provide a unique opportunity to expand our understanding of America's cultural heritage. The continued growth of these collections will ensure an even better understanding of the past for future generations.

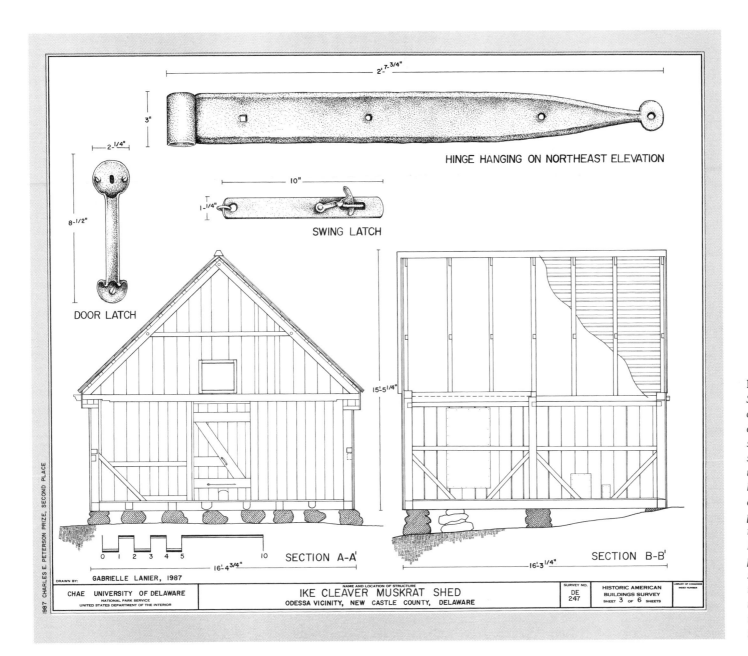

2'-7-3/4"

3"

HINGE HANGING ON NORTHEAST ELEVATION

2-1/4"

8-1/2"

DOOR LATCH

10"

1-1/4"

SWING LATCH

15'-5 1/4"

0 1 2 3 4 5   10

16'-4 3/4"

SECTION A-A'

16'-3 1/4"

SECTION B-B'

DRAWN BY: GABRIELLE LANIER, 1987

CHAE UNIVERSITY OF DELAWARE
NATIONAL PARK SERVICE
UNITED STATES DEPARTMENT OF THE INTERIOR

NAME AND LOCATION OF STRUCTURE
IKE CLEAVER MUSKRAT SHED
ODESSA VICINITY, NEW CASTLE COUNTY, DELAWARE

SURVEY NO.
DE
247

HISTORIC AMERICAN
BUILDINGS SURVEY
SHEET 3 OF 6 SHEETS

LIBRARY OF CONGRESS
INDEX NUMBER

Figure 1.17
Students at the University of Delaware measured and drew a muskrat skinning shed as part of a statewide study of vanishing vernacular building types. Their hand-drafted measured drawings won second place in the competition for the 1987 Charles E. Peterson Prize. An accompanying history of the shed and the material culture of the watermen who used it was also donated to HABS and incorporated into the collection.

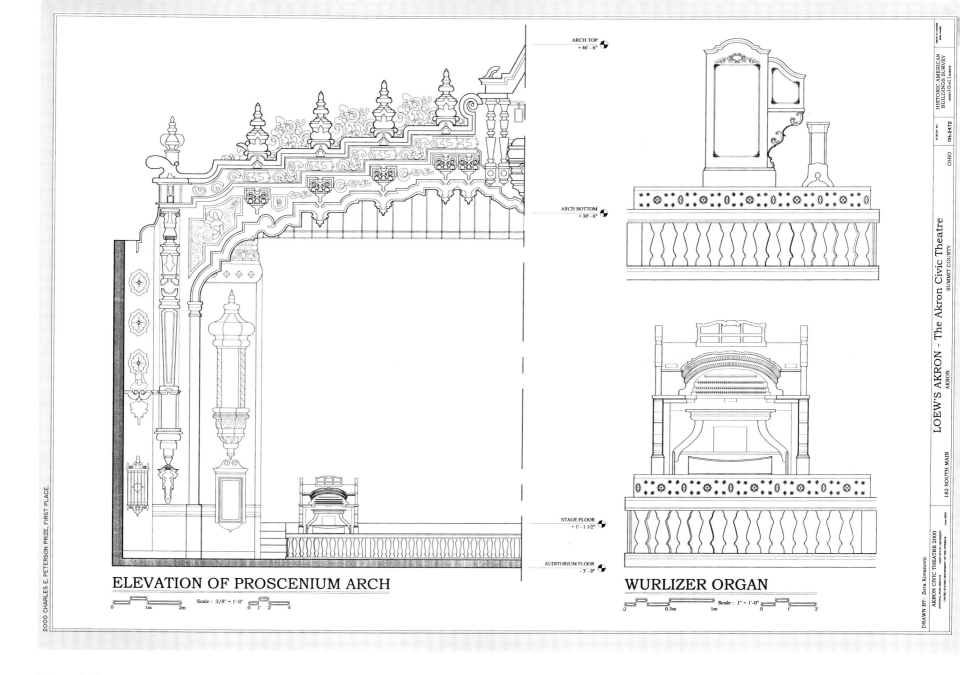

ELEVATION OF PROSCENIUM ARCH

Scale : 3/8" = 1'-0"

0   1m   2m   0 1' 2'   4'

WURLIZER ORGAN

Scale : 1" = 1'-0"

0   0.5m   1m   0   1'   2'

ARCH TOP
+ 46'- 6"

ARCH BOTTOM
+ 30'- 6"

STAGE FLOOR
+ 1'- 1 1/2"

AUDITORIUM FLOOR
- 3'- 0"

DRAWN BY: *Zora Kovacovic*

AKRON CIVIC THEATRE 2000
NATIONAL PARK SERVICE
KENT STATE UNIVERSITY
UNITED STATES DEPARTMENT OF THE INTERIOR
June 2000

182 SOUTH MAIN

LOEW'S AKRON - The Akron Civic Theatre
SUMMIT COUNTY
AKRON

OHIO

OH-2472

HISTORIC AMERICAN
BUILDINGS SURVEY
SHEET 10 OF 11 SHEETS

Figure 1.18

This CAD drawing of a proscenium at the 1929 Loew's Akron Theater, one of a set of eleven measured drawings, demonstrates the capability of CAD technology to depict intricate detail. The set of drawings, by students at Kent State University, won first place in the 2000 competition for the Charles E. Peterson Prize.

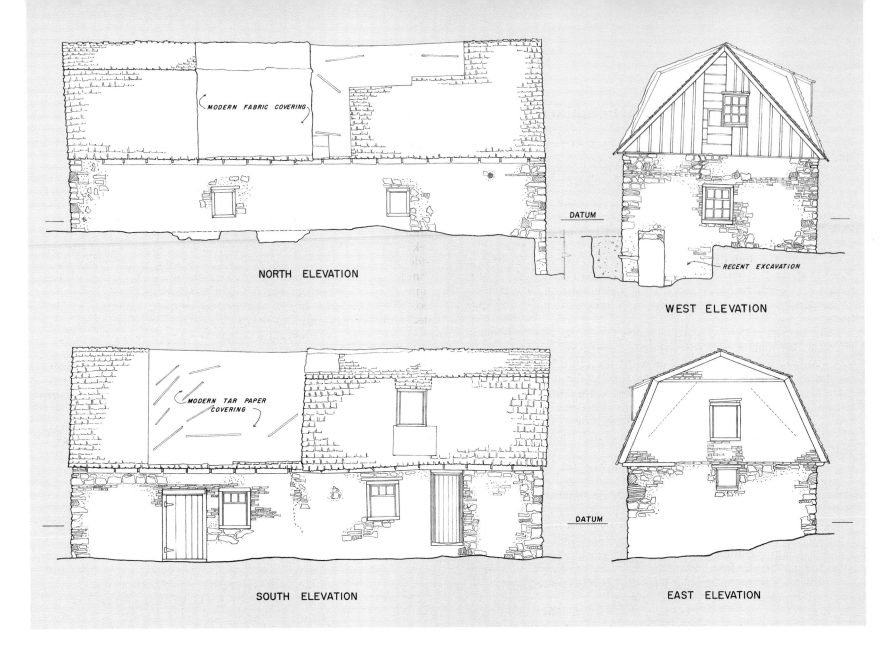

NORTH ELEVATION

MODERN FABRIC COVERING

DATUM

WEST ELEVATION

RECENT EXCAVATION

SOUTH ELEVATION

MODERN TAR PAPER COVERING

DATUM

EAST ELEVATION

Figure 1.19
Before work began on the Caleb Pusey House in Upland, Pennsylvania, the restoration architect produced drawings of existing conditions on HABS sheets as a historical record. The Friends of the Caleb Pusey House, Inc. then donated measured drawings, large-format photographs, and historical data to HABS.

Digital Access to HABS/HAER/HALS Collections

Archives everywhere are investing enormous sums of money and numerous resources to develop digital access to their collections. The Library of Congress project American Memory—Historical Collections for the National Digital Library posts distinctive documents related to U.S. history on the Internet, including documents from the HABS/HAER collections. The response to the online accessibility of the collections has been dramatic, with 3,000 researchers annually visiting the Prints and Photographs Division at the library and 3,000 users a week visiting the Built in America Web site. An approximately fiftyfold increase in use has been achieved without increased risk to the original documents, an archivist's dream. In fact, risk to the originals has been reduced because they no longer have to be handled to make reproductions.

The Library of Congress created the National Digital Library in a five-year, $65 million effort to make the essential documents of U.S. history available over the Internet. One of the first of the library's collections to be digitized and made available was the documentation in the Historic American Buildings Survey and the Historic American Engineering Record. The relief employment program conceived by Charles Peterson in the depths of the Great Depression had grown in size and stature to be considered critical to understanding the cultural patrimony of the United States.

The Web site Built in America (http://memory.loc.gov/ammem/hhhtml/hhhome.html) was created by the Library of Congress so that anyone with Internet access could download good-quality electronic copies of the measured drawings, photographs, and written data in the HABS/HAER collections. The original drawings are scanned at 400 dots per inch (dpi) and the original negatives at 500 to 1,000 dpi to create extremely high-resolution images. Smaller reference copies of the files are also available for faster download times. *Built in America* provides truly universal access to the collections and includes more than six terabytes of digital files available to the public.

Admittedly, the HABS/HAER collections were ideal for digitizing, as they are popular, in standardized formats, in the public domain, and stored in a preexisting computerized database. From the beginning, the collections were designed to be easily accessible and reproducible, which further eased the digital transformation.

The great limitation to universal access had been that the collections were housed in Washington, D.C. Various means of disseminating the collections more broadly included national, state, regional, and topical catalogs, publications, microfilm and microfiche editions, an online database, and exhibitions. Researchers still believed it was necessary to trek to Washington for serious research, however, illustrating the limited widespread use of the collections. American Memory—Historical Collections for the National Digital Library has changed all that, both increasing overall use and broadening use to audiences not previously recognized. One of the biggest surprises was that the collections are ideal for educational use in grades K-12.

There are resource limitations to digital access. File size and download times are proportional to the resolution of graphic images. The higher the resolution, the more unwieldy the files become, and the more slowly a page will download. Finding the balance between image quality and practicality become a major factor for digital archives. When an organization's products are quality drawings and photographs, image resolution is critical. However, it was noted that a prototypical user with a 17″ monitor was not going to have the ability to appreciate the image quality of a high-resolution digital file. Scholars and publishers, however, would want the highest resolution possible. In the end, images were made available in four resolutions so that researchers could choose the resolution most suitable to their needs: thumbnails, compressed JPEG and TIFF files, and uncompressed TIFF files.

To facilitate research, HABS/HAER developed a controlled vocabulary, hierarchical index, and keywords to provide a powerful search capability. Category fields are now limited to the controlled vocabulary, but the keyword field is more free-form to accommodate the rich variety of descriptive words used in the collections. For instance, *arch* is a controlled vocabulary word, but *brick arch* or *masonry arch* may be used in the keyword field. The HABS/HAER/HALS database and thesaurus are meant to be compatible with other collection databases in the Library of Congress to enable cross-collection and cross-institution searches.

CHAPTER 2

HISTORY

Alison K. Hoagland
Gray Fitzsimons

Historical research plays a central role in recording historic structures. Historians examine both physical remains and written documentation to acquire a greater understanding of a historic structure or site. In the HABS/HAER/HALS program, the products of the historian's work appear in three forms: written documentation, measured drawings, and selection of and captions for large-format photographs. While the focus of this chapter is on how to produce written documentation, a historian's work often involves close interaction with architects, for many of the questions posed by the historian are answered in graphic form in the architect's drawings. Conversely, many of the architect's questions about a site or structure are answered by the historian.

In producing written documentation for historic structures or sites, a historian should seek to impart information that explains why a specific historic structure or site is significant. Preparation of written documentation involves collecting historical information, analyzing the structure or site in question, investigating graphic documentation, and then synthesizing these elements to provide an understanding of the historical importance of the structure or site.

Because written documentation is more than mere fact collecting, the HABS/HAER/HALS staff has found that professional historians are generally better suited to this task. Historians are trained to direct their inquiries in a logical and systematic fashion, to research and evaluate a wide range of source materials, and to present the research findings and analysis in a cogent form. Because scholars of U.S. history represent diverse fields of study—ranging, for example, from political to social to economic history—this chapter is designed to aid historians trained not only in material cul-

ture or technological history, but also in more general fields. Moreover, this chapter is intended to remind architectural, technology, and landscape historians of the need to place specific structures or sites in a more general historical context.

Technological history, seemingly a very specialized field, actually embraces a wide range of human activities and historical subjects. Such disciplines as the history of science, economic history, labor history, social history, political history, and intellectual history, to name but a few, are often addressed when examining a specific topic in the history of technology. Many of the historian's traditional approaches—primarily the reliance on written documentation to provide factual evidence and substantiate historical theses—are also requisite for the historian of technology. However, while the field of technological history draws heavily on these "mainstream" disciplines and traditional approaches, it also requires an ability to understand and analyze topics in science, mathematics, and engineering and an ability to understand and evaluate mechanical objects and engineering structures. By combining these abilities with traditional historical methods—identifying the important avenues of inquiry, undertaking the research in a carefully thought-out and well-organized fashion, and presenting the findings in a clear and cogent form—a historian can produce a successful technological history.

This chapter outlines a general methodology for producing written historical documentation and underscores the major contributions that historians can provide in recording historic structures. Although the material presented largely constitutes the approach to historical documentation taken by the Historic American Buildings Survey, the Historic American Engineering Record, and the Historic American Landscapes Survey, this approach can be applied to many other kinds of historical investigations into the nation's architectural and engineering heritage. This chapter contains five parts, which discuss the steps involved in documenting a historic structure in approximately chronological order: historical information, description, significance, sources and methodology, and presentation. The fields of architectural history and the history of technology overlap somewhat, but differences are apparent in the kinds of questions asked and in the answers sought. Accordingly, the general discussion in this chapter presents the documentation of architecture, with separate discussions of issues particular to the documentation of engineering and industrial structures.

Historical Information

The historian should begin with an understanding of the significance of the structure under study. Some areas of significance may have been established through previous surveys or inventories. However, the research undertaken to prepare documentation for a structure or site will expand the historical, architectural, engineering, or landscape significance documented earlier and in some cases may redefine it.

The preliminary assessment of significance will determine the basic research. If a building is identified as important because it is an example of French Colonial construction, for instance, then the research should concentrate on the manner in which it was built. Not only should historians explore the building date, original owner, and possible builders, they should also interpret the construction by identifying it, for example, as *poteaux sur solle* (posts on sill), and by placing that fact in the context of French Colonial settlement. If a house is important because it has been identified as the home of a signer of the Declaration of Independence, then his relationship to the house and what the house can tell us about that time period should be early avenues of investigation.

This initial assessment of significance is frequently modified after more research. Sometimes the context will change. For example, a theater may have been identified as significant to its city because it was the last remaining example of a once-common building type, but research may reveal that it was the work of an architect known nationwide for designing theaters. In this case, the documentation should address both of these aspects of the theater's history. Similarly, a building identified as significant for stylistic reasons may, upon further investigation, be found to have unusual structural features that were not readily apparent. Archival resources, too, may point the researcher in unanticipated directions.

The ultimate purpose of an investigation is to develop a better understanding of the significance of a structure or site. Setting the structure into context is essential—how does it compare with what was going on around it? Such declarations as "first," "only," and "most" are extremely difficult to make but very effective when proven.

In addition, the product—the reason for producing the documentation—should guide the historian. If the basic question is when the roof was put on, then the research should be directed to sources that might answer that question: the building itself, contemporary drawings and photographs, contemporary descriptions, building permits, and so on. Time and money constraints will further define the task at hand. At a minimum, though, basic research questions of who, what, where, when, and why should be answered, and the significance of the building should be addressed.

Asking Questions

Writing history is a process of answering questions, and good research is a product of good questions. For every structure, there will be some basic questions common to all structures and others common to structures of its type. The characteristics of a particular site should provoke additional questions that suggest other avenues of inquiry.

When documenting a structure, specific questions relevant to that structure must be answered. Even if a structure is more significant for the people associated with it than for its architecture, it should be explained and identified. The structure is, after all, the object of the documentation. Basic questions about a structure that should occur to a researcher include the following:

1. Who designed it, who built it, who used it?

2. When was it built, altered, demolished?

3. What was it originally, what is it now, what was it meant to be?

4. Why was it built, why does it look the way it does?

5. How was it built, how has it been altered, how did it function?

6. Where was it, where is it?

To explain or define the significance of a site, additional questions may have to be asked. These questions derive from the nature and significance of the resource. Generally, they involve setting the resource in a larger context and focusing on particular features or elements. For example, a bank has been identified as significant to the business district because of its design. The researcher will first want to answer the basic questions of who designed it and when, how it was built, how banking functions were arranged on the interior, how long it was used as a bank, why it was located there, and so on. To set it in context, the researcher will probably want to look first at other banks in the city, their designs and locations, and then at other downtown buildings in the same style. An interesting item may turn up in the process of answering these questions—say, the architectural commission was awarded through a competition. This provokes other questions, all relevant to the significance of the design: why a competition, who competed, why this firm was selected, what program the firm was given, how this design compared to the others, who selected it (*see fig. 2.6*).

Engineering and Industrial Structures. Histories of engineering structures such as dams, bridges, or buildings emphasize design innovations, construction methods, and structural performance, while histories of industrial sites often focus on the process—how the system operated, how the goods were produced, or how the resource was extracted. To set an engineering structure or industrial complex in context, research requires questions that address specific engineering or technological issues: What were the precedents for the development of the technology? Was the technology unusual or common for its time? What impact did the technology have over time?

In the case of an industrial complex or factory where historic machinery survives, HAER often directs its questions along descriptive and analytical lines. For example, the study of a woolen mill in Missouri sought to answer several basic questions for each piece of machinery. The descriptive questions included the following: What was the historic name of the machine? Who manufactured it? When was it manufactured? How did it operate? What changes were made to the machine? What is its current condition? The analytical query focused on the significance of each piece of machinery: Was the machine technologically unique, or was it a common type? Did it reflect national technological advancement, or was it a local adaptation of a national type?

Answering Questions

Answering the many questions confronting historians requires a multitude of primary and secondary sources. To set the technological context for structures of technological historical interest, some of the reference works cited in the bibliography will be helpful. For buildings of local historical interest, secondary source material is often scarce and primary research is the only course. Sources vary from place to place, and no list could ever be exhaustive. Many local historical societies or other organizations have published guides on researching in their locality.

The effectiveness of the primary sources will depend on the questions being asked. It is important to evaluate progress constantly so that the researcher does not get sidetracked or fail to pursue something that could be significant. This evaluation could consist of writing research questions at the start and reviewing them periodically or writing an outline or first draft of the final product before the research is complete.

Historians should also evaluate the quality of sources to determine their accuracy and reliability. When were the data produced—contemporaneously with the resource itself (a primary source) or later (a secondary source)? Did the recorder have firsthand knowledge, or was it hearsay? What was the motivation and funding for producing the data? What were the recorder's biases? Keeping these questions in mind can prevent the historian from giving too much credence to unreliable sources (*see fig. 2.1*).

The researcher usually starts with secondary sources, such as published architectural guides and histories and technological reference works. Unpublished surveys also deserve investigation. The researcher will probably have to return to secondary sources after learning more about the structure through primary research, but as a starting point, secondary sources can save a lot of time. By identifying basic facts, such as year of construction, secondary sources can point the researcher to the best primary sources, such as the right tax books. In addition, a careful reading of the bibliography in a secondary source can reveal important sources the researcher might otherwise have missed.

Some secondary sources can change the thrust of the research approach. For example, if the initial research finds that a definitive study of the architect in question has been written, then the research might shift from investigating that architect's entire work to merely fitting the building into it. Such a definitive study could be referenced in the documentation rather than recounted. Nonetheless, it is important not to accept basic facts about a structure from a secondary source without verification. Construction dates and attributions in secondary sources have been known to be wrong, and if an error is accepted as a premise, the research will obviously be faulty.

Legal records are among the best primary sources. A chain of title, which establishes ownership of a property, can be constructed from deeds. Variations in the price of a property, or in some cases in the description of it, can indicate major construction or alterations. The effectiveness of chains of title varies from place to place, but for rural areas they are often the only key to ownership. Other legal records include tax records, which indicate ownership and changes in assessment; building permits, which are invaluable but usually available

Figure 2.1
Historic photographs are generally reliable sources. This 1923 photograph of the McLachlen Building (1910–11, J. H. de Sibour), in Washington, D.C., was found in a promotional publication of the architect's works. A comparison between it and the extant structure confirms that the building has changed little since its construction and reveals the original appearance of the storefronts.

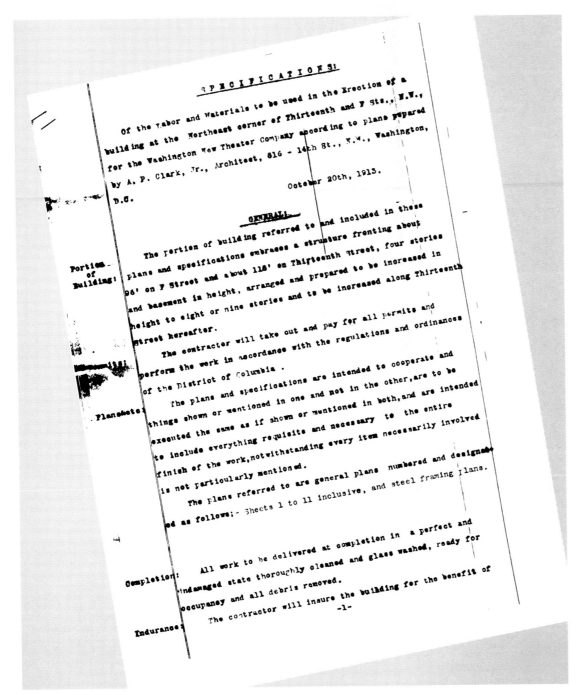

only in cities; and probate records, which often include explicit inventories of real and personal property.

Publications and documents contemporary with the structure are another important source (*see fig. 2.2*). Newspapers are helpful, but as they are often unindexed, pertinent articles and advertisements may be hard to find (*see fig. 2.3*). City directories can identify occupants and uses of a structure and are also helpful in determining construction dates (*see fig. 2.4*). Promotional publications such as real estate brochures and souvenir booklets can be helpful, but their self-serving nature should be taken into account. Letters, diaries, and corporate records, although difficult to locate, can be extremely rich resources (*see figs. 2.5 and 2.6*). The manuscript version of the U.S. Census, which contains detailed information on building occupants, is available but only for censuses taken more than seventy-two years ago. Real estate insurance maps give site plans, number of floors, and construction materials and often include information on power supply and machinery for industrial sites (*see fig. 2.7*). Issued every few years, they can help pinpoint construction dates and show alterations. Although these maps

Figure 2.2
Specifications for construction can be highly informative. In this example from the Homer Building (1913–14, Appleton P. Clark Jr.), the second paragraph specifies that the building will be four stories but "arranged and prepared to be increased in height . . . along Thirteenth Street hereafter." The extra height was not added, but the building was doubled in size with an addition to the north. More than sixty years after construction, the architect's original specifications were a critical part of the rationale to substantially increase the height of the now-historic building.

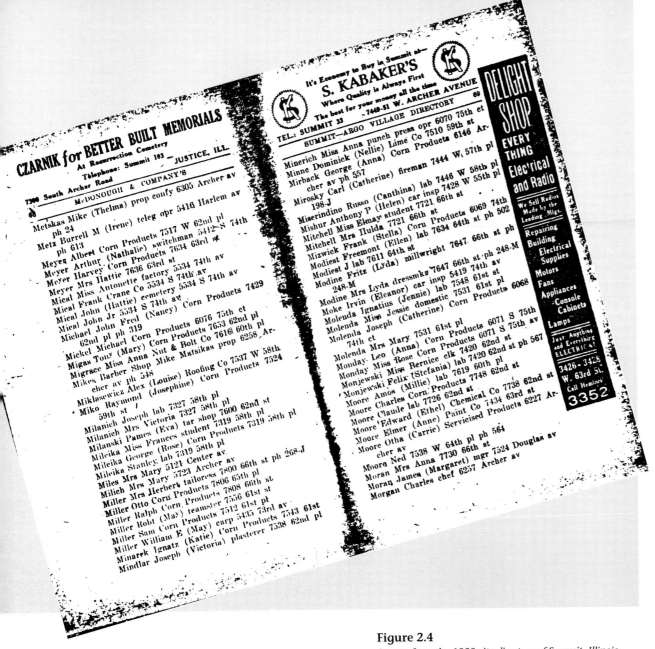

Figure 2.4

A page from the 1929 city directory of Summit, Illinois, indicates the blue-collar nature of the town. Corn Products is easily identifiable as the town's major employer.

generally are limited to urban areas, they often include industrial sites outside the city limits that posed a fire hazard and were likely to be insured.

Because a structure is the focus of the research, architectural and engineering records should not be overlooked. Original design and construction drawings are most likely to be found in the possession of the original architecture firm or its successor. They may also be found in the building itself, in the archives of the company for which it was built, or in the owner's papers. The National Union Index to Architectural Records in the Library of Congress and the Avery Index to Architectural Periodicals may provide good leads.

Other graphic sources should also be investigated. Historic illustrations can be extremely helpful, not only in identifying original appearance and subsequent alterations but also in identifying occupants and uses (*see fig. 2.8*). Published compilations of historic photographs, which usually concentrate on a specific area, are a good place to start. Otherwise, a local historical society and local newspaper files are probably the best sources. Postcards, manufacturers' catalogs, and other promotional illustrations can also be important graphic sources. Bird's-eye views and elaborated maps can be helpful but are not always entirely accurate because of their promotional nature (*see fig. 2.9*).

The historian should include copies of important graphic records with the written documentation. A careful selection should be made, depending on the preservation and accessibility of the records in their current repository. If the records are well preserved and well known, it is less important to include them with the documentation; a reference to their existence and location might suffice. A second consideration is the importance of the graphic records to the significance of the building. For example, a photograph that illustrates a building before major alterations or a landscape at a particular point in time will be important to include with the documentation (*see fig. 2.10*). Even if copied, a citation to the location of the original photograph is absolutely necessary, and copyright restrictions must be observed. Graphic material can be copied either by photography or with a photocopier, although a photograph is more easily reproducible for the next researcher. The archival stability of any type of copy should be consistent with the standard of the rest of the documentation.

People connected with the structure should be consulted, not only for their knowledge of the structure but also for their help in identifying other possible sources. While oral tradition is often suspect, it can provide good leads. Oral histories can be an especially useful source for more recent structures with few archival materials. If the researcher asks the informants how they happened to remember these facts, he or she may get an indication of their reliability. Data from oral tradition must be credited as such.

The structure itself is, of course, the most important resource. This includes not only archival materials stored there, such as company records or correspondence, but also the very structure, which reveals its alterations and uses. While the information for the architectural description is being gathered, the historian should also regard the structure as a document. On the exterior, interruptions in symmetrical fenestration patterns may indicate alterations, just as changes in moldings on the interior may indicate an altered room arrangement (*see fig. 2.11*). Basements and attics, traditionally unfinished spaces, can be a rich source of structural information (*see figs. 4.31 and 7.8*) and can also provide incidental clues, such as

Figure 2.5
Correspondence concerning building suppliers can provide valuable information, particularly for restoration work. This example, found in the collection of Scotty's Castle in Death Valley, California, gives the intended locations for each piece of metalwork.

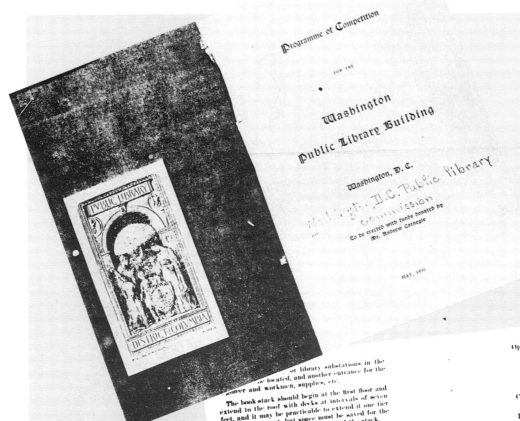

Figure 2.6
The Washington Public Library (1899–1903, Ackerman and Ross) was designed through a competition, as were many Carnegie libraries. The competition program provides insights into the Library Board's original intentions, as well as some of the constraints the architects faced.

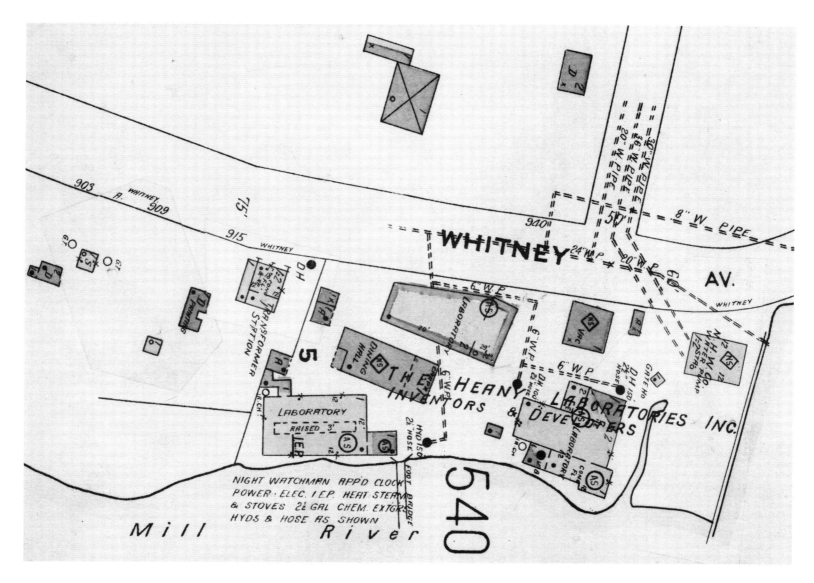

Figure 2.7
This Sanborn insurance map of the Eli Whitney Armory in Hamden, Connecticut, shows industrial areas along Whitney Avenue and the Mill River. Note the indications of utility services and the labels identifying various uses related to risk.

Figure 2.8
Three historic illustrations of the Leland Stanford House (1857, Seth Babson) in Sacramento, California, reveal the extensive alterations that were made to this building. The lithograph was printed in the California Farmer *of July 4, 1862, and showed the building shortly after construction. The pre-1870 photograph, from a book about Leland Stanford, likewise showed the original house. The 1902 photograph from the collection of the California Society of Pioneers depicts the building after 1871, when it was elevated onto a raised basement and a mansard roof and wings were added.*

Figure 2.9
This view of the Cambria Iron Works in Johnstown, Pennsylvania, is typical of the bird's-eye view genre. Published primarily as commercial ventures, they can be valuable although not always accurate renderings.

the dates of newspapers used for insulation. It is important to keep consulting the structure as information is turned up elsewhere. For example, if research suggests that alterations were made, the historian should determine if they are visible on the structure. Do not take the structure itself for granted; question every aspect of it.

Engineering and Industrial Structures. Among the sources most useful and readily available to the technological historian are professional engineering and scientific journals and industrial and engineering trade journals. The earliest of the indexes that provide a comprehensive list of citations in the trade journals is the *Engineering Index*. This annual index was first published in 1896 and groups the citations by subject, such as railroads, wastewater treatment plants, steel works, and so on. The *Industrial Arts Index*, published from 1913 to 1957, is an outstanding tool for researching the trade journals and, unlike the *Engineering Index*, lists citations by both geographic region and corporate name. American trade and professional journals of the nineteenth century tend to be indexed at best in the *Readers' Guide to Periodical Literature* and at the very least in the individual journals.

Engineering and industrial texts and treatises are often a neglected resource. These frequently provide the historian with an understanding of the state-of-the-art technology at a

Figure 2.10
This 1885 photograph not only captures the bridge from which it was taken, but documents the buildings and landscape along the waterfront. Landscapes, in particular, change rapidly, and historic views of landscapes make an especially valuable record of a specific point in time.

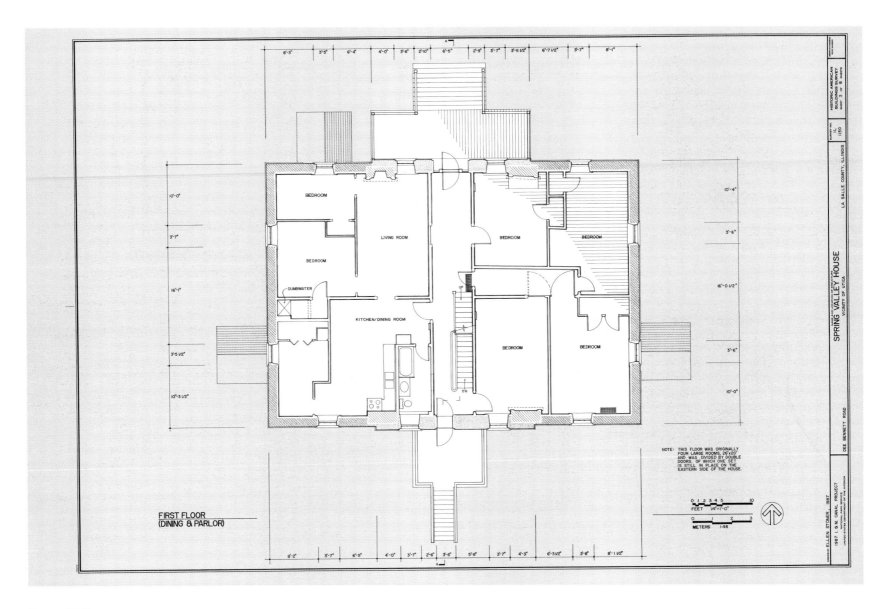

Figure 2.11

Measured drawings are excellent research tools. The partitions that have been added to the interior of this house might be confusing to someone on site, but in this HABS drawing they are distinct from the original walls. (The first floor of the 1850s Spring Valley House near Utica, Illinois, was originally divided into four large rooms with a central hall.)

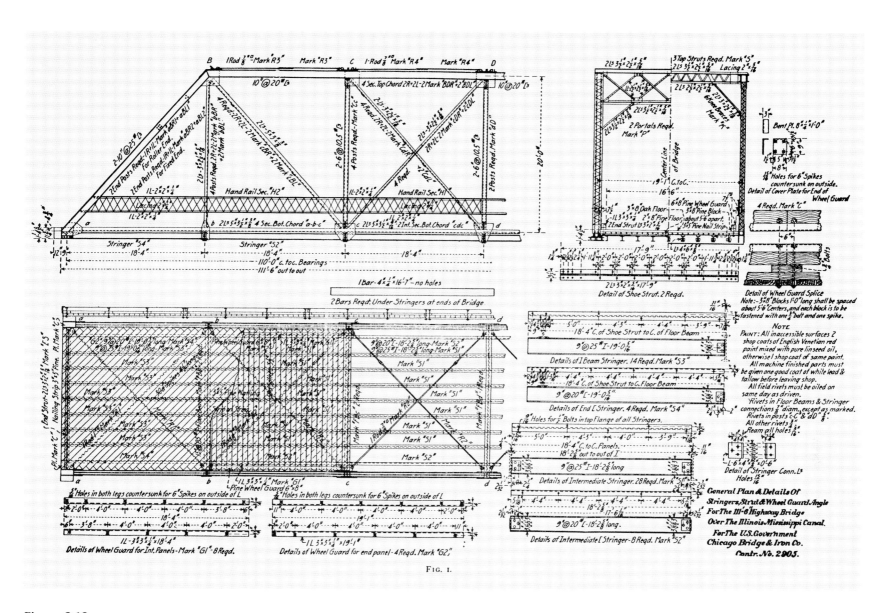

FIG. I.

Figure 2.12
This drawing from Milo S. Ketchum's Design of Highway Bridges, *published in 1908, exemplifies the wealth of information that can be found in historic engineering reference books.*

particular time and occasionally permit a glimpse of society's attitudes toward the technology. For example, Milo S. Ketchum's *Design of Highway Bridges,* published in 1908, is an excellent reference for bridge design, construction, and aesthetics of the late nineteenth and early twentieth centuries (*see fig. 2.12*). For a historian studying a mid-nineteenth-century flour mill, an indispensable work is Oliver Evans's *The Young Millwright and Miller's Guide,* first published in 1834 with several other editions issued through the late nineteenth century (*see figs. 2.13 and 2.14*). One frequently used reference from the late nineteenth century is *Appleton's Cyclopaedia of Applied Mechanics* (1880). This two-volume set provides a fine overview of major engineering works and mechanical equipment dating from the mid- to late nineteenth century.

An often neglected resource, patent records are frequently helpful for understanding how a mechanism or structure was intended to function (*see fig. 2.15*). Researching patent records has been greatly facilitated by the development of the Classification and Search Support Information System (CASSIS), available at select libraries in each state.

Description

A description of the structure that is the object of research is always necessary. Too often, historians take it for granted that the reader is as familiar with the object as the writer, or that drawings or photographs will suffice to describe the structure. The present appearance of a structure, though, should always be documented in the written history. A description should not only relate what a structure looks like, but also qualify that appearance.

Identify and define important characteristics of the building. These include qualities such as massing, shape, scale, rhythm, and texture, which particularly concern the three-dimensional character of a building—qualities that drawings or photographs do not always portray effectively. While each of these qualities can be interpreted literally, such as "four stories," the scale of the building has more to do with how these four stories are perceived. Similarly, describing the massing of a building is more than explaining the plan and bulk; the impression the bulk leaves on the viewer should be described also. In a way, these qualities are a means of interpreting the designer's intentions—for example, in selecting a particular fenestration pattern, what rhythm did the designer create? Examining these qualities helps the researcher comprehend a building.

A description of a building should include its size, shape, materials, and fenestration, as well as the shape and materials of the roof (*see fig. 2.8*). The actual structural system should be noted in addition to the exterior material. On the interior, plan and materials are important. Any significant features should receive special attention. A description of the site is also important, especially for relating the building to others around it or to landscape features that bear upon it, such as a mill's relation to a stream (*see figs. 11.19 and 11.20*).

The issue of categorizing architectural style has come under increasing debate in recent years. In some cases, the desire to assign a style to every structure has resulted in absurdity, with styles the designer never conceived assigned to buildings that bear little resemblance to the historical style. On the other hand, styles are of great importance to buildings that were conceived to represent them, such as the Greek Revival–style U.S. Patent Office in Washington,

D.C. Not to label the Patent Office "Greek Revival" in any description of it would show a severe misunderstanding of the significance of the building. In addition, style can provide a shorthand description to someone who speaks the language. For example, terming a country house "Georgian Revival" conveys a great deal about the appearance of the building, the era in which it was constructed, and the aspirations of its owner. Style names should be used when they serve a purpose and are accurate but should not be used to fill in a blank, to sound erudite, or when a building does not fit the style that is being assigned.

Vernacular building types should also be acknowledged, although without attempting to convert a type to a style by creating a new name. The phrase "three-bay row house" instantly conveys a picture of an attached dwelling three bays wide, probably two or three stories tall, and, more than likely, with a side hall entrance. When describing vernacular buildings, the historian should pay greater attention to structure, material, form, and plan.

A description can be augmented through research. For example, a hidden structural system may be identified by studying a building permit or construction photographs, rather than by destructive testing. Similarly, the origin of an element, such as a mantelpiece adapted from a pattern book, is included in a description if it is known.

Making interpretive statements, such as defining important characteristic features, identifying style, and employing research, should never be confused with, or take the place of, writing an actual description. A description of present appearance should be clearly limited to what can actually be seen, and interpretation or guesswork should be explicitly labeled as such.

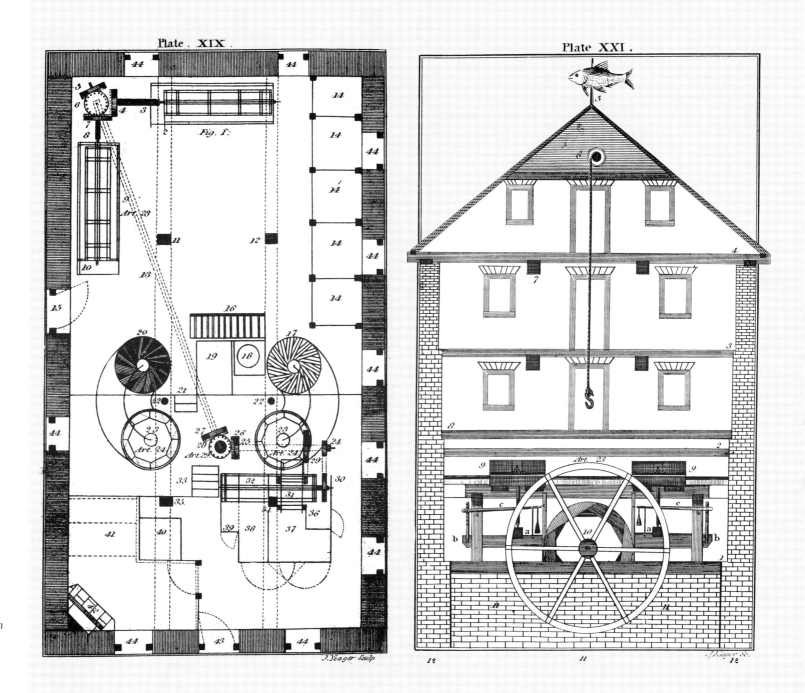

Figure 2.13
Engravings from Oliver Evans's Young Millwright and Miller's Guide *depict a prototypical mill in plan and section drawings. Compare these illustrations with fig. 2.14.*

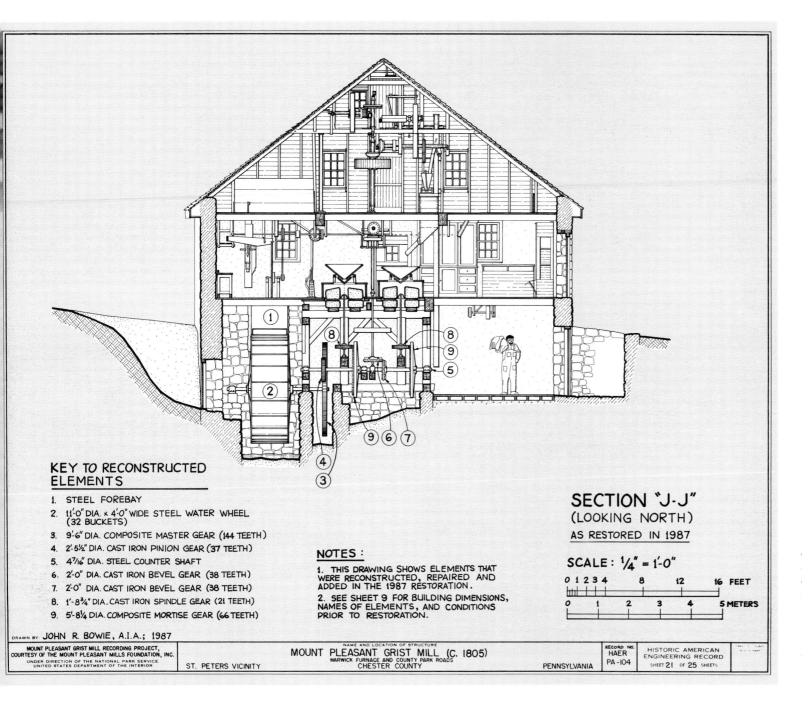

KEY TO RECONSTRUCTED ELEMENTS

1. STEEL FOREBAY
2. 11'-0" DIA. x 4'-0" WIDE STEEL WATER WHEEL (32 BUCKETS)
3. 9'-6" DIA. COMPOSITE MASTER GEAR (144 TEETH)
4. 2'-5½" DIA. CAST IRON PINION GEAR (37 TEETH)
5. 4⁷⁄₁₆" DIA. STEEL COUNTER SHAFT
6. 2'-0" DIA. CAST IRON BEVEL GEAR (38 TEETH)
7. 2'-0" DIA. CAST IRON BEVEL GEAR (38 TEETH)
8. 1'-8¾" DIA. CAST IRON SPINDLE GEAR (21 TEETH)
9. 5'-8¼" DIA. COMPOSITE MORTISE GEAR (66 TEETH)

DRAWN BY: JOHN R. BOWIE, A.I.A.; 1987

NOTES :

1. THIS DRAWING SHOWS ELEMENTS THAT WERE RECONSTRUCTED, REPAIRED AND ADDED IN THE 1987 RESTORATION.
2. SEE SHEET 9 FOR BUILDING DIMENSIONS, NAMES OF ELEMENTS, AND CONDITIONS PRIOR TO RESTORATION.

SECTION "J-J"
(LOOKING NORTH)

AS RESTORED IN 1987

SCALE : ¼" = 1'-0"

0 1 2 3 4   8   12   16 FEET

0   1   2   3   4   5 METERS

MOUNT PLEASANT GRIST MILL RECORDING PROJECT, COURTESY OF THE MOUNT PLEASANT MILLS FOUNDATION, INC.
UNDER DIRECTION OF THE NATIONAL PARK SERVICE. UNITED STATES DEPARTMENT OF THE INTERIOR

NAME AND LOCATION OF STRUCTURE
MOUNT PLEASANT GRIST MILL (C. 1805)
WARWICK FURNACE AND COUNTY PARK ROADS
ST. PETERS VICINITY   CHESTER COUNTY   PENNSYLVANIA

RECORD NO.
HAER
PA-104

HISTORIC AMERICAN ENGINEERING RECORD
SHEET 21 OF 25 SHEETS

Figure 2.14
A comparison of this HAER drawing with the engraving in fig. 2.13 reveals the ways in which the same functions in prototypical and actual settings are similar and different.

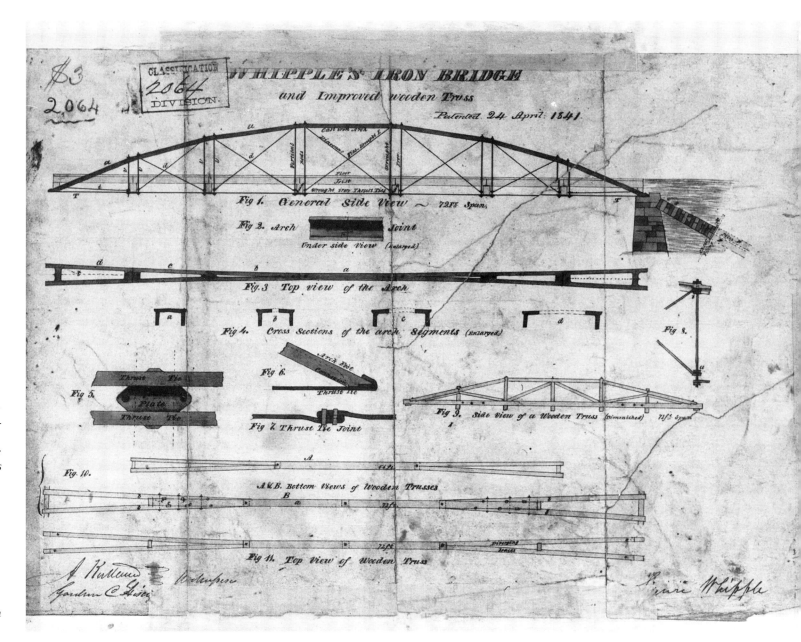

Figure 2.15

This watercolor of Squire Whipple's arch truss bridge, possibly by his hand, is the drawing he would have submitted to the Patent Office on application. Even though Whipple conceptualized the bridge as all iron, both the drawing and specifications included language about building the bridge in wood. The 1840s was a transitional period, when iron was first being used for bridges. Bridge building in the United States was still a wood tradition, and Whipple wanted to benefit regardless of which material was chosen.

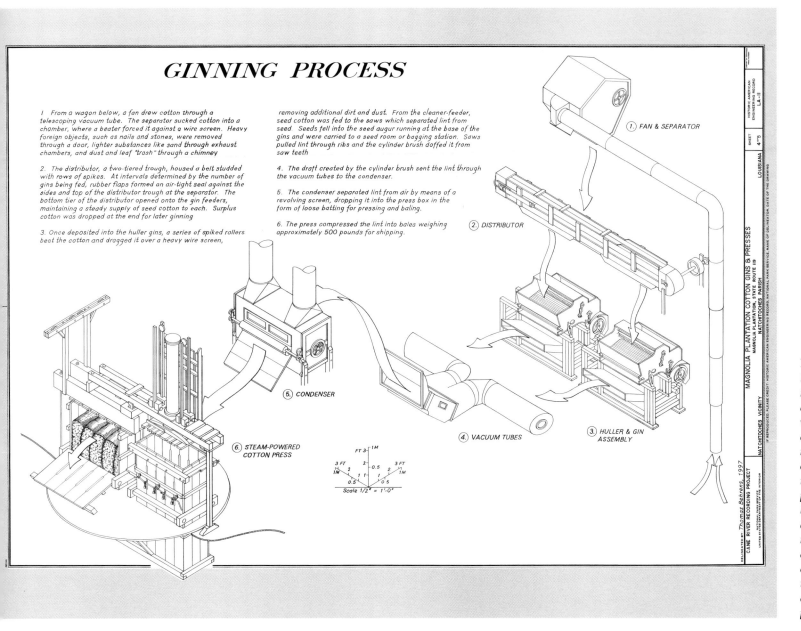

GINNING PROCESS

1   From a wagon below, a fan drew cotton through a telescoping vacuum tube. The separator sucked cotton into a chamber, where a beater forced it against a wire screen. Heavy foreign objects, such as nails and stones, were removed through a door, lighter substances like sand through exhaust chambers, and dust and leaf "trash" through a chimney

2. The distributor, a two-tiered trough, housed a belt studded with rows of spikes. At intervals determined by the number of gins being fed, rubber flaps formed an air-tight seal against the sides and top of the distributor trough at the separator. The bottom tier of the distributor opened onto the gin feeders, maintaining a steady supply of seed cotton to each. Surplus cotton was dropped at the end for later ginning

3. Once deposited into the huller gins, a series of spiked rollers beat the cotton and dragged it over a heavy wire screen,

removing additional dirt and dust. From the cleaner-feeder, seed cotton was fed to the saws which separated lint from seed. Seeds fell into the seed augur running at the base of the gins and were carried to a seed room or bagging station. Saws pulled lint through ribs and the cylinder brush doffed it from saw teeth

4. The draft created by the cylinder brush sent the lint through the vacuum tubes to the condenser.

5. The condenser separated lint from air by means of a revolving screen, dropping it into the press box in the form of loose batting for pressing and baling.

6. The press compressed the lint into bales weighing approximately 500 pounds for shipping.

1. FAN & SEPARATOR

2. DISTRIBUTOR

5. CONDENSER

6. STEAM-POWERED COTTON PRESS

FT 3 1M
3 FT   3 FT
1M   0.5   1M
    1   0   1
  0.5   2
      0.5
Scale 1/2" = 1'-0"

4. VACUUM TUBES

3. HULLER & GIN ASSEMBLY

DELINEATED BY: *Thomas Behrens, 1997*
CANE RIVER RECORDING PROJECT

MAGNOLIA PLANTATION COTTON GINS & PRESSES
MAGNOLIA PLANTATION, STATE ROUTE 119
NATCHITOCHES PARISH

NATCHITOCHES VICINITY   LOUISIANA

SHEET 4 "5

HISTORIC AMERICAN ENGINEERING RECORD
LA-11

Figure 2.16
Drawings can help explain industrial processes that are difficult to describe in words. Here, axonometric drawings of cotton ginning and baling machinery are arranged to show the flow of the ginning process and subsequent baling of the cotton. The drawings are supplemented by annotations and text. Further detail can be found in the text of the accompanying history and in the large-format photographs.

DOUBLE BOX STEAM PRESS

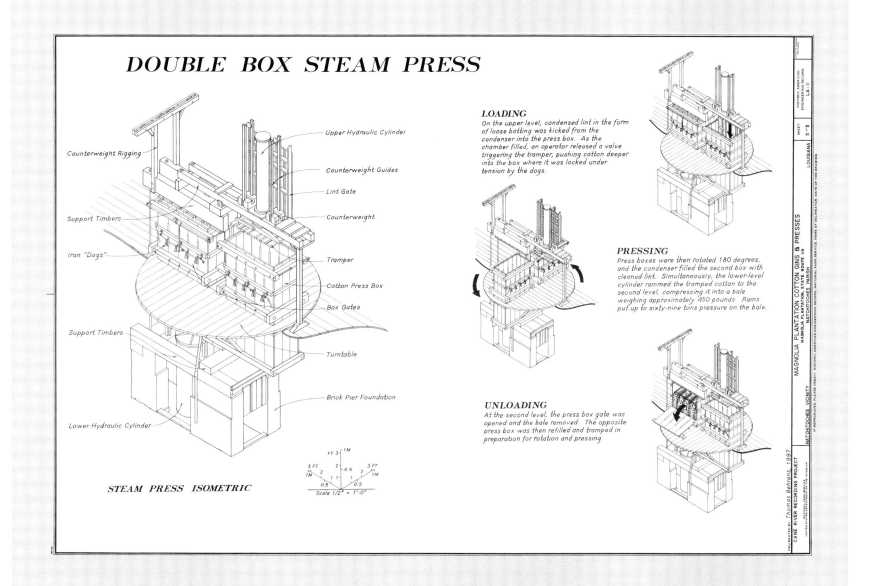

Counterweight Rigging

Upper Hydraulic Cylinder

Counterweight Guides

Lint Gate

Counterweight

Support Timbers

Iron "Dogs"

Tramper

Cotton Press Box

Box Gates

Support Timbers

Turntable

Brick Pier Foundation

Lower Hydraulic Cylinder

STEAM PRESS ISOMETRIC

FT 3 1M
3 FT 2 3 FT
1M 1 1M
0.5 0.5
0.5 1 0.5
Scale 1/2" = 1'-0"

LOADING
On the upper level, condensed lint in the form of loose batting was kicked from the condenser into the press box. As the chamber filled, an operator released a valve triggering the tramper, pushing cotton deeper into the box where it was locked under tension by the dogs.

PRESSING
Press boxes were then rotated 180 degrees, and the condenser filled the second box with cleaned lint. Simultaneously, the lower-level cylinder rammed the tramped cotton to the second level, compressing it into a bale weighing approximately 450 pounds. Rams put up to sixty-nine tons pressure on the bale.

UNLOADING
At the second level, the press box gate was opened and the bale removed. The opposite press box was then refilled and tramped in preparation for rotation and pressing

DELINEATED BY Thomas Behrens, 1997
CANE RIVER RECORDING PROJECT
UNITED STATES DEPARTMENT OF THE INTERIOR

MAGNOLIA PLANTATION COTTON GINS & PRESSES
MAGNOLIA PLANTATION, STATE ROUTE 119
NATCHITOCHES PARISH

NATCHITOCHES VICINITY   LOUISIANA

HISTORIC AMERICAN ENGINEERING RECORD
LA-11

SHEET 5 OF 5

IF REPRODUCED, PLEASE CREDIT: HISTORIC AMERICAN ENGINEERING RECORD, NATIONAL PARK SERVICE, NAME OF DELINEATOR, DATE OF THE DRAWING

Relating the description to the graphic material that will accompany it is crucial. Because a physical object is the subject of investigation, some graphic representation is always desirable (*see fig. 2.16*). However, before referring to the graphics or letting them take the place of description, make sure they actually will accompany the written material. Also, the quality of the graphic material is important; a 35 mm contact print will need to be amplified by far more verbal description than would an 8" × 10" print of a large-format negative. If the written information is to be complemented by good graphic documentation, then the description should concentrate on things that need to be emphasized or that the graphics represent poorly. If black-and-white photographs are the only graphic documentation, particular attention should be given in the written description to such features as color, materials, structural system, and plan. Details that will appear in the graphic material without explanation might also be emphasized, such as quoins, modillions, and inscriptions.

Interpreting drawings is also important. For example, when the written material is accompanied by floor plans, a convoluted description of spatial relationships is unnecessary. In fact, that type of description is rarely helpful. If a plan is complicated and there are no measured drawings, then the written description should be complemented by a sketch plan. A characterization of the floor plan, such as "center passage plan," is often sufficient (*see fig. 4.8*).

A description can be extremely detailed, and it is sometimes difficult to know where to stop. Infinitely detailed descriptions are rarely necessary, though, for if the specifics are that important, they should be illustrated. A written description should interpret the structure broadly. It should record the appearance of fea-

tures that graphic materials do not record, and it should interpret specific features of significance. If, for example, an auditorium is significant for its acoustics, the acoustic features should be described in detail. While these will be illustrated in the graphic material, their effectiveness will not be obvious to uninformed readers. Finally, a written description may be the best or only documentation of a structure. Do not overlook the obvious.

Engineering and Industrial Structures. Engineering and industrial structures generally fall into one of two categories: structural or mechanical. The structural category includes bridges, dams, and buildings. The mechanical category encompasses a larger range of objects, including textile machinery, steelmaking contrivances, hydroelectric equipment, chemical processing and industrial apparatuses, and so on. Resources in the structural category are often easier to describe than those in the mechanical. For example, the description of a metal truss bridge should include such basic information as the truss type, age, span length, and type of supporting structures (piers or abutments). Often the description of the truss type includes a discussion of the truss members (the material they consist of) and mention of any changes made to the trussing as well as to the rest of the bridge (*see fig. 6.6*). The historian should organize the description so that readers can better understand the form and function of the site or structure.

The descriptions of sites or structures included in the mechanical category are often more involved. However, whether describing a complex array of machinery in a textile mill or an intricate network of electronic components in an early computer, a historian should always proceed from the general to the specific, relating

the physical description to the way in which the machinery or equipment operated. Such basic information as the manufacturer (or inventor) of the machine should be noted, as well as its date of manufacture and installation and its production capabilities or output. Attention should also be given to the physical relationship of one machine to another, that is, how did an individual machine function as part of a larger industrial process? Relating the physical layout of the machinery or equipment to the people who used it is central to the description (*see fig. 4.4*).

Through the description, a historian can provide greater insight into the drawings of a structure. For instance, a truss bridge may be drawn showing details of the various truss members, but it is the description that makes sense of them by explaining their composition (their materials and the way in which they were fabricated) and their function (the way in which they behave under loads). When the description and analysis are well integrated with the drawings, each becomes a far more useful tool (*see fig. 6.5*).

Significance

Once the history of a structure has been researched and its present appearance assessed, this information should be analyzed and synthesized. Only then can a statement of significance be written. The significance should be derived from the history and design of the structure. While it is often easy to focus on a person or event associated with a structure, it is important to relate the structure itself to that person or event. For instance, does it look the way it did when that person lived there? It may be that after research has been conducted, a structure will have less significance than had been assumed in the preliminary assessment. There is nothing wrong with this; a structure's significance should not be exaggerated. Everything that is asserted in the significance statement should have been proven and amplified in the historical and descriptive sections.

A well-written significance statement should be clear, pithy, and supported by the evidence. As a rule, the more significant the building, the shorter the significance statement.

Sources and Methodology

No research work is complete without a list of the sources consulted and the whys and hows of documentation. A list of sources permits other historians to verify the research and gives appropriate credit to original thoughts. Standard scholarly procedure demands that sources be credited and quotations be referenced.

Information about the documentation project helps readers evaluate the research. For complicated projects, particularly where judgments have been made in the selection or evaluation of the buildings, a statement of methodology should be included. This states the assumptions and shows how the work was approached and undertaken. For simpler projects, a project information statement should be included that tells who did the work, when, and for whom. Inclusion of the affiliation of the researcher or the organization that funded the work implies the reasons behind the project, the constraints it may have faced, and the direction it took.

Presentation

Many formats can be used to present research. Some are closely prescribed, such as National Register nomination forms, which are preprinted and accompanied by specific instructions for their use. Others, like the standard HABS outline format, divide the information into specific categories. Some formats are not written at all, such as oral presentations to boards and commissions. All of them, with the possible exception of scholarly articles, should be presented so that they can be understood by an inexpert but interested audience. Avoid overly technical language whenever possible, and use the active voice, particularly when describing industrial processes.

Report findings selectively; do not include everything that was learned. For example, a historian researching a rural site may have had to trace a chain of title from the present back to 1810 to determine the original owner. There is no need to repeat the entire chain in the report if it is not informative. Instead, the specific deeds pertaining to the original owner should be cited, and the deed books with their location should be noted in the list of sources consulted. Likewise, although every occupant of a building may have been determined through city directory research, making generalities about these occupants, rather than listing them individually, is often sufficient.

Nevertheless, a problem more common than reporting too much of the research is that of omitting important aspects of a building or site from the investigation. For this reason, HABS uses an outline format wherein each heading reminds the writer of items to be covered. In addition, the reader can find answers quickly by going directly to the relevant section. A paragraph or more of information follows each heading. The HABS historian's guidelines discuss this issue in greater detail and should be consulted before writing information for submission to HABS.

(HAER, it should be noted, does not use this outline.)

HABS Outline

For each of the headings in the section on historical information in the HABS outline, a direct answer should be given first, then expanded upon. For example: "Date of erection: 1917–18. The foundation was laid in June 1917, according to the building permit (Permit #7548, June 8, 1917). The building was formally opened on September 9, 1918 (*Daily Planet*, September 10, 1918, p. 4 c. 1)." The section on original plans and construction is designed to permit discussion of the importance of the original design. The second part of this section, on historical context, is where the building should be placed in context—geographically, chronologically, stylistically, technologically, and so on. In addition, people and events associated with the structure should be discussed here.

The architectural information section of the outline is self-explanatory. In this format, the description proceeds logically from foundation to roof, and then to the interior, concluding with a description of the site.

Historians are encouraged to use sources other than published material, such as original architectural drawings, early views (photographs and drawings), and interviews. Each source, and its location if obscure, should be fully described in a bibliography. The concluding section on project information is a free-form description of the project, its goals and constraints, the people and organizations involved, and the date.

The disadvantage of the outline format is that writers feel constrained by it and limit their inquiry strictly to the categories that appear in the outline. Despite entreaties to add or delete categories as necessary, most writers adhere to

HABS Outline

Building name and HABS number
Location
Present owner
Present use
Significance

Part I. Historical information
A. Physical history
    1. Date of erection
    2. Architect
    3. Original and subsequent owners
    4. Builder, contractor, suppliers
    5. Original plans and construction
    6. Alterations and additions
B. Historical context

Part II. Architectural information
A. General statement
    1. Architectural character
    2. Condition of fabric
B. Description of exterior
    1. Overall dimensions
    2. Foundations
    3. Walls
    4. Structural system
    5. Porches
    6. Chimneys
    7. Openings
        a. Doorways and doors
        b. Windows and shutters
    8. Roof
        a. Roof shape, covering
        b. Cornice, eaves
        c. Dormers, cupolas, towers

C. Description of interior
    1. Floor plans
    2. Stairways
    3. Flooring
    4. Wall and ceiling finish
    5. Openings
        a. Doorways and doors
        b. Windows
    6. Decorative features and trim
    7. Hardware
    8. Mechanical equipment
        a. Heating, air-conditioning, ventilation
        b. Lighting
        c. Plumbing
D. Site
    1. General setting and orientation
    2. Historic landscape design
    3. Outbuildings

Part III. Sources of information
A. Original architectural drawings
B. Early views
C. Interviews
D. Bibliography
    1. Primary and unpublished sources
    2. Secondary and published sources
E. Likely sources not yet investigated
F. Supplemental material

Part IV. Project information

the rigid format instead of using it as a springboard. HABS therefore accepts written information in other formats.

HAER, and sometimes HABS, manuscripts appear in a narrative style with headings tailored by the historian for the individual structure or complex. For example, a HAER historian used a chronological approach in the history of a gristmill, with the following chapters: "Alexander's Mill (1855–1894)," "Wilson's Mill (1900–1940)," and "The Mill in 1940." Alternatively, when relating the history of a neighborhood, one historian divided the manuscript into the general HABS headings of history and description. Subheadings in the historical information section covered street railways, parks, water, gas and electricity, and paving. The architectural information included discussions of the buildings' floor plans, heating and lighting, and exterior and interior ornamentation.

HAER and HABS have also developed a one-page architectural and engineering data form appropriate for cases in which there is minimal information, or for structures of less-than-national significance. Not all of the blanks need to be filled in to make the form meaningful. Even limited information, if it is accurate, is better than none.

The complexity of the structure that is being recorded will determine which format is most appropriate. Regardless of the format chosen, the written documentation should complement and illuminate the measured drawings and photographs. When the documentation is complete, an understanding of the structure will emerge.

Figure 2.17
The organizational structure of the HABS outline format is apparent on the first page of the HABS history of the Washington Monument on the Mall in Washington, D.C.

HISTORIC AMERICAN BUILDINGS SURVEY

WASHINGTON NATIONAL MONUMENT
HABS No.   DC-428

Location: The Mall, on a lot bordered by Constitution Avenue to the north, the Tidal Basin to the south, Fourteenth and Fifteenth Street to the east, and Seventeenth Street to the west, Washington, D.C.

Present Owner: U.S. Government.

Present Use: Public monument.

Significance: Built to commemorate the first president of the United States, the monument has also become a hallowed symbol of the nation's government and the city in which it is located. Though the eminent nineteenth-century American architect Robert Mills conceived the initial design, the structure also reflects the technical knowledge and aesthetic judgement of Thomas Lincoln Casey, the Army Corps engineer charged with completing the project. Under Casey, a stagnant construction campaign emblematic of mid-century political and economic turmoil at long last produced the tallest building of its day and an enduring American icon.

Historian: Aaron V. Wunsch, HABS, summer 1994

PART I. HISTORICAL INFORMATION

A.   Physical History:

1.   Date of Erection: The monument was erected in two distinct phases, the first one occurring between 1848 and 1858, the second between 1878 and 1885. The Washington National Monument Society selected Mills' design in 1836, but construction did not begin for another twelve years. An 1848 Congressional resolution permitted the Society to erect the monument on public land within the city, and the Society chose a site near the intersection of the east-west axis through the Capitol and the north-south axis through the President's House (White House). The foundation was laid in June 1848, followed on July 4th by the cornerstone. Progress slowed dramatically in 1854 and halted altogether in 1858. Work resumed under federal direction in October 1878, and a second cornerstone was laid on August 7, 1880. The capstone was set on December 6, 1884, and the monument dedicated on February 21, 1885. Important additions and modifications occurred over the next few years.

CHAPTER 3

PHOTOGRAPHY

William L. Lebovich

For both professionals and amateurs, photography is the most popular means of documenting structures. It is the least expensive, fastest, and easiest method of documentation. When measured drawings and histories are prepared, photographs complement the other work. They are more easily understood and can convey information not normally included in the other forms of documentation (see figs. 3.1, 3.2, and 3.3).

A photograph can convey three-dimensional qualities, spatial relationships, current conditions, texture, and context. The size of an engine or the degree to which the main pavilion of a house projects beyond flanking side wings is more quickly comprehended in a photograph than from a lengthy written description or measured drawing (see fig. 3.4). Texture of materials is difficult to depict by drawing or writing. Certain aspects of current condition, such as minor cracks, spalling, or peeling paint, are too small or too time-consuming to draw (see figs. 3.5 and 3.6). A single photograph, taken from the right vantage point, establishes the environmental setting for a building or structure to be studied (see fig. 3.7). To achieve the same result with a history or drawing requires more effort than is necessary for a secondary aspect of the subject being documented. In making decisions about documenting a resource, it is critical to understand which aspects of a structure are best depicted by photographs, a history, or drawings.

The HABS/HAER/HALS Approach

Despite the popularity and demonstrated usefulness of photography, few documentary photographs display the technical and aesthetic qualities of the large-format photographs produced by the Historic American Buildings Survey (HABS), the Historic American Engineering Record (HAER), and the Historic American Landscape Survey (HALS). HABS/HAER has been doing large-format photography for seventy years and has developed approaches that can improve anyone's photographs of the built environment. This chapter explains those approaches and demonstrates, through words and photographs, what constitutes good documentary photography. These approaches are applicable to nearly all formats of photography. The strengths and weaknesses of 35 mm, medium-size, and large formats will be discussed to help readers pick the one best suited to their needs.

The HABS/HAER/HALS programs use large-format photography for official

WEST ELEVATION

Figures 3.1 and 3.2

It is easier to read the projections of the entrance and flanking wings in the photograph than in the measured drawing of the Maurice Bathhouse in Hot Springs National Park, Arkansas. The wings and mosaic panels between the second-story windows are also more apparent in the photograph, but the height of the roof is shortened and the tower is not visible. Notice the flagpole, which was not included in the measured drawing.

Figure 3.3

This perspective photograph clearly shows the depth of the entrance bay and flanking wings of the Maurice Bathhouse. It also shows the round-headed window in the wings and the gatepost with eagle, which are obstructed by a tree in the photograph in fig. 3.2. It had been deleted from the west elevation drawing (but is included in another drawing) and is not apparent in the west elevation photograph.

Figure 3.4
The worker gives scale to this photograph of the East Boston Pumping Station, making it possible to estimate the size of the horizontal Corliss engine.

Figure 3.5
Small details in a structure such as the rivet holes in the Statue of Liberty's face and the damage at the tip of her nose are more easily recorded through photography. (Rivets are used to attach the saddle holding the wrought-iron strap that supports the copper skin of the statue.) Photographic assignments, particularly for structures such as the Statue of Liberty, often require appropriate safety precautions for photographer and equipment (hard hat, safety ties, etc.).

HABS/HAER/HALS documentation of a building or structure. This formal photography is deposited in the Library of Congress as part of the permanent, archivally stable collections. Large format is defined by HABS/HAER/HALS as photography using cameras that produce 4″ × 5″, 5″ × 7″, or 8″ × 10″ negatives. The programs' staff photographers currently use 5″ × 7″, which seems to have been the most popular format since the founding of HABS in 1933. Staff architects and historians use smaller-format cameras to produce field photographs of the buildings and structures they are researching, measuring, and drawing. The resulting informal photography, consisting primarily of 35 mm negatives and contact sheets or small prints, is transmitted to the Library of Congress as field records. Informal photography should ideally meet the archival standards of the formal photographic documentation, although it is not required.

Formal HABS/HAER/HALS photographic documentation is done with black-and-white film, and the negatives and contact prints are archivally treated. The contact paper is fiber-based rather than resin-coated (RC), and the paper and negatives have been washed in water long enough to remove all processing chemicals. Archivally stable negatives and contact prints will last at least 100 years.

Beginning in 1996, the Library of Congress began accepting large-format color transparencies as part of the formal HABS/HAER collections to incorporate the many attributes of color photography into the permanent collections. Color films are less archivally stable than black-and-white films, so special transmittal and curation guidelines were developed to slow

Figure 3.6
Texture and tone are easily conveyed in black-and-white photographs.

Figure 3.7
This photograph of the tree-lined approach to Gunston Hall shows the house in the context of its setting.

the deterioration processes, including cold storage of the originals. Several thousand large-format color transparencies are now part of the collections.

Formal Versus Informal Photography

Why does HABS/HAER/HALS use one format for formal photography and another for informal photography? Along with most other professional architectural photographers, HABS/HAER/HALS photographers use large format because of its large negative size and extensive range of camera movements (*see fig. 3.8*). All other factors being equal, the larger the negative, the better the prints made from it. HABS/HAER/HALS sends contact prints rather than black-and-white enlargements to the Library of Congress. It is much easier to see details on a large-format contact print than it is on smaller 35 mm or medium-format contact prints. In addition, from the point of view of the Library of Congress, large-format negatives are considerably easier to handle and less likely to be damaged than medium-format or 35 mm negative strips.

On a large-format monorail camera, the front standard, which holds the lens, and the rear standard, which holds the film, can be raised, lowered, tilted, swung, and shifted laterally. These movements enable the photographer to eliminate the perspective distortion that commonly occurs in photography of tall buildings or structures. Perspective distortion is often apparent in photographs when the camera had to be inclined to include the entire subject in the

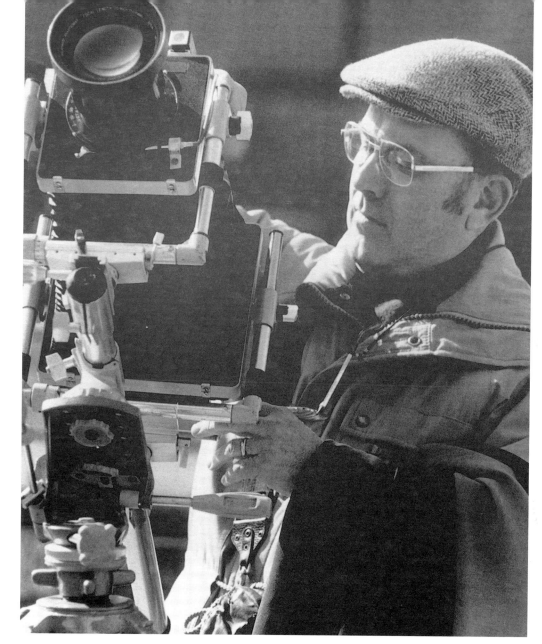

Figure 3.8
HABS photographer Jack E. Boucher loads the film holder in the rear of his 30-pound 5" × 7" monorail camera, which is supported by a 22-pound tripod.

Lens Covering Power

The advantages of a large-format camera for photographing large structures are limited by two factors: the characteristics of the camera and the characteristics of the lens. A large-format field or flatbed camera is less able to cover a tall building than a large-format monorail camera because most field cameras have no vertical fall with their rear film standards and relatively limited rise on their front lens standard. For example, the Calumet field camera permits 45 mm of front rise, while the Calumet monorail camera has a total rise (rising front and falling rear) of 95 mm. Even monorail cameras vary in the amount of total rise offered. The Toyo G permits a 115 mm total rise, while the Horseman permits a total rise of 60 mm (rising front and falling rear).

Even more important than the amount of rise and fall built into a camera is the coverage of the lens. Lens coverage is simply how large an area of film a particular lens will cover. When a camera is raised, lowered, or shifted too much for the particular lens being used, the corners of the image are darkened, creating a less-than-pleasing image. Such an effect is called vignetting (*see fig. 3.9*). The covering power of a lens should not be confused with the angle of view of a lens. The latter indicates how wide a view of the subject a particular lens projects onto the film plane.

Lens coverage is also independent of the lens's focal length (f). For example, Schneider produces two 90 mm lenses, f/5.6 and f/8. The f/5.6 lens has an angle of coverage of 105 degrees, and the f/8 lens has an angle of coverage of 100 degrees. Translated into practical terms, the f/8 lens will cover a 4″ × 5″ piece of film and the f/5.6 lens will cover a 5″ × 7″ piece of film. Used on a 4″ × 5″ camera, the f/5.6 lens, therefore, can be raised (lowered/shifted) more than the f/8 lens can before vignetting occurs. Even with the limited total rise and fall of the Horseman (in comparison with the Toyo), an image may show vignetting when using the 90 mm f/8 lens, whereas there would be none with the f/5.6 lens.

One advantage of most medium- and large-format cameras is that they may accept a holder for Polaroid film, which enables the photographer to make an exposure and see the image in less than a minute. The photographer uses the Polaroid to test exposure and check composition. With large-format cameras, it is very difficult to see what is happening in the four corners, which appear quite dark. The test exposure enables the photographer to spot and avoid annoying, irrelevant features such as overhead wires.

Figure 3.9
Note the vignetting in the upper corners of this photograph, caused by the lens being shifted beyond its covering power. Sometimes it is impossible to avoid vignetting in documentary photography, especially with tall structures like this abandoned iron furnace in a congested industrial complex.

field of view. In the resulting image, the structure appears trapezoidal.

The other type of large-format camera, the flatbed or field camera, permits fewer movements. Most importantly, the rear standard does not move on this type of camera, allowing less opportunity for perspective correction.

HABS/HAER/HALS does not use large format for informal photography for several reasons. First, the architects and historians working in the field often use their personal equipment, which is seldom larger than a 35 mm camera. Such cameras are usually equipped with a perspective-correction wide-angle lens, which gives results similar to those achieved with large format, except that the negatives are smaller. In addition, 35 mm equipment is more portable, less expensive, and easier to operate, and it offers a wider selection of lenses, film, and accessories. These advantages are compelling for those who do not need or cannot afford the higher-quality images that can be produced with large-format equipment.

Copy Photography
In addition to the structures themselves, HABS/HAER/HALS photographers are sometimes called upon to shoot old photographs, drawings, or lithographs (see examples in chapter 2). This is done only with the owner's permission and waiver of any copyright restrictions. As available collections are usually too numerous to copy in their entirety, the most informative representative examples should be selected. The earliest American architectural photographs date from the 1840s, and although the HABS program's early recording efforts focused on pre–Civil War structures, HABS/HAER/HALS has since begun to record more post–Civil War structures, making such historic drawings and construction photographs more important.

To obtain the best results, historic drawings, photographs, and other types of illustrations should be sent to a graphic reproduction service, which has the appropriate copy lenses, filters, special films, lighting, and horizontally mounted cameras. However, historic documents often cannot be removed from the site and must be photographed in the field.

Principles of Architectural Photography

Photographers often seem more concerned with camera equipment than with subject matter. Perhaps they make an unconscious assumption that composition comes naturally if one has the right equipment. Every photographer needs a certain amount of equipment and a certain level of expertise to take good photographs, but much more is needed to produce high-quality documentary photographs.

Understanding the Subject
Photographers must understand the subject and have a clear concept of what they are trying to accomplish. They must know, for example, why a certain residence or blast furnace is worth documenting. They must understand the historical context and key elements of the structure being photographed (*see fig. 3.10*). They use that knowledge to decide what to photograph, and from what vantage point, so that the resulting images convey the importance of the structure. If a photographer lacks such understanding, a historian or other person knowledgeable about the subject can assist.

Misunderstanding the subject can lead to glaring errors in a photograph, from cutting off the tops of skyscrapers to leaving out bridge abutments and approaches—elements integral to understanding the structure and its design

(*see fig. 3.11*). Only slightly less problematic are the numerous instances in which the photographer has not bothered to find a camera position that will provide an unobstructed view of the facade, interior space, or detail being photographed. Not only do some photographers fail to change the camera position or shift the lens (or front standard) to avoid cars and trees, but columns, pipes, or shadows obstruct important elements in many interior shots.

A more subtle problem occurs when a photographer uses an extremely wide-angle lens and then moves too close to the subject. The result is either distortion of the edges or obstruction of parts of the building. If a house is photographed from too close, for example, the eave blocks any view of the roof.

A photographer with inadequate understanding of the resource is also unlikely to photograph all of its important aspects or to take photographs from positions that emphasize these aspects (*see figs. 3.12, 3.13, and 3.14*). For example, someone unfamiliar with steel production would not recognize the key machines, operations, and structures in a large plant or which vantage point would best show the way the machines work (*see fig. 3.15*). Likewise, someone unfamiliar with architectural history would not know the importance of photographing the simple but important rustic detailing of a bungalow-style house (*see fig. 3.10*).

The photographs in the HABS collection taken in the 1930s and '40s, many with lenses, films, and cameras considered primitive today, exemplify the importance of understanding the subject matter. Many of these photographs are still striking because the photographer understood the building, was familiar with principles of composition, and knew how to use natural lighting to create a dramatic image (*see figs. 3.16 and 3.17*).

Figure 3.10
This photograph illustrates the simple detailing of a bungalow. Good coverage would require having a close-up of the timber roof that shows how it is finished and how it is joined to the other structural elements.

Components of a High-Quality Photograph

Assuming a photographer has knowledge of pertinent architecture, engineering, industrial, or landscape history, and the necessary photographic equipment and the skill to use it, what are the specific components of a high-quality documentary photograph? Put simply, a good documentary photograph is an accurate, informative record of a structure or landscape. The photograph should not distort straight lines, a problem caused by tilting the camera (*see fig. 3.18*). To ensure that the image is sharp and suitable for enlarging, a tripod is used, and the camera is carefully leveled (using one or more spirit levels) and focused on the image. The lens is then stopped down to ensure sharp focus.

Lighting. Whenever possible, the angle of the sun and camera position are chosen to avoid casting details into deep shadows, thus obscuring them. Artificial lighting can lighten shadows cast on the exterior of a building. Another means of revealing shadowed details is to lower the contrast of the image when processing or printing the negative, although this may be more difficult to control. Building interiors are illuminated to avoid creating harsh shadows and to simulate natural lighting (*see fig. 3.19*). An additional benefit of using artificial lighting to open up shadows is that the negative will yield a higher-quality enlargement (*see fig. 3.34*). A few excellent architectural photographers working in black-and-white do not use artificial lighting because they do not like the look of artificially lit photographs or do not want to carry the additional equipment. Professional architectural photographers shooting in color almost always use artificial lighting because color film is more sensitive to changes in light levels. If color film is used, the natural lighting coming in through the windows or

Figure 3.11
Notice how the elevated camera position gives an unobstructed overall view of the Chicago Stock Exchange building. The cropping of the top of the building actually occurred when the negative was printed, rather than when the photograph was taken, but is illustrative of what can happen when equipment limitations prevent coverage of an entire building. The spandrel detail from the building is a strongly composed and dramatically lit photograph. However, it would have served better as documentation if it had been taken straight on from an elevated position, with fill flash to provide greater shadow detail.

open doors, the ambient lighting from lamps and light fixtures, and the artificial lighting must be color-balanced to match the film for accurate color reproduction.

To get accurate exposures, a light meter is essential. Large-format cameras do not have built-in light meters, so a photographer must use a handheld one. Some professional photographers use a separate light meter even when using 35 mm or medium-format cameras with meters. HABS/HAER/HALS photographers use one high-quality light meter, which can measure either reflected or incident light and has an accessory spot-metering attachment. Some photographers carry as many as three meters: one for reading incident light (the light striking the subject), a spot meter (which reads a small angle of light reflected off the subject), and an electronic flash meter (for measuring the light produced by the flash).

Scaling. To enable the viewer to sense the scale and size of the subject being photographed, scale sticks can be placed in the field of view. Because these sticks are painted in alternating blocks of black and white, each one foot in height, they are easy to read and give a quick approximation of the size of the object they are placed against (*see figs. 3.20, 4.11, and 4.17*). The HABS/HAER/HALS guidelines stipulate that when photographing Level I structures (the most important resources), the photographer should take two shots of each view, one with the scale stick and one without. For photography of Level II and III structures, at least one photograph showing the scale stick, usually of the principal facade, should be made. Field photographs often have a scale stick in every view.

Technical points. If a photograph is of high technical quality, the viewer will concentrate on the subject matter, not on the photographic

Figure 3.12
This view of the south elevation of the conservatory at Borough House in Stateburg, South Carolina, was taken with a wide-angle lens (121 mm lens on 5" × 7" camera).

Figure 3.13

When the subject in fig. 3.12 was shot from twice as far away with a normal lens (210 mm lens on 5" × 7" camera), a reality very different from that in fig. 3.12 is presented. Not only do more details of the walls flanking the conservatory become apparent, but, most importantly, the roof and upper section of the main house are visible.

Figure 3.14

This image was shot from same camera station as fig. 3.13, but with the wide-angle lens used for fig. 3.12. No other details about the house are visible, and the relationship between the conservatory and the main house is unchanged. However, the wider lens at this camera station provides a better sense of the environment of Borough House.

Figure 3.15
The photographer used flash to supplement existing light for this photograph at a steel plant in Cleveland. Shown are roughing stands for the 84-inch strip mill, which is used to remove extraneous materials from steel slabs processed in the bar mill.

Figure 3.16
This crisp, pleasing, and informative image of an iron balustrade in Savannah, Georgia, exemplifies simple photographic documentation of an architectural detail.

Figure 3.17
Notice the absence of harsh, distracting shadows in this image. Instead, the photographer created an image in which the details are not obscured by shadows cast by the lighting source, and there is a natural look to the photograph.

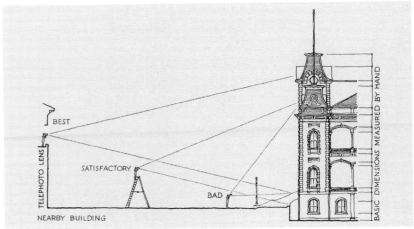

Figure 3.18
This diagram shows how camera location can be used to minimize distortion in photographs.

Figure 3.19
This photograph of a stair at Winthrop College in South Carolina demonstrates the effective use of artificial lighting to simulate natural lighting.

medium (*see fig. 3.21*). The photographer can enhance the potential impact of an image by paying attention to technical considerations such as leveling the camera; using the proper exposure, lighting, and film; and filtering properly. A checklist can help eliminate technical mistakes.

Aesthetics. In addition to technical knowledge of photography and scholarly knowledge of the subject, high-quality documentary photography requires an eye for aesthetics. As HABS photographer Jack E. Boucher has written, "Follow standard elements of composition—for example, have structures photographed from a perspective positioned off center, so [the viewers of the photograph] 'look in' to the photograph,

Figure 3.20
Notice how the scale stick enables the viewer to gauge the approximate size of the vessel's features. The scale stick is held vertically (i.e., parallel to the film plane) to eliminate perspective diminution, which would reduce the accuracy of measurements by foreshortening the scale stick.

Figure 3.21
This photograph of an incline skip (which carries raw materials to the top of a blast furnace and unloads them into it) is an excellent example of a technically perfect illustration. The most important element, the incline skip, occupies a prominent position, yet it is clear how it relates to the surrounding machinery. The negative has been exposed and printed properly, so no detail is too dark.

Figure 3.22

The photographer selected a camera station, lens length, and camera angle that draw the viewer into this image. This strong composition is not at the expense of the subject; the photograph conveys a great deal of information about the building.

not out! Eliminate or minimize distracting foreground, such as pavement, in favor of sky" (*see fig. 3.22*).

Aesthetic considerations, meaning strong composition, are important because they make a photograph more compelling and, therefore, more likely to hold a viewer's attention. When looking at a weak photograph, a viewer unconsciously assumes that the subject is uninteresting, not that the photograph is technically or aesthetically inept. No matter how important a bridge or house is, the qualities that make the structure significant will not be apparent unless a photograph is compelling enough to hold the viewer's attention long enough to study it (*see fig. 3.23*).

Historians and architects know that their depictions of a structure are interpretation, but they assume that a photographer's illustration is impartial. Yet a photographer can exaggerate, distort, or conceal spatial relationships and prominence of features, thereby influencing whether a viewer finds the subject attractive or worthy of documentation.

A photographer, therefore, has a two-part obligation: First, he or she must provide technically good and aesthetically pleasing photographs—properly exposed, properly focused, well lit, effectively composed, undistorted, and rich in detail (*see fig. 3.24*). Second, the photographer must provide photographs that convey the importance of the structure and give enough information for viewers to make their own analysis of it.

Planning and Producing Photographic Documentation

Before embarking on a documentation project, photographers must seek out the background information required to understand the subject matter and make a number of decisions about the equipment needed.

How Much Equipment?

Some photographers feel strongly about not wanting to miss a shot because they are not carrying the necessary equipment. The difficulty with this approach is that it can be physically demanding and time-consuming for photographers who work alone to get all of their equipment to a site (*see fig. 3.25*). When documenting Buffalo Bill Dam in Cody, Wyoming, the HABS photographer had to lower his equipment by rope and then climb down to get a certain vantage point.

In general, the amount of equipment to be carried should be based on how important the resource is, how comprehensive the documentation will be, and how the photography will be used. One slide of a relatively insignificant structure, to be used for a lecture, should require much less equipment than images of a National Historic Landmark intended for publication.

Which Format?

As discussed previously, HABS/HAER/HALS standards require large-format (4″ × 5″, 5″ × 7″, or 8″ × 10″) negatives for formal documentation. Often photographers shift to smaller formats if their subject is extremely isolated and inaccessible. For instance, in Alaska, the HAER photographer who shot the railroad bridge shown in figure 3.26 used a 4″ × 5″ camera rather than the bulkier 5″ × 7″ equipment he usually uses (*see fig. 3.26*).

If the intended use of the photography is not HABS, HAER, or HALS documentation but lecturing, then 35 mm would be the obvious choice because 35 mm slide projectors are

Figure 3.23

This detail of a windmill in New York State is an aesthetically pleasing photograph that also captures the structural system of the windmill. The worn stairs suggest the great age of the structure.

widely available and 35 mm cameras and lenses are less cumbersome in the field. If the documentation is to be used in a publication, medium-format (120/220 mm) negatives are preferable.

Digital cameras have become an integral part of the recording process as their resolution has increased. While not considered archival, digital images are ideal for incorporation into PowerPoint presentations and can be used to help produce CAD drawings. The Library of Congress uses digital files in the form of high-resolution scans to provide access to the HABS/HAER/HALS collections through the Built in America Web site. However, permanent, formal documentation is still prepared in hard copy. As was the case with color transparencies, digital originals will not be accepted into the collections until questions about their permanence can be resolved.

Which Film?

The only film suitable for permanent documentation purposes is black-and-white film, which is archivally stable. Of the panchromatic, continuous-tone black-and-white films available, the slower the film (lower ASA/ISO designation), the less grainy it is; and the less grain, the better the enlargements of the negative. Grain in a negative consists of clumps of silver particles that make up the image. Faster films

Figure 3.24
Built into the Lake Lynn Dam near Morgantown, West Virginia, in two stages (1913–14 and 1925–26), the power plant's generators provide electricity for a number of towns in the region. A carefully selected camera location, lens, and composition capture both the machinery and the surrounding structure.

Figure 3.25

Photographer Jack Boucher's camera equipment and the van he uses to haul it. This photographer prefers to drive rather than fly because of the amount of equipment he requires.

Figure 3.26

This Pennsylvania through-truss bridge carried the Copper River and Northwestern Railroad between two glaciers. One span collapsed during the Alaska earthquake of 1964. The photographer took this shot with a 4″ × 5″ camera and 300 mm lens, rather than bulkier equipment, because of the site's inaccessibility.

have bigger clumps, and when the negative is enlarged, the grain becomes visible. This is especially distracting in continuous-tone areas such as sky or blank walls, where the grain is clearly visible as a salt-and-pepper pattern. Grain is not a serious consideration with large-format equipment because the negative is already so large that the grain is finer in enlargements.

HABS and HAER photographers have favored 5″ × 7″, 400 ASA black-and-white film, which makes tremendous enlargements possible. The same speed film in 35 mm cannot be enlarged much beyond 8″ × 10″ before the image becomes unacceptably grainy. To appreciate this, consider that enlarging a 4″ × 5″ image to an 8″ × 10″ print requires projection at a scale of slightly more than 2 to 1 linearly (4 to 1 by area), while enlarging a 35 mm image to an 8″ × 10″ print requires projection at a scale of 8.5 to 1 linearly (60 to 1 by area) (*see figs. 3.27 and 3.28*).

Figure 3.27
These reproductions of 4″ × 5″ and 35 mm negatives are shown actual size for comparison.

Figures 3.28
These two photographic enlargements were made from the negatives in fig. 3.27—the one on the left with a 35 mm Nikon camera with 28 mm PC lens and the one on the right with a 4″ × 5″ Horseman camera with 90 mm Schneider lens. Note the crisp detail in the enlargement from the 4″ × 5″ negative.

Large-Format Photography

HABS, HAER, and HALS continue to use large-format photography for two major reasons. First, the large negative permits maximum enlargement without the film's grain reducing the sharpness of the image (*see fig. 3.28*). It is, therefore, possible to make substantial enlargements of small details to understand features that would be too difficult to describe in words or too small to understand in person or on a drawing. Second, the large-format monorail camera allows more movement to correct for perspective than is possible with any other format or type of camera. By comparison, a 35 mm camera with perspective control lens can be moved up, down, and sideways (and on a few lenses it is even possible to tilt it), but the degree of movement is limited to a shift of approximately 11 mm.

Because the large-format camera consists of a lens mounted on a front standard, connected by a flexible bellows to a rear standard that holds the film, it is possible to substantially raise or lower the front and rear standards, shift them horizontally, and even tilt them. In comparison with the limited rise possible on a 35 mm camera, some large-format cameras offer a rise (front rise and rear drop) of nearly 100 mm. The range and extent of movement on a large-format camera permit the photographer to capture tall or wide structures without distortion, to increase depth of field (called the Scheimpflug effect), and to displace obstructions blocking the view of the structure being photographed.

For the photographer using large-format equipment, 4″ × 5″ is the most popular size, offering the most film types, lenses, and accessories. HABS and HAER photographers, however, have traditionally used the larger 5″ × 7″ camera, despite its greater weight and fewer offerings in terms of lenses or films. The larger negative is nearly twice the size of the 4″ × 5″ negative, offering an additional 15 square inches. It is easier to see all the details in a 5″ × 7″ contact print than in a 4″ × 5″ contact print. This point is especially important because users of the HABS/HAER collection at the Library of Congress view these contact prints rather than enlargements. Also, because a 5″ × 7″ negative is less square than a 4″ × 5″ negative, some photographers consider it a better-proportioned size for photographing architectural and engineering structures.

There are photographers who employ even larger or more specialized equipment than HABS/HAER/HALS for documenting architecture and engineering. Although 8″ × 10″ cameras are considered studio cameras, some photographers use them in the field. A few architectural photographers use panoramic cameras, with moving lenses or camera bodies. These are capable of capturing extremely wide expanses, such as the downtown of a city, and can produce a very distinctive image. A banquet camera is another type of wide-field camera, producing a negative more than twice as wide as it is high. Its name comes from the type of photograph it was designed for: banquet and graduating-class pictures.

Photographic Stability

The issue of archival stability is not a simple one. Too many variables affect negatives and prints for experts to do more than speak about general time periods. Knowledgeable people talk about stability in terms of short lifetime (10 years), medium lifetime (between 10 and 100 years), and long lifetime (more than 100 years). Ilford, Eastman Kodak, Fuji, and Polaroid, as manufacturers of color negative materials or color prints, provide information on the stability of their products. In general, each manufacturer believes its products are becoming more stable and that the major causes of fading or color changes are high temperature, high humidity, strong light, atmospheric pollution, and careless handling.

Professional users extend the life of color negatives, transparencies, and prints by using cold storage (with low humidity) or by making black-and-white separations from color images. The process of making a separation, which involves creating three black-and-white negatives that can be recombined at any point to produce a color image, is expensive, as is having special cold storage facilities. Specific information is available in the publications of the American National Standards Institute (New York City) and the Society of American Archivists (Chicago).

What About Lighting Equipment?
When interiors are photographed, substantial lighting equipment is necessary. Continuous lighting and the larger electronic strobes provide a great deal of light but require electricity, and many historic properties—especially those that are unoccupied—do not have enough, if any, electricity. It is possible to generate the needed electricity with portable gas-powered generators, but these are heavy. Truly portable but less powerful battery-powered electronic strobes are available, as are continuous lighting and photoflash bulbs. HABS/HAER/HALS photographers carry strobe, continuous lighting, and photoflash bulbs. Photoflash bulbs are fragile and do not always fire, but they produce tremendous illumination and do not require electricity (*see figs. 3.29, 3.30, and 3.31*).

Even when interiors are not to be shot, it is advisable to carry a portable flash to provide fill lighting in exterior areas (such as porches, doorways, and under eaves), which might otherwise be cast in shadows that would obliterate details. However, where there is a risk of explosion, as in grain elevators and ammunition or chemical plants, any flash might be too dangerous.

What About Other Equipment?
It is probably impossible to come up with an all-inclusive equipment list for a photographer who will be documenting structures. A fairly complete one, though, would include tripod, light meter, filters (especially a yellow filter for black-and-white photography), extra batteries, powerful flashlight, knife, repair tools, gaffer tape for holding small objects in place, scale stick, compass (essential for captioning photographs), name and telephone numbers of property owners, log for recording information on shots, plenty of film, film holders for large format or extra film backs for medium format, a Polaroid back for making test exposures, and changing bag/portable darkroom for loading and unloading film holders (*see fig. 3.25*).

What About Background Research?
HAER photographer Jet Lowe says he tries to learn everything he can about a project before he goes out to photograph it. He sees this preparation as a way of narrowing the assumptions he will make about the assignment. In addition to the photographic request form filled out by the project historian or leader (*see fig. 3.32*) and discussions with the project historian, Lowe recommends reading general texts on the subject. For example, Lowe has tried to become knowledgeable in the fields of bridge construction and steel fabrication to aid him in photographing bridges and steel plants (*see fig. 3.33*). Over the last thirty years HABS photographer Jack E. Boucher has read extensively in, and acquired an extensive personal library on, local and architectural history. In the field, photographers employ the expertise they have acquired to capture all the salient characteristics of a structure (*see fig. 3.34*).

Most photographers do not prepare for an assignment to the degree that HABS/HAER/HALS photographers do, but all photographers make assumptions about the subject they are about to photograph. These assumptions concern how important the subject is and what condition it is in. Based on them, photographers make working estimates as to approximately how many shots will be made and approximately how long it will take. This process all takes place before the photographer sees the property to be photographed.

Figure 3.29
The photographer used strobe to ensure even lighting in this photograph of the Inskip powerhouse generator, built in 1910 as part of the Battle Creek hydroelectric project in California.

Figure 3.30
To light this tunnel, the photographer used a technique called painting with light. He walked down the tunnel firing a total of eight flashbulbs, one at a time, with the lens shutter left open. If the tunnel had not been so dark, he would have had someone cover the lens between firings of the flashbulbs; otherwise the lightest areas of the image would have been overexposed.

Once on site, photographers need to make a visual reconnaissance—to walk around and through the site. This inspection can correct erroneous assumptions about the significance and condition of the subject and about the number of shots and amount of time required.

Some architectural photographers always take certain shots of a building. Such standard shots are not always worth taking, especially when they replace shots that would convey more information about the property being photographed. The visual inspection often reveals uncommon, unanticipated "targets of opportunity" such as exposed structural systems. If a photographer does not consider the possibility of seeing such features and does not search for them, they will not be photographed.

In summary, whether photographers are shooting their tenth bridge or hundredth house, each bridge and each house needs to be approached afresh. Otherwise, the photographer unconsciously starts shooting by rote, photographing each bridge and each house from the same angles, with the same views.

The high cost of producing large-format photographs forces photographers to plan shots carefully, avoiding those that are redundant or insignificant. With 35 mm photography, which allows much more mobility at a much lower cost, photographers are much freer to experiment and shoot lots of film, but they still need to know what the key or essential shots are.

The visual reconnaissance serves a purpose beyond ensuring that a photographer will not miss an important shot. A walk around and through the site reveals environmental limitations imposed on the photographer. The two most common are foliage and the compass orientation of the structure. In the summer it is virtually impossible to get unobstructed photographs of residences, whether rural or

Figure 3.31
The photographer placed his lighting to accentuate floor wear from the workers' repetitive routine.

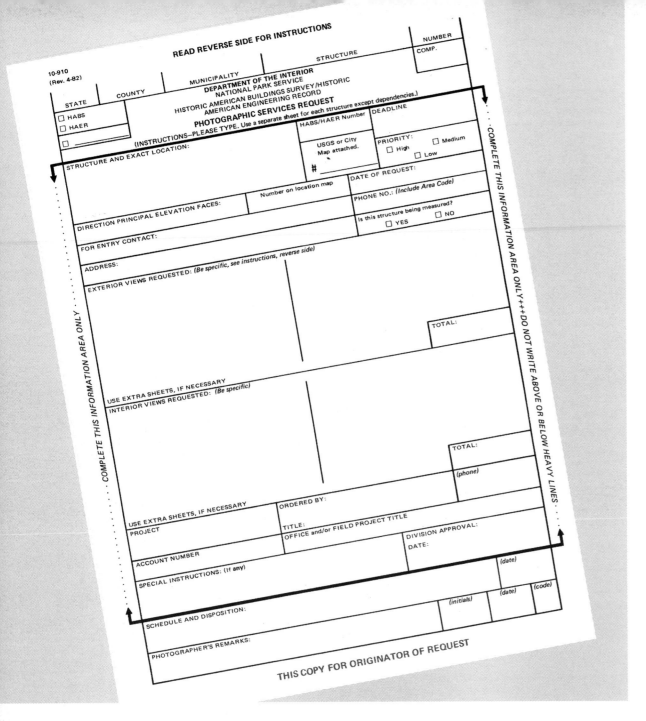

urban, because of foliage. This is not a problem with industrial structures, such as steel mills, but can be a problem with other engineering structures, such as bridges whose abutments are concealed by vegetation. The northern facade of any structure is almost always in shadow, making it difficult to get a photograph with sufficient contrast. It is therefore often necessary to shoot in the early morning or late afternoon, when a northern facade is illuminated (see fig. 3.35). Commercial architectural photographers sometimes shoot the north front of a building at night, using streetlights and the building's lights to illuminate and add interest to the photograph. This approach is most effective in photographing storefronts and small office buildings. Landscape photography presents further challenges in the seasonal and temporal changes of plant materials. Other constraints on the photographer are (1) adjacent buildings that block unobstructed shots of the elevations, (2) operating machinery, or (3) abandoned, decayed buildings, which can pose safety hazards. In shooting bridges or other potentially hazardous structures, the photographer should use safety devices such as a hard hat and a harness to minimize risks.

The most common and probably most cumbersome constraint is that of time—very rarely do photographers get to spend as much time at a site as they would like.

Figure 3.32
This specialized form serves the needs of program photographers. Others might need only a simplified version of this document.

Figure 3.33
Knowing the characteristics of cast iron, the photographer recorded the unique but structurally insignificant Egyptian Revival detailing on diagonals of the Reading–Halls Station Bridge in Lycoming County, Pennsylvania.

Figure 3.34
Combining knowledge of the subject and the capabilities of the medium, the photographer lighted this well-composed image of a stairwell to suggest even, natural lighting and to highlight the grain in the wood.

Figure 3.35
The photographer took this photograph in the spring of 1976, on one of the few days of the year when sunlight illuminates the north side of the White House. He photographed the White House again in 1987 and 1988, when the paint had been removed, revealing the original stone surfaces.

Processing the Film

There are two key aspects to the processing phase: proper darkroom procedures and systematic and complete labeling.

Processing exposed film into a negative and making a print from that negative are two distinct darkroom procedures, but the same standards must be applied to both. A conscientious darkroom worker always uses clean containers and trays to avoid chemical contamination. All chemicals must be fresh and kept at the proper temperature, and the manufacturer's recommendations for processing must be followed. The proper handling of negatives cannot be overemphasized. Any other part of processing—contact prints or enlargements—can be redone in the darkroom, but damage to the negative, ranging from scratches and dust to chemical stains, is permanent and can rarely be concealed.

HABS/HAER/HALS standards for archival processing of prints and negatives require complete removal of the chemicals used to develop and fix an image. Remnants of these chemicals on the negative or print will cause discoloration and, eventually, deterioration. After they have been treated with hypo remover (a chemical that facilitates washing)—one of the last steps in darkroom processing—the negatives and prints are washed for a long period to remove any remaining traces of hypo or other chemicals. (Adding a small amount of selenium toner to the hypo remover increases archival stability.) Once processed, the negatives must be stored in archival sleeves. An archivally permanent print has all chemicals removed and is made on fiber-based rather than resin-coated paper, as the latter is considered chemically active and thus is expected to deteriorate over time.

Once processed, negatives and prints must be accurately and adequately identified. The

Figure 3.36

Jack Boucher's shooting log for the Higgins Armory records the address, compass orientation, number and description of shots, whether a filter was used, and the date of the photographs. Each image has a letter and number in a box; this code corresponds to a number Boucher exposes on the film before going into the field. The same number is written on the film holder. This numbering procedure is necessary because sheet film (for large-format photography), unlike roll film (for 35 mm and medium format), does not come from the factory with sequential numbering in the margin.

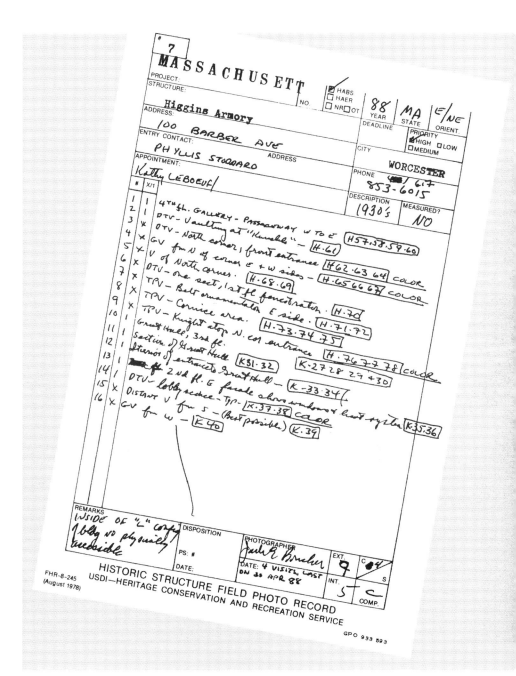

Figure 3.37
The number K 29 in the upper left corner identifies this image as "Great Hall, 3rd fl." on the photo log shown in fig. 3.36.

following information should be provided: (1) the name and location of the structure, (2) a descriptive caption of the subject covered in the particular photograph, (3) the name of the photographer, and (4) the time and date the photograph was taken (*see figs. 3.36 and 3.37*). Too often, photographers rely on their memories to identify photographs taken weeks or even months earlier—a system that simply does not work. The importance of taking the time in the field to keep a good photographic log cannot be stressed strongly enough.

For photographs to be included in the HABS, HAER, or HALS collection at the Library of Congress, the following procedures are followed. The negatives, archival sleeves, archival contact prints, and archival photo mount cards are all labeled with the HABS, HAER, or HALS number for the property. A caption list is prepared for each set of negatives and contact prints. This sheet lists the name and precise location of the subject, the name of the photographer, the date the photograph was taken, the description of each image, and the HABS, HAER, or HALS number. The negatives in holders, contact prints on photo mount cards, and captions (all archival) are transferred to the Library of Congress, where they are maintained under archivally stable conditions (*see fig. 3.38*). Any of the photographs can be retrieved by the staff, and the public can easily find out if a particular building, structure, or site has been recorded by HABS, HAER, or HALS as long as the name and location are known. These two features—archival stability and ease of retrieval—are standards that everyone should try to achieve, whether the photographs are to be deposited in a local library or university or are to remain as working records in the office of an architect, historian, photographer, or government agency.

Specialized Techniques

Techniques such as computer enhancement of photographs, X-ray photography, and infrared photography make it possible to glean more information from photographs than HABS and HAER normally need. Two techniques that provide precise information are rectified photography and stereophotogrammetry. These techniques are described briefly here but, because they are used to produce measured drawings, are discussed in greater detail in chapter 4.

Rectification attempts to eliminate the slight distortion that is inevitable even in large-format photography when the camera's film plane is not perfectly parallel to the building. It is possible to make an accurate measured drawing of elements in the main subject plane of a rectified photograph. This is accomplished by taking measurements directly from the photograph (*see figs. 3.39, 3.40, and 3.41*).

Stereophotogrammetry takes rectified photography one step further (*see fig. 3.42*). To reduce the possibility of imprecision caused by distortion, stereophotogrammetry uses two cameras, rather than one, very precisely placed in relation to each other and the facade being photographed. The resulting glass plate negatives can be plotted to produce accurate measured drawings. Unlike rectified photography, depth can be measured from the resulting photograph because a stereo image is produced. Convergent photogrammetry is a form of photogrammetry in which the camera axes are not parallel but converge.

X-ray photography (radiography), infrared photography, and the computer enhancement of photographs are three highly specialized techniques of great value in the right circumstances. Restoration architects have used

Figure 3.38
Sample HABS photograph showing large-format negative, archival negative sleeve, and photograph in archival mount card.

portable X-ray equipment to uncover what was inside a wall without destroying the interior or exterior finishes (*see figs. 3.43, 3.44, and 3.45*). David M. Hart, AIA, a restoration architect and expert in the use of radiography, has written:

> Historic buildings containing the usual building materials such as plaster and lath, wood and steel or iron can usually be easily examined non-destructively by the use of portable x-ray machines. Masonry walls and partitions composed of brick or stone, thick cementitious plasters or stucco, and earth-type structures are not easily examined by x-rays.
>
> Radioactive isotopes have also been used, but safety issues are a factor which preclude widespread use of this method.
>
> The examination of buildings can reveal information in the following categories:
>
> 1. Structural systems, to illustrate the location, size, configuration, and joints of components. Structural conditions of components can also be determined.
>
> 2. Construction details of finish materials for historical and dating purposes. The configuration and ages of components can be determined by comparative methods. Changes and alterations within the building fabric can also be ascertained by the same method.

In infrared photography, a special film with corrective filters is used. The resulting images—

Figure 3.39
Targets are placed in the field of view of this rectified photograph of Stan Hywet Hall, Akron, Ohio.

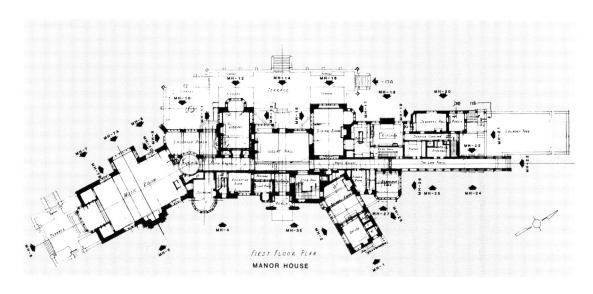

Figure 3.40
This partial view of the floor plan of Stan Hywet Hall was annotated by restoration architects Chambers & Chambers to show the locations of various rectified photographs.

Figure 3.41
An unrectified photograph of the same section of Stan Hywet Hall as that shown in fig. 3.39. A comparison of the rectified and unrectified photographs demonstrates that each conveys different information about the subject.

whether in color or black and white—have tones or colors different from those produced with normal film. The unusual pattern of tone and/or colors in infrared film reveals characteristics not visible on normal film or to the eye. One of the most effective uses has been in aerial infrared photography, which reveals belowground structures that would not otherwise be apparent without conducting an archaeological dig.

Computer enhancement of photographs is a technique developed by the National Aeronautics and Space Administration (NASA) to improve the clarity of photographs sent back from space. The same technique can make historic photographs less fuzzy and therefore more informative. The once-exotic software is now widely available for manipulating digital images.

When done carefully, photography justifies its popularity. Photographs of buildings, bridges, landscapes, or almost any structure can be aesthetically pleasing and informative. Although photography is not a substitute for drawings, histories, or actually seeing a structure or site, it offers a unique viewpoint and another way of preserving structures into the future.

Figure 3.42
A Wild C-120 stereometric camera was mounted in a cherry picker to take this photogrammetric view of the north elevation of the Dorchester Heights Monument in Boston. It is obvious how difficult and dangerous it would have been to hand-measure this 115-foot monument, so photogrammetry was a more appropriate technique.

Figure 3.43
The X-ray generator is activated for approximately five seconds to record the image on a film cassette placed in position for exposure. Cassettes are developed subsequently in a lab.

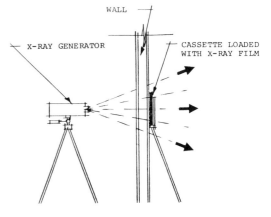

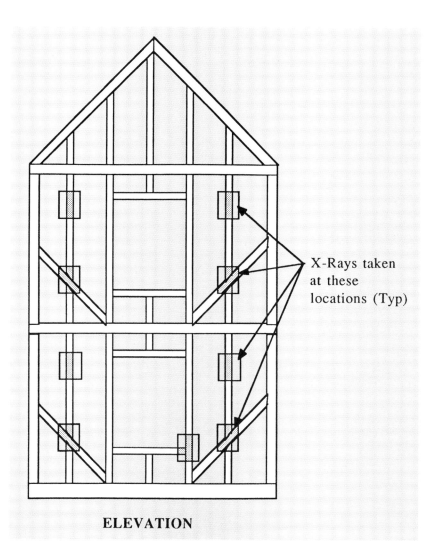

ELEVATION

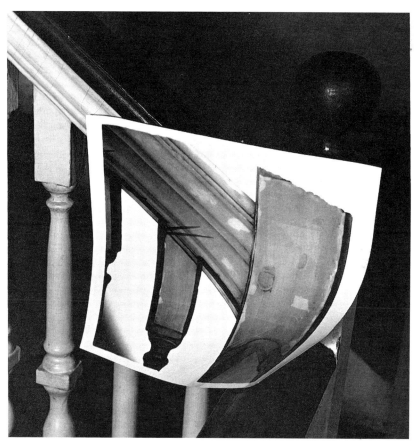

Figure 3.44
Radiographs of strategically located small sections of structural components can be used to determine the overall structural system of a wood-frame building. In this example, radiographs taken at the location of 45-degree wind braces determined their configuration. The entire structural system was then derived from this small amount of information.

X-Rays taken at these locations (Typ)

Figure 3.45
Radiographs of finish materials make it possible to date components by comparison with known dated materials. The wooden peg used to attach the handrail to the newel post in this example is evidence of early construction. The use of hand-wrought nails to attach the balusters to the rail confirms the stylistically established late-eighteenth-century date of the assembly.

MEASURED DRAWINGS

John A. Burns

Measured drawings constitute a third type of formal HABS/HAER/HALS documentation, which complements the format photographs and written documentation discussed in the preceding chapters. This chapter will explain what measured drawings are and how to plan and execute a set of them. Decisions on what to draw, the types of drawings to use, how to obtain the measurements, the levels of accuracy required, and the appropriate scales for the drawings will be discussed.

Measured drawings are one of the most expensive forms of architectural and engineering documentation because of the length of time they take to produce. There are many reasons for producing them, however. Measured drawings can be used as the basis for planning restoration or rehabilitation work, to record a structure facing imminent demolition, to aid in the normal maintenance of a structure, to protect against catastrophic loss, or as part of a scholarly study. The subjects recorded with measured drawings vary widely. The HABS, HAER, and HALS measured drawings collections represent an encyclopedic range of the built environment, from mansions to dollhouses, corncribs to skyscrapers, windmills to steel mills, ships and canals to missile test facilities, and small gardens to large cultural landscapes.

What Are Measured Drawings?

Measured drawings are line drawings that follow standard drafting conventions to portray a three-dimensional structure or site in two dimensions. Measured drawings are similar to as-built architectural drawings, except that they are generally produced years after a structure was built, not immediately after construction. Measured drawings portray conditions at the time of documentation, including the accretions, alterations, and deletions made to the original. Hidden elements, exploded views, sequences of construction, and functional processes are easily portrayed in a drawing.

HABS/HAER/HALS drawings are produced as a documentary record of a given structure, although they often serve another purpose as well. For example, they can be used as an easement document, as the basis for restoration work, or as interpretive drawings to explain how something works.

HABS/HAER/HALS measured drawings are accurate, detailed, scaled drawings that portray or interpret the significant features of the recorded structure in a standardized format on an archivally stable medium. HABS/HAER/HALS drawing sheets come in three sizes: 19″ × 24″, 24″ × 36″, and 34″ × 44″, with preprinted title block and borders that reduce the actual drawing areas to 15¾" × 20⅛", 21¾" × 31¾", and 31⅞" × 40", respectively.

The principal medium for HABS/HAER/HALS drawings is polyester film, referred to by the trade name Mylar. The ink used for hand delineation is archival quality, and designated for use on plastic drawing films. CAD drawings are laser or electrostatic plots on Mylar. HABS/HAER/HALS Mylar is 4 mils thick (a mil is equal to a thousandth of an inch) with a drawing surface on both sides. Rag paper and vellum with ink and pencil have been used in the past. The key test of these materials is the archival stability of the medium. Ink-on-Mylar drawings and laser or electrostatic plots on Mylar should meet a performance standard of 500 years. While drafting media and technologies have changed over the years, it is important to remember that HABS/HAER/HALS standards and guidelines are graphic standards that define and describe the completed drawing, not the means for producing it.

The extent and level of detail of HABS/HAER measured drawings are related to the nature and significance of the subject being recorded. For instance, drawings of a balloon-frame house should include not only plans, elevations, sections, and details but also information on the walls and how they were constructed (*see fig. 4.1*). Measured drawings of a building with highly significant interiors should emphasize large-scale detail drawings of room elevations and interior decorative finishes (*see figs. 4.2 and 4.3*). Drawings of a significant machine shop should concentrate on the machinery and process of work (*see fig. 4.4*). Landscape drawings should locate, identify, and state breast height or crown diameters for plant materials (*see fig. 4.43*). Measured drawings can be heavily annotated and dimensioned for restoration work or unadorned for publication purposes.

Figure 4.1
This axonometric drawing illustrates how a balloon-frame house is constructed. Axonometric drawings are particularly useful for depicting how structural components fit together.

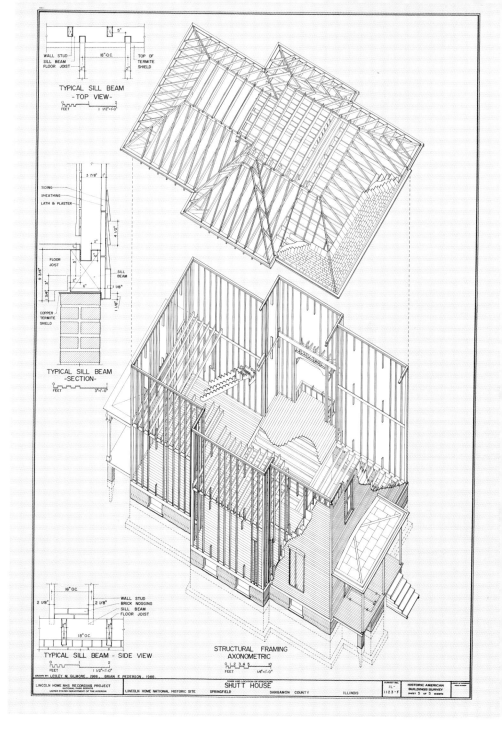

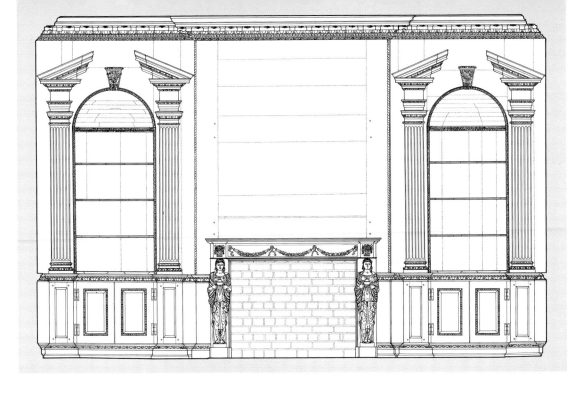

Figures 4.2 and 4.3
The elaborate interior woodwork at Gunston Hall in Fairfax County, Virginia, designed by William Buckland, is the most dramatic element of the house. The exterior gives little hint of these interior finishes, which are the most significant architectural features of the house.

Figure 4.4 (right)
This HAER drawing was intended to capture the overall machine layout of Ben Thresher's Mill in Barnet Center, Vermont. Each machine is identified and briefly described. Note that the architectural features of the structure are minimized, without dimensions or annotations. Annotations relate only to the machinery and function of the mill. The power transmission system for the machinery was recorded in a separate drawing (see fig. 4.34).

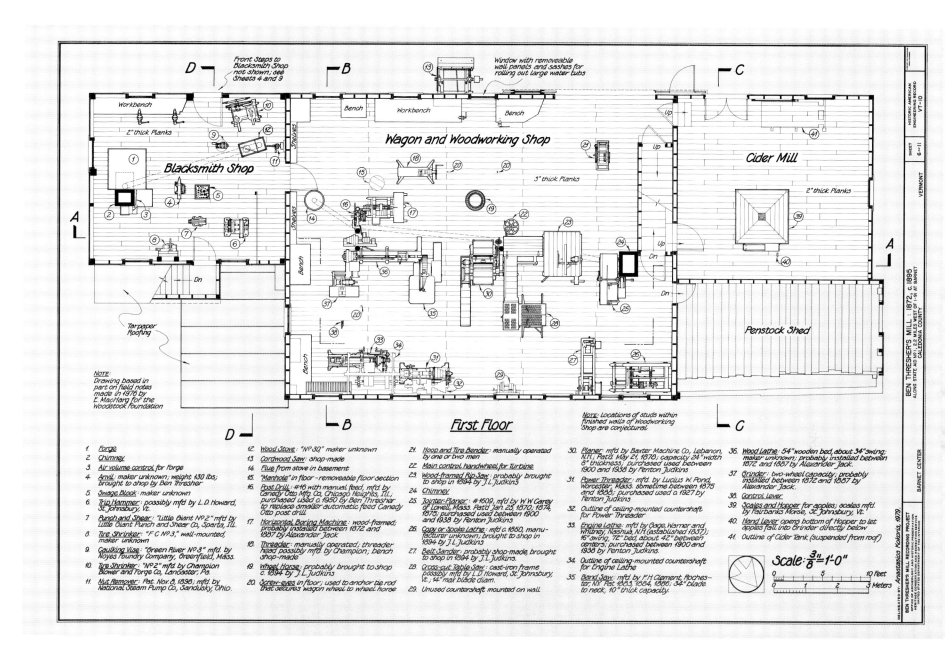

Front Steps to Blacksmith Shop not shown; see Sheets 4 and 9

Window with removeable wall panels and sashes for rolling out large water tubs

Workbench

2" thick Planks

Blacksmith Shop

Bench

Workbench

Bench

Wagon and Woodworking Shop

Cider Mill

2" thick Planks

3" thick Planks

Shelves

Shelves

Bench

Dn

Tarpaper Roofing

Bench

Dn

Penstock Shed

NOTE:
Drawing based in part on field notes made in 1976 by E. MacHarg for the Woodstock Foundation

NOTE: Locations of studs within finished walls of Woodworking Shop are conjectural

First Floor

1. Forge
2. Chimney
3. Air volume control for forge
4. Anvil: maker unknown; weight 130 lbs; brought to shop by Ben Thresher
5. Swage Block: maker unknown
6. Trip Hammer: possibly mfd by L.D. Howard, St. Johnsbury, Vt.
7. Punch and Shear: "Little Giant No 2" mfd by Little Giant Punch and Shear Co, Sparta, Ill.
8. Tire Shrinker: "F C No 3", wall-mounted, maker unknown
9. Caulking Vise: "Green River No 3" mfd by Noyes Foundry Company, Greenfield, Mass.
10. Tire Shrinker: "No 2" mfd by Champion Blower and Forge Co, Lancaster, Pa.
11. Nut Remover: Pat. Nov. 8, 1898; mfd. by National Steam Pump Co, Sandusky, Ohio.

12. Wood Stove: "No 30" maker unknown
13. Cordwood Saw: shop-made
14. Flue from stove in basement
15. "Manhole" in floor - removeable floor section
16. Post Drill: #16 with manual feed, mfd by Canedy Otto Mfg. Co, Chicago Heights, Ill.; purchased used c.1950 by Ben Thresher to replace smaller automatic feed Canedy Otto post drill.
17. Horizontal Boring Machine: wood-framed; probably installed between 1872 and 1887 by Alexander Jack.
18. Threader: manually operated; threader head possibly mfd by Champion; bench shop-made
19. Wheel Horse: probably brought to shop c. 1894 by J.L. Judkins
20. Screw-eyes in floor; used to anchor tie rod that secures wagon wheel to wheel horse

21. Hoop and Tire Bender: manually operated by one or two men
22. Main control handwheel for Turbine
23. Wood-framed Rip Saw: probably brought to shop in 1894 by J.L. Judkins
24. Chimney
25. Jointer-Planer: #1609, mfd by W W Carey of Lowell, Mass. Pat'd Jan. 25, 1870; 1874, 1875; purchased used between 1900 and 1938 by Fenton Judkins
26. Copy or Spoke Lathe: mfd c.1850, manufacturer unknown; brought to shop in 1894 by J.L. Judkins
27. Belt Sander: probably shop-made, brought to shop in 1894 by J.L. Judkins.
28. Outline of ceiling-mounted countershaft
29. Unused countershaft mounted on wall.

30. Planer: mfd by Baxter Machine Co, Lebanon, N.H.; Pat'd. May 21, 1878; capacity 24"width 8" thickness; purchased used between 1900 and 1938 by Fenton Judkins
31. Power Threader: mfd by Lucius W. Pond, Worcester, Mass. sometime between 1875 and 1888; purchased used c.1927 by Fenton Judkins
32. Outline of ceiling-mounted countershaft for Power Threader
33. Engine Lathe: mfd by Gage, Warner and Whitney, Nashua, N.H. (established 1837); 16"swing, 72" bed, about 42" between centers; purchased between 1900 and 1938 by Fenton Judkins.
34. Outline of ceiling-mounted countershaft for Engine Lathe
35. Band Saw: mfd by F.H. Clement, Rochester, N.Y. Pat 1883, 1884, 1886; 34" blade to neck, 10" thick capacity.

36. Wood Lathe: 54"wooden bed, about 34"swing; maker unknown; probably installed between 1872 and 1887 by Alexander Jack.
37. Grinder: two-wheel capacity; probably installed between 1872 and 1887 by Alexander Jack.
38. Control Lever
39. Scales and Hopper for apples; scales mfd. by Fairbanks Morse, St. Johnsbury, Vt.
40. Hand Lever opens bottom of Hopper to let apples fall into Grinder directly below
41. Outline of Cider Tank (suspended from roof)

Scale: $\frac{3}{8}$" = 1'-0"

0   5   10 Feet
0   1   2   3 Meters

DELINEATED BY Anastasios Kokoris, 1979.

BEN THRESHER'S MILL RECORDING PROJECT
OFFICE OF ARCHEOLOGY AND HISTORIC PRESERVATION
HERITAGE CONSERVATION AND RECREATION SERVICE
UNITED STATES DEPARTMENT OF THE INTERIOR

BEN THRESHER'S MILL : 1872, c. 1895
ALONG STATE AID No 1 ; 2.2 MILES WEST OF I-91 AT BARNET
CALEDONIA COUNTY

BARNET CENTER

VERMONT

HISTORIC AMERICAN ENGINEERING RECORD
VT-10

SHEET 6 OF 11

VT-10

Types of Architectural and Engineering Drawings

Architects and engineers use drawings to portray buildings and structures as they progress from conceptualization to completion. These drawings can be useful in preparing HABS/HAER measured drawings. The types of drawings you may encounter are outlined below:

- Conceptual drawings are intended to depict how an object is to work, be used, or appear. Also called schematics, they are diagrammatic drawings of the essential elements of a design. Conceptual drawings are small-scale, single-line drawings (walls drawn as a single line) with little detail and few dimensions. They most closely resemble sketches in appearance.

- Preliminary drawings, sometimes called preliminaries, work out the arrangement of spaces, circulation, and massing. They are double-line drawings (walls drawn as two parallel lines) drawn at a larger scale than conceptual drawings. They include plans, elevations, and sections. Preliminaries fix and describe the size and character of the entire design.

- Design and bid drawings work out the details, aesthetics, dimensions, and costs for construction or manufacture. They include detail drawings of design features.

- Construction, working, and shop drawings are the drawings actually used in construction or manufacturing. They are dimensioned completely and accurately and include annotations.

- As-built drawings are produced after construction is complete and show the structure as it was actually built, incorporating changes made as construction progressed. As-built drawings are usually produced by modifying a reproducible copy of the construction drawings.

Collectively, these drawings show how a structure was conceived, designed, and produced. They are commonly called "original drawings," because they are important records of the original designs and conditions at a site. They could be used to build another identical structure. Note that they may not show a structure as it was finally built. They also do not include information on later changes, whether major or minor, as do the following types of drawings:

- Alteration drawings are generally very specific, dealing only with the portion of the structure being altered or added to. They are less informative about the overall structure but are nevertheless useful as a historical record.

- Existing-condition drawings are just that. They record the physical fabric and conditions of a structure at a given point in time. They are often produced as the first step in the rehabilitation or restoration of a historic structure. HABS/HAER measured drawings are a specialized subset of existing-condition drawings.

- Restoration drawings can be highly informative about the historic fabric of a structure because they are frequently adapted from existing-condition or HABS/HAER measured drawings. They are somewhat less useful as a historical record because they primarily depict present-day treatments.

Measured drawings are based primarily on physical evidence but may rely on other sources of information. Documentary sources can provide evidence of former conditions and may help to interpret physical fabric. Historic views, whether drawn or photographed, can be invaluable. Key features in any HABS/HAER/HALS measured drawing are citations to the sources for the measurements. Such sources include hand measurements, photographs, original drawings, and restoration drawings.

Can Original Drawings Be Substituted for Measured Drawings?

A basic assumption in producing measured drawings is that other sources for drawings do not meet the needs of the project being undertaken. The discovery of original drawings for a structure about to be hand-measured is usually a great relief; however, the term "original drawings" can refer to many drawing types (see sidebar). Only rudimentary sketches were developed to guide the craftsmen of the oldest buildings, while more recent structures may have dozens or even hundreds of detailed drawings. Any existing drawings should be studied carefully to make sure they are reliable and accurate, and can fulfill the same needs as a measured drawing. Original drawings of one house that HABS planned to document revealed, upon close inspection, that the dimensions shown were for the structural elements of the house. The elaborate interior finishes were not included in these drawings because they were contracted separately. To produce new drawings, HABS hand-measured the interior details to complement the basic measurements of the house obtained from the structural drawings (see fig. 4.5). In this case, the original drawings, while extremely useful, did not adequately describe or interpret the significance of the site.

Original drawings of engineered or industrial structures such as a bridge, a steel mill, or

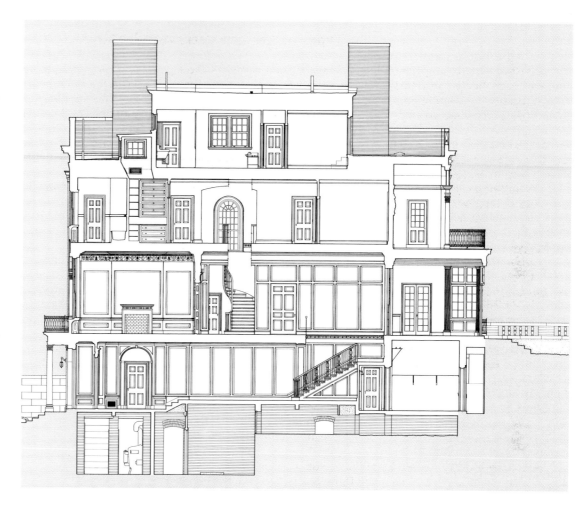

Figure 4.5
The original construction drawings were found in a vault in the 1915 Woodrow Wilson House in Washington, D.C. Because they did not include the interior finishes, they were of limited use in preparing this measured drawing of the completed interior. Prints of the original drawings were used in taking field measurements, and copies were included in the field records for the house.

a machine may make preparation of contemporary measured drawings unnecessary. However, engineering drawings may be so dense with dimensions, notations, and other information that they confuse and obscure a basic understanding of the structure. Such drawings are intended for construction or manufacture, not for interpretation. Even if original drawings can be copied, interpretive drawings may still be necessary to explain an industrial process, a construction technique, the function of a machine, or how a landscape has evolved over time.

Copying original and other drawings for HABS/HAER/HALS can be accomplished in several ways. In most cases, the drawings are copied from other accessible sources by making 8″ × 10″ copy negatives and contact prints. The reproduction is thus a photograph of the original drawing. HABS/HAER/HALS generally does not photographically copy or scan other drawings onto a measured drawing sheet unless there is some reason to do so—for instance, if the drawing is deteriorating or inaccessible to the public. When a drawing is copied onto a HABS/HAER/HALS drawing sheet, this fact must be clearly labeled on the sheet so that there is no confusion regarding the source of the drawing. Program staff routinely trace or otherwise adapt drawings to produce measured drawings, always clearly citing what is copied and what is new. Since all HABS/HAER/HALS records are in the public domain, owner permission and copyright restrictions may limit the reproduction of historic materials for the programs' collections.

Why Produce Measured Drawings?

HABS/HAER/HALS measured drawings are produced for any or several of the following reasons:

- To establish existing conditions when restoration or rehabilitation work is planned

- As part of normal conservation and maintenance of a structure

- For research

- To keep a permanent record for future generations when demolition is planned

- As insurance against catastrophic loss, should something happen to the structure

- For public information or interpretation

While measured drawings are utilitarian, HABS/HAER/HALS measured drawings must additionally meet all HABS/HAER/HALS standards for content, quality, materials, and presentation. A HABS/HAER/HALS measured drawing project begins with an assessment of the need for measured drawings, which is based on the significance of the structure to be recorded. Information for a preliminary assessment of significance can be gleaned from written sources such as local guidebooks, company histories, National Register of Historic Places nominations, or preliminary archival research. A site visit to reconnoiter the structure in its context and to inspect it inside and out and from bottom to top is imperative (see chapter 2). The physical fabric of a structure may both provide answers and prompt further questions. What was its period of significance and what remains from that period? Does the structure retain its integrity? Is it threatened by development or neglect? Observations are recorded and compared with the written history uncovered, and rough measurements are taken for planning the scale and composing the drawings.

Traditionally, associative historical value and architectural importance have been the determinants of significance. For the most part, however, the built environment was not

designed by a prominent architect or engineer and was not associated with a famous person or event. Under HABS/HAER/HALS standards, an individual structure does not have to be nationally significant to be recorded with measured drawings. For instance, a two-story army barracks with a gable roof and pent eaves is ordinary until you consider that its standardized construction had a considerable impact on the construction industry and that thousands of them were built and still exist. It represents a plan and construction type of national significance (*see fig. 4.6*).

Once the decision to produce measured drawings has been reached, the type of information essential for inclusion in the finished drawings must be considered:

- What drawings will best explain and illustrate the significant features of the site?

- What kind of detail is required in the finished drawing? This will determine the scale of the drawing. At the common scale of ¼″ = 1′-0″, the smallest distance that can be accurately drawn or plotted at map scale is approximately 1 inch.

- How many dimensions and annotations are necessary?

- What level of accuracy is needed in the measurements? Dimensions to the nearest inch are perfectly adequate for site plans but inadequate for details, where measurements to the nearest ¹⁄₁₆″ or ⅛″ are required.

- What sheet size should be used? For planning purposes, the area inside the borders of a small HABS sheet (15¾″ × 20⅛″) scales 63′-0″ × 80′-6″ at ¼″ = 1′-0″. Most domestic and similarly scaled structures will fit com-

fortably on this sheet size. The area inside the borders of a D-size HABS, HAER, or HALS sheet (21¾″ × 31¾″) scales 87′-0″ × 127′-0″, and an E-size sheet (31⅞″ × 40″) scales 127′-6″ × 160′ at the same scale. Some structures or complexes may require several large sheets to accommodate a single elevation or plan at an appropriate scale. Do not mix sheet sizes in a single set of drawings. (Note that HAER does not use the smaller sheets.)

After the type of measured drawings has been decided, a source for the measurements needed to produce those drawings is the next consideration. The following questions can help determine how best to obtain measurements.

- Do any drawings exist, or must they be produced?

- If drawings exist, are they accurate and useful to the current need?

- If measurements must be taken, what tools and expertise are available?

- Does the structure itself (its size, condition, use, and accessibility) dictate the manner in which it can be measured?

Measured drawings require varying levels of detail and annotation, depending on their ultimate use. Drawings that are intended to provide the basis for restoration will require extensive dimensions and annotations to record the necessary historical and conditional information, while drawings intended for maintenance purposes may require little more than material indications and dimensions for calculating gross areas needing treatment. Measured drawings produced as mitigation are the "last

Figure 4.6
The simple character and plain appearance of this 63-man barracks belies its significance as a representative of the thousands of similar temporary wooden structures built during the mobilization for World War II. The standardized designs, standardized construction techniques, economy of materials, and ease of erection for relatively unskilled labor significantly affected the postwar construction industry.

Figure 4.7

Independence Hall is one of the most famous and significant structures in the United States. Interestingly, given the amount of attention the building has received over the years, its most pristine parts were never recorded in detail. The central hall and stair tower had not been altered or restored, so there was no need for detailed measurements and drawings. In addition, although drawings of varying quality were produced over the years for different purposes, there was no complete, accurate set for the entire structure. Several driving forces led to a HABS project to document the structure: maintenance, restoration, interpretation, public requests for drawings, and catastrophic loss protection. The significance of Independence Hall is such that if it was damaged or destroyed, in all likelihood it would be rebuilt as faithfully as possible. Accurate, detailed documentation would be imperative for reconstruction.

rites" for a structure slated for demolition, recording all its salient features for future generations. Drawings intended to serve as protection from catastrophic loss must be detailed enough to allow the exact replication of a highly significant structure should that structure be destroyed (*see fig. 4.7*).

Sketch plans are an alternative to measured drawings when a structure does not warrant measured drawings, or when time or money is not available to produce measured drawings. Sketch plans do not have to be accurately scaled, but they should show elements in proper proportion to each other. They are generally drawn on 8½" × 11" archival paper (*see fig. 4.8*). HABS/HAER/HALS treats these sketches as data pages, including them with the formal written data. Sketches may include the primary and typical floor plans, site plans, and, less frequently, sections and details. Sketches of floor plans can also be used to key locations of photographs. Sketch plans should always include basic dimensions, approximate scale, a north arrow, the name of the delineator, and the date. Elevations are better shown in photographs.

After decisions have been made about the type and quantity of measured drawings to be made, as well as their level of detail, scales, accuracy, and sheet layout, the fieldwork can begin.

Gathering Information

The raw materials assembled for producing measured drawings constitute the field records. Field records are valuable because they contain all the detailed information on methodology, dimensions, and notes made at the time of recording. They are a primary resource and may be consulted by subsequent researchers

Figure 4.8
This sketch conveys the basic information necessary for understanding the room arrangements and appearance of this town house. It is simple and easily understood. Major dimensions are included along with a north arrow to give orientation. The sketch plan provides highly useful information with a minimum of effort and skill.

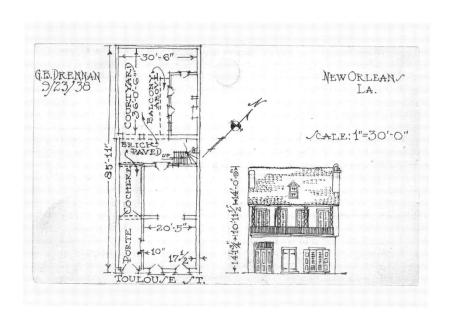

because of their great detail. Field notes are invariably more comprehensive than the given dimensions and annotations on a finished drawing. For this reason, some people consider the field notes more important than the final drawing. A complete measured drawing cannot be more accurate than the field records from which it was produced.

The quality of the fieldwork has a substantial impact on the quality of the completed documentation. Fieldwork must be thought out in advance in order to organize the recording efficiently and to minimize the chances for mistakes. Field notes must be accurate and comprehensive. They must be carefully annotated and neatly labeled so that others can understand the information. Hasty or sloppy fieldwork invariably includes errors and omis-

sions that cause repeated trips to the site or flaws in the final drawings.

Field records may consist of copies of original drawings annotated to include later alterations, dimensioned sketches, photographs, and whatever else may be needed to produce a finished drawing. Sketches and measurements made in the field are recorded on graph paper and organized in what are called field notebooks to be filed as part of the field records. HABS/HAER/HALS field records are considered to be informal documentation because they are not rigorously archival (although archival materials and processes are used) and are not easily reproducible. Field records are retained by HABS/HAER/HALS and transmitted to the Library of Congress along with other completed documentation.

A Step-by-Step Approach to Hand Measuring

Planning

- ❏ Establish type and number of measured drawings to be produced.
- ❏ Develop methodology for taking measurements, including quality control checks.
- ❏ Assess site constraints:
    - Floor level
    - Rooms square
    - Access and lighting
    - Safety

Measuring

- ❏ First sketch the areas to be measured and establish the locations for the principal reference points and overall dimensions. These sketches will become the basis for the field notes.
- ❏ Establish datum lines and planes as points of reference for taking measurements. Locate datum lines and planes in relation to each other and note their locations on sketches.
- ❏ Begin by locating major points in relation to each other and any datum lines and planes. Take major dimensions. Record both in field notes.
- ❏ Double-check accuracy of initial measurements, since all subsequent measurements will rely on them.
- ❏ Systematically take and record measurements to fill in the necessary dimensions for each drawing. Periodically tie your measurements back to the principal reference points or datum lines and planes to ensure continued accuracy.

Checking

- ❏ An effective way to verify the accuracy of your measurements is to block out the major dimensions on a drawing while still in the field, then check how the component parts will fit into the overall drawing.
- ❏ Preliminary drawings should be produced in the field to ensure the accuracy and completeness of the field measurements.

Obtaining Measurements

Dimensions for measured drawings have traditionally come from three sources: documents, hand measurements, and photographs. Laser scanning is a more recent technology that most closely resembles stereophotogrammetry. Like a photogrammetric camera, a laser scanner captures ungeneralized, line-of-sight data that can be converted to xyz coordinates that can serve as the basis for a measured drawing. Documentary measurements come from original or alteration drawings, old views, published accounts, previous surveys, specifications, and so on. A more thorough discussion of documentary sources is included in the history chapter.

The tools and techniques used for taking measurements by hand vary in their sophistication. The measurements are produced by taping distances, surveying (measuring angles and distances, often with the help of surveying instruments and electronic distance measuring equipment), or measuring and counting repetitive materials (*see fig. 4.9*).

Photography offers a wide variety of information-gathering capabilities that are discussed in great detail in the previous chapter. Field photographs are used as an adjunct to field measurements and are invaluable for double-checking accuracy. In addition, they are very cost-effective. As a rule of thumb, the less accessible a site is for checking measurements, the

Figure 4.9
Counting repetitive materials is a way to determine measurements that are inaccessible, such as for the tower on this city hall. The dimensions of the brick coursing were recorded ("Note: 10 brick courses are 2'-4" in height") so that the dimensions of the tower could be calculated.

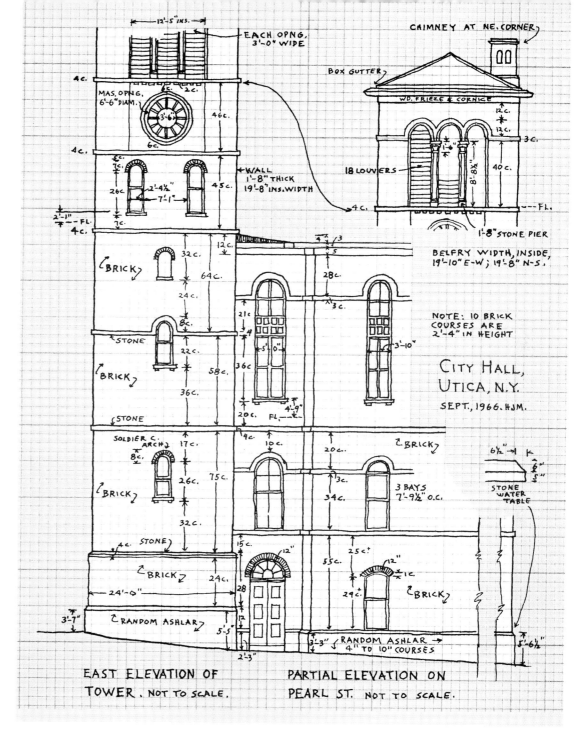

Figure 4.10
Note the mix of general and detail views and the systematic coverage of the entire exterior surface of the springhouse in these contact prints of field photographs. The interiors were documented on another roll of film.

more field photographs should be taken. Even a simple structure like a springhouse may require an entire roll of film to record all its details (*see fig. 4.10*). Large-format photographs are sharper and clearer than 35 mm photographs. Great detail is discernible, even in contact prints, when large-format photographs are viewed under a jeweler's loupe or magnifying glass. A measuring stick placed in the field of view of a photograph can be used to scale distances (*see fig. 4.11*). Other, less common ways to produce measurements using photographs include the techniques of rectified photography, mono- and stereophotogrammetry, and convergent and analytical photogrammetry, all discussed later in this chapter.

Obtaining Measurements from Documentary Sources

The easiest way to obtain measurements is to find a source that has already recorded them. Historical research should include a search for drawings, specifications, building permits, and other sources of dimensional information. If they are found, the reliability and accuracy of the dimensions must be assessed, as must their usefulness to the current project. Important questions include: Who produced the measurements and for what purpose? Do the drawings reflect the structure as it was actually built and exists today? If not, how and why are the drawings different? Are some but not all of the drawings reliable?

The recorder must verify the accuracy of the information against the structure itself. If the drawings have few given dimensions, it may be possible to scale from the drawings. Scaled dimensions must be checked in both directions on a drawing to make sure there is no differential distortion. Paper will elongate or shrink differently along the grain than across the grain. Prints made by wrapping the drawing and print paper around a tubular light source, the exposure method found in most blueprint machines, are elongated in the direction of travel. For a 4-mil-thick HABS/HAER/HALS drawing sheet and a 2-inch-diameter light source, the elongation would be approximately $\frac{5}{32}$" in 3', or the equivalent of 8 scale inches at $\frac{1}{4}$" = 1'-0". Drawings on thicker paper produce more elongation; drawings on thinner paper produce less. Some large-format scanners and some graphic software make it possible to change the x and y axes of a drawing separately, allowing uniformly distorted drawings to be "undistorted."

Hand Measuring

Hand measuring is the most common way to obtain dimensions for measured drawings. Hand measuring can be highly accurate when carefully planned and executed. The number of drawings, their accuracy, the scale used, and the sheet layout should be determined before the measuring is planned because those decisions help determine the best way to measure a structure. Hand measuring records only what is consciously measured and written down, making a methodical, systematic approach essential. Otherwise, errors of omission and commission will be difficult to avoid. Proceeding in a systematic manner not only gives organization to the measuring process, but also highlights errors when they do occur. Plan more than one way to obtain each measurement—for example, by direct measurement, by calculation from other points, or by trigonometry—so that all dimensions will be verifiable (*see fig. 4.12*).

The number of people required for hand-measuring a structure varies. Three is an ideal number, two people to measure and one to record the dimensions. In teams of two, one person can measure while the other records the dimensions. It is difficult, however, and potentially dangerous for one person to measure any-

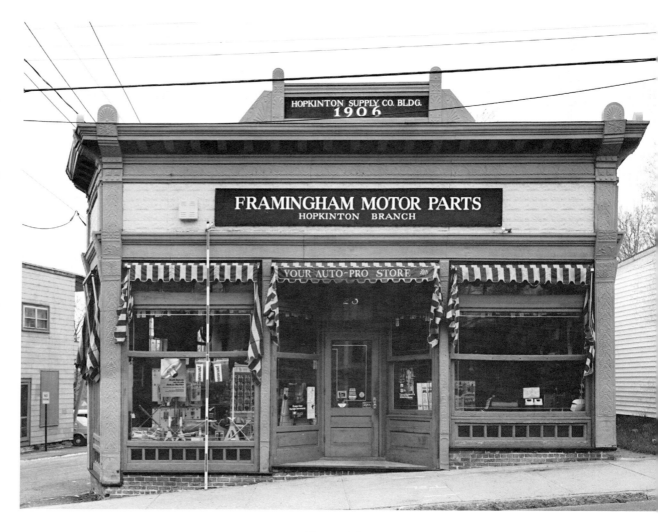

Figure 4.11

For structures unlikely to be recorded in measured drawings, a scale stick placed in the field of view of the photographs provides basic dimensional information. Note that the recessed entry and projecting cornice will be distorted in relation to the distance they are displaced from the plane of the facade.

Measuring Tips

A few points are important to remember when making hand measurements (*see figs. 4.13a and 4.13b*):

■ It cannot be assumed that rooms or buildings are square or that floors are level. Taking diagonal measurements and checking levels will allow you to determine if there is any distortion.

■ Establish datum lines and planes as points of reference for the measurements.

■ Cumulative measurements are more accurate than consecutive measurements because they use a common zero point and thus do not require the tape to be relocated after each measurement.

■ Hold the tape taut when making measurements. Temperature, tension, and wind can affect the accuracy of measurements by causing the tape to stretch, shrink, or sag.

■ Know where the zero point is on the tape. It is not always at the end.

■ Horizontal distances must be measured with the tape held level. Use a plumb line to measure points displaced vertically.

■ Triangulate to features on inclined or curved surfaces from fixed points.

■ Remember that the minimum distance from a point to a line is always in a direction perpendicular to the line, so if you set the end of a tape at the point and swing it near the line, the minimum measurement is the true dimension. Similarly, the distance from a point to a plane follows the same geometric rule.

■ Use the utmost care in transcribing dimensions. Use a standardized system of notation to reduce the chance of error. For instance, the dimension 1'-8" is similar to 18" both visually and literally.

■ The use of surveying instruments and other measuring tools can both speed up measuring and increase accuracy.

Hand measuring can be broken down into a three-step process (see "Step-by-Step Approach" sidebar). After the principal dimensions have been accurately determined, repeat the process at the next higher level of detail until the entire structure has been measured at the level of detail necessary to produce the planned drawings.

Figure 4.12

Dimensions recorded on field notes are the primary source material for a measured drawing. In this example, compare the many dimensions and notes in the field drawing to the finished drawing. The information in the field notes makes it possible to gauge the accuracy of the completed drawing.

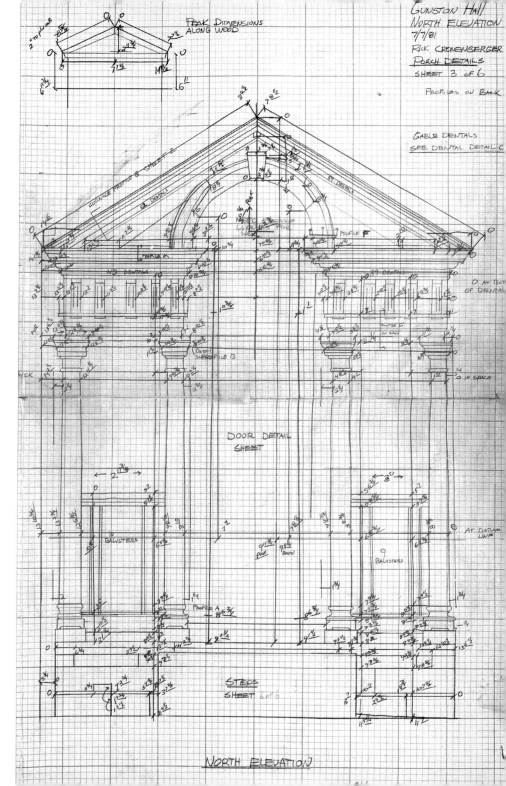

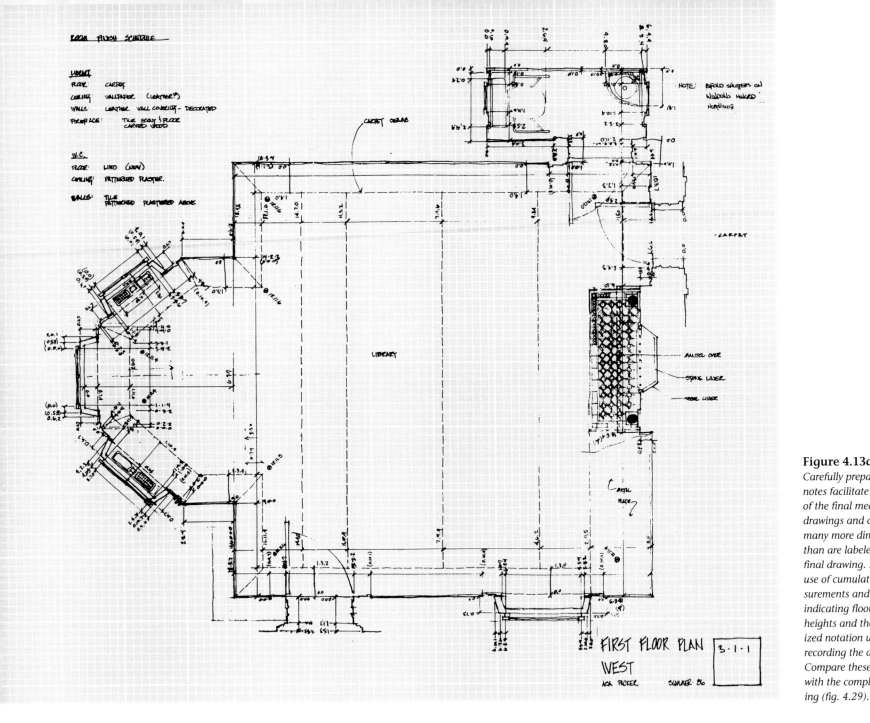

Figure 4.13a
Carefully prepared field notes facilitate production of the final measured drawings and contain many more dimensions than are labeled on the final drawing. Note the use of cumulative measurements and targets indicating floor-to-ceiling heights and the standardized notation used for recording the dimensions. Compare these field notes with the completed drawing (fig. 4.29).

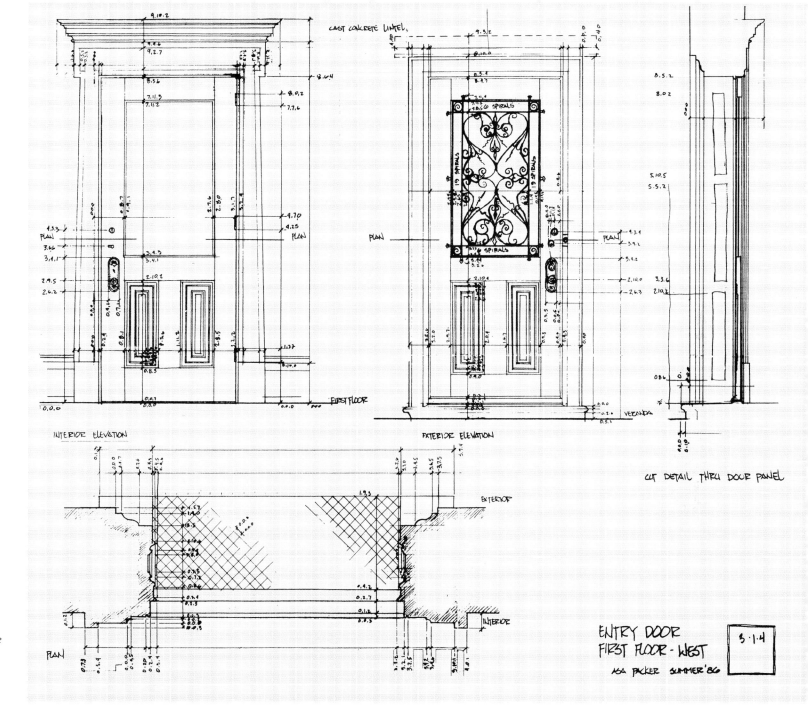

Figure 4.13b
The field notes for this door were made at a large scale because the final drawing will be at a large scale to show the necessary detail.

INTERIOR ELEVATION

EXTERIOR ELEVATION

CAST CONCRETE LINTEL

CUT DETAIL THRU DOOR PANEL

ENTRY DOOR
FIRST FLOOR - WEST
ASA PACKER SUMMER '86

3·1·4

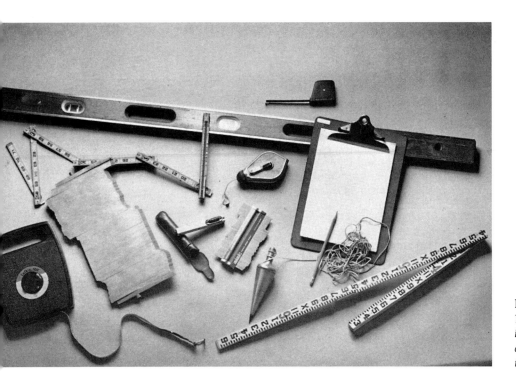

Figure 4.14
Traditional hand-measuring equipment is readily available and easily transported.

level is to inspect it. Does it look level or feel level when you walk on it? If your observations indicate the floor may be level, check it more carefully with a carpenter's level or by using the techniques described in the following paragraphs. An advantage to using the floor as a datum plane is that it requires only one vertical measurement (from the floor up instead of both up and down from a datum plane). Another consideration is whether the floor elevation changes from room to room or from wing to wing. Even if all the floors are level, changes in elevation may necessitate a common datum plane from which to measure.

If the floor is level, a convenient height for measuring is at waist level. It does not require you to stoop and is high enough to pass across most window openings. Remember to keep the tape level when measuring.

If the floor is not level, you must establish a datum plane independent of the structure. A horizontal datum line accurate enough to use for most small structures can be established by leveling a taut string with a carpenter's spirit level. The longer the level and the tighter the string, the more accurate the level line will be. The spirit level should be at least 2 feet long for optimum accuracy. The string should be tight enough to remove visible sags, which can be observed by sighting along the string. Also note if the string is hung up on anything. (A small bubble level designed to hang on a string is significantly less accurate than this method. A chalk line can be used, but it may leave a permanent mark on some materials, so obtain permission before using one.) By repeating the process, you can carry the datum line around a structure to establish a datum plane. To check accuracy, periodically tie back or relate subsequent datum lines to the first one.

A water level (consisting of a water-filled tube, like a hose, with transparent ends through

thing other than small features or details. Large structures are documented more efficiently with several two- or three-person measuring teams rather than one large team.

Tools for Hand Measuring. The most common tools for hand measuring are a retractable steel tape stiff enough to extend across openings or up to ceilings (a 1-inch-wide, 25-foot tape is recommended), a 100-foot steel tape, a 6-foot folding carpenter's rule, a plumb bob or similar weight and string, a carpenter's spirit level, graph paper, a large clipboard, and a pencil (*see fig. 4.14*). Accurate measurements can be

made and recorded with these simple tools and a knowledge of geometry. Additional equipment might include a profile gauge, magnetic compass, scale stick for field photographs, flashlight, and ladders or scaffolding. Safety equipment such as hard hats and ropes should be used as needed.

Establishing Datum Lines and Planes. The first step in hand measuring is to establish datum lines and planes from which to take measurements. In some structures it may be possible to use the floor as a datum plane if it is found to be level. The first step in determining if a floor is

which the water level can be viewed) can also be used to demarcate a horizontal datum plane that can be carried from room to room or from the interior to the exterior of a structure. It works on the principle that water seeks its own level. Advantages of water levels are that they are accurate and flexible in that they can go around corners and through openings. They are also inexpensive and can be homemade. One problem with the technique is that if water spills, you must both reset the level to compensate for the lost water and clean up the mess.

Vertical datum lines and planes can be established by running a plumb line up or down from known points. Horizontal relationships from floor to floor can be determined using this technique.

Aboard ships, the use of a transit to set datum planes may be essential (especially if the ship is afloat) for measuring the compound curves of the decks. Plumb bobs and levels are useless unless the vessel is in a dry dock or otherwise supported out of water on land. See the chapter on recording historic ships in the case study section for more detailed information.

Hand Measuring Conventions. All measurements are assumed to be made in either horizontal or vertical planes. Vertical measurements can be made most accurately by using a plumb line to ensure the verticality of the tape. When taking horizontal measurements, keep the tape taut to avoid sags. (Surveyors use a standard of 20 pounds of tension when taking measurements with steel tapes.) If you are using a transit to sight in a datum plane, the minimum dimension read in the scope, as you swing a tape from a point to the scope sight line, is in a direction perpendicular to the datum plane.

When direct horizontal measurements are not possible, inclined dimensions can be taken and converted to horizontal dimensions using trigonometry. Horizontal measurements made with one end of the tape higher than the other will actually measure a longer distance because of the inclination of the tape. It may be easier to measure inclined distances by breaking the slope into a series of stepped horizontal measurements. Vertical alignment of the tape at each step can be ensured by using a plumb line.

Specialized Hand-Measuring Tools. HABS/HAER uses several other types of hand-measuring tools that are extremely useful. The Leitz SK telescoping digital measuring pole allows one person to measure heights up to 26 feet with a direct read-out of the dimension in feet, inches, and eighths of an inch (*see fig. 4.15*). The pole can also be used horizontally. It is just over 4 feet long when collapsed and weighs 4 pounds. Made of nonconducting materials, the pole nevertheless must be used with extreme caution around power lines.

A second Leitz measuring tool is the builder's mini rod, similar to an oversized folding carpenter's rule. It comes in both 6½- and 9½-foot lengths, with numbers that read vertically, making it useful as a scale stick in photographs. The shorter rod is just over 15 inches long when folded and fits easily in a briefcase; the longer rod is 22 inches long when folded (*see fig. 4.14*). Marking one side of the rule in alternating black-and-white 1-foot increments increases its usefulness as a scale stick when photographed from a distance.

Another measuring tool is a telescoping fiberglass rod (with an oval cross section) that is about 5 feet long but extends to 25 feet. It has gradations marked every ¼ inch on one side and alternating red and white 1-foot increments on the other (*see fig. 4.11*).

Basic Surveying. A rudimentary understanding of surveying techniques can make hand mea-

Figure 4.15
A Leitz SK telescoping digital measuring pole simplifies taking vertical measurements by hand.

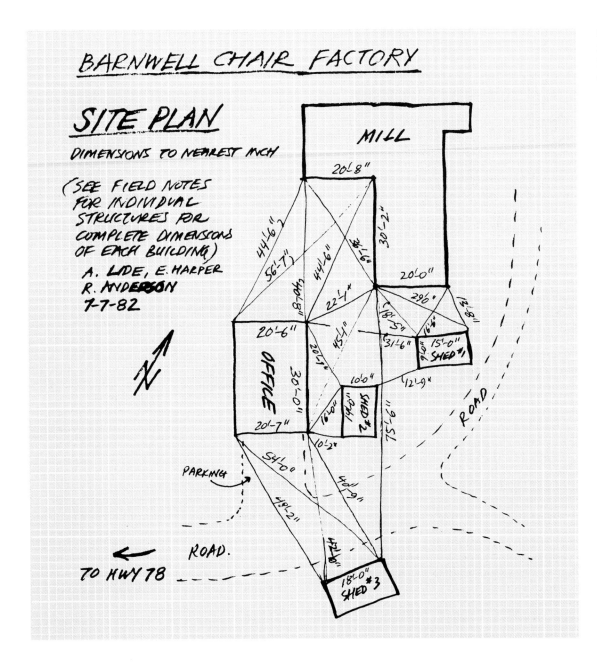

BARNWELL CHAIR FACTORY

SITE PLAN

DIMENSIONS TO NEAREST INCH

(SEE FIELD NOTES
FOR INDIVIDUAL
STRUCTURES FOR
COMPLETE DIMENSIONS
OF EACH BUILDING)
A. LIDE, E. HARPER
R. ANDERSON
7-7-82

MILL

OFFICE

SHED #1
SHED #2
SHED #3

PARKING

ROAD

ROAD.
TO HWY 78

suring faster, easier, and more accurate. Survey-ing is based on geometry and is an efficient method of establishing levels, measuring angles, and measuring distances. For more information on surveying, see the books listed in the bibliography.

The simplest form of surveying is triangula-tion, a technique suitable for hand measuring. Any point on a site can be located accurately by establishing its distance from two other points. An entire site can be measured by using a series of triangles and measuring the distances along their sides (*see fig. 4.16*). To ensure accuracy, you must periodically tie back to known points. This technique is particularly effective for flat sites, less so for sloping or hilly sites. The com-pensation for inclined measurements must be calculated using either the angle of inclination or the difference in height between the two points being measured. Both calculations are simple trigonometric functions. This technique is especially useful in irregular structures, for site plans, or on board ships.

Plane surveying should be used for docu-menting historic sites with a transit or other sur-veying instrument. Plane surveying does not compensate for the curvature of the earth,

Figure 4.16
Measuring a series of triangles can locate structures in relation to one another without the use of surveying equip-ment. The technique is accurate when all the measure-ments are taken in a level plane. On a sloping site, the measurements must be either taken in vertically displaced level planes or calculated by converting inclined measure-ments to level measurements mathematically.

Field Photographs

Field photographs should include a scale stick or measuring tape to give approximate scale to elements in the view (*see fig. 4.17*). Another technique, especially useful for irregular features such as stonework or log walls, is to place a grid of known dimension over the subject being photographed. Such a grid can be made from a rigid frame of pipe, 5 feet square, with a string grid at 1-foot intervals. Objects in or close to the plane of the tape or grid can be scaled relatively accurately. Objects in front of or beyond the plane of the tape or grid are either enlarged or diminished in relation to their displacement from the plane.

Figure 4.17
The measuring stick allows the viewer to understand the scale of the adobe bricks, which are much larger than regular bricks. Without the scale stick as a reference, it is difficult to estimate the size of the masonry units.

Architectural photogrammetry combines principles of photography and geometry in a method for creating scaled drawings from photographs. The process makes use of photographs taken from known locations to create an optical model that can be scaled in all directions. There are several kinds of photogrammetry, which vary in technique, accuracy, and expense.

Rectified Photography. Rectified photography uses optical means to rectify or correct a photograph so that one plane of the subject is recorded without distortion. Because its accuracy is limited to one plane, rectified photography is best used for flat facades and room elevations (*see fig. 4.18*). The rectification can be in either exposure of the negative or the printing process. If the photographer has access to a darkroom, the latter is easier.

Rectifying a negative requires the photographer to establish a grid on the object being photographed and to position the camera in relation to the grid so that the central axis of the lens is perpendicular to the center point of the grid and the film plane is parallel to the grid plane. This is a difficult and time-consuming task. However, the resulting negative can be enlarged conventionally to any desired scale.

The second technique rectifies the photograph in a darkroom by manipulating the negative as it is printed. This is usually accomplished by tilting the print easel in relation to the negative to remove the distortions. This is ideally done with a rectifying enlarger designed for such work, but reasonably accurate results can be achieved with an ordinary photographic enlarger (*see figs. 4.18 and 4.19*). Again, the negative can be enlarged to any desired scale.

With either technique, prints should be made on resin-coated (RC) paper because it is

which is a negligible factor even in large historic sites. All distance measurements are assumed to be either horizontal or vertical. Vertical measurements are taken in the direction of gravity, which can be determined by using a plumb line. Horizontal measurements are defined as being perpendicular to the direction of gravity. Inclined measurements up a hill, for instance, must be corrected to a horizontal measurement using trigonometry. A pocket calculator with trigonometric functions simplifies the mathematics. Total station surveying instruments can record angles and distances and export coordinates directly into a CAD program.

Architectural Photogrammetry

Measurements obtained from photographs can offer certain advantages over other methods of measurement. Photographs are generalized, that is, they record information without constraints. Everything seen by the camera is documented; conversely, anything not seen by the camera is not documented. Photographs also convey information on condition and texture.

Figures 4.18 and 4.19

This photograph is an enlargement of the original field photograph, made so that the image of the facade is to the same scale as the drawing of the facade. A perspective-corrected 35 mm negative, normal photographic enlarger, and resin-coated (RC) enlarging paper were used to make the print. While not as accurate as rectified photography can be, this simple technique allowed the delineator to accurately position and rotate the window openings in the drawing. Notice the difference in the length of the gable ridge. In the photograph, it is diminished significantly in size because it is so far beyond the image plane of the facade.

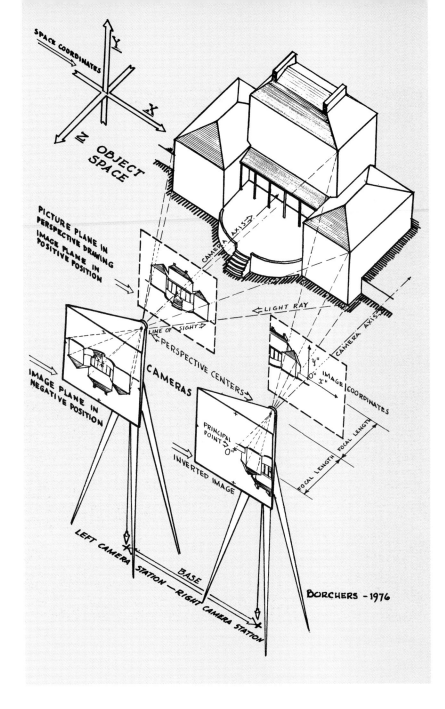

Figure 4.20

This diagram illustrates a typical setup for producing glass plate photogrammetric stereopairs using two camera stations. Note that it is the area of overlap of the two photographs, in this case the right half of the building, that can be measured from the plates.

much less likely than fiber-based papers to change shape when immersed in developing chemicals, washed, and dried. Note, however, that resin-coated papers are not archivally stable.

Monophotogrammetry is a more accurate version of rectified photography. It makes use of metric cameras, the same type used in stereophotogrammetry, to make photographs without the optical distortions found in most camera systems. Metric cameras are heavy, rigid cameras with fixed, distortion-free, high-resolution lenses that produce extremely high-quality photographs on glass plates. Glass plates are used because they are rigid, distortion-free, and dimensionally stable. The characteristics of the camera are precisely measured and recorded. Metric cameras have internal masks that place points called fiducial marks on each negative. The location of the fiducial marks is part of the known characteristics of the camera used in plotting the plates.

Perspective distortion is still present in monophotogrammetry, however, because metric cameras have fixed lenses. The perspective distortion is corrected in a special enlarger, called a rectifier, designed for that purpose. The resulting positive, made on another glass plate, is undistorted and may be scaled accurately in its principal image plane. Less expensive paper prints can be made, but they will be less accurate.

Stereophotogrammetry. Stereophotogrammetry is the most accurate widely used type of photogrammetry (*see fig. 4.20*). Two or more overlapping photographs are taken at successive camera positions or stations, normally with the axes parallel. The locations of the camera stations are carefully measured in relation to the building, the specifications of the camera are noted, and some points and

Figure 4.21

The documentation of Grant's Tomb presented problems of geometry (it is round), size (143' high), and access (scaffolding would have been prohibitively expensive). Stereophotogrammetry was an ideal choice. The open site, photographed after the leaves had fallen, allowed the necessary angles of view, and the technique easily accommodated the size and shape of the monument. The perspective distortion apparent in the plate was corrected when the plates were plotted.

Figure 4.22

St. Mary's Seminary in Baltimore was threatened with imminent demolition, and photogrammetry was the only practical means to record it, given the limited amount of time and money available. The circled and labeled targets are known and measured survey control points that allow other dimensions to be determined using a photogrammetric plotter. The survey control points also allow adjacent plates to be related precisely to each other by comparing points visible in both plates.

dimensions are established on the structure or in the space before it. These data are known as survey control.

Paired photographs (stereopairs) are placed in a plotting instrument to produce an optical model that is scalable in three dimensions. The technique is highly specialized and requires the use of expensive cameras and plotting instruments operated by trained technicians. It is especially useful for structures that are too irregular, large, inaccessible, or dangerous to measure by hand (*see fig. 4.21*). The technique is limited by the fact that the cameras document only what is in their field of view. Objects hidden by foliage or projections are not measurable and must be recorded in some other manner.

One use for photogrammetry is in the preparation of stereopairs and survey control data that will be plotted and drawn only as necessary. Since plotting and drawing is the most expensive aspect of photogrammetry, this will make it possible to document more buildings for a given expenditure, retaining the capability to produce measured drawings in the future (*see fig. 4.22*). Two problems with this approach are that the informational content is neither easily reproducible (glass plates are fragile and require special handling) nor independently verifiable without putting the plates in a plotter.

Stereophotogrammetry may be either terrestrial or aerial. Terrestrial photogrammetry is used for showing individual buildings or groups of buildings in elevation. It is the best way to record small dimensions since the camera-to-subject distances are short.

Aerial photogrammetry is used for mapping and making plans for districts. Survey control in this case includes some targeting or knowledge of elevations, distances, and direction of points on the ground as well as the course, altitude, and speed of the plane and the time between successive exposures. Aerial photographs are generally taken with the axis within 3° of perpendicular to the ground. A specialized type of aerial photogrammetry is low-level oblique, in which the photographs are taken from low altitudes with the camera turned to the side to record elevations. The camera-to-subject distance is large, so the level of detail is not great. The technique is ideal, however, for recording large areas in a short time.

The products of both terrestrial and aerial processes are photographic stereopairs, which when placed in a plotting machine present the illusion of a three-dimensional optical model. (The same principle is at work in a child's View-Master.) Using the survey control, this model can be accurately measured and points can be plotted on a drawing at any desired scale. A drafter then joins these points to produce a measured drawing in standard orthographic projection.

The number of stereopairs needed to document a site depends on the nature of the structure and its environment. Elevation drawings are best made from stereopairs taken perpendicular to the building, while oblique views are best for determining measurements of features in more than one plane, such as cornices or roofs. Repetitious views taken from several distances and angles may therefore be required. Large areas can be covered by series of pairs of photographs, which can be arranged in a mosaic by relating common points visible in adjacent pairs. Trees, adjacent structures, and other obstacles that obscure the view may also increase the number of stereopairs needed.

Analytical Photogrammetry. An analytical photogrammetry technique called reverse perspective analysis can be used to prepare drawings for structures that have been damaged or demolished but for which photographs remain and a few dimensions can be determined (*see figs. 4.23, 7.5, and 7.14*).

The technique uses ordinary contemporary or historic photographs, sometimes in conjunction with contemporary photogrammetry. It combines the use of one or more photographs for which the camera position can be determined with geometric calculation of the major dimensions of the structure. Accuracy depends on the quantity and quality of photographs available and the number of known dimensions. The process is easier if historic photographs can be combined with contemporary photogrammetry.

CAD/photogrammetry is the HABS/HAER/HALS term for its photogrammetric documentation, which evolved from the digital convergent photogrammetry the program first experimented with in 1989. Now the predominant photogrammetric technique used by the program, CAD/photogrammetry is discussed in more detail in the case study on recording monuments and in the sidebar on digital documentation technologies in the overview.

HABS/HAER/HALS Measured Drawings

HABS/HAER/HALS measured drawings all have common elements of identification (*see fig. 4.24*). The title block includes the name of the project or sponsor; the name of the structure; the address, including city or vicinity, county, and state; the HABS, HAER or HALS number; and the sheet number. Information in the drawing area includes the name of the delineator, date of the drawing, graphic scales in both English and metric units, and north arrow on plans. Dimensions, materials indications, and annotations are also standard.

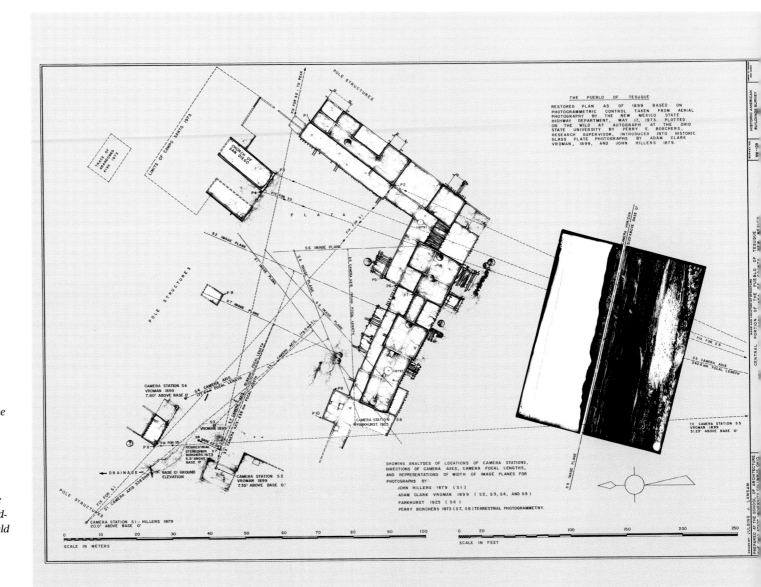

Figure 4.23
Using aerial photogrammetric glass plates from 1973, reverse perspective analysis was used to plot the camera stations, axes, and focal lengths for historic photographs of the Pueblo of Tesuque made in 1879, 1899, and 1925. Using known dimensions from the 1973 photogrammetric studies, measured drawings could be prepared for the three earlier views. This drawing shows the locations of the earlier views superimposed on the 1973 plan of the site.

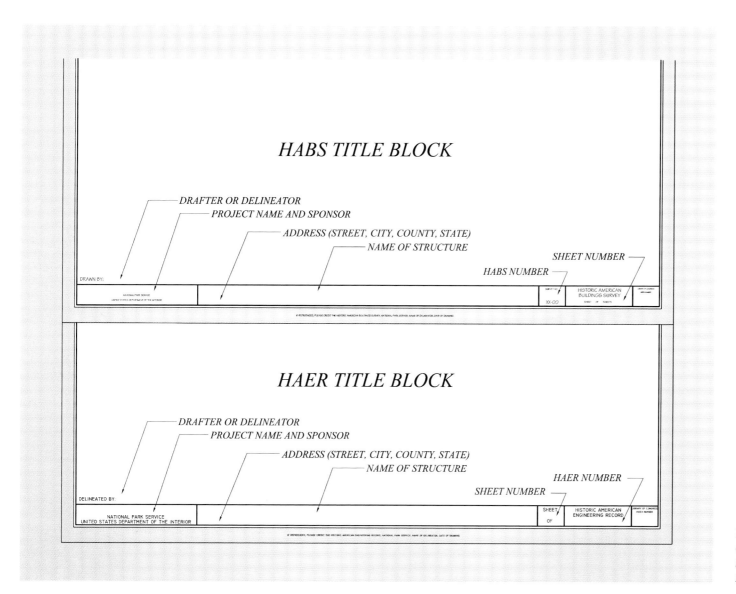

HABS TITLE BLOCK

DRAFTER OR DELINEATOR
PROJECT NAME AND SPONSOR
ADDRESS (STREET, CITY, COUNTY, STATE)
NAME OF STRUCTURE
SHEET NUMBER
HABS NUMBER

DRAWN BY:

NATIONAL PARK SERVICE
UNITED STATES DEPARTMENT OF THE INTERIOR

HISTORIC AMERICAN
BUILDINGS SURVEY

XX-00   SHEET   OF   SHEETS

IF REPRODUCED, PLEASE CREDIT THE HISTORIC AMERICAN BUILDINGS SURVEY, NATIONAL PARK SERVICE, NAME OF DELINEATOR, DATE OF DRAWING

HAER TITLE BLOCK

DRAFTER OR DELINEATOR
PROJECT NAME AND SPONSOR
ADDRESS (STREET, CITY, COUNTY, STATE)
NAME OF STRUCTURE
HAER NUMBER
SHEET NUMBER

DELINEATED BY:

NATIONAL PARK SERVICE
UNITED STATES DEPARTMENT OF THE INTERIOR

SHEET

OF

HISTORIC AMERICAN
ENGINEERING RECORD

IF REPRODUCED, PLEASE CREDIT THE HISTORIC AMERICAN ENGINEERING RECORD, NATIONAL PARK SERVICE, NAME OF DELINEATOR, DATE OF DRAWING

Figure 4.24
Common elements of identification in HABS and HAER measured drawings.

Drawing Scales and Drawing Accuracy

HABS/HAER/HALS uses common architectural and engineering scales in its drawings (see sidebar). Other scales can be used, although though they are not common. An example would be a drawing done at ³⁄₁₆″ = 1′-0″ because it would not fit on a standard HAER Mylar at ¼″ = 1′-0″.

Metric Scales

Metric scales are expressed in decimal ratios. Typical metric scales are very similar to English scales in the level of detail given. The metric scale commonly used for floor plans, 1:50, is only 4 percent smaller than the English scale of ¼″ = 1′-0″ (1:48). Since few historic structures in the United States were built using the metric system, HABS/HAER/HALS rarely uses metric measurements except as a convenience to subsequent researchers. The most common HABS/HAER/HALS use of the metric system is the inclusion of a metric graphic scale on measured drawings.

Before Drafting

All of the measured drawings in a set should be designed before the drafting begins. The composition of each sheet should be planned so that there is room for the drawing, the common information listed above, dimensions, and annotations. While it is sometimes possible to place more than one drawing on an individual sheet, a single drawing of a large structure or site may require several sheets. Do not mix sheet sizes in a single set of drawings. HABS/HAER/HALS achieves a unity of design throughout a set of measured drawings by establishing and following consistent drafting conventions regarding line weights, lettering, dimensions, annotations, materials indications, labels, north arrows, scales, and title blocks.

Hand-delineated ink-on-Mylar HABS/HAER/HALS measured drawings are frequently tracings of preliminary drawings made from field measurements. The consistency and accuracy of the set are worked out before the inking begins. The preliminary drawings are frequently done in pencil on Mylar. Pencil is used because it is easy to use and erase and is cheaper than ink. Mylar is preferred to tracing paper or vellum because of its dimensional stability. Paper and vellum change shape, particularly with changes in humidity, reducing the accuracy of a field drawing and the final drawing that will be traced from it. In addition, the translucency of Mylar facilitates overlay drafting and checking. Drawings can be overlaid to reduce the amount of repetitive drafting and to check accuracy. For instance, the horizontal dimensions for an elevation or section drawing can be traced from a floor plan.

HABS/HAER/HALS measured drawings should always be produced so that the drawing will remain legible when reproduced at a smaller size. At the Library of Congress, the public views page-size copies of HABS/HAER/HALS measured drawings, which fit in three-ring binders. Similarly, researchers using the Built in America Web site will most commonly print downloaded drawings at page size. The drawings reproduced in this book are significantly smaller than the originals. Extremely fine lines (smaller than 0.25 mm or a 3×0 Rapidograph), small lettering (smaller than ⅛″), and closely spaced parallel lines are to be avoided if possible. When necessary, they should be used with caution. When reproduced at a reduced scale, fine lines tend to fade out, small lettering becomes illegible, and closely spaced lines bleed together and read as a solid mass. E-size sheets, which are reduced more, should have higher tolerances to remain legible

at page size (0.3 mm or a 00 Rapidograph for lines and ³⁄₁₆″ lettering).

Title Sheet

The title sheet for the measured drawings component of the HABS/HAER/HALS documentation traditionally includes at least a site plan, statement of significance, and project information statement (*see fig. 4.25*). In some cases, particularly on the larger sheet size, there is room to include one of the measured drawings on the title sheet. The site plan includes enough of the surrounding area to establish the setting for the structure or object being recorded. There is no HABS/HAER/HALS requirement for specific site plan sources or scales because they are variable. Site maps frequently follow the civil engineering practice of measuring in feet and hundredths and drawing at engineering scales such as 1″ = 20′.

Site plans do not have to be measured by hand. The scale should be determined by the location, size, and significance of the site. Cities often have detailed maps locating individual structures and lots. These can be copied, and the source, scale, and date cited (*see fig. 4.26*). HABS/HAER/HALS discourages photographically copying maps onto measured drawings because the resulting photographic image is not archivally stable.

For rural sites, maps should include enough of the surrounding area to make it possible to reliably locate the structure. HABS/HAER/HALS typically copies U.S. Geological Survey (USGS) 7.5 minute maps as site maps. They are available for the entire country in both printed and digital form and are in a convenient scale (1″ = 2,000′ or 1:24,000). If a USGS map is used, the latitude and longitude or Universal Transverse Mercator (UTM) coordinates for the site should be determined and the corresponding grid marked with ticks along the neat lines (border) of the map (*see fig. 4.27*).

It may be possible to include the site immediately around a building as part of the first-floor plan. Sites with elaborate or significant grounds may warrant a site plan on a separate sheet or sheets, drawn at a scale large enough to illustrate the significant features of the site. Refer to the chapter on historic landscape documentation in the case study section for more detailed information.

The statement of significance, as in the written portion of the documentation, summarizes the significance of a site and often includes a brief interpretation. A reader should be able to determine from this statement why a structure was judged significant enough to warrant measured drawings. The length of statements of significance varies. The significance of Mount Vernon, for example, can be simply and concisely stated. A coal mine, by contrast, may require several paragraphs to explain its features and operation.

The project information statement describes the history of a recording project. It includes the concept behind the documentation, the organizers and sponsors, persons and organizations completing the work, and the scope and limitations of the research. Academic as well as financial sponsors should be credited along with any cooperating agencies. Documentation is rarely a one-person effort, and it is always appropriate to give credit where credit is due.

Plans
Plans are an essential element of measured drawings, as they cannot be documented adequately in photographs. Plan drawings are horizontal cuts through a structure that portray the arrangement and progression of spaces so that an observer can perceive what is being

Architectural Scales

SCALE	RATIO	SMALLEST UNIT*	USE
¹⁄₁₆″ = 1′-0″	1:192	4″	Drawings of large structures without details. Materials shown in plan only.
¹⁄₈″ = 1′-0″	1:96	2″	Little detail possible. Materials shown in plan, only large units in elevation.
¹⁄₄″ = 1′-0″	1:48	1″	The most common architectural scale. Reasonable amount of detail possible. HABS/HAER shows door and window frames, materials in both plan and elevation. At this scale, line weights can adversely affect accuracy. A 3×0 (0.25 mm) line is approximately ¹⁄₂″ thick.
³⁄₄″ = 1′-0″	1:16	³⁄₈″	Most common scale for door/window elevations and other features of similar scale.
1¹⁄₂″ = 1′-0″	1:8	³⁄₁₆″	Details of door/window jambs/frames, large tools, small machines, etc.
3″ = 1′-0″	1:4	³⁄₃₂″	Details of objects such as hardware, tools, etc. and molding profiles.
Full Size	1:1		Small or intricate objects, elaborate moldings and ornamentation

*The smallest unit that can be drawn relates to the surveying practice of a drawing accuracy of ¹⁄₅₀″ at map scale. This converts to approximately 1″ at the scale of ¹⁄₄″ = 1′-0″ (a ratio scale of 1:48).

Engineering and Map Scales

SCALE	RATIO	SMALLEST UNIT*	USE
1″ = 5,280′	1:62,500	104′	USGS 15 minute maps
1″ = 2,000′	1:24,000	40′	USGS 7.5 minute maps
1″ = 40′	1:480	0.8′	Site maps
1″ = 20′	1:240	0.4′	Very common scale for residential-size site plans (at this scale a half-acre lot fits comfortably on a legal-size page in a deed book). Distances given in feet and hundredths.
1″ = 16.66′	1:200	0.33′	Site maps
1″ = 10′	1:120	0.2′	Small site maps
1″ = 8.33′	1:100	0.166′	Small site maps

*The smallest unit that can be drawn relates to the surveying practice of a drawing accuracy of ¹⁄₅₀″ at map scale. This converts to approximately 5″ at the scale of 1″ = 20′ (a ratio scale of 1:240).

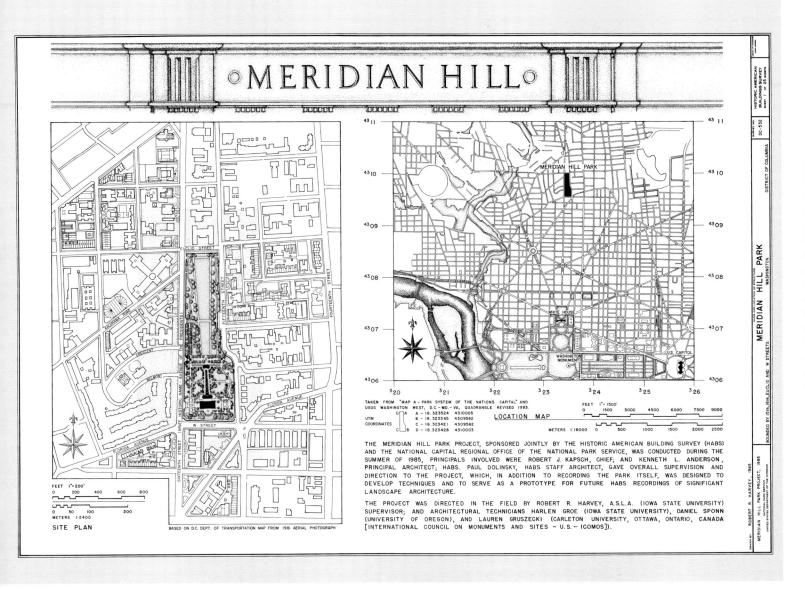

Figure 4.25
The title sheet for drawings of Meridian Hill Park in Washington, D.C., includes not only a U.S. Geological Survey location map but also a larger-scale site plan for placing the park in a neighborhood context. The decorative detail across the top of the sheet is the frieze from the 16th Street fountain. All title sheets should include a brief statement of significance, as well as credits and acknowledgments.

Figure 4.26
Urban sites with easily located street addresses have less need than others for a detailed map of the surrounding area. In this instance, four historic maps were used to illustrate the development of a block over time.

ATLANTIC BUILDING

CAST·IRON SIGN

FEET   3"=1'-0"   1:4

CENTIMETERS   1:4

920·930 F STREET NORTHWEST {COMMERCIAL BUILDINGS}

920, 922-24 AND 926 F STREET NORTHWEST ARE THREE SMALL-SCALE, BRICK COMMERCIAL STRUCTURES WHICH ILLUSTRATE THE TRADITIONAL BUILDING PATTERNS ASSOCIATED WITH THE LATE-19TH AND EARLY-20TH CENTURY COMMERCIAL DISTRICT. DESIGNED WITH RETAIL SPACES ON THE GROUND LEVEL AND OFFICES OR RESIDENTIAL SPACE ABOVE, THEY CONTINUE TO PRESENT THE MERCANTILE IMAGE OF A TURN-OF-THE-CENTURY DOWNTOWN. AS AN ENSEMBLE, THESE BUILDINGS HAVE BEEN RECOGNIZED AS INTEGRAL ELEMENTS OF THE HISTORIC F STREET STREETSCAPE AND ARE CITED BY THE D.C. HISTORIC PRESERVATION DIVISION AS CONTRIBUTING TO THE SIGNIFICANCE OF THE DOWNTOWN HISTORIC DISTRICT AND THE PENNSYLVANIA AVENUE NATIONAL HISTORIC SITE.

THE SCHWARTZ BUILDING, AT 920 F STREET NORTHWEST, WAS DESIGNED IN 1911 BY SAMUEL R. TURNER FOR BENJAMIN SCHWARTZ. FOUR STORIES TALL, THIS BRICK BUILDING FEATURES A THREE-STORY OCTAGONAL ORIEL AND A CAST-IRON DENTILLED CORNICE. THE BUILDING HOUSED SCHWARTZ'S TAILOR SHOP ON THE GROUND FLOOR AND VARIOUS INDEPENDENT OFFICES ON THE UPPER FLOORS UNTIL THE 1920S WHEN IT RECEIVED MAJOR ALTERATIONS TO ACCOMMODATE ITS CONVERSION TO HOTEL USE.

DATING TO THE 1870S, 922-24 F STREET NORTHWEST IS THE OLDEST OF THE THREE SMALL STRUCTURES. THIS BUILDING FEATURES A PRESSED BRICK FRONT AND CAST-IRON CORNICE BELOW THE MANSARD ROOF OF THE ATTIC STORY, CHARACTERISTIC OF THE SECOND EMPIRE STYLE POPULAR IN WASHINGTON AT THAT TIME. DESIGNED FOR COMMERCIAL USE ON THE GROUND FLOOR, THE BUILDING WAS OCCUPIED BY THE EVANS DINING ROOM FROM 1879 TO 1897, FOLLOWED BY THE EVANS DRUG STORE FROM 1901 TO 1910. IN 1912, THE SINGLE RETAIL SPACE AT STREET LEVEL WAS ALTERED TO ACCOMMODATE TWO SEPARATE STORES.

926 F STREET NORTHWEST WAS DESIGNED IN 1891 BY NOTED LOCAL ARCHITECT LEON DESSEZ AS OFFICES FOR THE PROMINENT LAW FIRM OF WOLF AND COHEN. THREE STORIES TALL, THIS BRICK BUILDING FEATURES DECORATIVE BRICK LINTELS AND A CORBELLED BRICK CORNICE. IN 1909, SALVATORE DESIO, A JEWELER, RELOCATED TO THE BUILDING AND CONTRACTED ARCHITECTS HUNTER AND BELL TO REMODEL THE STRUCTURE, INCLUDING LOWERING THE FIRST LEVEL AND ADDING AN ELABORATE STOREFRONT, SINCE REMOVED.

THE ATLANTIC BUILDING, AT 928-30 F STREET NORTHWEST, WAS DESIGNED IN 1887 BY PROMINENT WASHINGTON ARCHITECT JAMES GREEN HILL FOR THE ATLANTIC BUILDING COMPANY. HILL HAD SERVED AS SUPERVISORY ARCHITECT OF THE U.S. TREASURY AND WAS THE DESIGNER, AS WELL, OF NUMEROUS FINE PRIVATE BUILDINGS IN THE NATION'S CAPITAL. THE ATLANTIC BUILDING COMPANY WAS A SYNDICATE OF LOCAL INVESTORS, AND THE BUILDING IS NOTABLE AS ONE OF THE EARLIEST LARGE-SCALE COMMERCIAL DEVELOPMENTS IN WASHINGTON TO BE FINANCED BY LOCAL MONEY.

DESCRIBED IN THE CONTEMPORARY PRESS AS "ONE OF THE MOST MAGNIFICENT OFFICE STRUCTURES ON THE CONTINENT" AND AS "PRONOUNCED BY GOOD JUDGES AS IN MANY RESPECTS THE FINEST OFFICE BUILDING IN THE WORLD," THE ATLANTIC BUILDING REMAINS ONE OF THE FINEST EXAMPLES OF THE ROMANESQUE REVIVAL STYLE IN THE DISTRICT. ITS SKILLFULLY COMPOSED FACADE IS CONSTRUCTED OF BRICK AND BROWNSTONE WITH TERRA COTTA ORNAMENT, AND IRON AT THE FIRST FLOOR.

EIGHT STORIES TALL WITH AN ATTIC, THE ATLANTIC BUILDING WAS ONE OF THE LAST BUILDINGS OF ITS SIZE TO BE CONSTRUCTED OF LOAD-BEARING MASONRY WALLS IN WASHINGTON. THESE BRICK BEARING WALLS, WHICH INCLUDE ALL INTERIOR PARTITIONS, RANGE IN THICKNESS FROM 39" AT THE FOUNDATIONS TO 13" AT THE EIGHTH FLOOR. FLOOR STRUCTURE THROUGHOUT THE BUILDING CONSISTS OF WOOD FRAMING, EXCEPT FOR LIMITED AREAS OF THE FIRST AND SECOND FLOORS WHERE BRICK VAULTS RESTING ON IRON BEAMS WERE USED IN AN ATTEMPT TO PROVIDE FIREPROOFING AND SECURITY. ELSEWHERE, THE USE OF IRON FRAMING IS LIMITED TO SUPPORTING THE FACADE, THE ROOF, AND THE BRICK PARTITION WALLS ABOVE THE STORES AND THE REAR ROOM ON THE FIRST FLOOR.

ONE OF THE FIRST HIGH-RISE OFFICE BUILDINGS IN WASHINGTON, THIS SPECULATIVE STRUCTURE FEATURES TWO PASSENGER ELEVATORS PAIRED WITH A SUBSTANTIAL WOODEN STAIRCASE WRAPPED AROUND A SKYLIT STAIRWELL, AND COMMODIOUS OFFICE SPACES ON ALL EIGHT FLOORS. THE PLAN OF A TYPICAL FLOOR OF THE ATLANTIC BUILDING CONSISTS OF A DOUBLE-LOADED CORRIDOR,

WITH ALL OFFICES CONNECTED INTERNALLY AS WELL AS TO THE CORRIDOR, TO FACILITATE SUITE ARRANGEMENTS. LIGHT WELLS, BOTH EXTERNAL AND INTERNAL, ARE USED TO PROVIDE LIGHT TO OFFICES ON THE LOWER FLOORS. THE PLAN WAS MODIFIED ON THE EIGHTH FLOOR TO PROVIDE TWO LARGE ASSEMBLY ROOMS. THESE ROOMS HAVE BEEN NOTED AS THE LOCATION OF NUMEROUS IMPORTANT PUBLIC MEETINGS, INCLUDING ONE AT WHICH THE NATIONAL ZOOLOGICAL PARK WAS FOUNDED. THE ATTIC CONSISTS OF AN APARTMENT FOR THE BUILDING'S CARETAKER.

THE ATLANTIC BUILDING IS LISTED INDIVIDUALLY ON THE NATIONAL REGISTER OF HISTORIC PLACES AND IS A PROMINENT MEMBER OF THE DOWNTOWN HISTORIC DISTRICT AND THE PENNSYLVANIA AVENUE NATIONAL HISTORIC SITE.

DOCUMENTATION OF THESE STRUCTURES WAS MANDATED BY THE DISTRICT OF COLUMBIA AS ONE OF THE REQUIREMENTS FOR OBTAINING A PARTIAL DEMOLITION PERMIT UNDER THE D.C. HISTORIC LANDMARK AND HISTORIC DISTRICT PROTECTION ACT OF 1978.

THIS DOCUMENTATION WAS PRODUCED UNDER A COOPERATIVE AGREEMENT BETWEEN THE HISTORIC AMERICAN BUILDINGS SURVEY / HISTORIC AMERICAN ENGINEERING RECORD OF THE NATIONAL PARK SERVICE, ROBERT J. KAPSCH, CHIEF, AND CLOVER F STREET ASSOCIATES, L.P., EDWARD L. DANIELS, PRESIDENT. THE MEASURED DRAWINGS WERE EXECUTED UNDER THE DIRECTION OF HABS/HAER ARCHITECT JOHN A. BURNS, A.I.A., BY SUPERVISORY ARCHITECT MARK SCHARA, GRADUATE OF THE UNIVERSITY OF VIRGINIA; DRAFTING FOREMAN CHRISTINE B. VINA, GRADUATE OF TEXAS TECH UNIVERSITY; AND ARCHITECTURE TECHNICIANS MARY ELLEN DIDION, GRADUATE OF THE CATHOLIC UNIVERSITY OF AMERICA, THOMAS P. FORDE, JR., VIRGINIA POLYTECHNIC INSTITUTE AND STATE UNIVERSITY, AND DORIS MICHAELA GROSSING, TECHNICAL UNIVERSITY OF VIENNA (ICOMOS/AUSTRIA). THE RECORDING WAS ASSISTED BY ARCHITECTURAL AND HISTORICAL DATA MADE AVAILABLE BY PATRICK BURKHART, A.I.A. OF SHALOM BARANES ASSOCIATES ARCHITECTS AND EMILY EIG OF TRACERIES. THE LARGE FORMAT PHOTOGRAPHS WERE TAKEN BY HABS PHOTOGRAPHER JACK E. BOUCHER.

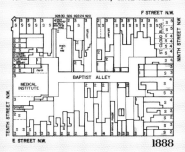

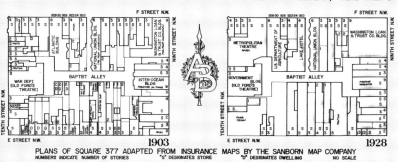

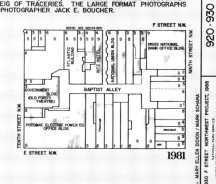

1888

1903

1928

1981

PLANS OF SQUARE 377 ADAPTED FROM INSURANCE MAPS BY THE SANBORN MAP COMPANY
NUMBERS INDICATE NUMBER OF STORIES   "S" DESIGNATES STORE   "D" DESIGNATES DWELLING   NO SCALE

920-930 F STREET NORTHWEST (COMMERCIAL BUILDINGS)
WASHINGTON   DISTRICT OF COLUMBIA

DRAWN BY: MARY ELLEN DIDION / MARK SCHARA
920-930 F STREET NORTHWEST PROJECT, 1988
NATIONAL PARK SERVICE
UNITED STATES DEPARTMENT OF THE INTERIOR

recorded. Plans are cut at a consistent height; the convention is to cut through openings such as doors, windows, and fireboxes. Plans should be projected views; that is, where "horizontal" surfaces are inclined or curve, as in the deck of a ship, they should be projected into a horizontal plane. Ideally, all plans should be drawn at the same scale so that the relationship between levels is consistent.

Plans are arranged in a logical progression. HABS/HAER/HALS orders them from the bottom up (the lowest level comes first, the highest level last) except with ships, where the order is reversed. HABS records building plans from foundation to roof, although most sets of floor plans include only basement to top floor.

Plans of attics and basements (often thought not worth recording or drawn at a smaller scale) can record valuable information. Basements are paradoxical. While they are usually the most abused and changed spaces in a structure, they often contain a great deal of information about the structural and mechanical systems of a building (see fig. 7.8). They are rarely finished as elaborately as the rest of a building and may be damp, dirty, and difficult to measure. They are nevertheless worth documenting, especially if they reveal important information about a structure. There can be analogous spaces in industrial structures and aboard ships.

Traditionally, unfinished attics and basements usually allow access for measuring and recording. Foundations, on the other hand, are rarely accessible, and the resulting lack of information generally precludes their documentation. However, when information on footings and foundations is available, consideration should be given to recording that important information (see fig. 7.5). The foundations of engineering and industrial structures can be

particularly significant. Large machines may require special footings to isolate the surrounding structure from vibrations. Bearing points for bridges must accommodate the lateral movement of expansion and contraction in the bridge structure (see fig. 4.28).

First-floor plans can fulfill several documentation needs. The first floor is frequently the most important floor in a structure (see fig. 4.29). It is sometimes the only floor plan documented with a measured drawing. In addition, site plan information can be added to a first-floor plan to explain the relationship between interior and exterior spaces.

Upper floors are documented with measured drawings when they are significant enough to justify the effort. In houses, the second floor is where the private rooms are located. In commercial buildings, the upper floors are often given over to office space that may be completely different in character from first-floor commercial space. In both instances, the differences are significant enough to justify additional measured drawings. Where similar floor plans are repeated many times, as in tall buildings or row houses, repetitive plans may be recorded in a single drawing of a typical floor, annotated to explain the differences between floors (see fig. 4.30).

Attic plans are similar to basement plans in that they can reveal a great deal of information about a structure (see fig. 4.31). Like basements, they can be uncomfortable to work in. Common drawbacks are low headroom, protruding nails, dirt, poor lighting, and the possibility of bird and insect infestations. Moreover, they are often cold in the winter and hot in the summer. Discomforts notwithstanding, attics are worth documenting if they provide useful information.

Roof plans provide information about the arrangement and massing of a structure, partic-

ularly for large buildings and complexes. They can be included, albeit at a small scale, on the site plan. Roofs can, of course, be difficult and dangerous to measure.

Elevations

Elevation drawings show facades, room elevations, and other vertical elements of a structure projected into a vertical plane. Elevations show structures as we see them, upright and facing straight ahead (but without perspective). Buildings look like their elevation drawings more than any other measured drawing. The illusion of depth is provided by varying line weights, not by diminishing size as in a perspective drawing (see figs. 1.3, 4.2. and 4.7).

For buildings, the front facade is the most commonly drawn because it is usually the most important. Rear facades are usually secondary, as are side facades. Location is an important determinant. The land and river facades of a plantation house are both important, as would be the front and side facades of a commercial building on a corner. Secondary facades may be adequately recorded with large-format photography. In such instances, dimensional information could be obtained from plans and section drawings.

The facades of industrial buildings, which usually have little significance compared to their interiors, can also be adequately recorded with large-format photography. Technological objects are recorded with elevation drawings similar to building elevations. A machine may

Figure 4.27
Title sheets for rural structures often need several maps at different scales to locate the site in relation to adjacent properties, nearby towns, or major landscape features.

EISENHOWER FARM TWO

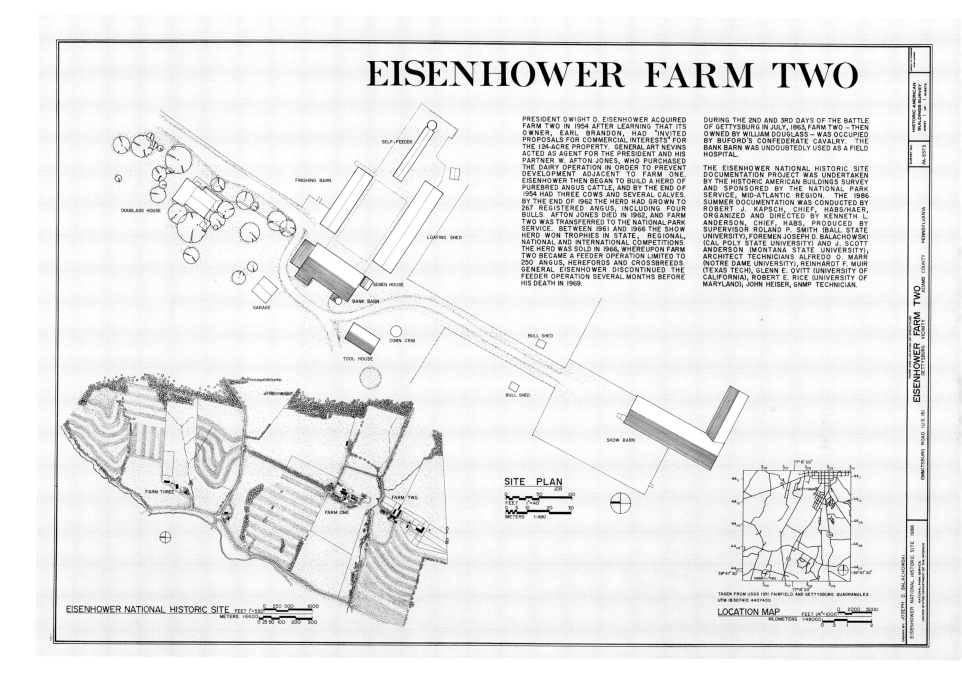

PRESIDENT DWIGHT D. EISENHOWER ACQUIRED FARM TWO IN 1954 AFTER LEARNING THAT ITS OWNER, EARL BRANDON, HAD "INVITED PROPOSALS FOR COMMERCIAL INTERESTS" FOR THE 124-ACRE PROPERTY. GENERAL ART NEVINS ACTED AS AGENT FOR THE PRESIDENT AND HIS PARTNER W. AFTON JONES, WHO PURCHASED THE DAIRY OPERATION IN ORDER TO PREVENT DEVELOPMENT ADJACENT TO FARM ONE. EISENHOWER THEN BEGAN TO BUILD A HERD OF PUREBRED ANGUS CATTLE, AND BY THE END OF 1954 HAD THREE COWS AND SEVERAL CALVES. BY THE END OF 1962 THE HERD HAD GROWN TO 267 REGISTERED ANGUS, INCLUDING FOUR BULLS. AFTON JONES DIED IN 1962, AND FARM TWO WAS TRANSFERRED TO THE NATIONAL PARK SERVICE. BETWEEN 1961 AND 1966 THE SHOW HERD WON TROPHIES IN STATE, REGIONAL, NATIONAL AND INTERNATIONAL COMPETITIONS. THE HERD WAS SOLD IN 1966, WHEREUPON FARM TWO BECAME A FEEDER OPERATION LIMITED TO 250 ANGUS, HEREFORDS AND CROSSBREEDS. GENERAL EISENHOWER DISCONTINUED THE FEEDER OPERATION SEVERAL MONTHS BEFORE HIS DEATH IN 1969.

DURING THE 2ND AND 3RD DAYS OF THE BATTLE OF GETTYSBURG IN JULY, 1863, FARM TWO — THEN OWNED BY WILLIAM DOUGLASS — WAS OCCUPIED BY BUFORD'S CONFEDERATE CAVALRY. THE BANK BARN WAS UNDOUBTEDLY USED AS A FIELD HOSPITAL.

THE EISENHOWER NATIONAL HISTORIC SITE DOCUMENTATION PROJECT WAS UNDERTAKEN BY THE HISTORIC AMERICAN BUILDINGS SURVEY AND SPONSORED BY THE NATIONAL PARK SERVICE, MID-ATLANTIC REGION. THE 1986 SUMMER DOCUMENTATION WAS CONDUCTED BY ROBERT J. KAPSCH, CHIEF, HABS/HAER, ORGANIZED AND DIRECTED BY KENNETH L. ANDERSON, CHIEF, HABS, PRODUCED BY SUPERVISOR ROLAND P. SMITH (BALL STATE UNIVERSITY), FOREMEN JOSEPH D. BALACHOWSKI (CAL POLY STATE UNIVERSITY) AND J. SCOTT ANDERSON (MONTANA STATE UNIVERSITY), ARCHITECT TECHNICIANS ALFREDO O. MARR (NOTRE DAME UNIVERSITY), REINHARDT F. MUIR (TEXAS TECH), GLENN E. OVITT (UNIVERSITY OF CALIFORNIA), ROBERT E. RICE (UNIVERSITY OF MARYLAND); JOHN HEISER, GNMP TECHNICIAN.

SITE PLAN

EISENHOWER NATIONAL HISTORIC SITE

LOCATION MAP

TAKEN FROM USGS 1951 FAIRFIELD AND GETTYSBURG QUADRANGLES
UTM 18.307410.4407400

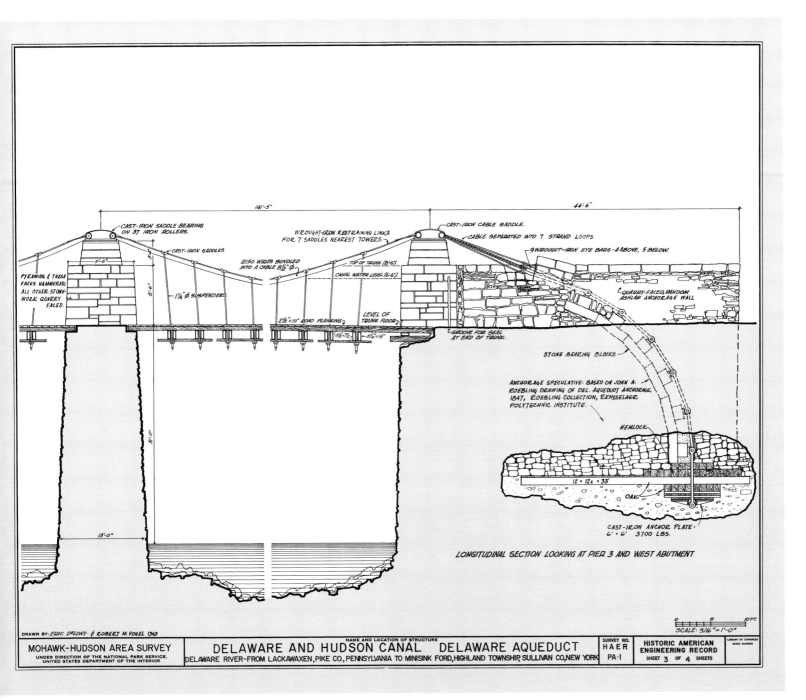

Figure 4.28
In this section of the Delaware and Hudson Canal Delaware Aqueduct, the site measurements were complemented with information on the cast-iron plate, wooden timber, chain link, and curved stone arch anchorage system for the wire cables taken from an 1847 drawing by John A. Roebling, designer of the aqueduct. Note the citation for the drawing of the anchorage with the comment that the information is speculative. The information contained on the drawing obviously cannot be confirmed. While the anchorage probably was constructed as drawn, that conclusion can be assessed by the user of the documentation.

Figure 4.29

The plans of this elaborate late nineteenth-century house were recorded in detail, down to the porch floorboards and seams in the strip carpeting. A potential disadvantage of showing this much detail is that it can make the floor plan harder to read. The graphic density of the closely spaced floorboards tends to draw the viewer's eye away from the carpeted major rooms. Also, the contrast between the flooring in the kitchen and the carpeting in the other rooms visually disguises the original symmetrical shape of the house. Compare the drawing with the field notes in figs. 4.13a and 4.13b.

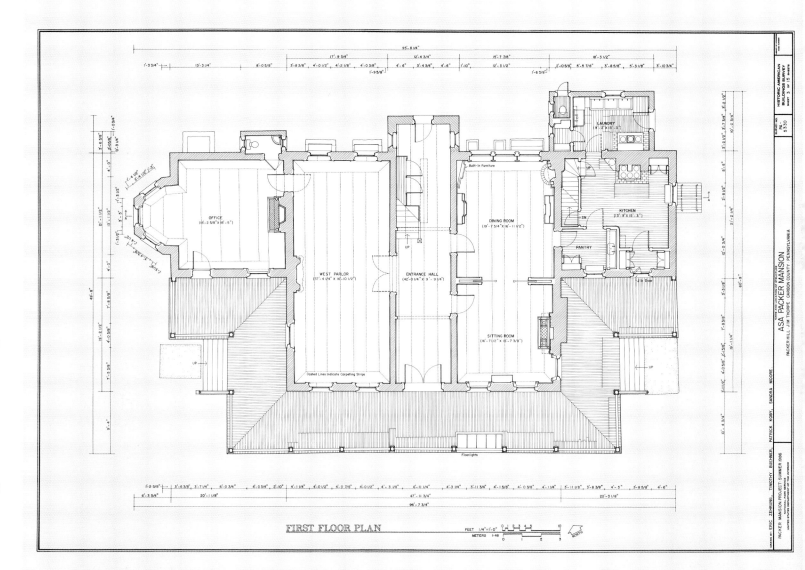

FIRST FLOOR PLAN

need four elevation drawings to reveal its complexities, while a ship may need only a starboard profile.

Sections
Section drawings are vertical cuts through a structure or site that show the vertical arrangement of spaces and objects at a particular plane(s) (*see fig. 4.32*). What you see in a section drawing of a building is a series of room elevations in accurate relation to one another but separated by walls, floors, and ceilings. They are cut in one plane but may jog horizontally from floor to floor to reveal different information. The locations of section cuts are indicated on each floor plan so that they can be related. Section drawings are useful because they provide vertical information: floor-to-floor heights, ceiling heights, roof height, and the vertical progression of spaces. They are also valuable for structural details, interior decorative finishes, and the relation of functions.

Sections are similar to floor plans, except that they are cut perpendicular to the floor. Instead of the floor, the visible surface beyond the horizontal cut line of a plan, room elevations are the visible surfaces beyond the vertical cut line of a section.

Large-Scale Details
Large-scale detail drawings explain how objects fit or work together. A door or window detail may include a plan, interior and exterior elevations, and jamb, lintel, and sill sections (*see fig. 4.33*). A detail of a power supply system in a mill will show how power is transferred through a series of shafts, pulleys, and belts to individual machines (*see fig. 4.34*). Exploded-view drawings allow a drafter to pull apart an object to show how its component parts fit together. Often an exploded view is the only way to

explain the intricacies of a heavy-timber framing joint or a pin connection in a bridge truss (*see figs. 4.35, 6.2, 6.14b, and 6.21*). Large-scale drawings are appropriate for depicting complex objects, such as machines, that cannot be delineated adequately at a small scale (*see fig. 4.36*). The tools used in an industrial process are an important component of the work (*see fig. 4.37*). Remember, however, that it is difficult to portray the motion inherent in machinery operations in a two-dimensional drawing. Other objects such as mantels and newels can be recorded adequately with a large-format photograph using a scale stick in the field view (*see fig. 4.38*).

Interpretive Drawings
Interpretive drawings can be produced in various ways. A documentary drawing can be annotated to explain information that may not be apparent from the delineation, as when the air circulation system of a theater is superimposed on a section drawing. In one case, research on a mill building uncovered few written records, so the most efficient way to explain the evolution of the site was through the use of Sanborn (*see fig. 2.7*) and other historical maps to produce a drawing that portrayed the chronological development of the mill (*see fig. 4.39*). In another example, the design evolution of an architecturally significant house was interpreted in a drawing that reproduced several historical drawings along with copies of the HABS measured drawings of the plan and elevation (*see fig. 4.40*).

HAER makes extensive use of interpretive drawings to explain industrial processes and structural systems. At the site of an iron furnace, the blast machinery was found to be in ruinous condition. The pieces were measured and graphically assembled in a drawing to

show how the machinery produced compressed air for the furnace (*see fig. 4.41*). In another example, the production of smokeless gunpowder at a military arsenal was explained in a series of drawings that followed the process step by step (see the industrial process case study). The structural subsystems of a bridge were depicted in a series of schematic drawings that identified each of the major components (*see fig. 4.35 and the case study on recording bridges*).

Drawing techniques can help interpret what is being recorded. Axonometric and isometric projections are two common forms of delineation that help explain volume and mass (*see fig. 7.1*). Cutaway views graphically remove portions of a subject to reveal details underneath (*see figs. 1.7 and 4.1*). Often several techniques can be combined in one drawing (*see fig. 4.42*). See the case study on recording an industrial process for more information.

Historic Landscape Documentation
Prior to the establishment of HALS in 2000, most historic landscapes were recorded as part of a project to document a historic structure or industrial site. HABS and HAER did document historic landscapes and parks by themselves, however. HABS recorded existing conditions in a botanical garden in a project that located and identified all plant materials in a series of detailed drawings to provide a benchmark against which to measure future changes (*see fig. 4.43*). An urban park was documented with both existing condition drawings and interpretive drawings depicting the original design at maturity. HAER projects to record roads and bridges made significant contributions to cultural landscape documentation. See the case study on recording historic landscapes for more information.

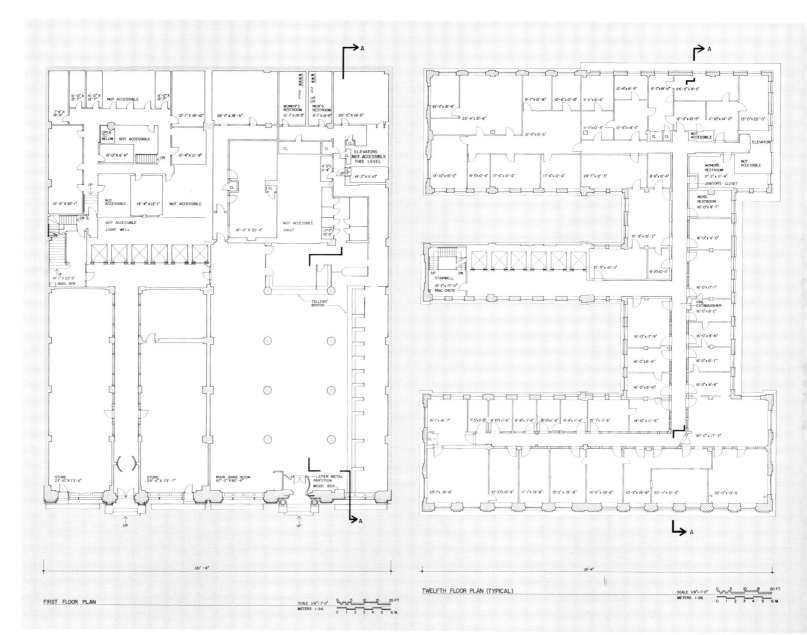

Figure 4.30
Tall buildings like the Munsey Building in Washington, D.C., commonly have a large number of identical or nearly identical floors. It is duplicative to record each floor individually; instead, a typical floor is recorded, then annotated to indicate the features that vary from floor to floor. Note how the upper floors differ from the first-floor plan, which covers the entire site; to be marketable as office space, the upper floors needed light wells. The Munsey Building plan is typical of commercial buildings of the early twentieth century, when offices depended on natural light and air circulation.

FIRST FLOOR PLAN

SCALE 1/8"=1'-0"
METERS 1:96

TWELFTH FLOOR PLAN (TYPICAL)

SCALE 1/8"=1'-0"
METERS 1:96

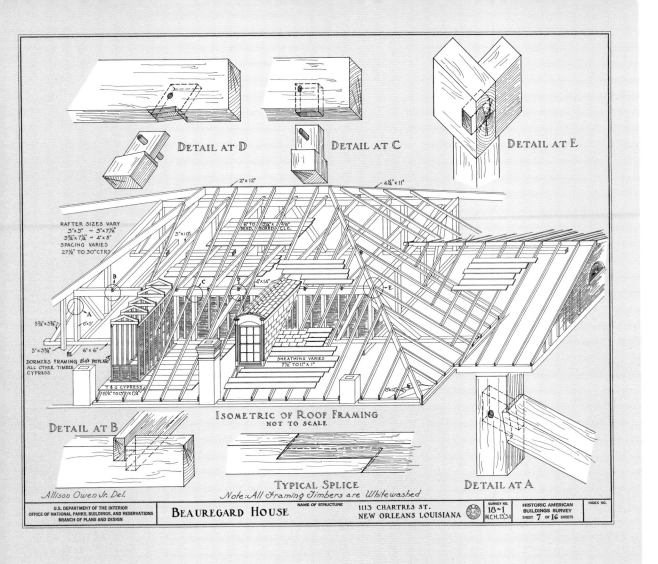

DETAIL AT D

DETAIL AT C

DETAIL AT E

2"x 12"

4¼"x 11"

RAFTER SIZES VARY
3"x 5" ~ 3"x 7½"
3⅜"x 7¼" ~ 4"x 5"
SPACING VARIES
27½" TO 30"CTRS

3"x10"

6" TO   1¾"x   ⅜"
BEAD.   BOARD   CLG.

B

C

D

4"x14"

E

5¾"x 5¾"

6"x 5"

A

5"x 5¾"

6"x 6"

DORMERS FRAMING 2:4? POPLAR
ALL OTHER TIMBER
CYPRESS

SHEATHING VARIES
7½" TO 11"x 1"

6"x12"

T & G CYPRESS
1⅛" 8½" TO 3⅝"x1¼"

ISOMETRIC OF ROOF FRAMING
NOT TO SCALE

DETAIL AT B

DETAIL AT A

Allison Owen Jr. Del.

TYPICAL SPLICE
Note: All Framing Timbers are Whitewashed

U.S. DEPARTMENT OF THE INTERIOR
OFFICE OF NATIONAL PARKS, BUILDINGS, AND RESERVATIONS
BRANCH OF PLANS AND DESIGN

BEAUREGARD HOUSE

NAME OF STRUCTURE
1113 CHARTRES ST.
NEW ORLEANS LOUISIANA

SURVEY NO.
18~1
M.C.H.13-34

HISTORIC AMERICAN
BUILDINGS SURVEY
SHEET 7 OF 16 SHEETS

INDEX NO.

Historic Ship Documentation

Historic vessels are recorded with many of the same techniques used for architectural and industrial struct ures. However, specialized adaptations in field procedures may be required to record decks and profiles or for lines lifting. Some measured drawing conventions specific to ships, such as lines drawings and construction plans, may have to be produced. See the chapter on historic ship documentation in the case study section for more information.

In addition to the specialized measured drawings used to document historic ships, land-scapes, and industrial processes, other specialized recording techniques and methods are used to document unusual sites. In the next section, case studies explain the approaches used to produce HABS/HAER/HALS documentation for seven disparate types of historic resources.

Figure 4.31
This drawing shows how the attic space of the Beauregard House in New Orleans was utilized and how the structure was arranged to carry the roof load. Joint and splice details illustrate representative construction technology of the period, and the roof and dormer cutaways show typical construction practices.

Figure 4.32

This section drawing shows the 1984 appearance of the central portion of the original Smithsonian Institution building and reveals where additions were made to the original structure. The interior originally had two floors—one large space, the Great Hall, on the first floor, and three rooms on the second floor. The left three bays have had two intermediate floors added to house the papers of the first secretary of the Smithsonian, Joseph Henry. The right three bays had one floor added to provide office space. The original height of the second floor is visible in the left two bays. If you follow the cornice line across the drawing, you can see where the returns define the original room sizes. Masonry groin vaults support the first floor. The original second floor, now called the third floor, is supported on iron beams with brick barrel vaults.

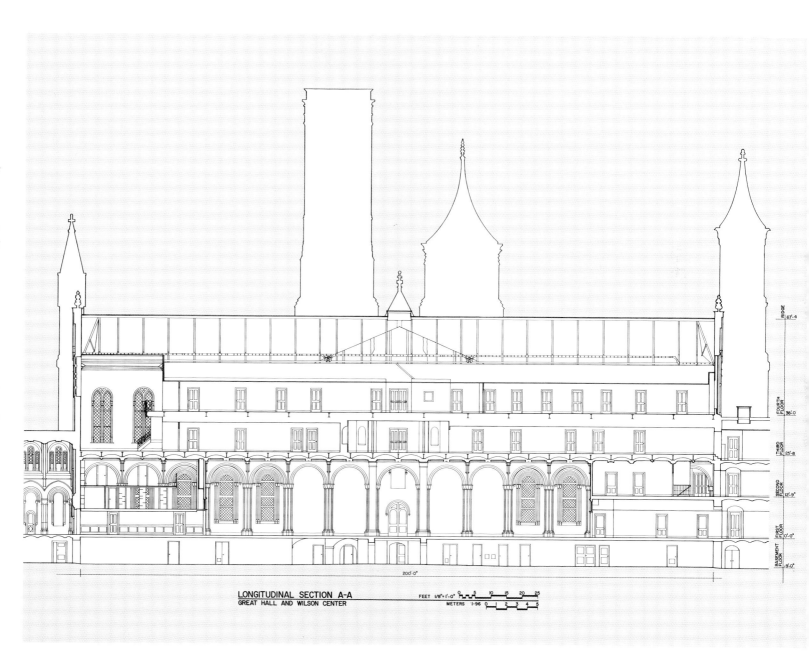

LONGITUDINAL SECTION A-A
GREAT HALL AND WILSON CENTER

FEET 1/8"=1'-0"
METERS 1:96

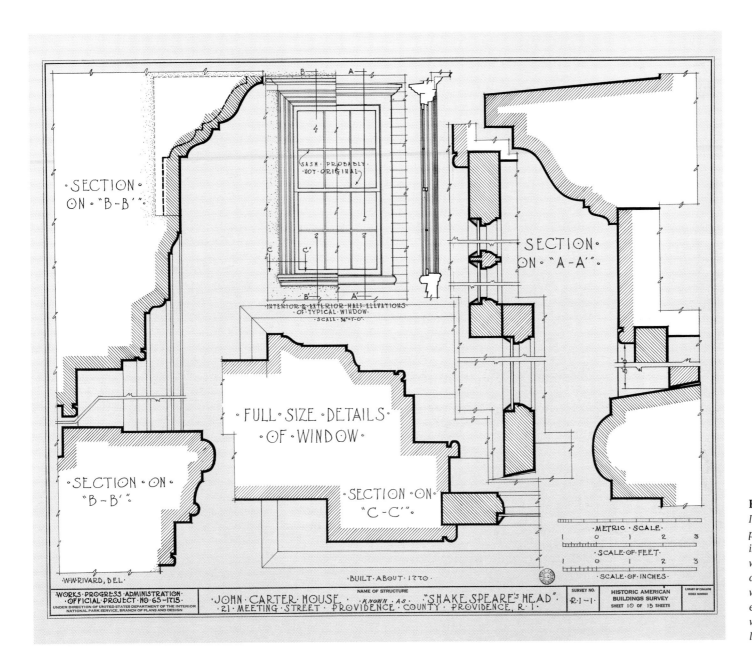

Figure 4.33
In these window details, profiles of the exterior and interior sills and heads as well as jamb and sash details are drawn full size, with an exterior/interior elevation drawing of the window indicating the location of each detail.

Figure 4.34

This schematic drawing illustrates power transmission in Ben Thresher's Mill in Vermont (also shown in fig. 4.4). Power was formerly transmitted in mills with a series of shafts, pulleys, and belts. The main drive shaft was designed to operate at a constant speed. Individual line shaft speeds could be varied from the main shaft speed by using different-sized pulleys. Machine speeds could be further controlled by changing their pulley sizes. The original power source in this example was a waterwheel. Some mills later converted to water turbines or steam engines to drive the shafts. Ultimately, the introduction of machinery driven by electric motors eliminated the need for this type of power transmission.

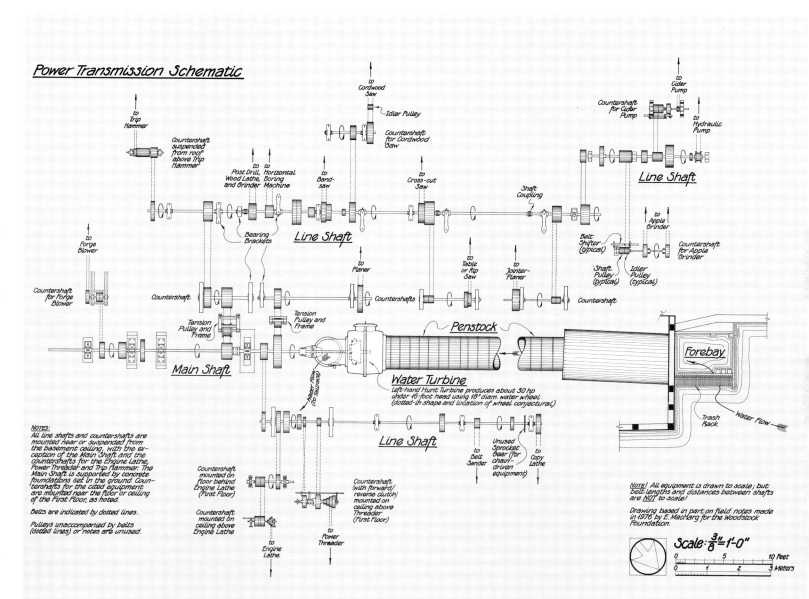

Power Transmission Schematic

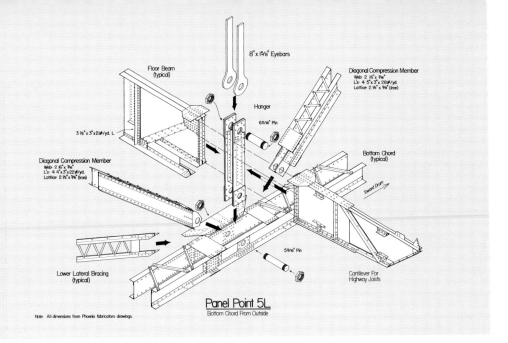

8" x 1⅝" Eyebars

Floor Beam
(typical)

Diagonal Compression Member
Web 2 ½" x ⅞"
Ls 4 5" x 3" x 28#/yd.
Lattice 2 ½" x ⅜" (Iron)

Hanger

6⅝" Pin

3 ½" x 3" x 21#/yd. L

Bottom Chord
(typical)

Diagonal Compression Member
Web 2 ½" x ⅞"
Ls 4 4" x 3" x 22#/yd.
Lattice 2 ½" x ⅜" (Iron)

Toward Drum

5⅞" Pin

Lower Lateral Bracing
(typical)

Cantilever For
Highway Joists

Panel Point 5L
Bottom Chord From Outside

Note   All dimensions from Phoenix fabricators drawings.

Figure 4.35
The only way to adequately document a pin connection in a truss is to graphically explode the joint, pulling the members apart so that each component can be drawn and the fit of the assembly explained. This bridge panel point actually has two pin connections, making it possible for the floor beams and deck to move independent of the primary truss. Note that the dimensions were taken from fabrication drawings for the bridge.

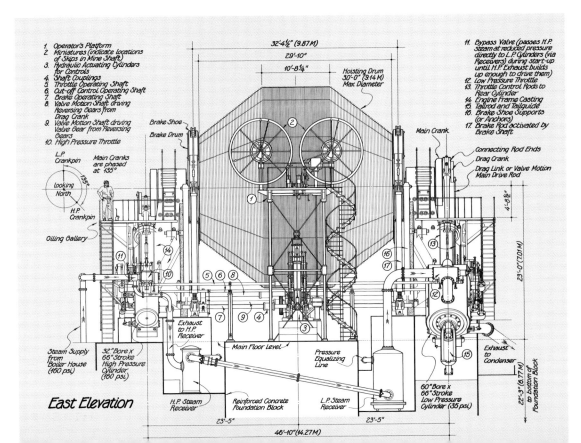

East Elevation

Figure 4.36
The steam-powered cross-compound condensing hoist with a cylindro-conical drum for the no. 2 shaft of the Quincy copper mine in Hancock, Michigan, was manufactured by the Nordberg Manufacturing Company. Placed in operation in 1920, the hoist was the largest in the world at the deepest mine in the Western Hemisphere. This drawing shows a longitudinal elevation with the individual parts labeled and major dimensions given. The drawing was based on original drawings, field-checked by HAER, and shows the hoist in original condition.

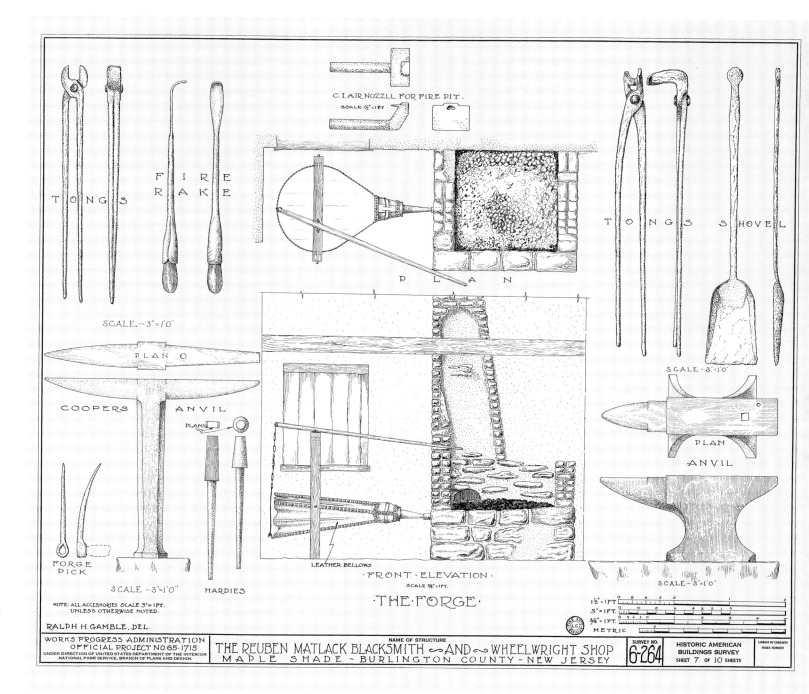

Figure 4.37

Measured drawings of a blacksmith's tools help explain and interpret the work of a blacksmith more completely than would a measured drawing of the forge itself.

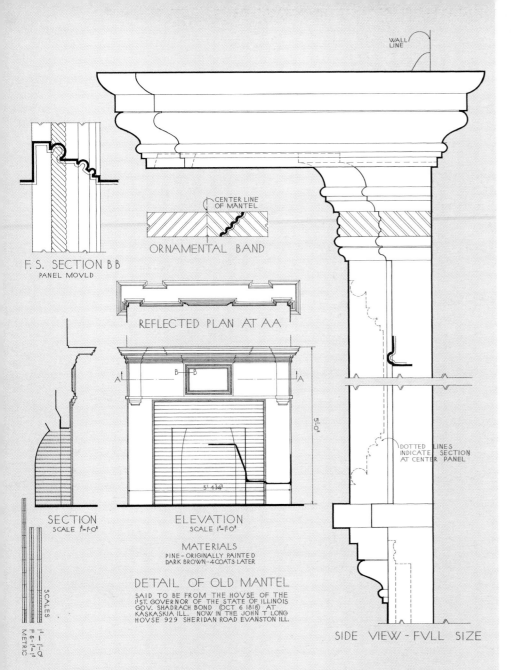

F. S. SECTION BB
PANEL MOVLD

ORNAMENTAL BAND

CENTER LINE
OF MANTEL

REFLECTED PLAN AT AA

A | B | B | A

5'-0"

5' 4¾"

SECTION
SCALE 1"=1'-0"

ELEVATION
SCALE 1"=1'-0"

MATERIALS
PINE - ORIGINALLY PAINTED
DARK BROWN - 4 COATS LATER

DETAIL OF OLD MANTEL
SAID TO BE FROM THE HOVSE OF THE
1ST. GOVERNOR OF THE STATE OF ILLINOIS
GOV. SHADRACH BOND (OCT 6 1818) AT
KASKASKIA ILL. NOW IN THE JOHN T LONG
HOVSE 929 SHERIDAN ROAD EVANSTON ILL.

SCALES
1"=1'-0"
F. S.=1'-1"
METRIC

WALL
LINE

DOTTED LINES
INDICATE SECTION
AT CENTER PANEL

SIDE VIEW - FVLL SIZE

Figure 4.38
Basic dimensions can be determined from this photograph with reasonable accuracy using the two scale sticks placed on the mantel. The accuracy was enhanced when the photographer positioned the camera near the center point and perpendicular to the plane of the subject. Compare the photograph with the measured drawing (at left) to determine the types of information available from each recording technique.

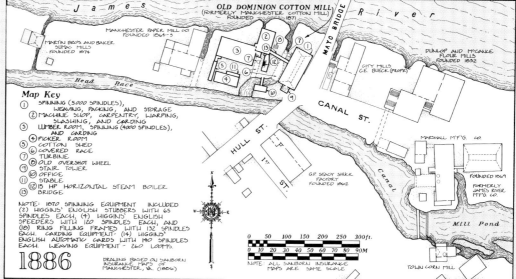

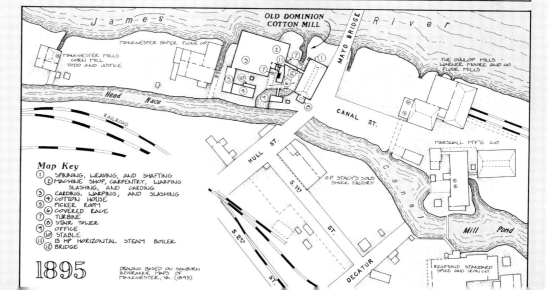

Figure 4.39

Manchester Mill was one of the few Richmond, Virginia, mills to survive the Civil War. Research turned up a substantial amount of graphic information, ranging from a Mathew Brady photograph in the National Archives to Sanborn insurance maps. Written records were found to be nearly nonexistent. The graphic records thus provided most of the clues, but not all of the answers, to the history of the mill. This drawing is one of two sheets, adapted from historic maps, that illustrate the evolution of the site.

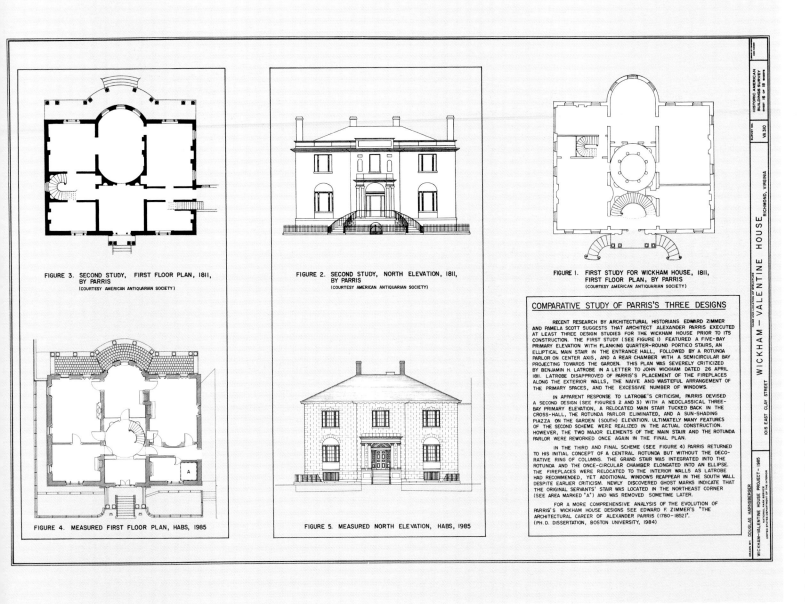

FIGURE 3. SECOND STUDY, FIRST FLOOR PLAN, 1811, BY PARRIS
(COURTESY AMERICAN ANTIQUARIAN SOCIETY)

FIGURE 2. SECOND STUDY, NORTH ELEVATION, 1811, BY PARRIS
(COURTESY AMERICAN ANTIQUARIAN SOCIETY)

FIGURE 1. FIRST STUDY FOR WICKHAM HOUSE, 1811, FIRST FLOOR PLAN, BY PARRIS
(COURTESY AMERICAN ANTIQUARIAN SOCIETY)

FIGURE 4. MEASURED FIRST FLOOR PLAN, HABS, 1985

FIGURE 5. MEASURED NORTH ELEVATION, HABS, 1985

COMPARATIVE STUDY OF PARRIS'S THREE DESIGNS

RECENT RESEARCH BY ARCHITECTURAL HISTORIANS EDWARD ZIMMER AND PAMELA SCOTT SUGGESTS THAT ARCHITECT ALEXANDER PARRIS EXECUTED AT LEAST THREE DESIGN STUDIES FOR THE WICKHAM HOUSE PRIOR TO ITS CONSTRUCTION. THE FIRST STUDY (SEE FIGURE 1) FEATURED A FIVE-BAY PRIMARY ELEVATION WITH FLANKING QUARTER-ROUND PORTICO STAIRS, AN ELLIPTICAL MAIN STAIR IN THE ENTRANCE HALL, FOLLOWED BY A ROTUNDA PARLOR ON CENTER AXIS, AND A REAR CHAMBER WITH A SEMICIRCULAR BAY PROJECTING TOWARDS THE GARDEN. THIS PLAN WAS SEVERELY CRITICIZED BY BENJAMIN H. LATROBE IN A LETTER TO JOHN WICKHAM DATED 26 APRIL 1811. LATROBE DISAPPROVED OF PARRIS'S PLACEMENT OF THE FIREPLACES ALONG THE EXTERIOR WALLS, THE NAIVE AND WASTEFUL ARRANGEMENT OF THE PRIMARY SPACES, AND THE EXCESSIVE NUMBER OF WINDOWS.

IN APPARENT RESPONSE TO LATROBE'S CRITICISM, PARRIS DEVISED A SECOND DESIGN (SEE FIGURES 2 AND 3) WITH A NEOCLASSICAL THREE-BAY PRIMARY ELEVATION, A RELOCATED MAIN STAIR TUCKED BACK IN THE CROSS-HALL, THE ROTUNDA PARLOR ELIMINATED, AND A SUN-SHADING PIAZZA ON THE GARDEN (SOUTH) ELEVATION. ULTIMATELY MANY FEATURES OF THE SECOND SCHEME WERE REALIZED IN THE ACTUAL CONSTRUCTION. HOWEVER, THE TWO MAJOR ELEMENTS OF THE MAIN STAIR AND THE ROTUNDA PARLOR WERE REWORKED ONCE AGAIN IN THE FINAL PLAN.

IN THE THIRD AND FINAL SCHEME (SEE FIGURE 4) PARRIS RETURNED TO HIS INITIAL CONCEPT OF A CENTRAL ROTUNDA BUT WITHOUT THE DECORATIVE RING OF COLUMNS. THE GRAND STAIR WAS INTEGRATED INTO THE ROTUNDA AND THE ONCE-CIRCULAR CHAMBER ELONGATED INTO AN ELLIPSE. THE FIREPLACES WERE RELOCATED TO THE INTERIOR WALLS AS LATROBE HAD RECOMMENDED, YET ADDITIONAL WINDOWS REAPPEAR IN THE SOUTH WALL DESPITE EARLIER CRITICISM. NEWLY DISCOVERED GHOST MARKS INDICATE THAT THE ORIGINAL SERVANTS' STAIR WAS LOCATED IN THE NORTHEAST CORNER (SEE AREA MARKED "A") AND WAS REMOVED SOMETIME LATER.

FOR A MORE COMPREHENSIVE ANALYSIS OF THE EVOLUTION OF PARRIS'S WICKHAM HOUSE DESIGNS SEE EDWARD F. ZIMMER'S "THE ARCHITECTURAL CAREER OF ALEXANDER PARRIS (1780-1852)". (PH.D. DISSERTATION, BOSTON UNIVERSITY, 1984).

Figure 4.40
Research completed shortly before production of the HABS drawings of the Wickham-Valentine House in Richmond uncovered drawings showing the evolution of the design of the house. This sheet compares and contrasts the different designs by the architect, Alexander Parris, with the house as it existed in 1985.

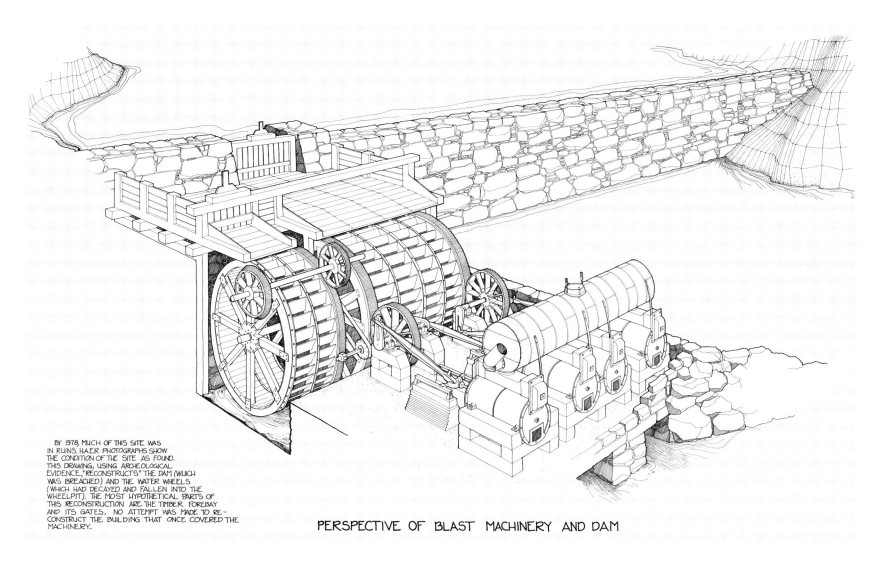

BY 1978, MUCH OF THIS SITE WAS
IN RUINS. H.A.E.R. PHOTOGRAPHS SHOW
THE CONDITION OF THE SITE AS FOUND.
THIS DRAWING, USING ARCHEOLOGICAL
EVIDENCE, "RECONSTRUCTS" THE DAM (WHICH
WAS BREACHED) AND THE WATER WHEELS
(WHICH HAD DECAYED AND FALLEN INTO THE
WHEELPIT). THE MOST HYPOTHETICAL PARTS OF
THIS RECONSTRUCTION ARE THE TIMBER FOREBAY
AND ITS GATES. NO ATTEMPT WAS MADE TO RE-
CONSTRUCT THE BUILDING THAT ONCE COVERED THE
MACHINERY.

PERSPECTIVE OF BLAST MACHINERY AND DAM

Figure 4.41

*The blast machinery and dam of the Adirondack Iron and
Steel Company in Tahawus, New York, were in ruins when
recorded by HAER in 1978. The physical remnants were
studied, measured, and graphically reassembled to pro-*
*duce this interpretive drawing of the original conditions.
No attempt was made to draw the sheltering structure over
the machinery. Conjectural portions of the drawing were
identified in the note.*

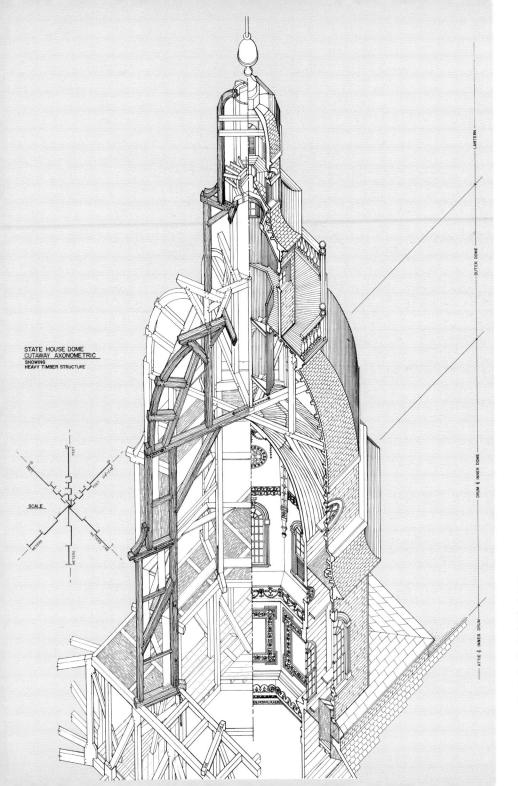

STATE HOUSE DOME
CUTAWAY AXONOMETRIC
SHOWING
HEAVY TIMBER STRUCTURE

SCALE

Figure 4.42
This axonometric drawing of the Maryland State House dome is cut away in two ways, to reveal information on the structural system on the left and the finish materials on the right.

Figure 4.43
One problem in landscape recording is noting the names and sizes of all the plant material without having the drawing dominated by notes. The solution devised for this garden was to use abbreviations of the scientific and common names, separated by a slash, followed by the diameter of the trunk at breast height, a dimension that would be too small to draw accurately at this scale. Crown diameters were easier to draw and to measure from the drawing, so they were left undimensioned. Adjacent plantings with the same name were tied to a single label by using fine lines. If the diameters varied, they were labeled individually. A key map was used to locate this section in relation to the overall garden.

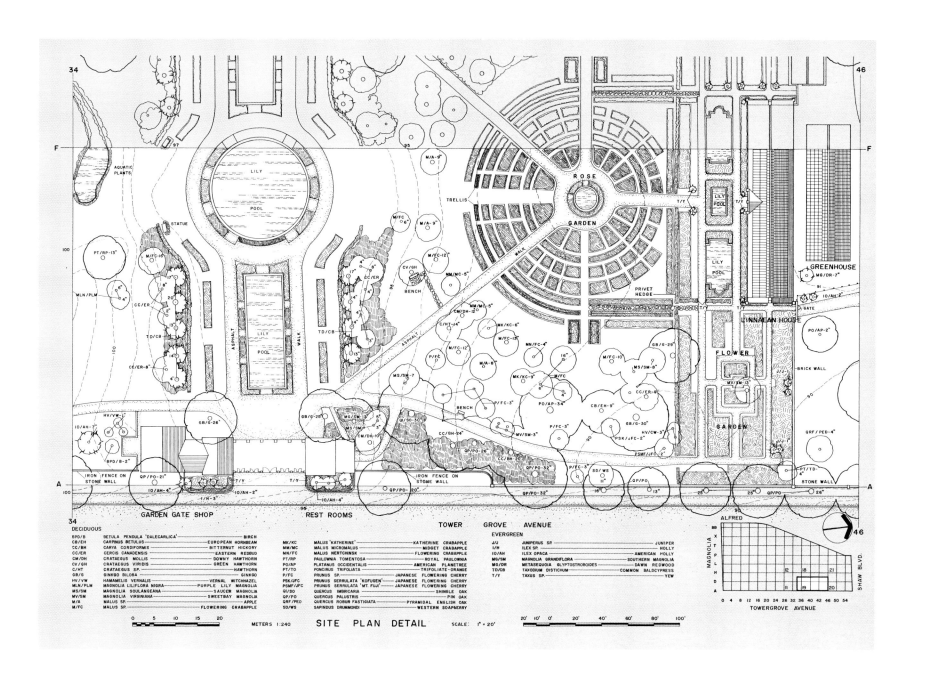

34

46

F — — — F

AQUATIC
PLANTS

LILY
POOL

STATUE

ROSE
GARDEN

TRELLIS

M/A-9"
M/FC
6"
M/A-9"

M/FC-12"

CV/GH
BENCH
CC/ER
8"

MM/MC-5"

CM/DH-12"
MM/MC-5"

C/HT-14"

MK/KC-6"

GREENHOUSE
MG/DR-7"

10/AH-2"

PRIVET
HEDGE

PT/RP-13"

M/FC-16"

17"

20"

13"

14"

TD/CB

CC/ER-8"

4"

MLN/PLM

8"
4"

CC/ER

2"

LILY
POOL

8"

CC/ER

TD/CB

3"

14"

3"

M/FC-13"

M/FC-12"

M/A-8"

MS/SM-7

MN/FC-4"

MK/KC-9"

M/FC-10"
MS/SM-8"

M/FC

GB/G-29"

PO/AP-2"

LINNAEAN HOUSE

FLOWER

MV/SM-13

BRICK WALL

J/J-1

HV/VW-1"

GB/G-26"

GB/G-25"

MG/SM-13

MS/SM-13

CM/DH-10"

QI/SO-30"

BENCH

P/FC-3"

CC/ER-9"

PO/AP-34"

CB/EH-9"

MK/KC-9"

QRF/PED-4"

10/AH-7"

BPD/B-2"

QP/PO-21"

10/AH-4"

1/H-3"

T/Y
T/Y

10/AH-2"

10/AH-4"

QP/PO-20"

IRON FENCE ON
STONE WALL

CC/BH-24"

QP/PO-26"

CC/BH-20"

QP/PO-32"

MV/SM-3"

GB/G-30"

HV/CW-3"

PSK/JFC-2"

PSMF/JFC-2"

P/FC-3"

P/FC-3"

SD/WS
11"

P/FC-3"

16"

QP/PO

13"

GARDEN

J/J-1

MV/SM-13

PT/TD-
4"

STONE WALL

QP/PO-32"

16"

11"

25"

25"

QP/PO

26"

A — — — A

GARDEN GATE SHOP

REST ROOMS

TOWER   GROVE   AVENUE

ALFRED

MAGNOLIA

BB
X
T
P
L
H
D
A

SHAW BLVD.

12
18
21

11
19
20

0 4 8 12 16 20 24 28 32 36 40 44 48 52 54

TOWERGROVE AVENUE

DECIDUOUS

BPD/B	BETULA PENDULA 'DALECARLICA'	BIRCH
CB/EH	CARPINUS BETULUS	EUROPEAN HORNBEAM
CC/BH	CARYA CORDIFORMIS	BITTERNUT HICKORY
CC/ER	CERCIS CANADENSIS	EASTERN REDBUD
CM/DH	CRATAEGUS MOLLIS	DOWNY HAWTHORN
CV/GH	CRATAEGUS VIRIDIS	GREEN HAWTHORN
C/HT	CRATAEGUS SP.	HAWTHORN
GB/G	GINKGO BILOBA	GINKGO
HV/VW	HAMAMELIS VERNALIS	VERNAL WITCHHAZEL
MLN/PLM	MAGNOLIA LILIFLORA NIGRA	PURPLE LILY MAGNOLIA
MS/SM	MAGNOLIA SOULANGEANA	SAUCER MAGNOLIA
MV/SM	MAGNOLIA VIRGINIANA	SWEETBAY MAGNOLIA
M/A	MALUS SP.	APPLE
M/FC	MALUS SP.	FLOWERING CRABAPPLE

MK/KC	MALUS 'KATHERINE'	KATHERINE CRABAPPLE
MM/MC	MALUS MICROMALUS	MIDGET CRABAPPLE
MN/FC	MALUS NERTCHINSK	FLOWERING CRABAPPLE
PT/RP	PAULOWNIA TOMENTOSA	ROYAL PAULOWNIA
PO/AP	PLATANUS OCCIDENTALIS	AMERICAN PLANETREE
PT/TO	PONCIRUS TRIFOLIATA	TRIFOLIATE-ORANGE
P/FC	PRUNUS SP.	JAPANESE FLOWERING CHERRY
PSK/JFC	PRUNUS SERRULATA 'KOFUGEN'	JAPANESE FLOWERING CHERRY
PSMF/JFC	PRUNUS SERRULARIA 'MT. FUJI'	JAPANESE FLOWERING CHERRY
QI/SO	QUERCUS IMBRICARIA	SHINGLE OAK
QP/PO	QUERCUS PALUSTRIS	PIN OAK
QRF/PEO	QUERCUS ROBUR FASTIGIATA	PYRAMIDAL ENGLISH OAK
SD/WS	SAPINDUS DRUMMONDI	WESTERN SOAPBERRY

EVERGREEN

J/J	JUNIPERUS SP.	JUNIPER
I/H	ILEX SP.	HOLLY
10/AH	ILEX OPACA	AMERICAN HOLLY
MG/SM	MAGNOLIA GRANDIFLORA	SOUTHERN MAGNOLIA
MG/DR	METASEQUOIA GLYPTOSTROBOIDES	DAWN REDWOOD
TD/CB	TAXODIUM DISTICHUM	COMMON BALDCYPRESS
T/Y	TAXUS SP.	YEW

0   5   10   15   20
METERS 1:240

SITE   PLAN   DETAIL

SCALE: 1" = 20'

20' 10' 0'   20'   40'   60'   80'   100'

Certain historic resources possess special characteristics that call for adaptation of the precepts and guidelines described in earlier chapters of this book. These characteristics may be found in the evolution of a site over time; the distinctive features of a designed landscape; the structural details of a bridge; an industrial process that requires interpretation; a distinctive building type; a historic ship, whose hull is curved; or a complex building significant for its structural and mechanical systems as well as its aesthetic design. New technologies may be required to produce documentation under challenging conditions or time limitations.

In recording historic resources, special attention must be paid to those characteristics that are different or distinctive. These add to the significance of a resource and may challenge the would-be recorder. This section describes seven different types of special resources and the approaches used by the Historic American Buildings Survey, Historic American Engineering Record, and Historic American Landscapes Survey to document them. Case studies are given for a vernacular building type, bridges, a building with multiple areas of significance that include its mechanical systems, historic ships, major monuments, a significant industrial process, and cultural landscapes.

PART 2

CASE STUDIES

CHAPTER 5

RECORDING VERNACULAR BUILDING FORMS
Catherine L. Lavoie

*A*t the inception of the Historic American Buildings Survey in 1933, the documentation of regionally specific vernacular structures and more commonplace building types constituted the backbone of the program. While landmark structures are important as exemplary models of architectural style or as venues for conveying seminal events in our nation's history, alone they present a skewed perception of our culture. Vernacular building forms more accurately exemplify the diversity of ethnic heritage, lifestyles, and folkways in the United States. The significance of vernacular structures resides not so much in their individual merit as in their ability to reflect larger patterns in our nation's historical and architectural development. Therefore, it is important to record for the HABS collection exemplary or representative examples of various vernacular forms.

In contrast to the fairly straightforward approach taken in identifying and recording a single, uniquely significant landmark structure, recording vernacular building types presents new challenges. The most effective means for selecting and evaluating representative building forms are field survey and contextual study. Survey is an effective mechanism for amassing data for a larger sampling of historic resources. Collectively, survey information offers insight into patterns of development and provides a general understanding of the resources under study. The data constitute both a valuable record for analysis and a useful tool for identifying structures worthy of further investigation. In short, the field survey allows for the inclusive examination and careful selection of representative building forms suitable for documentation through written history, measured drawings, and large-format photography.

Recording Friends Meeting Houses

A recent example of the HABS field survey and contextual study approach is the effort to record Friends meeting houses in the Delaware Valley (*see fig. 5.1*). The Delaware Valley region encompasses parts of Pennsylvania, Delaware, and New Jersey and is under the care of the Philadelphia Yearly Meeting of the Religious Society of Friends. The meeting houses are an important resource for a number of reasons: As artifacts of the built environment, they serve as tangible reminders of the vast contributions Friends have made to the history of Pennsylvania and the greater Delaware Valley. As religious structures, they speak directly to the

Friends' legacy of religious tolerance, a central theme in the region's development. From an architectural standpoint, they include many well-preserved colonial-era structures, providing a venue for studying the area's early vernacular architecture. In particular, the meeting houses reflect building traditions particular to the ethnic heritage and religious tenets of the Friends who settled in Pennsylvania, most notably their aesthetic taste for plainness and simplicity. And finally, the meeting houses of the Delaware Valley range in date from as early as 1695 to as late as the 1970s, collectively presenting an unparalleled opportunity to document the evolution of a significant American building type.

From the time the Society of Friends was founded in England in 1652 until the passage of the 1689 Act of Toleration, Friends in England and its colonies were unable to worship openly without fear of reprisal. The followers of George Fox, founder of the Quaker movement, were forced to meet in houses, barns, and other buildings adapted for use as meeting places. Only rarely before 1690 did English Friends attempt to build structures explicitly for the purpose of holding Quaker worship. Friends began immigrating to New Jersey in the 1670s, and in 1681 to the Pennsylvania colony established by fellow Quaker William Penn. The religious tolerance guaranteed as part of Penn's "Holy Experiment" meant that colonial Friends were at liberty to develop building forms conducive to silent worship and separate men's and women's business meetings. Meeting house design evolved over time to reflect the changing expressions of the American Friends' faith and practice. With this history in mind, a HABS project was formulated to identify and record structures that exemplified various phases in the evolution of meeting house design in the Delaware Valley.

Figure 5.1
Old Kennett Meeting House (c. 1731) was included in a multiresource study that inventoried and selectively recorded Friends meeting houses in the Delaware Valley. An aid to photographic recording is the scale stick, which appears to the left in this image.

Figure 5.2

Plainness is a hallmark of the architectural style of Quaker meeting houses. While rubble work was favored over a more decorative pattern of ashlar block, the skill applied to the masonry work was generally of exceptional quality. Simple doorway hoods, like those at Caln Meeting House in Chester County, Pennsylvania, were a common feature in meeting house design.

Planning the Survey

The project to record Friends meeting houses began with preliminary research and information gathering, and site visits to a sampling of structures. The Quaker Information Center in Philadelphia supplied a list of contacts for all current meetings. An initial literature search revealed that the records of the Philadelphia Yearly Meeting and its constituent meetings are held in two local repositories: the Friends Historical Library at Swarthmore College, Swarthmore, Pennsylvania, and the Quaker Collection at Haverford College, Haverford, Pennsylvania. Among the holdings of these institutions are minutes and other primary records of the individual meetings, photographic collections, manuscripts, maps, and a vast collection of related journals and other secondary source publications. The information in these materials helped the project leaders formulate not only a basic understanding of meeting house structures but also of the meeting processes they were intended to facilitate.

Like their English counterparts, colonial Quakers rejected the elaborate ornamentation and iconography of Anglican churches in favor of the plainness dictated by their religious tenets (*see fig. 5.2*). Furthermore, because Quaker practice has no pastoral ministry, rituals, or sacraments, there is no need for many of the features found in other forms of ecclesiastical architecture, such as the nave, sanctuary, altar, and pulpit. Instead, meeting house plans were influenced by Quaker practices such as meetings for business and the designation of ministers and elders. Quaker meetings consist of a period of worship during which members sit in silence awaiting divine insight. Formerly, men and women separated after meeting for worship to conduct their individual meetings for business. The women's meeting could take place in a dif-

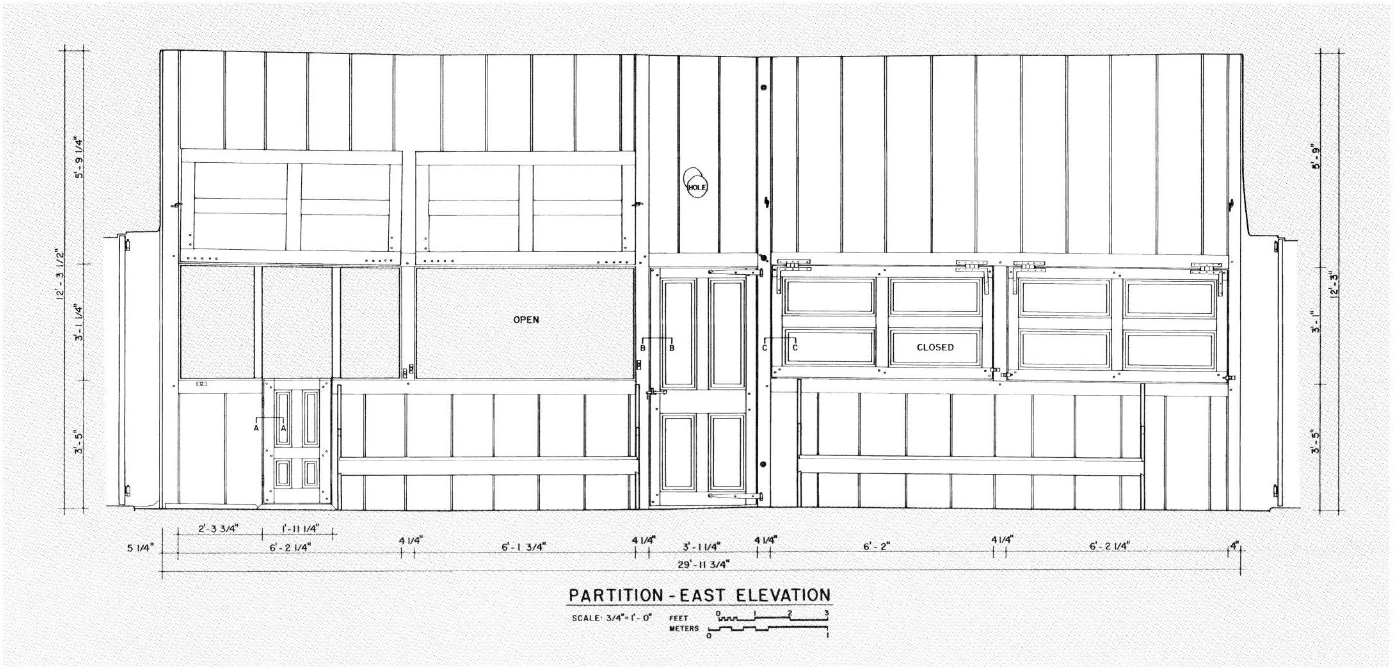

Figure 5.3
Retractable wood partitions were used to separate men and women during their business meetings. This drawing is of the partition at Chichester Meeting House in Boothwyn, Pennsylvania.

PARTITION - EAST ELEVATION
SCALE: 3/4" = 1'-0" FEET METERS

ferent structure, but often the principal meeting room was divided with a retractable paneled wood partition (*see fig. 5.3*). Early on, Friends developed a system of ministers, elders and, later, overseers to preside over the meeting for worship and attend to the affairs of the meeting. These individuals were seated in tiered benches referred to as the "facing benches," which were located along one wall of the meeting room (*see fig. 5.4*). Facing benches and retractable partitions became characteristic features of meeting houses on both sides of the Atlantic.

Once a general understanding of the meeting house structure and the meeting process

had been formulated, parameters were set to ensure that the survey would yield a picture of the evolution of meeting house design in this region. To achieve this, it was decided to survey all structures built under the care of the Philadelphia Yearly Meeting from the earliest times to the present. This comprised a range of structures built over the course of three centuries, with a geographical distribution over parts of three states.

A survey form was developed to facilitate the fieldwork and to establish a uniform measure or standard for comparing the buildings (*see fig. 5.5*). The form calls for historical and descriptive data, including name and location,

date of construction, building configuration and dimensions, and basic interior and exterior architectural description. It also has space for a brief description of the design and plan of each meeting house; this information was meant to help determine how the building functioned in response to the Quaker meeting program. The field surveyors paid particular attention to those features identified through preliminary research as characteristic of most meeting houses. Finally, subsidiary structures extant on the site that were associated with the meeting houses were also inventoried. These included privies, (horse) mounting blocks, carriage sheds, burying grounds, and walls. A "Historical Notes"

Figure 5.4
During meeting for worship, meeting members sit in silence awaiting divine insight. Until the twentieth century, meeting was presided over by designated ministers, elders, and overseers seated in tiered benches facing the other members. These facing benches are from Germantown Meeting House in the Germantown neighborhood of Philadelphia, Pennsylvania.

section on the form was used to record information available on-site from sources such as date stones, historical markers, and caretakers or other individuals present during the HABS site visit. These sections were later supplemented with historical data gathered through research, such as construction dates (when not indicated by date stones), accounts of prior meeting houses on the site, and affiliations with other meetings. As part of the field survey, black-and-white 35 mm photographs and color slides were taken.

Before the fieldwork began, lists of meeting houses under the purview of the Philadelphia Yearly Meeting were compiled by location. Since Friends keep information only for active meetings, historical sources, including maps, were needed to identify all of the meeting houses under study. Current county atlases were used to pinpoint meeting houses in the field. Due to the extreme size of the study area, the survey was divided geographically by county or by meeting "quarter"—the basic regional and administrative unit within the organizational structure of the Society of Friends.

Equally important in the planning that led up to the field survey were the initial questions of the project historians, such as these: What are the distinguishing features of a Quaker meeting house? Is there a standard form for Quaker meeting houses? If so, does it change over time or with various Quaker factions? Is there evidence of diffusion of either structural or stylistic

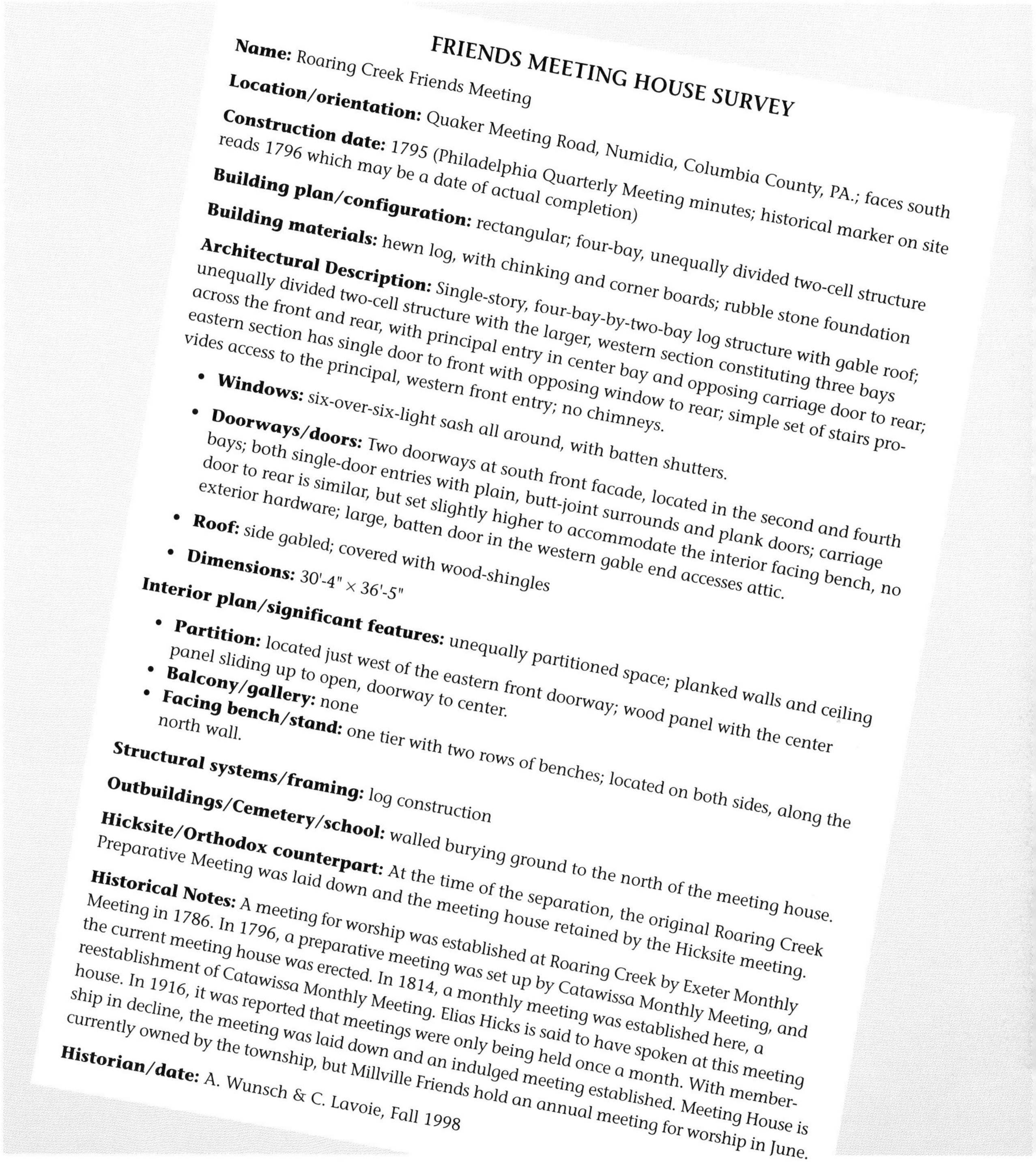

Figure 5.5
A survey format was developed to facilitate the field survey process and to provide a uniform measure for the comparison of meeting houses in the study area.

FRIENDS MEETING HOUSE SURVEY

Name: Roaring Creek Friends Meeting

Location/orientation: Quaker Meeting Road, Numidia, Columbia County, PA.; faces south

Construction date: 1795 (Philadelphia Quarterly Meeting minutes; historical marker on site reads 1796 which may be a date of actual completion)

Building plan/configuration: rectangular; four-bay, unequally divided two-cell structure

Building materials: hewn log, with chinking and corner boards; rubble stone foundation

Architectural Description: Single-story, four-bay-by-two-bay log structure with gable roof; unequally divided two-cell structure with the larger, western section constituting three bays across the front and rear, with principal entry in center bay and opposing carriage door to rear; eastern section has single door to front with opposing window to rear; simple set of stairs provides access to the principal, western front entry; no chimneys.

- **Windows:** six-over-six-light sash all around, with batten shutters.
- **Doorways/doors:** Two doorways at south front facade, located in the second and fourth bays; both single-door entries with plain, butt-joint surrounds and plank doors; carriage door to rear is similar, but set slightly higher to accommodate the interior facing bench, no exterior hardware; large, batten door in the western gable end accesses attic.
- **Roof:** side gabled; covered with wood-shingles
- **Dimensions:** 30'-4" × 36'-5"

Interior plan/significant features: unequally partitioned space; planked walls and ceiling

- **Partition:** located just west of the eastern front doorway; wood panel with the center panel sliding up to open, doorway to center.
- **Balcony/gallery:** none
- **Facing bench/stand:** one tier with two rows of benches; located on both sides, along the north wall.

Structural systems/framing: log construction

Outbuildings/Cemetery/school: walled burying ground to the north of the meeting house.

Hicksite/Orthodox counterpart: At the time of the separation, the original Roaring Creek Preparative Meeting was laid down and the meeting house retained by the Hicksite meeting.

Historical Notes: A meeting for worship was established at Roaring Creek by Exeter Monthly Meeting in 1786. In 1796, a preparative meeting was set up by Catawissa Monthly Meeting, and the current meeting house was erected. In 1814, a monthly meeting was established here, a reestablishment of Catawissa Monthly Meeting. Elias Hicks is said to have spoken at this meeting house. In 1916, it was reported that meetings were only being held once a month. With membership in decline, the meeting was laid down and an indulged meeting established. Meeting House is currently owned by the township, but Millville Friends hold an annual meeting for worship in June.

Historian/date: A. Wunsch & C. Lavoie, Fall 1998

Figure 5.6
Arney's Mount (1776) exemplifies an unaltered, regionally specific meeting house form. This two-story, single-cell type was particular to this part of southern New Jersey. The occurrence of regionally specific forms is one indication that Philadelphia Yearly Meeting allowed individual meetings the freedom to build meeting houses according to their own plans.

building traditions originating abroad or from within the region? How does the form or plan facilitate meeting function? Who designed and constructed these buildings? What role did the Philadelphia Yearly Meeting or its constituent quarterly and monthly meetings play in determining meeting house form and meeting program? The fieldwork was conducted in a series of weeklong trips by a team of historians who worked together to expedite navigation, field measurement and analysis, and photography. In all, more than 150 structures were surveyed.

Analysis

The field survey provided preliminary answers to many questions and yielded data used for identifying representative meeting houses to receive closer examination during the documentation process. Once the survey was complete, information was compiled and examined both chronologically and by quarter to reveal specific types, periods, and patterns in meeting house development. A number of interesting observations could be made at this point. Meeting houses located within the same quarterly or monthly meeting exhibited similarities but often varied greatly in form and/or detail from those in neighboring quarters. Identifiable local characteristics were most clearly defined though use of indigenous materials and variations in exterior design. Plan was less defined by location than by time period. Differences in meeting house plan were most pronounced among structures erected during the first century of Quaker settlement.

Localized variations in design and plan were among the most noteworthy aspects of the Delaware Valley meeting houses (*see fig. 5.6*). This fact suggests that the local meeting community played a more significant role in determining building form than the yearly meeting did. The range of diversity among meeting houses was somewhat unexpected. Although the survey revealed a preponderance of meeting houses of a two-cell type, arranging the survey forms chronologically revealed that this type took nearly a century to appear (*see figs. 5.7 and 5.8*). Furthermore, its evolution could be traced through incremental changes in the design of meeting houses built prior to the development of the two-cell type. The two-cell type was the most prevalent form from the late eighteenth century through the mid-nineteenth century. Despite its eventual decline, the influence of the two-cell type is discernible in later building forms.

Ongoing research conducted during the course of the survey included gathering information on structures no longer standing in order to ensure that the selection of those to be recorded did, in fact, represent all periods. This research would prove particularly important to the understanding of the early period of meeting house design. For example, it was discovered that seemingly unique forms were actually rare survivors of earlier meeting house types and reflected larger patterns of development. Further research also focused on the social and political context in which these meeting houses were created, in the hope of determining the reasons for changes in meeting house design.

Through field survey and the examination of surviving records, a general pattern of meeting house development in the Delaware Valley became clear. Immigrant Friends often began with a small, log structure, of which no early examples survive. The early period was one of experimentation, reflecting the lack of prescribed design standards in that era (*see fig. 5.9*). The earliest permanent meeting houses in the Delaware Valley generally followed one of two basic plans, although they varied greatly in

Figure 5.7
Buckingham, erected in Lahaska, Pennsylvania, in 1768, was the first of the two-cell form that became a prototype for American Friends meeting house design from the late eighteenth century through the mid-nineteenth century.

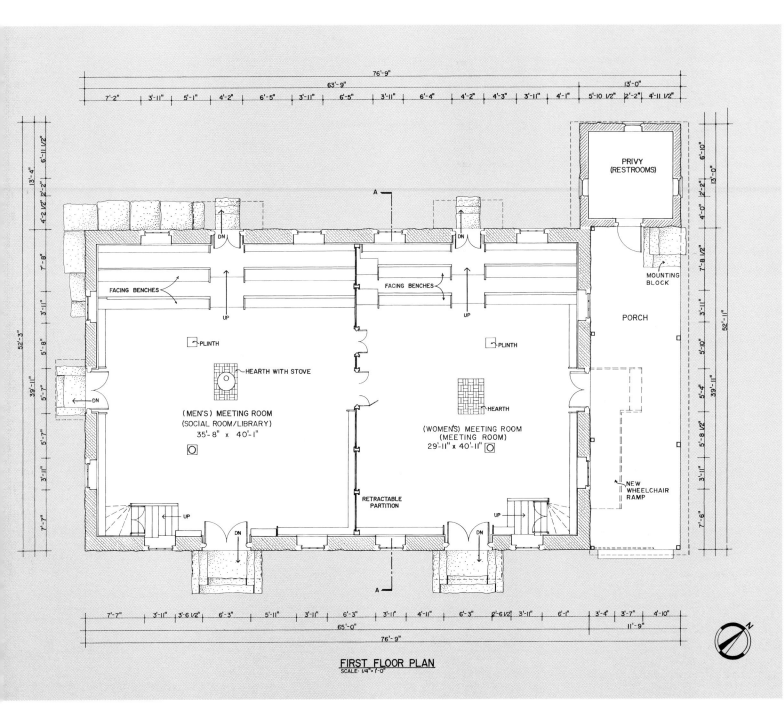

Figure 5.8

The plan of Buckingham Meeting House provided identical apartments for men and women and reflected a significant change in the Friends meeting program. Colonial Friends had adhered to a pattern of meeting established by the English, in which men and women met in a single room for worship after which the women would remove to another area. At meeting houses such as Buckingham, however, men and women met together in meeting for worship and raised a partition to divide the room when they held meeting for business. This pattern required a space that could be split in equal parts and a minister's facing bench in both sections rather than just one.

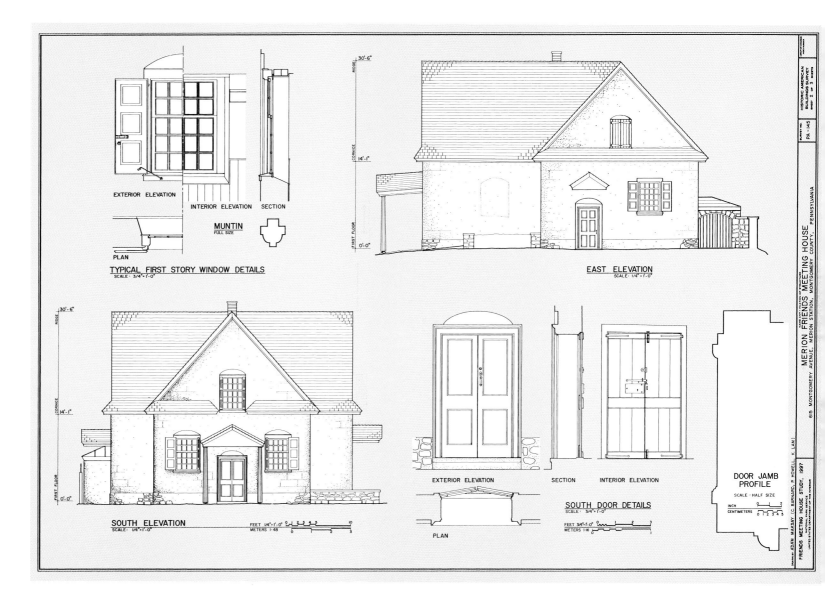

Figure 5.9
Merion Meeting House (c. 1695–1714) is the earliest extant meeting house in the Delaware Valley. Its virtually unprecedented T shape reflects the lack of prescribed design standards during the early Quaker period in Pennsylvania.

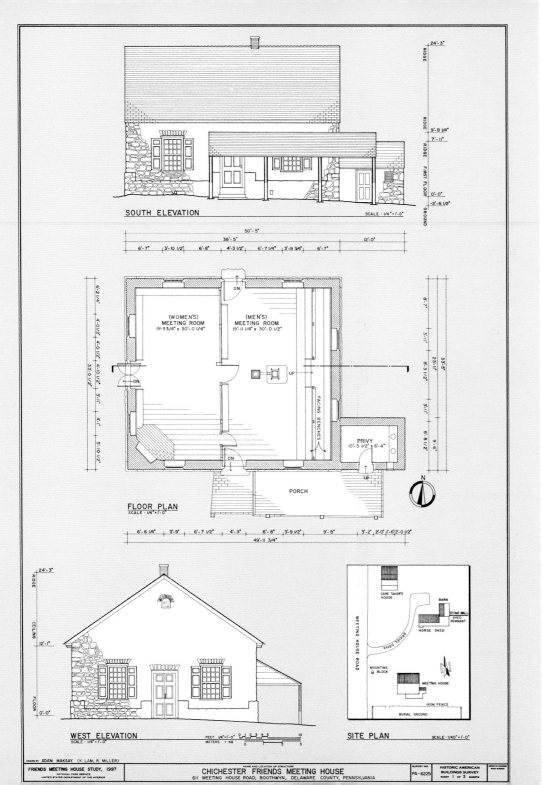

SOUTH ELEVATION · SCALE · 1/4"·1'-0"

FLOOR PLAN · SCALE · 1/4"·1'-0"

(WOMEN'S) MEETING ROOM 15'-3 3/4" x 30'-0 1/4"

(MEN'S) MEETING ROOM 19'-11 1/4" x 30'-0 1/2"

FACING BENCHES

PRIVY 10'-5 1/2" x 6'-4"

PORCH

WEST ELEVATION · SCALE · 1/4"·1'-0"

SITE PLAN · SCALE · 1/40"·1'-0"

CARE TAKER'S HOUSE

BARN

STONE WALL

SHED REMNANT

HORSE SHED

MEETING HOUSE ROAD

GRAVEL DRIVE

MOUNTING BLOCK

MEETING HOUSE

IRON FENCE

BURIAL GROUND

DRAWN BY: ADAM MAKSAY (K. LAM, R. MILLER)

FRIENDS MEETING HOUSE STUDY, 1997
NATIONAL PARK SERVICE
UNITED STATES DEPARTMENT OF THE INTERIOR

NAME AND LOCATION OF STRUCTURE
CHICHESTER FRIENDS MEETING HOUSE
611 MEETING HOUSE ROAD, BOOTHWYN, DELAWARE COUNTY, PENNSYLVANIA

SURVEY NO. PA-6225

HISTORIC AMERICAN BUILDINGS SURVEY
SHEET 1 OF 3 SHEETS

form and detail. One plan consisted of a roughly square structure containing back-to-back meeting rooms separated by a partition, with a facing bench in the larger of the two rooms. This form was similar to plans developed by English Friends (*see fig. 5.10*). The other meeting house type consisted of a single-cell or one-room structure with an entryway at the center of the principal facade. Single-cell meeting houses were often enlarged later with an addition subordinate to the main structure intended for the use of the women of the group (*see fig. 5.11*). The addition gradually became better integrated into the main structure, eventually resulting in the ubiquitous two-cell meeting house form that includes equal apartments for men's and women's business meetings separated by a retractable partition. Due to the increasingly pervasive influence of mainstream culture, a schism occurred in 1827, marking the beginning of changes in American Friends' faith and practice. By the latter part of the nineteenth century, change had begun to manifest itself in meeting house architecture (*see fig. 5.12*). By the early twentieth century, elements once considered essential to meeting house design, such as facing benches and partitions, had been eliminated from building plans. Also during this time, meeting houses were trans-

Figure 5.10
Chichester (1769) is a pristine example of the influence of the English program on colonial meeting house design. While the single-cell form is similar to other colonial designs, the interior plan is conducive to the English pattern of meeting in which men and women met in a single room for worship and the women removed themselves to another area to conduct gender-specific business meetings. Very few examples of this plan have survived.

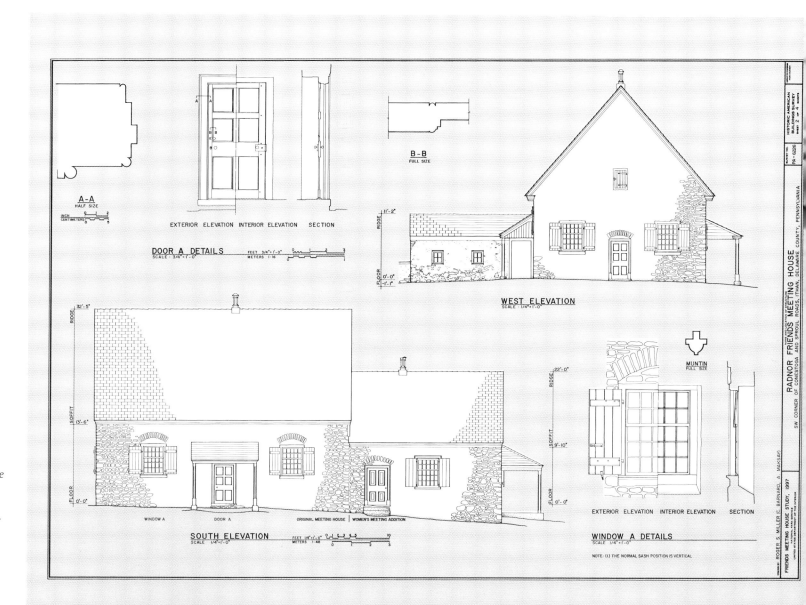

Figure 5.11
The telescoping form of Radnor Meeting House (begun in 1718) is the result of an addition to the main block of a structure intended for use by the women's meeting for business. This is the only remaining example of what was a common meeting house type in the Delaware Valley during the eighteenth century (and likely before).

A-A
HALF SIZE

INCH
CENTIMETERS

EXTERIOR ELEVATION   INTERIOR ELEVATION   SECTION

B-B
FULL SIZE

DOOR A DETAILS
SCALE: 3/4"=1'-0"
FEET 3/4"=1'-0"
METERS 1:16

WEST ELEVATION
SCALE: 1/4"=1'-0"

RIDGE 11'-2"

FLOOR 0'-0"
       -1'-1"

RIDGE 32'-5"

SOFFIT 13'-6"

FLOOR 0'-0"

WINDOW A   DOOR A   ORIGINAL MEETING HOUSE | WOMEN'S MEETING ADDITION

SOUTH ELEVATION
SCALE: 1/4"=1'-0"
FEET 1/4"=1'-0"
METERS 1:48

RIDGE 22'-0"

SOFFIT 9'-10"

FLOOR 0'-0"

MUNTIN
FULL SIZE

EXTERIOR ELEVATION   INTERIOR ELEVATION   SECTION

WINDOW A DETAILS
SCALE 1/4"=1'-0"

NOTE: (1) THE NORMAL SASH POSITION IS VERTICAL

DRAWN BY ROGER S. MILLER (C. BARNARD, A. MAKSAY)
FRIENDS MEETING HOUSE STUDY, 1997

RADNOR FRIENDS MEETING HOUSE
OF CONESTOGA AND SPROUL ROADS, ITHAN, DELAWARE COUNTY, PENNSYLVANIA
SW CORNER

SURVEY NO.
PA-6226

HISTORIC AMERICAN
BUILDINGS SURVEY
SHEET 2 OF 4 SHEETS

formed into multiuse structures (*see fig. 5.13*) to accommodate other Quaker activities.

Because the Friends adhered to the tenet of simplicity in all things, both temporal and spiritual, it was less important for the categorizing process of the survey to define meeting houses stylistically. The survey demonstrated that building *design* was clearly driven by vernacular building traditions and the use of indigenous materials. Building *plan*, on the other hand, played a more significant role in identifying particular building forms. Plan was essential to facilitating the meeting program and, therefore, differences discernible in the surveyed meeting houses were based on different programmatic needs.

The field survey and preliminary research provided the information needed to choose buildings for the study group. Criteria for selection included the architectural integrity of a structure and whether it embodied a particular stage in the evolution of meeting house design. More in-depth study was then conducted of the meeting houses in the representative sampling. This research into individual structures helped pinpoint the dates of initial construction and subsequent changes and revealed patterns of meeting within individual groups. Investigation into the social, political, and organizational history of Friends revealed that changes in their meeting houses were tied to shifts in their faith and practice, which were in turn precipitated by significant events or movements in Quaker history.

Figure 5.12

The design of Little Egg Harbor Meeting House (1863) more closely resembles that of a rural chapel than the predominant Quaker building forms of the era. As such, it reflects the increasingly pervasive influence of mainstream culture on Friends' faith and practice by the latter part of the nineteenth century.

Figure 5.13

West Grove Meeting House (1903) reflects the twentieth-century trend of expanding meeting houses to accommodate additional activities within a single, multiuse structure. Like others of this type, West Grove's design included preparative and quarterly meeting rooms, space for social and educational activities, a kitchen, and restroom facilities.

HABS Recording

During the summer of 1997, a field team of architectural technicians working under the direction of HABS architects produced measured drawings. At the same time, HABS historians and a photographer prepared written histories and large-format black-and-white photographs of the first six meeting houses chosen for further study. These were Merion (c. 1695–1714), Radnor (1718), Buckingham (1768), Chichester (1769), Caln (1726, rebuilt 1782), and West Grove (1903).

Due to the number of buildings and the vernacular nature of their design, the measured drawing component was formulated to convey the characteristic features of each meeting house. Drawn were floor plan(s), elevations of the front and one side, structural elements (often communicated through a sectional drawing), and essential details such as windows, doorways, bench-end profiles, and partitions. Because only representative elements were delineated, the layout of the drawing sheets was characterized by a rich composition of parts, recalling the drawings created during the early years of the HABS program in the 1930s. Likewise, smaller-scale elements such as doorway hoods, shutters, hardware, date stones, carved graffiti, and (horse) mounting blocks were recorded, adding to the aesthetic and visual complexity of the layout.

The accompanying historical reports conveyed the significance of each building in the evolution of meeting house design in the Delaware Valley. The histories included a discussion of the social and political events responsible for the changes in Friends' faith and practice that were manifested in meeting house forms. Large-format black-and-white photographs were used to record the general setting and all elevations, interiors, details, and other essential

Figure 5.14

As one of the most recently built meeting houses in the Delaware Valley, Southampton (1969) marks the end of the continuum in the evolution of design in the Delaware Valley. Its design reflects the elimination of once-essential features of meeting house design in response to programmatic changes. The practice of holding a joint business meeting rather than separate men's and women's meetings eliminated the need for a partition. Likewise, the diminishing role of the ministers, elders, and overseers led to the removal of the facing benches. At Southampton, the focus once provided by the facing benches was replaced by a picture window that opens onto the woods that surround the meeting house.

or noteworthy elements. Significant outbuildings such as carriage sheds and privies and features such as mounting blocks and burying grounds were photographed as well.

In the summer of 1999 a second team was fielded to record the meeting houses at Sadsbury (c. 1747), Frankford (1775), Arney's Mount (1775), Downingtown (1806), Little Egg Harbor (1863), Germantown (1869), Middletown (remodeled 1888), and Southampton (1969). In an effort to round out the selection, large-format photography and short historical reports were also prepared for an equally sizable selection of meeting houses, ranging in date from 1708 to 1931. Each of the latter structures reflects at least one important historical element, such as significant changes in faith and practice as manifested in the architecture, regionally significant building forms, or seminal events in Quaker history (see figs. 5.14 and 5.15).

The methodology developed for the study of Friends meeting houses in the Delaware Valley can be applied to other vernacular building forms. The techniques of field survey and contextual study are effective means for identifying and evaluating large groups of structures. Documenting select structures makes it possible to record information that pertains to a much larger sampling of vernacular building forms. When considered in historical context, this information can be used to establish the cultural and architectural significance of these building forms. The meeting house study also underscores the value of an interdisciplinary, history-driven approach. Contextual study is crucial to understanding structures of all types, and it is the most effective way to ensure that the buildings most true to form and most reflective of the nation's diverse cultural heritage are recorded.

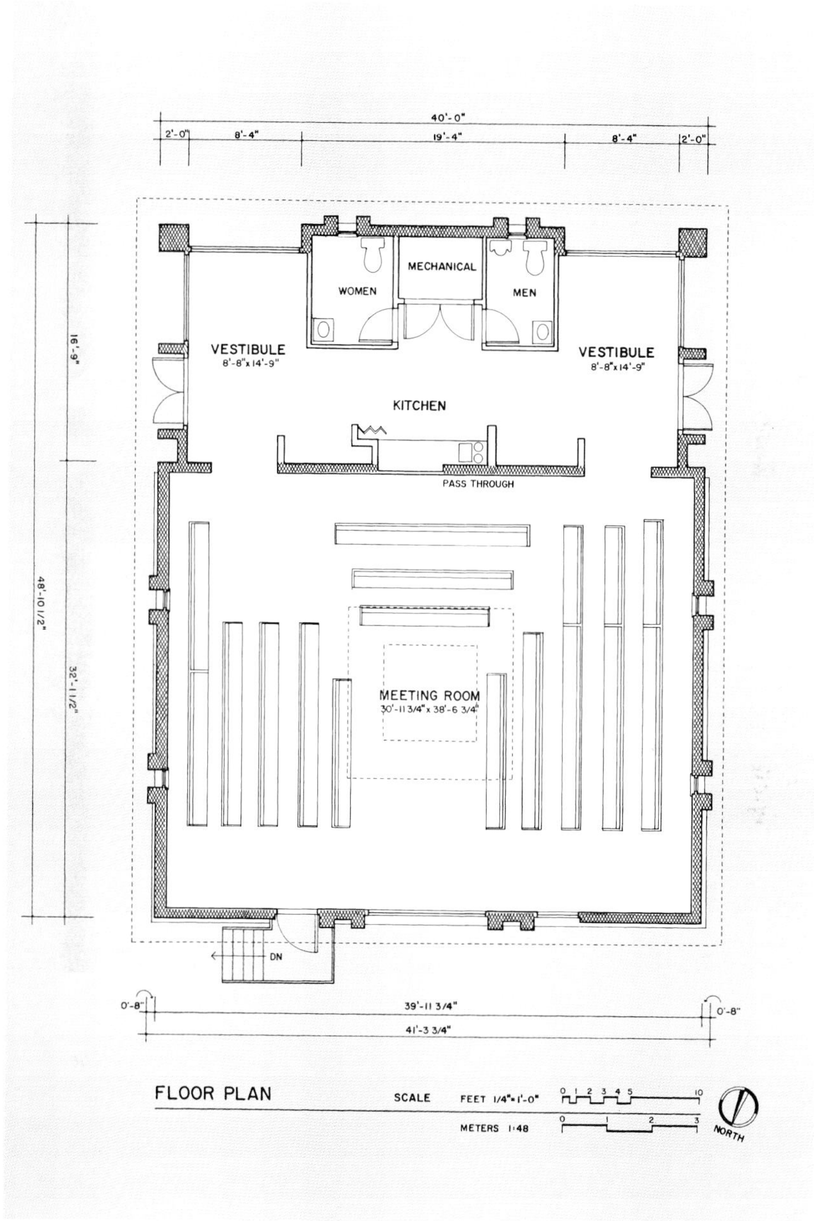

Figure 5.15
The plan of Southampton Meeting House is representative of many contemporary meeting houses that include space for the larger functions of the Society of Friends.

CHAPTER 6

DOCUMENTING HISTORIC BRIDGES

Eric N. DeLony

Of the 7,500 properties in the Historic American Engineering Record collection at the Library of Congress, bridges number 2,500. Many of these are civil engineering icons such as the Brooklyn, Eads, and Golden Gate bridges, while others are notable for their commonality. All are part of the rich civil engineering heritage of the United States.

Since the beginning of the program, bridges have figured prominently in the types of sites HAER records. Two important examples were documented during the program's pilot project, the Mohawk Hudson Area Survey in 1969. One was Squire Whipple's famous bowstring arch truss spanning the Normanskill just outside Albany, New York. Dating from 1867, it was one of the first bridges in the United States to be scientifically designed (see figs. 6.1, 6.2, 6.3 and 2.15). The other was John A. Roebling's Delaware Aqueduct (1849), one of the oldest suspension bridges in the world and a precursor to the Brooklyn Bridge (see figs. 6.4 and 6.13).

HAER drawings illustrate what a bridge looks like in traditional plan, section, and elevation views. In addition, exploded isometric drawings illustrate how members fit together, and diagrams explain engineering phenomena such as which members work in tension and compression.

Production of HAER drawings has been significantly enhanced in recent years by the use of computer-aided drafting (CAD). As the new technology became available, many HAER constituents were concerned that CAD delineation would be unable to replicate the quality of the traditional hand-rendered ink-on-Mylar HAER drawings. Fortunately, this has not been the case. In the hands of skilled CAD delineators, these drawings can be as textured and detailed as the drawings rendered by hand.

The transition from hand to CAD delineation of HAER projects took just three years, rather than the five predicted. In the summer of 2002, all HAER field team architects used CAD delineation, which not only facilitated the production of complicated isometric and perspective views but increased productivity. Creating traditional hand drawings, HAER architects averaged four 24" × 36" sheets over a twelve-week summer. CAD enables production of five to six sheets per architect, and this rate is likely to increase as students improve their CAD skills and more sophisticated programs become available.

HAER teams are able to document about twenty bridges during a typical twelve-week summer survey. This level of productivity requires a team of five or six architects, three historians, one or two engineers, and a part-time photographer. Each historian researches and writes about six to eight bridges. Architects and engineers measure, draw, and analyze four to five, depending on available records and the complexity of the bridge.

The bridge teams pioneered engineering analysis, another innovation in HAER documentation that benefited from new computer technologies. We know that many nineteenth-century bridge designs were based on empirical methods and approximate calculations, but little technical information survives to reveal exactly how this process was carried out. Current structural analysis and modeling programs, however, make it possible to create virtual models of any bridge. Researchers can impose loads as if the model bridge were carrying a variety of stationary and moving loads and then observe how it responds. The actual load-carrying mechanisms of the bridge are thus demonstrated, suggesting the approximate design methods of the bridge designer.

Computer modeling and analysis have increased understanding of how designers conceptualized bridges and how they reconciled their theoretical designs with the practicality of constructing efficient, buildable products. The new computer tools can be used to describe bridge performance and design efficiency and to compare similar bridge forms, such as metal bowstring and concrete arches, and one-of-a kind forms such as truss-stiffened suspension bridges and quinticular trusses (*see fig. 6.5*).

Field Research

Bridges are challenging subjects for research, and there is a fairly steep learning curve for HAER team members who document them. Rarely do any of the disciplines bring complete proficiency, training, or experience to a project. For architects, the crew has to work out the most efficient way to gather the dimensions, measurements, and details needed to develop drawings. Engineers must coordinate with the

Figure 6.1
This photograph illustrates the quintessence of Squire Whipple's revolutionary bowstring truss bridge. Every member was mathematically sized to handle its respective load, resulting in an extremely light, material-efficient, gravity-defying structure.

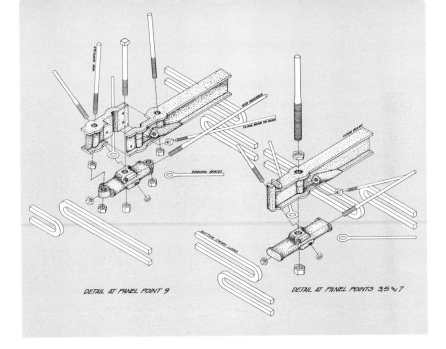
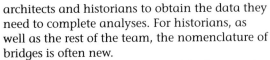

Figure 6.2

These connecting blocks and link chords, two parts of the Whipple bowstring, exemplify the craft of cast- and wrought-iron bridges. The connection block is beautifully sculpted, a complicated casting dependent on the skill and collaboration of the designer, pattern maker, mold maker, and foundry man. The link chords are made in the tradition of the blacksmith. Iron rods, square or round, are feathered at the ends and heat-welded to form a continuous elongated loop.

DETAIL AT PANEL POINT 9

DETAIL AT PANEL POINTS 3,5 % 7

architects and historians to obtain the data they need to complete analyses. For historians, as well as the rest of the team, the nomenclature of bridges is often new.

Many problems encountered in documenting historic bridges arise from lack of information. The primary artifact, the bridge itself, provides information about the structure, including, if you know what to look for, information on its manufacture, fabrication, and assembly at the site. The documentation team, exploiting the various skills and points of view of its members, has the opportunity to "read" the bridge. Nonetheless, information gleaned from the physical artifact alone is not sufficient for a comprehensive record.

Traditional historical documents, primary and secondary, are required for a complete understanding and interpretation of a bridge. A typical paper trail starts with primary sources such as strain sheets, contracts, or the minutes from a county commissioners' meeting. Such documents often provide interesting contextual information such as the infrastructure budget for other public works in the jurisdiction, the relative cost of a particular bridge compared with others, the reasons for building (or in some

Figure 6.3

Whipple's patent did not claim that he invented the bowstring arch, only the cast-iron segmental arch in combination with the diagonals, designed to sustain the shape against the effects of unequal loadings, and the bottom chord or string, which he called the "thrust tie." He also claimed the lateral bracing detail in his patent, a separate system to keep the arch from moving laterally. This detail did not appear in the patent drawing, but all Whipple bowstrings of moderate span (120–150 feet) have a lateral bracing member at the top of the arch.

Figure 6.4
This foreshortened perspective provides an artistic view of the Delaware Aqueduct as it appeared in the summer of 1969, when HAER first recorded it. At this time, the bridge was privately owned and used as a vehicular toll bridge.

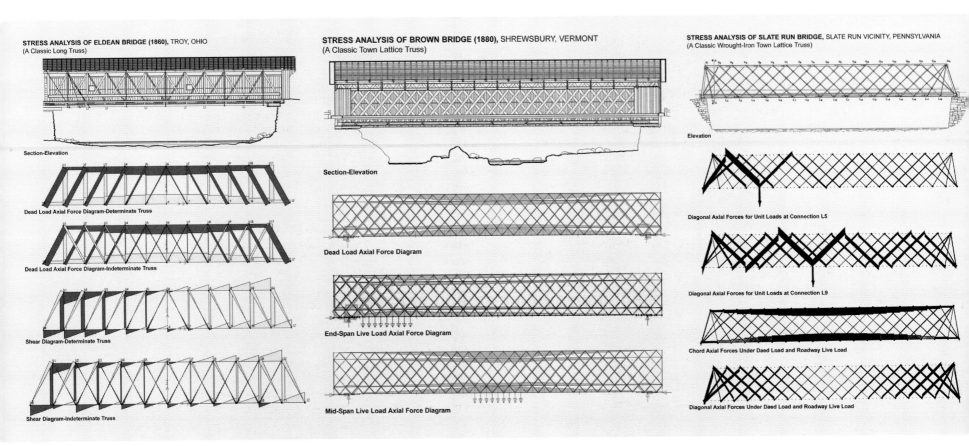

STRESS ANALYSIS OF ELDEAN BRIDGE (1860), TROY, OHIO
(A Classic Long Truss)

Section-Elevation

Dead Load Axial Force Diagram-Determinate Truss

Dead Load Axial Force Diagram-Indeterminate Truss

Shear Diagram-Determinate Truss

Shear Diagram-Indeterminate Truss

STRESS ANALYSIS OF BROWN BRIDGE (1880), SHREWSBURY, VERMONT
(A Classic Town Lattice Truss)

Section-Elevation

Dead Load Axial Force Diagram

End-Span Live Load Axial Force Diagram

Mid-Span Live Load Axial Force Diagram

STRESS ANALYSIS OF SLATE RUN BRIDGE, SLATE RUN VICINITY, PENNSYLVANIA
(A Classic Wrought-Iron Town Lattice Truss)

Elevation

Diagonal Axial Forces for Unit Loads at Connection L5

Diagonal Axial Forces for Unit Loads at Connection L9

Chord Axial Forces Under Daed Load and Roadway Live Load

Diagonal Axial Forces Under Daed Load and Roadway Live Load

Figure 6.5
*To better illustrate the performance and behavior of
bridges, stress diagrams were juxtaposed with the elevation of various bridge forms to reveal the axial forces in the
members. The bridges illustrated were all documented by
HAER and include a Long truss, a Town lattice truss, and a
riveted wrought-iron lattice (also known as a multiple-
intersection Warren or quinticular truss).*

Reading a Bridge

You can feel a truss bridge work by standing and holding the members as an automobile crosses. The deck gives way under the weight of the load but regains its original level once the car has passed. The wrought-iron diagonals stretch and the upper chord deflects slightly, then they too return to their original configurations. The bridge is an organism, and it functions as it does because of the elastic properties of its materials, the quality of its workmanship, and the way its parts are assembled. When you consider how many times a bridge is asked to flex over a 100-year period, you can begin to appreciate its remarkable qualities.

Unlike houses, where the studs, floor joists, wiring, plumbing, and heating and ventilating systems are concealed within the walls or hidden in the attic or basement, bridges (with the exception of reinforced concrete girders) reveal just about everything. In terms of engineering, bridges are discussed by design or type (beam, arch, truss, cantilever, suspension, or movable), length (usually in terms of clear or overall span), and materials (stone, wood, cast and wrought iron, concrete, and steel). The composition of the members—angles, channels, I-beams, lacing bars, plates; every connection, whether riveted, bolted, or pinned; and how members fit together—is there to be seen.

The essential difference among bridge types is the way they bear their own weight (the "dead load") and that of a person, train, wind, or snow (the "live load"). For beam, truss, and girder bridges, the weight bears directly downward from their ends onto the ground, piers, or abutments. Arch bridges thrust outward as well as down, acting in compression. The cables of suspension bridges act in tension, pulling inward against their towers and anchorages.

A more complex form of the beam is the truss, a rigid self-supporting system of triangles that transfers both dead and live loads to the abutments or piers. A more complex form of the girder is the cantilever, in which trussed and anchored ends of the girder support a central span. These were favored for deep gorges or wide, fast-flowing streams where false work (a temporary structure, usually of timber, erected to assist in the construction of the permanent bridge) is impossible to build.

The three principal types of bridges—beam, arch, and suspension—often were combined to form composite structures. The bridge design depended on the nature of the crossing, the span required, the materials at hand, and the type of load anticipated—pedestrian, vehicular, railroad, or a channel of water, as in aqueducts.

In terms of material, wood and stone are easily identified, but only an experienced eye can differentiate between cast and wrought iron and steel. Cast iron is a molten, poured material that is extremely strong in compression but essentially useless in tension. It is a brittle material that easily cracks when it is pulled apart, as in tension, or subjected to bending. Therefore, cast iron is used only in members carrying compressive forces, such as the vertical posts or the upper chord of a bridge. A pattern is needed to make a cast-iron part, so marks from the mold are another clue toward identification. There are very few all-cast-iron bridges in the United States. The best examples are the five cast-iron arches in Central Park in New York that separate the equestrian paths from the pedestrian walkways.

More common are composite cast- and wrought-iron bridges, of which approximately seventy remain around the country. They were used for about thirty years between the 1840s and the mid-1870s. Generally, the beefier, heavier members carried compression while the thinner, lighter members carried tensile loads. Wrought iron is a forged material that is heated, pounded, and shaped under a forging hammer, making it an extremely strong, ductile material that resists both tension and compression. Initially, wrought iron was used primarily for tension members because of its higher cost. One of the best examples of a composite truss is the Bollman Bridge at Savage, Maryland, discussed in this case study. Note the elaborate, decorative architectural members, such as the octagonal upper chord, the vertical posts, and the heavy grouped column towers at the end of the truss (see fig. 6.9), made of cast iron. The lighter, thinner members, such as the panel bracing rods and the diagonal eyebars radiating from the top of the towers, are made of wrought iron.

After the introduction of composite cast- and wrought-iron construction, a number of bridge failures resulted in loss of life and property, usually due to failure of a cast-iron part. Consequently, by the 1880s, engineers were building bridges with both compression and tension members fabricated from wrought iron, although some bridge parts were still made from cast iron. There followed a brief period of ten years in the 1880s and 1890s, when engineers built bridges entirely of wrought iron. By the 1890s, however, the Bessemer process had reduced the cost and improved the consistency and reliability of steel, and just about any bridge dating from the mid-1890s and later is probably steel.

It is nearly impossible to tell the difference between wrought iron and steel without testing. Engineers send specimens of metal, known as "coupons," to testing laboratories for identification. The strength and other properties of the metal can also be determined through testing, and if a bridge is to be rehabilitated, testing is crucial, as it is the only way to definitely identify a metal and determine its strength. Old metal bridges can be a lot stronger than one would normally suspect.

cases rebuilding) a bridge, and the relative importance of the bridge to local commerce, industry, and transportation.

Sometimes researchers are lucky to find the original drawings or a cache of old albumen photographs illustrating the construction process. Other important sources include bridge company catalogs and engineering journals. Old newspaper articles in the local historical society often reveal the reason for building the bridge, the process used to solicit bid proposals and award contracts, and discussions of workmanship and inspection to ensure that the bridge was built according to plans and specifications.

Historical research can also be frustrating. Fire and floods have destroyed many county courthouses and the records in them. Often, small-town governments are hard-pressed for storage space and discard such documents, not realizing their value to future historians. Information on large urban bridges is usually abundant, while reference material on bridges on smaller, farm-to-market roads is scarce.

Data on archaic materials such as cast and wrought iron or the design formulas used by engineers in the nineteenth century are not available in contemporary engineering texts. However, a lot can be learned from studying bridge patents. By comparing the "unbuilt" patents with the successful designs that were actually constructed, we can better understand the technologies that worked. Because patents were granted to individuals, there is also a chance of finding information on the background, training, and experience of inventors.

Identifying Bridges to Record

When asked about old bridges, most people think of covered wood bridges and stone arch bridges. The United States has more covered wood bridges than any other country (about 810), but many metal trusses, concrete arches, cantilevers, and suspension spans are just as important and worthy of research and preservation. Most of the surviving historic bridges are metal trusses. Erected by the thousands by bridge fabricating companies during the last quarter of the nineteenth century, these bridges are in jeopardy. Thus, it should come as no surprise that most of the bridges in the HAER collection are metal trusses (see fig. 6.6). Recent statistics suggest that more than half the metal truss bridges identified as eligible for the National Register of Historic Places have been destroyed in the last twenty years, a period in which the awareness and appreciation of historic resources supposedly was at its height.

Since it is not practical to record all historic bridges, there must be some criteria for selection. Generally, HAER chooses to document bridges from inventories completed by engineering consulting firms with some expertise in historic bridges. These databases generally result from contracts with state departments of transportation (DOTs). Just about every state has completed a survey of its historic bridges, making bridges one of the first structure types to be comprehensively evaluated throughout the United States. The exception is railroad bridges. Because state highway departments generally are not responsible for railroads, these bridges have rarely been included in statewide surveys. Other input comes from historians working with state historic preservation offices, the environmental quality divisions of the state DOTs, and experts on historic bridges in the state.

The reason bridges comprise nearly a third of the HAER collection is simple. The 1967 collapse of the Silver Bridge spanning the Ohio River due to the failure of one of its fracture-critical members resulted in the loss of forty-six lives. In response to this disaster, Congress passed legislation charging states to regularly inspect bridges to identify and remedy hazards. Unfortunately, most bridges identified as structurally deficient and functionally obsolete were also historically significant. HAER recognized that the new legislation and subsequent billions of dollars in federal and state funding to eliminate these bridges also threatened to eliminate the physical evidence of the U.S. bridge-building legacy. In response to this threat, HAER launched a national initiative in 1975 to identify and document historically significant bridges in the United States. For the last quarter century, HAER has fielded at least one, and often two, bridge teams every summer.

Documenting a Bridge

In this case study, five common bridge types illustrate the evolution of the HAER bridge documentation program: covered wood, metal truss, reinforced concrete girder, suspension, and two movable spans. While the approach to bridge documentation is similar regardless of type, each structure has nuances due to its location, construction materials, structural behavior, and method of construction. For example, the configuration of wood members and metal trusses and the way they are joined together are of particular interest in bridges constructed of those materials. For concrete bridges, the formwork, falsework, disposition of reinforcing, and

Figure 6.6
HAER's truss posters were developed in the mid-1970s to assist engineers and scholars in identifying various truss types.

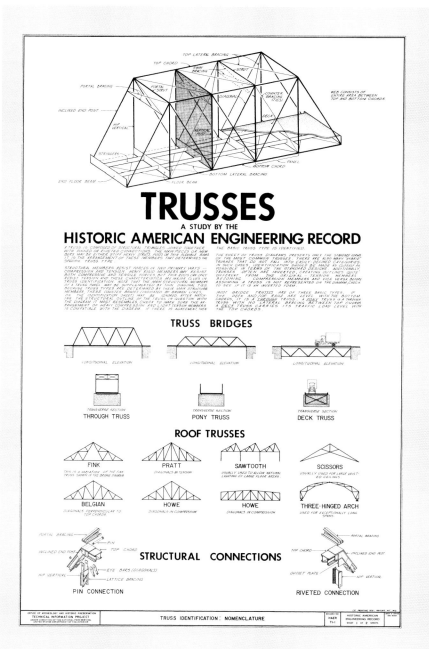

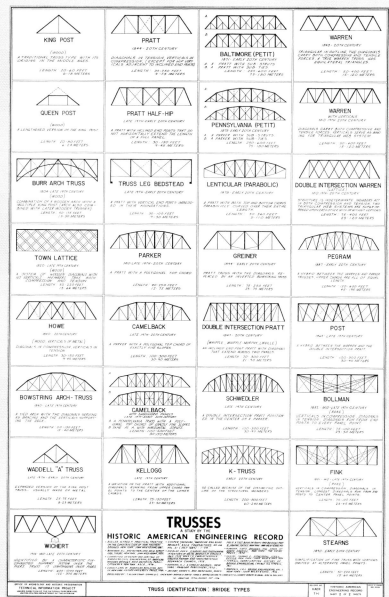

sequence of pouring are primary. The cable saddles, anchorages, suspenders, and stiffening trusses are of particular interest for suspension bridges. The machinery, gears, and lift and locking mechanisms are important for movable bridges.

Eldean Bridge (1860)

States possessing the most significant examples of covered wood bridges are those with large forested regions—New Hampshire, Vermont, and Maine in New England; Ohio, Indiana, and Iowa in the Midwest; Alabama, Georgia, and North Carolina in the South; and Oregon and California in the West. Pennsylvania has the most of any state, with about 260. Most of these

states have organizations of enthusiasts who advocate for the preservation of these bridges.

Many covered bridges are outstanding examples of wood construction technology, craftsmanship, and engineering. Consequently, wood framing and structural engineering are the focus of HAER documentation of the covered spans. In 2002 HAER received multiple-year funding from the Federal Highway Administration (FHWA) to document U.S. covered bridges. This is part of the National Historic Covered Bridge Preservation (NHCBP) program, established by Congress to help the states preserve, rehabilitate, and restore covered bridges around the country. HAER's primary role is to document a selection of the most outstanding examples.

During the first year, four of the earliest forms—Burr arch, Town lattice, and Long and Howe trusses—were measured, drawn, and structurally evaluated (*see fig. 6.7*).

The Eldean Bridge (1860), spanning the Great Miami River near the town of Troy in southeastern Ohio, is a particularly good example of a Long truss. The form was patented in 1830 by Colonel Stephen Harriman Long of the U.S. Army Topographical Engineers. It features diagonal compression and vertical tension members, an ingenious system superior in strength, solidity, permanence, and ease of repair, and far advanced for its time. It was simpler to build than the earlier and more popular Burr arch truss.

The Long truss is historically significant because it is the first wood truss system based on an understanding of structural theory. Colonel Long was the first American engineer to size the members of his trusses based on the magnitude of the forces each would have to carry. He was the first to understand the advantages of pre-stressing to eliminate tension in certain members, an advantage since tension connections are extremely difficult to fashion in wood. Pre-stressing prevented the joints from working in tension with the passage of moving loads and ensured that the members, which were liable to change stresses as the load advanced across the bridge, remained in compression (*see fig. 6.8*).

Bollman Iron Suspension and Trussed Bridge (1869)

One of the first iron truss types to be universally adopted by a railroad was Wendel Bollman's suspension and trussed bridge, a pioneering design that revolutionized railroad bridge construction. Patented in 1852, Bollman's system is a composite cast- and wrought-iron truss. It resembles the Pratt configuration but with radiating wrought-iron diagonal eye-bars extending from the ends of the top chord to each panel point and with no lower chord. The members along the bottom of the truss are cast-iron spacers holding the deck beams in place, rather than the lower tension chord member typical of other rectilinear forms such as the Pratt truss. Deck beams were hung from the truss framework on wrought-iron chain links at the panel points. Bollman adopted this connection so that the rest of the truss would remain intact if one of the deck beams failed (*see figs. 6.9a and 6.9b*).

Bollman's bridge design is significant because it is the first patented all-metal truss bridge to be built consistently by an American

Figure 6.7
Using traditional hand plotting and delineation, a skilled draftsman would have needed the better part of a summer to draw these complicated perspective views of covered bridges. Computer-aided drawing (CAD) programs make it easier for architects to project plan, section, and elevation views into three-dimensional perspective drawings, which provide a more graphic representation of complicated truss forms.

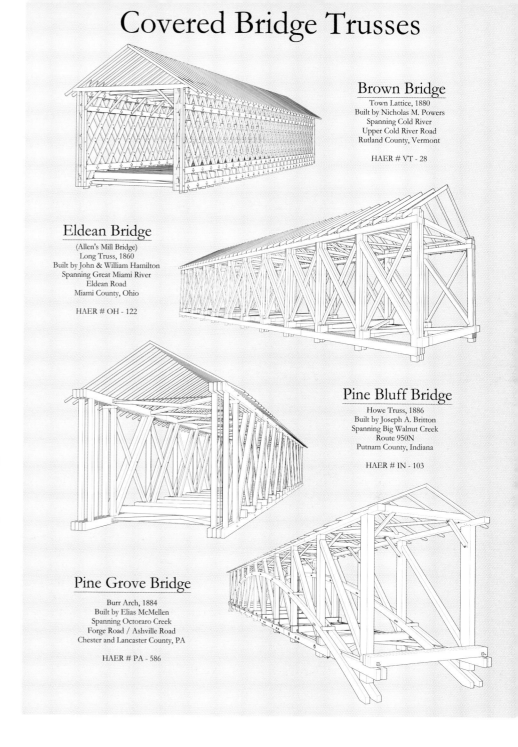

Covered Bridge Trusses

Brown Bridge
Town Lattice, 1880
Built by Nicholas M. Powers
Spanning Cold River
Upper Cold River Road
Rutland County, Vermont

HAER # VT - 28

Eldean Bridge
(Allen's Mill Bridge)
Long Truss, 1860
Built by John & William Hamilton
Spanning Great Miami River
Eldean Road
Miami County, Ohio

HAER # OH - 122

Pine Bluff Bridge
Howe Truss, 1886
Built by Joseph A. Britton
Spanning Big Walnut Creek
Route 950N
Putnam County, Indiana

HAER # IN - 103

Pine Grove Bridge
Burr Arch, 1884
Built by Elias McMellen
Spanning Octoraro Creek
Forge Road / Ashville Road
Chester and Lancaster County, PA

HAER # PA - 586

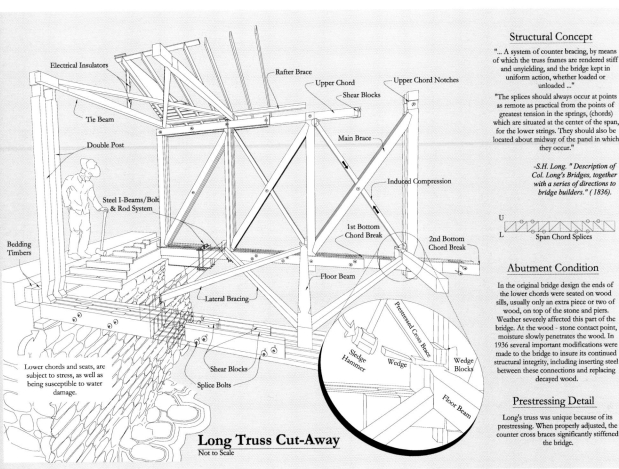

Electrical Insulators

Rafter Brace

Upper Chord

Upper Chord Notches

Shear Blocks

Tie Beam

Double Post

Main Brace

Induced Compression

Steel I-Beams/Bolt & Rod System

1st Bottom Chord Break

Bedding Timbers

2nd Bottom Chord Break

Lateral Bracing

Floor Beam

Lower chords and seats, are subject to stress, as well as being susceptible to water damage.

Shear Blocks

Splice Bolts

Prestressed Cross Brace

Sledge Hammer

Wedge

Wedge Blocks

Floor Beam

Long Truss Cut-Away
Not to Scale

Structural Concept

"... A system of counter bracing, by means of which the truss frames are rendered stiff and unyielding, and the bridge kept in uniform action, whether loaded or unloaded ..."

"The splices should always occur at points as remote as practical from the points of greatest tension in the springs, (chords) which are situated at the center of the span, for the lower strings. They should also be located about midway of the panel in which they occur."

-S.H. Long. "Description of Col. Long's Bridges, together with a series of directions to bridge builders." (1836).

U
L
Span Chord Splices

Abutment Condition

In the original bridge design the ends of the lower chords were seated on wood sills, usually only an extra piece or two of wood, on top of the stone and piers. Weather severely affected this part of the bridge. At the wood - stone contact point, moisture slowly penetrates the wood. In 1936 several important modifications were made to the bridge to insure its continued structural integrity, including inserting steel between these connections and replacing decayed wood.

Prestressing Detail

Long's truss was unique because of its prestressing. When properly adjusted, the counter cross braces significantly stiffened the bridge.

Figure 6.8

The essential feature distinguishing Long's truss from the multiple king-post and other common truss types of the time was a system of counterbraces, one per panel, that served to stiffen the bridge against deflection and, in effect, prestressed the structure. Loading the frame to produce some deflection, leaving a gap between the counterbrace and the horizontal upper and lower chord members,

was the first step in prestressing the counterbraces. With the bridge loaded to half its maximum limit, wedges were inserted, locking the joints so that each counterbrace acted in compression rather than tension when the load was removed. This HAER drawing illustrates how Long prestressed his bridges.

railroad. HAER recorded Bollman trusses on two occasions. First was the bridge spanning the Little Patuxent River at Savage, Maryland (*see fig. 6.10*). Originally constructed circa 1869, this bridge was moved in 1887 from the Main Stem of the B&O to an industrial spur serving the textile mill at Savage. It is the sole surviving example of its type.

The second Bollman truss recorded by HAER was the remains of the famous Y-bridge crossing of the Potomac at Harpers Ferry, West Virginia (*see fig. 6.11*). Situated at the strategic convergence of the Shenandoah and Potomac rivers, and the location of a U.S. military arsenal, the bridge suffered from multiple attempts at sabotage during the Civil War. Following the conflict, it was rebuilt. When the B&O main line was relocated on a new alignment in the early twentieth century, the bridge was converted to vehicular use that lasted until it was washed out by a flood in 1937. HAER recorded the Harpers Ferry span in 1987 following several years of drought that had left the Potomac at its lowest level in years, revealing remnants of the bridge in the bed of the river. Harpers Ferry National Historical Park arranged to have the parts salvaged from the river and sponsored a HAER team to document and help the park interpret the bridge (*see fig. 6.12*).

Figures 6.9a and 6.9b

A comparison of these 1969 and 1987 HAER drawings of the link pin details of the Savage and Harpers Ferry Bollman bridges shows how the main deck beams were suspended from the larger truss superstructure. Bollman may have developed this curious detail so that the deck beams would be independent of the rest of the superstructure should one of the deck beams fail.

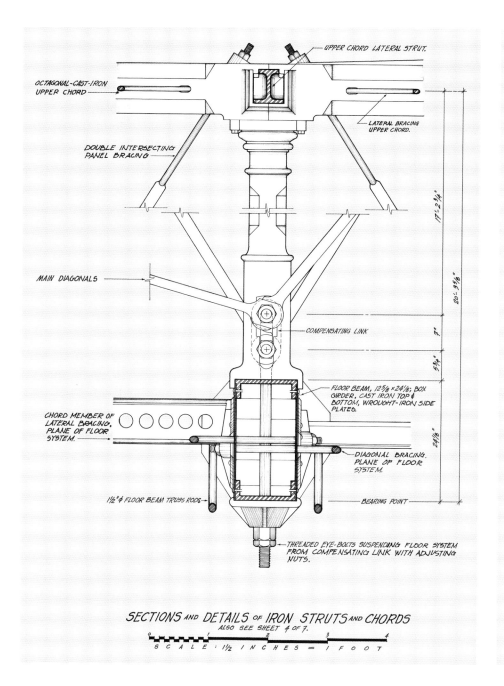

OCTAGONAL-CAST-IRON UPPER CHORD

UPPER CHORD LATERAL STRUT.

LATERAL BRACING UPPER CHORD.

DOUBLE INTERSECTING PANEL BRACING

MAIN DIAGONALS

COMPENSATING LINK

FLOOR BEAM, 12⅝ × 24⅛; BOX GIRDER, CAST IRON TOP & BOTTOM, WROUGHT-IRON SIDE PLATES.

CHORD MEMBER OF LATERAL BRACING, PLANE OF FLOOR SYSTEM.

DIAGONAL BRACING, PLANE OF FLOOR SYSTEM.

1½"ø FLOOR BEAM TRUSS RODS

BEARING POINT

THREADED EYE-BOLTS SUSPENDING FLOOR SYSTEM FROM COMPENSATING LINK WITH ADJUSTING NUTS.

17'-2¼"

20'-3⅛"

7"

5¼"

24⅛"

SECTIONS and DETAILS of IRON STRUTS and CHORDS

ALSO SEE SHEET 4 OF 7.

S C A L E : 1½ I N C H E S = 1 F O O T

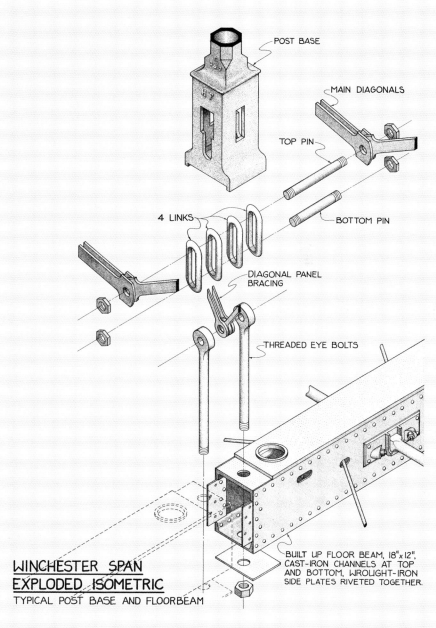

POST BASE

MAIN DIAGONALS

TOP PIN

4 LINKS

BOTTOM PIN

DIAGONAL PANEL BRACING

THREADED EYE BOLTS

WINCHESTER SPAN
EXPLODED ISOMETRIC
TYPICAL POST BASE AND FLOORBEAM

BUILT UP FLOOR BEAM, 18"×12", CAST-IRON CHANNELS AT TOP AND BOTTOM, WROUGHT-IRON SIDE PLATES RIVETED TOGETHER.

Figure 6.10
This photograph records Howard County's restoration of the sole remaining Bollman truss bridge, located in Savage, Maryland. The work involved rebuilding the floor beams for the pedestrian walkway and the wooden housings protecting the connections at the ends of the upper chord. The ironwork was cleaned and painted iron oxide red, and the wood housings were painted white.

Delaware Aqueduct (1849)

The Delaware Aqueduct is located in the valley of the upper Delaware River, a scenic and recreational river protected by the National Park Service (*see figs. 6.4 and 6.13*). One of the first bridges HAER recorded, it is the oldest suspension bridge in the United States. The bridge was designed and constructed by preeminent American engineer John Augustus Roebling. When completed for the Delaware & Hudson Canal at Lackawaxen, Pennsylvania, the aqueduct bridge consisted of four spans averaging 131

feet in length and suspended from two cables 8½ inches in diameter. Each cable was made up of 2,150 individual wires about as thick as a pencil lead. The cables carried a heavy wood trunk full of water.

HAER first recorded the Delaware Aqueduct in summer 1969, when it was a privately owned toll bridge (*see fig. 4.28*). The structure had been converted to vehicular use when the canal was abandoned in the early twentieth century (*see fig. 6.4*). Twenty years later, after the National Park Service had acquired the aqueduct and

rehabilitated and restored it to interpret the aqueduct's function for the public, HAER recorded the bridge a second time. Using Roebling's original drawings, the park had reconstructed the wood canal trunk and cantilevered towpaths, refurbished the wire-cable suspension system, and restored the wood nosing protecting the cutwaters on the piers (*see fig. 6.13*). These changes were substantial enough to justify updating the record.

A 1987 HAER drawing shows the replicated canal trunk and towpaths (*see fig. 1.10*). In addition, it shows the steel panels and bracing in the canal trunk walls that stiffen the truss structure, and the 8-inch-thick concrete slab that helps replicate the weight of the water, thus adding more stiffness to the suspension system and allowing its continued use as a vehicular bridge. The drawing also shows the sacrificial timber nosing on the pier, included in the restoration to save the stone masonry piers from deteriorating due to wear and tear from ice floes.

McKee Street Bridge (1932)

It should not be surprising that Texas, the second largest state, would have the largest number of bridges. HAER spent two summers documenting fifty-four of them. While Texas bridges are not as old as those in the eastern United States, the state has many interesting examples, several of them unique. One is the McKee Street Bridge, a continuous concrete girder spanning Buffalo Bayou in Houston. Not a typical rectangular concrete girder, the bridge is unusual in that its designer, city engineer J. G. McKenzie, designed the girders to follow the bending moment curve, resulting in a bridge that resembles a roller coaster, with curved girders of undulating, variable depth (see fig. 6.14a).

The McKee Street Bridge documentation is particularly interesting because it shows the disposition of the reinforcing bars in the bridge (see fig. 6.14c). Usually embedded in concrete, where it is not visible, rebar cannot be depicted unless original drawings are available. Fortunately, the city had a complete set of engineering drawings, specifications, and some construction photographs, which were used as the basis for the HAER drawings (see figs. 6.14a, 6.14b, and 6.14c). Constructed some thirty years after the introduction of concrete, McKee Street illustrates decades of development in reinforced-concrete technology.

Figure 6.11
This historic view of the Bollman bridge Y-crossing of the Potomac River at Harpers Ferry shows the truss after it was rebuilt following the Civil War. Although the photograph is black-and-white, it is apparent the bridge was polychromed; salvaged fragments were recorded by HAER fifty years later (see fig. 6.12).

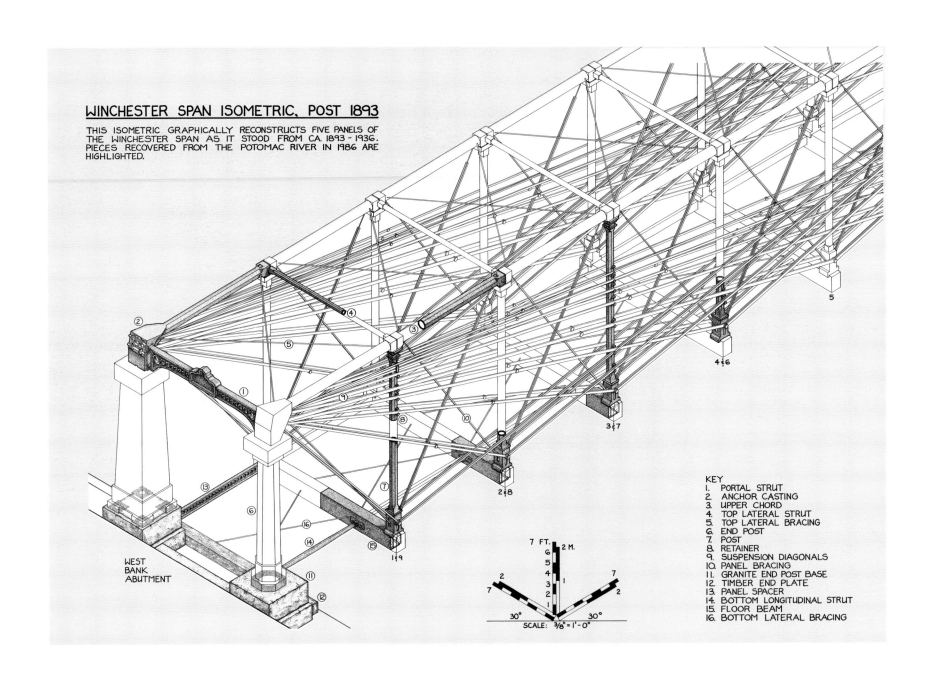

WINCHESTER SPAN ISOMETRIC, POST 1893

THIS ISOMETRIC GRAPHICALLY RECONSTRUCTS FIVE PANELS OF THE WINCHESTER SPAN AS IT STOOD FROM CA. 1893-1936. PIECES RECOVERED FROM THE POTOMAC RIVER IN 1986 ARE HIGHLIGHTED.

WEST BANK ABUTMENT

7 FT.
6
5
4
3
2
1
2 M.

7
2
30°

7
2
30°

7
2

SCALE: 3/8" = 1'-0"

KEY
1. PORTAL STRUT
2. ANCHOR CASTING
3. UPPER CHORD
4. TOP LATERAL STRUT
5. TOP LATERAL BRACING
6. END POST
7. POST
8. RETAINER
9. SUSPENSION DIAGONALS
10. PANEL BRACING
11. GRANITE END POST BASE
12. TIMBER END PLATE
13. PANEL SPACER
14. BOTTOM LONGITUDINAL STRUT
15. FLOOR BEAM
16. BOTTOM LATERAL BRACING

Willamette River Bridges, Portland

The bascule or draw span was developed during the Middle Ages, and the late nineteenth century saw a resurgence of interest in movable bridges. Reliable electric motors and techniques for counterbalancing the massive weights of the bascule, lift, and swing spans marked the beginning of modern movable bridge construction. Usually found in flat terrain, where the cost of approaches to gain high-level crossings is prohibitive, these bridges are characterized by rapidity of operation and an ability to vary the opening depending on the size of vessels. In addition, the bridges can be designed to accommodate congested areas adjacent to factories, warehouses, and other bridges.

Movable bridges fall equally in the realms of mechanical and civil engineering. Machinery for lifting or opening is the distinguishing feature of these types of spans. The bascules over the Chicago River in Chicago are well known, but Portland, Oregon, has an equally interesting and more diverse collection of movable spans.

Figure 6.13
This 1989 view of the Delaware Aqueduct shows the replicated canal trunk and the protective wood nosing on the upstream face of the piers. The cantilevered towpaths had not yet been restored when this photograph was taken.

Figure 6.12
The HAER team carefully measured the parts of the Harpers Ferry Bollman bridge salvaged from the river and constructed a drawing that placed them in their relative positions on the original bridge truss. The intention was to develop an interpretive exhibit on this important nineteenth-century railroad structure. Today, one of the portal castings is displayed in a small exhibit on the bridge crossing at Harpers Ferry.

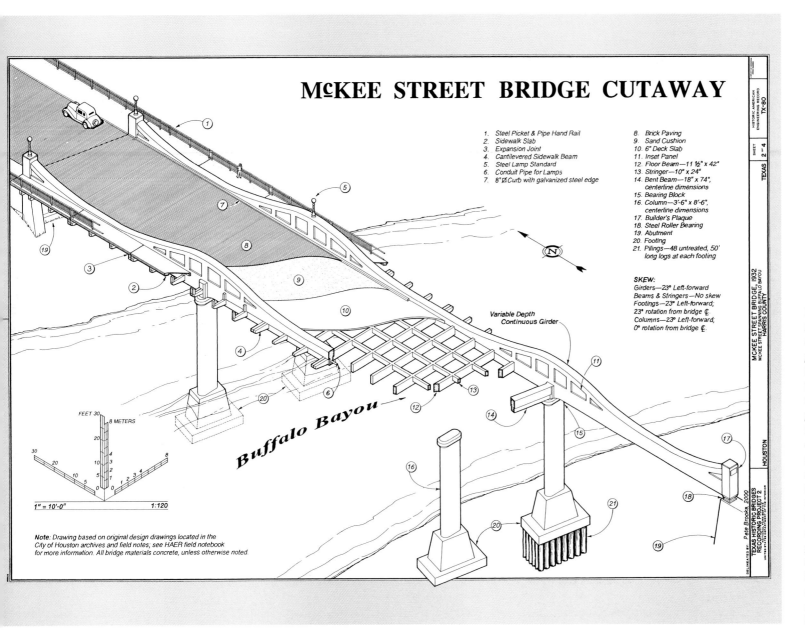

McKEE STREET BRIDGE CUTAWAY

1. Steel Picket & Pipe Hand Rail
2. Sidewalk Slab
3. Expansion Joint
4. Cantilevered Sidewalk Beam
5. Steel Lamp Standard
6. Conduit Pipe for Lamps
7. 8" Ø Curb with galvanized steel edge

8. Brick Paving
9. Sand Cushion
10. 6" Deck Slab
11. Inset Panel
12. Floor Beam—11 ½" x 42"
13. Stringer—10" x 24"
14. Bent Beam—18" x 74", centerline dimensions
15. Bearing Block
16. Column—3'-6" x 8'-6", centerline dimensions
17. Builder's Plaque
18. Steel Roller Bearing
19. Abutment
20. Footing
21. Pilings—48 untreated, 50' long logs at each footing

SKEW:

Girders—23° Left-forward
Beams & Stringers—No skew
Footings—23° Left-forward;
23° rotation from bridge ₵
Columns—23° Left-forward;
0° rotation from bridge ₵.

Variable Depth Continuous Girder

Buffalo Bayou

FEET 30   8 METERS

1" = 10'-0"   1:120

Note: Drawing based on original design drawings located in the City of Houston archives and field notes; see HAER field notebook for more information. All bridge materials concrete, unless otherwise noted.

MCKEE STREET BRIDGE, 1932
MCKEE STREET SPANNING BUFFALO BAYOU
HARRIS COUNTY

TEXAS 2"4

HISTORIC AMERICAN ENGINEERING RECORD
TX-60

SHEET

HOUSTON

DELINEATED BY Pete Brooks, 2000
TEXAS HISTORIC BRIDGES
RECORDING PROJECT 2

Figure 6.14a

Figures 6.14a, b, and c are three of the best interpretive drawings of a bridge in the HAER collection. The cutaway view of the McKee Street Bridge provides a visual context for the main features of a concrete bridge structure: (1) the substructure consisting of the pilings and footings, (2) the superstructure, comprising the main deck beams, variable-depth continuous girder, floor beams, stringers, and cantilevered sidewalks, and (3) decorative features such as the railing and light standards.

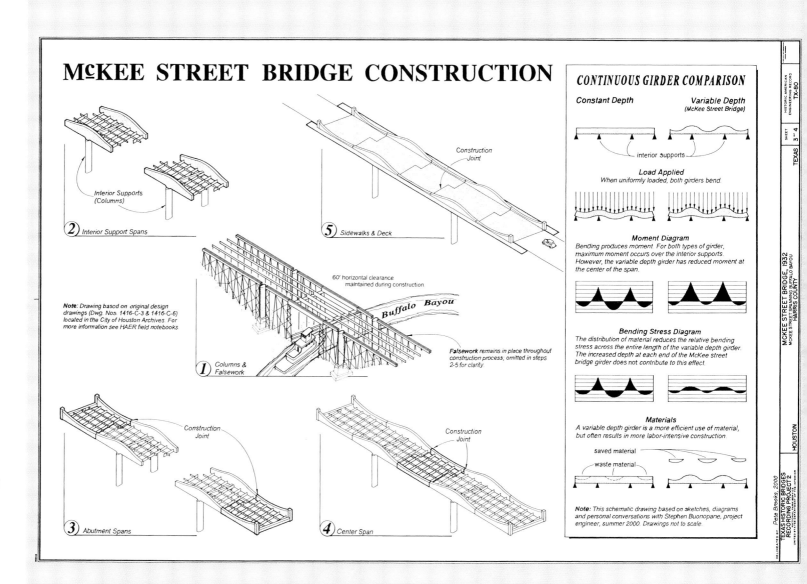

Figure 6.14b

This drawing sheet shows how the McKee Street Bridge was constructed, including the sequencing of the concrete pours, and includes structural diagrams that reveal the basis of the design. Original engineering drawings and specifications and some period photographs were used as the basis for this HAER drawing.

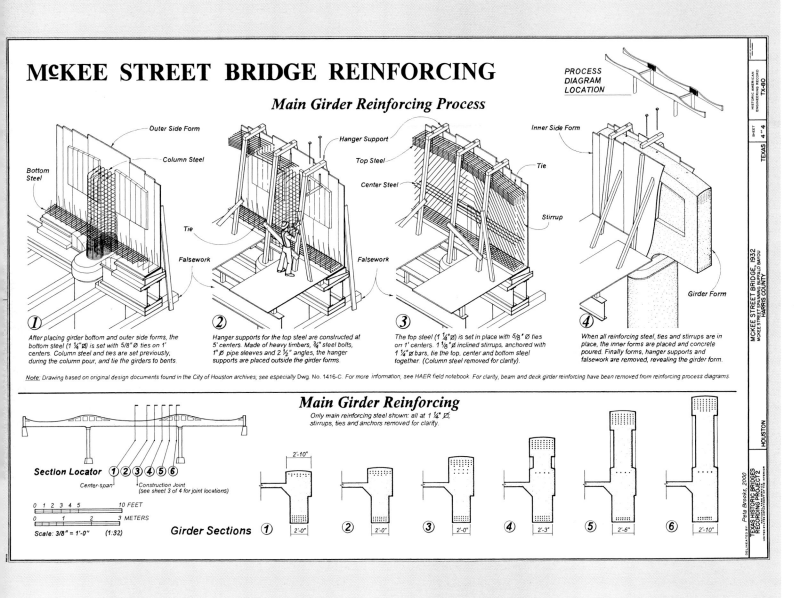

McKEE STREET BRIDGE REINFORCING

Main Girder Reinforcing Process

PROCESS DIAGRAM LOCATION

Outer Side Form

Column Steel

Bottom Steel

Tie

Falsework

Hanger Support

Top Steel

Center Steel

Falsework

Inner Side Form

Tie

Stirrup

Girder Form

① After placing girder bottom and outer side forms, the bottom steel (1 ¼" Ø) is set with 5/8" Ø ties on 1' centers. Column steel and ties are set previously, during the column pour, and tie the girders to bents.

② Hanger supports for the top steel are constructed at 5' centers. Made of heavy timbers, ¾" steel bolts, 1" Ø pipe sleeves and 2 ½" angles, the hanger supports are placed outside the girder forms.

③ The top steel (1 ¼" Ø) is set in place with 5/8" Ø ties on 1' centers. 1 ⅛" Ø inclined stirrups, anchored with 1 ¼" Ø bars, tie the top, center and bottom steel together. (Column steel removed for clarity).

④ When all reinforcing steel, ties and stirrups are in place, the inner forms are placed and concrete poured. Finally forms, hanger supports and falsework are removed, revealing the girder form.

Note: Drawing based on original design documents found in the City of Houston archives; see especially Dwg. No. 1416-C. For more information, see HAER field notebook. For clarity, beam and deck girder reinforcing have been removed from reinforcing process diagrams.

Main Girder Reinforcing

Only main reinforcing steel shown: all at 1 ¼" Ø; stirrups, ties and anchors removed for clarity.

Section Locator ① ② ③ ④ ⑤ ⑥

Center-span   Construction Joint (see sheet 3 of 4 for joint locations)

0 1 2 3 4 5   10 FEET
0   1   2   3 METERS

Scale: 3/8" = 1'-0"   (1:32)

Girder Sections ① 2'-0"   ② 2'-0"   ③ 2'-0"   ④ 2'-3"   ⑤ 2'-6"   ⑥ 2'-10"

2'-10"

MCKEE STREET BRIDGE, 1932
MCKEE STREET SPANNING BUFFALO BAYOU
HARRIS COUNTY

TEXAS   SHEET 4" 4

HISTORIC AMERICAN ENGINEERING RECORD   TX-80

HOUSTON

Pete Brooks, 2000

TEXAS HISTORIC BRIDGES RECORDING PROJECT 2

Figure 6.14c
The construction and structural character of the main girders of the McKee Street Bridge, shown on this sheet, demonstrate the size and placement of the reinforcing rods and the formwork of the bridge. Notice the difference in the number of reinforcing rods in the top and bottom of the girder depending on whether it is ruled by compression or shear. The drawings along the bottom explain how the number of reinforcing rods changed along the length of the girder depending on the bending moments.

The Willamette River courses through the heart of Portland, and within a 5-mile stretch of the river is a remarkable collection of movable bridges. The Oregon Department of Transportation asked HAER to document these ten structures, which represent a veritable who's who of turn-of-the-century bridge designers. Many outstanding U.S. bridge engineers are represented along Portland's waterfront, including J. A. L. Waddell and John L. Harrington, Ira G. Hedrick, Joseph B. Strauss, Ralph Modjeski, Holton D. Robinson, David B. Steinman, and Gustav Lindenthal. Four of the bridges are movable spans dating from the first two decades of the twentieth century. The Steel Bridge (1912) and the Broadway Bridge (1913) are particularly interesting because of their unusual mechanical movements.

The Steel Bridge is a vertical lift span conceptualized and patented by John Alexander Low Waddell, perhaps the most notable American consulting bridge engineer at the turn of the century. The detailing and final design were developed by his partner, John Lyle Harrington, a mechanical engineering genius who developed the gearing, counterweights, and lift mechanisms (see fig. 6.15). The bridge is of interest because of its unusual mechanical mechanism and its massive scale. Designed to carry both vehicular and railroad traffic, the size of its individual members is impressive (see fig. 6.17). Of even more interest is the mechanical movement, whereby the vertical members of the lower railroad deck, when raised, telescope into the trusses supporting the upper vehicular deck (see fig. 6.18). The Steel Bridge was constructed when oceangoing vessels included tall-masted ships, hence the double lift (see fig. 6.16).

The Broadway Bridge (1913) was the first bascule span built in Portland and at the time the longest bascule in the United States. The

Figure 6.15

Waddell & Harrington developed the Steel Bridge in Portland, Oregon, as a vertical lift span to accommodate two levels of traffic: the lower deck carries the Union Pacific–Southern Pacific Railroad, while the upper carries street traffic. This view shows the bridge with the lower railroad deck raised—its normal stance. As few trains or tall ships pass the bridge on any given day, the verticals that carry the railroad deck actually telescope inside the vertical elements of the upper deck truss structure to permit virtually uninterrupted vehicular and river traffic.

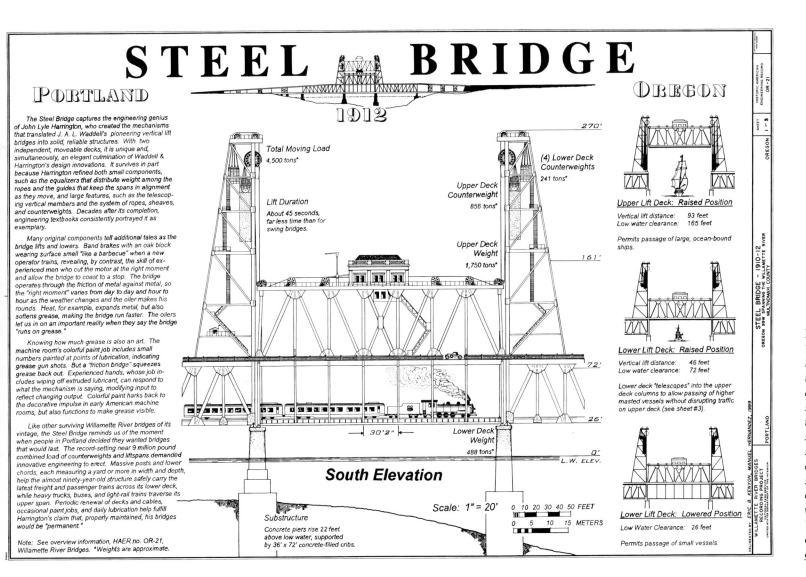

Figure 6.16
The title sheet of the Steel Bridge drawings includes the south elevation and diagrams of the bridge showing the various positions of the vertical lift span. The highest lift stage was required to accommodate tall-masted ships, common in the early twentieth century, when the bridge was built. Today, it is raised only to allow the largest ocean-going vessels to pass.

earliest successful bascules constructed in the United States were the Scherzer rolling lift and the Rall, of which the Broadway is one of the few surviving examples. The Broadway Bridge was designed by Ralph Modjeski, and its bascule spans were manufactured by the Strobel Steel Construction Company of Chicago, which had a license to manufacture the Rall patent bascule.

Bascules may be single or double leaf, the single used for short spans and the double for longer ones (*see fig. 6.19*). The advantage of the double is that it has smaller leaves, which can be raised more quickly and thus require lighter counterweights and moving parts. For the Rall type, the leaves are designed to roll backward as they swing upward, a complicated mechanical movement that probably was the reason for its limited use (*see figs. 6.20, 6.21, and 6.22*). The most common types were the simple trunnion or Chicago bascule and the multiple trunnion or Strauss. The Scherzer rolling lift was used by the railroads because its mechanics and lift mechanism were suited for heavier loads.

HAER has worked with the National Park Service, the Federal Highway Administration, state departments of transportation, the engineering community, the National Trust for Historic Preservation, and the Advisory Council on Historic Preservation for more than a quarter century to make the public aware of the country's outstanding legacy of historic bridges. In 1987 surface transportation legislation singled out historic bridges for special treatment, requiring that bridge replacement and rehabilitation be implemented "in a manner that encourages the inventory, retention, rehabilitation, adaptive reuse, and future study of historic bridges." Despite all the attention, recent statistics indicate that over half the historic bridges in the United States have been destroyed during the

Figure 6.17
This isometric view of the Steel Bridge illustrates the tower and lift deck configuration, showing the cable, sheaves, counterweight, and motor mechanisms.

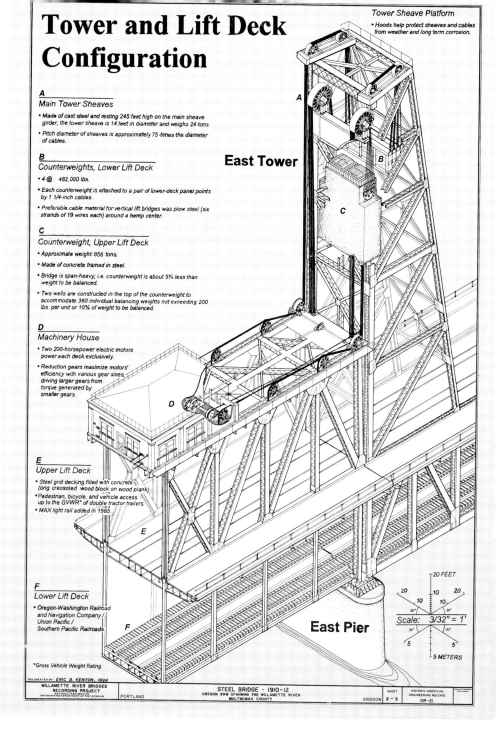

Tower and Lift Deck Configuration

Tower Sheave Platform
• Hoods help protect sheaves and cables from weather and long term corrosion.

A
Main Tower Sheaves
• Made of cast steel and resting 245 feet high on the main sheave girder, the tower sheave is 14 feet in diameter and weighs 24 tons.
• Pitch diameter of sheaves is approximately 75-times the diameter of cables.

B
Counterweights, Lower Lift Deck
• 4 @ 482,000 lbs.
• Each counterweight is attached to a pair of lower-deck panel points by 1 1/4-inch cables.
• Preferable cable material for vertical lift bridges was plow steel (six strands of 19 wires each) around a hemp center.

C
Counterweight, Upper Lift Deck
• Approximate weight: 856 tons.
• Made of concrete framed in steel.
• Bridge is span-heavy; i.e. counterweight is about 5% less than weight to be balanced.
• Two wells are constructed in the top of the counterweight to accommodate 360 individual balancing weights not exceeding 200 lbs. per unit or 10% of weight to be balanced.

D
Machinery House
• Two 200-horsepower electric motors power each deck exclusively.
• Reduction gears maximize motors' efficiency with various gear sizes, driving larger gears from torque generated by smaller gears.

E
Upper Lift Deck
• Steel grid decking filled with concrete. (orig. creosoted wood block on wood plank)
• Pedestrian, bicycle, and vehicle access up to the GVWR* of double tractor trailers.
• MAX light rail added in 1985.

F
Lower Lift Deck
• Oregon-Washington Railroad and Navigation Company / Union Pacific / Southern Pacific Railroads.

*Gross Vehicle Weight Rating

East Tower

East Pier

Scale: 3/32" = 1'

DELINEATED BY: ERIC B. KENYON, 1999
WILLAMETTE RIVER BRIDGES RECORDING PROJECT
NATIONAL PARK SERVICE
UNITED STATES DEPARTMENT OF THE INTERIOR
PORTLAND

STEEL BRIDGE - 1910-12
OREGON 99W SPANNING THE WILLAMETTE RIVER
MULTNOMAH COUNTY

OREGON 2-3

SHEET

HISTORIC AMERICAN ENGINEERING RECORD
OR-21

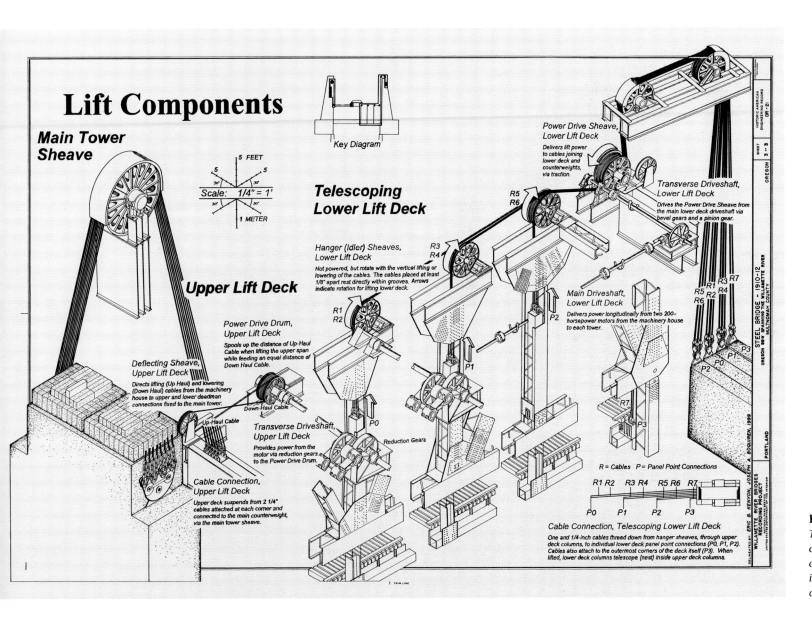

Lift Components

Main Tower Sheave

Key Diagram

5 FEET
5 | 5
30° | 30°
Scale: 1/4" = 1'
30° | 30°
1 METER

Telescoping Lower Lift Deck

Upper Lift Deck

Power Drive Sheave, Lower Lift Deck
Delivers lift power to cables joining lower deck and counterweights, via traction.

Hanger (Idler) Sheaves, Lower Lift Deck
Not powered, but rotate with the vertical lifting or lowering of the cables. The cables placed at least 1/8" apart rest directly within grooves. Arrows indicate rotation for lifting lower deck.

Transverse Driveshaft, Lower Lift Deck
Drives the Power Drive Sheave from the main lower deck driveshaft via bevel gears and a pinion gear.

Main Driveshaft, Lower Lift Deck
Delivers power longitudinally from two 200-horsepower motors from the machinery house to each tower.

Power Drive Drum, Upper Lift Deck
Spools up the distance of Up-Haul Cable when lifting the upper span while feeding an equal distance of Down Haul Cable.

Deflecting Sheave, Upper Lift Deck
Directs lifting (Up Haul) and lowering (Down Haul) cables from the machinery house to upper and lower deadman connections fixed to the main tower.

Down-Haul Cable

Up-Haul Cable

Transverse Driveshaft, Upper Lift Deck
Provides power from the motor via reduction gears to the Power Drive Drum.

Reduction Gears

Cable Connection, Upper Lift Deck
Upper deck suspends from 2 1/4" cables attached at each corner and connected to the main counterweight, via the main tower sheave.

R = Cables   P = Panel Point Connections

Cable Connection, Telescoping Lower Lift Deck
One and 1/4-inch cables thread down from hanger sheaves, through upper deck columns, to individual lower deck panel point connections (P0, P1, P2). Cables also attach to the outermost corners of the deck itself (P3). When lifted, lower deck columns telescope (nest) inside upper deck columns.

R5 R6   R3 R4   R1 R2   P2   P1   P0   R7   P3

R5 R1 R3 R7
R6 R2 R4

R1 R2   R3 R4   R5 R6   R7
P0   P1   P2   P3

TRIM LINE

Figure 6.18
The cable, sheaves, and counterweight operation of the lift span are shown in this isometric drawing of the Steel Bridge.

Figure 6.19

A contextual view of the Portland, Oregon, Broadway Bridge in the raised position illustrates the need for a movable span by revealing that the Willamette is a working river with grain elevators and cement storage and loading terminals along its banks.

Figure 6.20

This HAER photograph of the Broadway Bridge depicts the Rall-hinged trunnion, wheel, and track mechanism around which the lift span rolled and rotated to the open position.

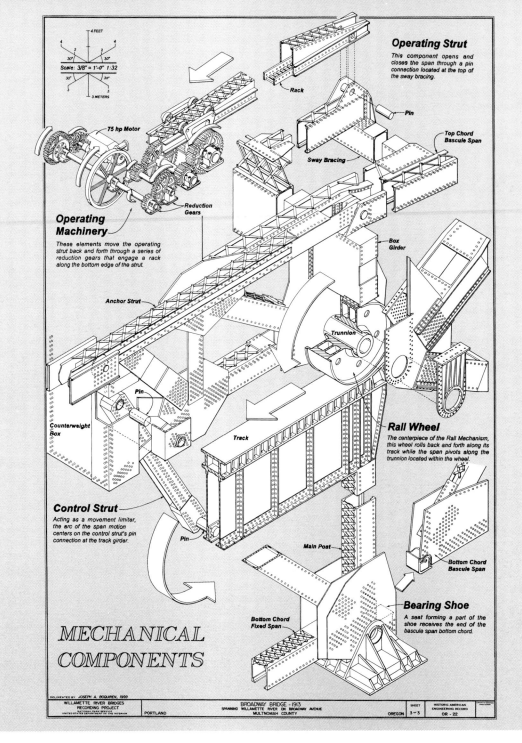

Operating Strut
This component opens and closes the span through a pin connection located at the top of the sway bracing.

Rack

Pin

Top Chord Bascule Span

Sway Bracing

Operating Machinery
These elements move the operating strut back and forth through a series of reduction gears that engage a rack along the bottom edge of the strut.

75 hp Motor

Reduction Gears

Anchor Strut

Box Girder

Trunnion

Pin

Counterweight Box

Track

Pin

Rail Wheel
The centerpiece of the Rail Mechanism, this wheel rolls back and forth along its track while the span pivots along the trunnion located within the wheel.

Control Strut
Acting as a movement limiter, the arc of the span motion centers on the control strut's pin connection at the track girder.

Pin

Main Post

Bottom Chord Bascule Span

Bearing Shoe
A seat forming a part of the shoe receives the end of the bascule span bottom chord.

Bottom Chord Fixed Span

MECHANICAL COMPONENTS

DELINEATED BY: JOSEPH A. BOQUIREN, 1999

WILLAMETTE RIVER BRIDGES RECORDING PROJECT
NATIONAL PARK SERVICE
UNITED STATES DEPARTMENT OF THE INTERIOR

PORTLAND

BROADWAY BRIDGE - 1913
SPANNING WILLAMETTE RIVER ON BROADWAY AVENUE
MULTNOMAH COUNTY

OREGON

SHEET 3 OF 3

HISTORIC AMERICAN ENGINEERING RECORD
OR - 22

last twenty years. To address this alarming situation, HAER continues to work with the engineering profession, transportation agencies, and other preservation organizations to improve the feasibility of preserving historic bridges. Certainly there can be no argument against preserving a selection of the country's best and most representative historic spans. Until sufficient funding is available and highway officials and the public view the preservation of historic bridges as an integral part of the overall vision of the nation's transportation system, HAER will continue to respond to the imperative to record historic bridges.

Figure 6.21
In combination with the previous photograph, this drawing suggests the appearance of the Rall mechanism of the Broadway Bridge. Some mechanical movements are so complicated that the only way to understand their operation is a three-dimensional model or motion picture interpretation.

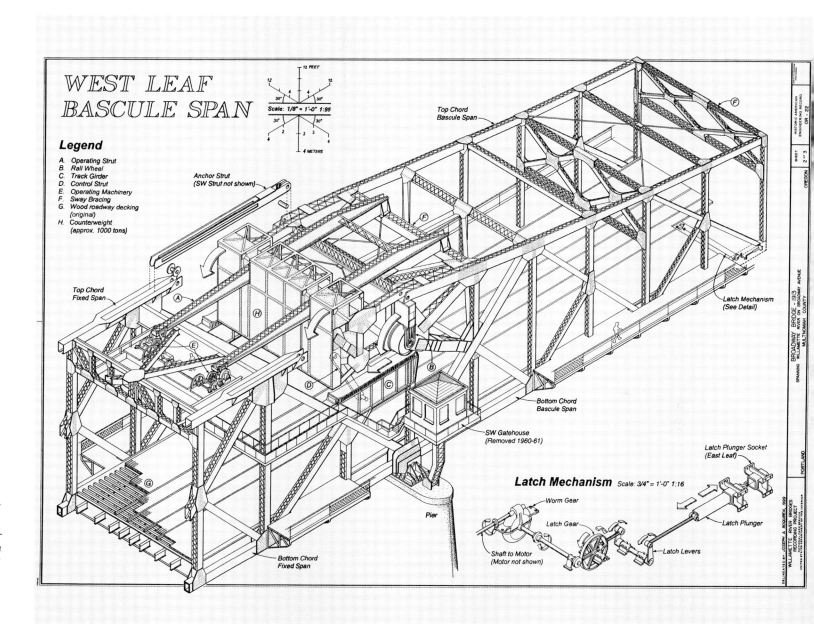

Figure 6.22

This isometric drawing illustrates the entire bascule component of the Broadway Bridge, including the latch mechanism that makes the leaves of the two movable spans continuous, creating a homogeneous bridge in the closed position.

WEST LEAF BASCULE SPAN

Scale: 1/8" = 1'-0" 1:96

12 FEET

12   12
30°   30°
4
30°   30°
4   2   2   4
4 METERS

Legend

A. Operating Strut
B. Rail Wheel
C. Track Girder
D. Control Strut
E. Operating Machinery
F. Sway Bracing
G. Wood roadway decking (original)
H. Counterweight (approx. 1000 tons)

Top Chord Bascule Span

Anchor Strut (SW Strut not shown)

Top Chord Fixed Span

Latch Mechanism (See Detail)

Bottom Chord Bascule Span

SW Gatehouse (Removed 1960-61)

Bottom Chord Fixed Span

Pier

Latch Mechanism Scale: 3/4" = 1'-0" 1:16

Latch Plunger Socket (East Leaf)

Worm Gear

Latch Gear

Latch Plunger

Shaft to Motor (Motor not shown)

Latch Levers

BROADWAY BRIDGE - 1913
SPANNING WILLAMETTE RIVER ON BROADWAY AVENUE
MULTNOMAH COUNTY
PORTLAND   OREGON
HISTORIC AMERICAN ENGINEERING RECORD
SHEET 2 of 3   OR - 22
DELINEATED BY JOSEPH A. BOQUIREN 1999
WILLAMETTE RIVER BRIDGES RECORDING PROJECT

CHAPTER 7

RECORDING STRUCTURAL AND MECHANICAL SYSTEMS

John A. Burns, FAIA

At the time of its completion in 1890, the Auditorium Building in Chicago (now Roosevelt University) was the largest structure of its kind in the United States. The program included a hotel, an auditorium, and offices, with the hotel and office building wrapping around the theater in the center (see fig. 7.1). Economics had dictated three different uses for the site. The developers planned to include income-producing functions to offset the large deficits expected in operating the theater. The Auditorium Building was thus an early example of mixed-use development. The arrangement of the various functions was determined by real estate market conditions, light and ventilation requirements, and the characteristics of the site. The challenge to architects Dankmar Adler and Louis H. Sullivan was to integrate the three disparate functions, each with different needs, into a cohesive design (see fig. 7.2).

It is a common misconception that Dankmar Adler was the sole engineering genius behind the Auditorium Building, but responsibility for designing the foundations, structural framing, and heating and plumbing systems was shared by numerous consultants. The design of much of the elevator, electrical, and service facilities was apparently the work of the equipment manufacturers. There was no general contractor on the project, but Adler, who directed most of the construction work, acted much like a modern-day project manager. Full-time supervision of the work was handled by an experienced builder.

The challenges encountered during documentation of the Auditorium Building are becoming more prevalent as HABS takes on a greater number of structures built since the late nineteenth century. At the beginning of the nineteenth century, building technologies were limited to masonry bearing-wall or heavy-frame construction, with fireplaces for heating and outdoor privies. By the end of the century, technologies had evolved to include steel skeleton and light-frame construction, as well as central heating and other mechanical systems such as plumbing and electricity. Architecture and engineering developed as professions during the century, along with many specialized building trades. As a result, buildings generally grew more complex in terms of materials, structure, and function, and large buildings became common.

The Auditorium Building exemplifies these changes in building technology. It is a large building that is significant in many areas: design and construction, structural systems, mechanical systems, and aesthetics. It is also a structure for which a great many documentary records exist, another increasingly common phenomenon.

The HABS documentation of the Auditorium Building demonstrates the evolution of approaches, techniques, and technologies used to

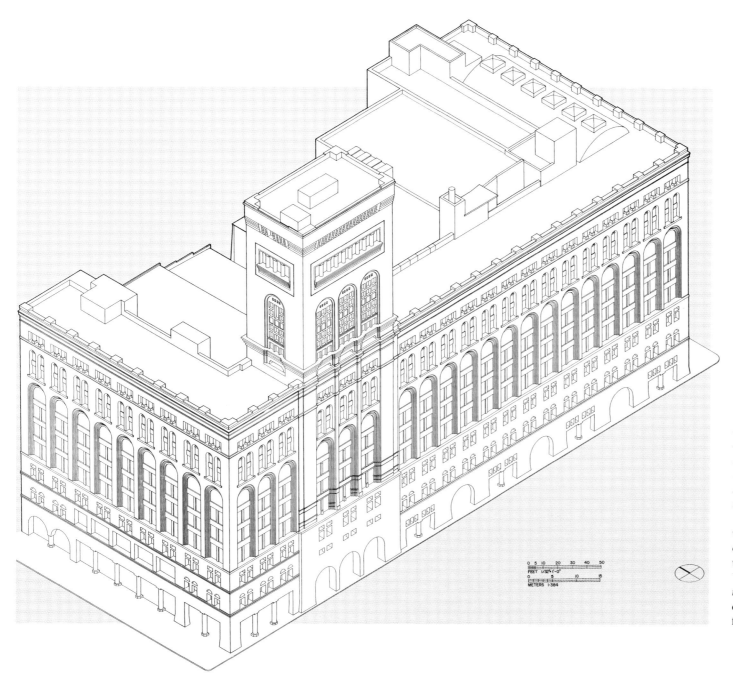

Figure 7.1
*The program for the
Auditorium Building in
Chicago combined three
unrelated functions—a
theater, a hotel, and an
office building. The
design solution placed the
theater in the interior,
wrapped the hotel around
two sides, and added an
office space along the
third side, with one
entrance on each street
elevation. An aerial iso-
metric drawing was used
to portray the arrange-
ment and massing of the
three functional areas.
The particular angle of
view in this drawing was
chosen to delineate the
west and south facades.
The east facade was
recorded in a separate
elevation drawing (see
fig. 7.3).*

Figure 7.2
The imposing stone exterior of the Auditorium Building offers little hint of its interior complexities. This view of the Michigan Avenue facade, taken shortly after the building's completion in 1890, is not yet marred by fire escapes and shows the weather station on top of the tower, since removed. Note that the ground-level camera station does not reveal the functional massing of the building. Compare this perspective-corrected photograph with the photogrammetric image in fig. 7.4.

record historic structures over the past forty years. The first HABS documentation was compiled in 1963 as part of a larger project to record significant Chicago School buildings, one of the earliest forays into the documentation of large-scale buildings. The completed records comprised six measured drawings, six photographs, and ten data pages. The measured drawings were composed on the original small HABS sheets, requiring an extremely small scale and a correspondingly limited amount of detail. The one floor plan showed the building before a 20-foot arcade was cut through the southern side to allow the widening of Congress Street. The one elevation drawing (*see fig. 7.3*) was produced with photogrammetry from glass-plate stereopairs (*see fig. 7.4*) and an analog plotter. An interesting feature in the latter drawing is the graphic reconstruction of the observation platform on the top of the tower, the dimensions of which were derived from historic photographs and contemporary glass plate images (compare figs. 7.2 and 7.4) using a technique called reverse perspective analysis. (See the "Measured Drawings" chapter for more information about this technique.) The section drawing was derived from an 1888 drawing published in *Inland Architect* and a 1961 drawing by Skidmore, Owings and Merrill, who had been retained by Roosevelt University for restoration and remodeling work. As with the elevation, the section drawing was augmented by photogrammetric reconstruction of the observation platform. Two detail drawings showed the hotel dining room in restored condition. In all instances, the HABS drawings cite their sources and describe how they were modified.

Half of the six photographs were details, and more than half of the ten data pages consisted of bibliography. Taken out of context, the documentation seems inadequate for a nationally significant building. However, the overall Chicago School project was efficient and pro-

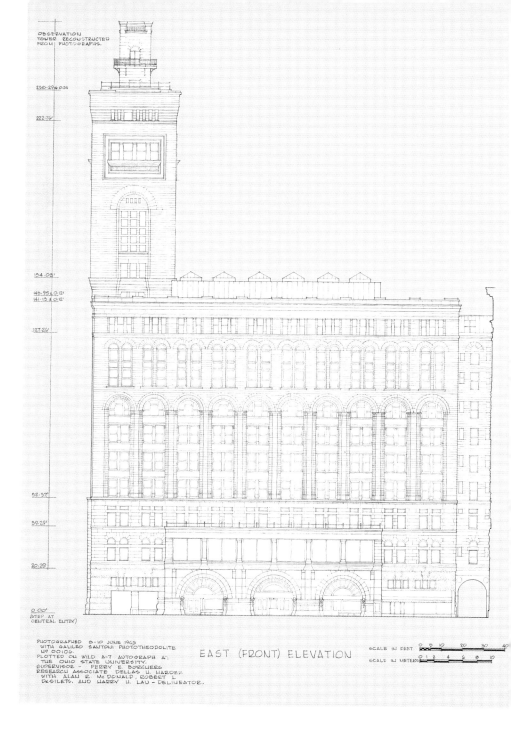

Figure 7.3
The Michigan Avenue facade of the Auditorium Building was recorded in 1963 using stereophotogrammetry. Combining historic photographs of the observation tower, which is no longer extant, and information from the photogrammetric plates made it possible to include the tower in the drawing.

Figure 7.4
The Michigan Avenue facade drawing was produced from 5″ × 7″ glass plate stereopairs. Fiducial marks around the perimeter of each image are part of the photogrammetric survey control, precisely locating the image in relation to the known geometry of the phototheodolite (camera) and optical characteristics of the lens. Note that the photograph is not perspective-corrected. Perspective distortion is corrected in the plotting process to produce an orthographic drawing. Compare this image with fig. 7.2, which is perspective-corrected.

duced a substantial amount of documentation in a short time. It proved the viability of architectural photogrammetry, made effective use of the large amount of available historical records, photographed tantalizing glimpses of the collective significance of Chicago School buildings, and provided a solid bibliographic record for subsequent researchers.

In 1979 Roosevelt University asked HABS/HAER to produce a comprehensive documentary record as the basis for its stewardship of the building. This documentation would enable the university to consider historical significance and integrity when planning for the changing needs of the school. While Roosevelt University had access to extensive archival materials, it did not have a complete, consistent, and accurate set of drawings showing existing conditions in the building, which had undergone numerous alterations and additions after its construction. In fact, the volume of records available to review, cross-check, and verify presented a logistical problem. Nevertheless, this source material made possible the compilation of an extensive graphic and written history and description of the building. Historic photographs and drawings were located. Selected examples were photographically copied if permission could be obtained, and the remainder were cited in the bibliography. The resulting documentation presents a unique holistic assessment of all the significant features and systems of the Auditorium Building.

The university identified two specific goals for the measured drawings: (1) to locate structural members and (2) to record existing floor plans and room functions. Because of budget constraints, floor plans for the theater were beyond the scope of the project, although the theater was recorded in the section drawings. For the same reasons, the project did not produce measured drawings of the decorative elements of the building.

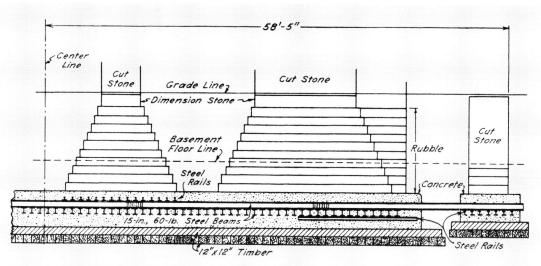

DETAIL I : TOWER FOUNDATION OF AUDITORIUM

Architectural research traditionally focuses on the architect as the principal person responsible for a building. Although the Auditorium Building research went beyond Adler and Sullivan, it was difficult to find detailed information on most of the other people associated with the design and construction of the building. Time and budget constraints precluded an exhaustive search. Budgets notwithstanding, the key point is that structures with multiple areas of significance will probably require multiple areas of historical research if a complete history is to be compiled. For instance, information on the roof trusses over the theater was found in an article on building construction details in *The Engineering and Building Record,* the plumbing specifications were found in a book called *Industrial Chicago,* and drawings and a description of the foundation were found in an engineering pamphlet on settlement of buildings in Chicago (*see fig. 7.5*). A book with drawings and a description of the precedent for the hydraulic stage

Figure 7.5

Documentary records other than original drawings and specifications are rarely available for foundations. This illustration of the Auditorium Building foundation, from a 1955 engineering pamphlet titled Observed and Computed Settlements of Structures in Chicago, *was probably based on a drawing published in the* Inland Architect *in July 1888. The widely varying point and linear loads of the Auditorium Building foundations and poor bearing capacity of the soil necessitated the use of spread footings. The center and left footings in this illustration, which are part of one large footing that carries the seventeen-story masonry tower, are considerably larger than the right footing, which supports the ten-story exterior wall.*

equipment (at the Budapest Opera House in Hungary) was serendipitously found in a used-book store in Pennsylvania. Additional information was found in court records detailing the troubled financial history of the building, including allegations of structural deficiencies.

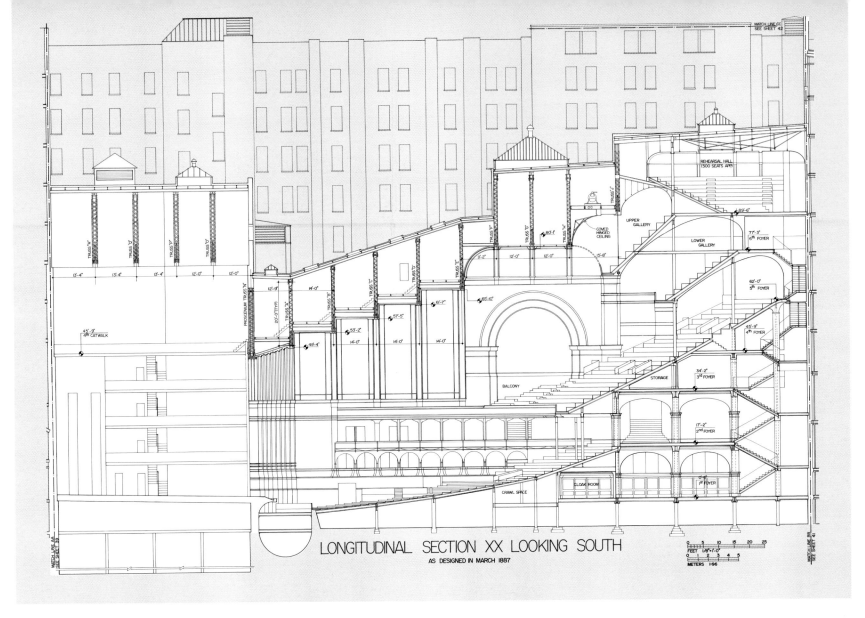

LONGITUDINAL SECTION XX LOOKING SOUTH

AS DESIGNED IN MARCH 1887

Figures 7.6 and 7.7

Two section drawings were necessary to portray the major changes made in the Auditorium Building design as construction progressed. These two sheets show only the theater portion as it was originally designed and as it was eventually completed four years later. Similar changes were made in the hotel and office portions of the building. In the stage house, note the hydraulic equipment added under the stage and the four floors of service space over the roof trusses. In the hall, the orchestra pit was modified, truss A was raised to accommodate the new organ, and a hinged ceiling was installed over the lower gallery. The roof trusses over the rehearsal hall were changed from Fink trusses to built-up plate girders. Above the roof of the theater, the banquet hall was supported by two large trusses spanning the full width of the theater. These changes placed more weight on the foundations, which had been designed to support the earlier configuration.

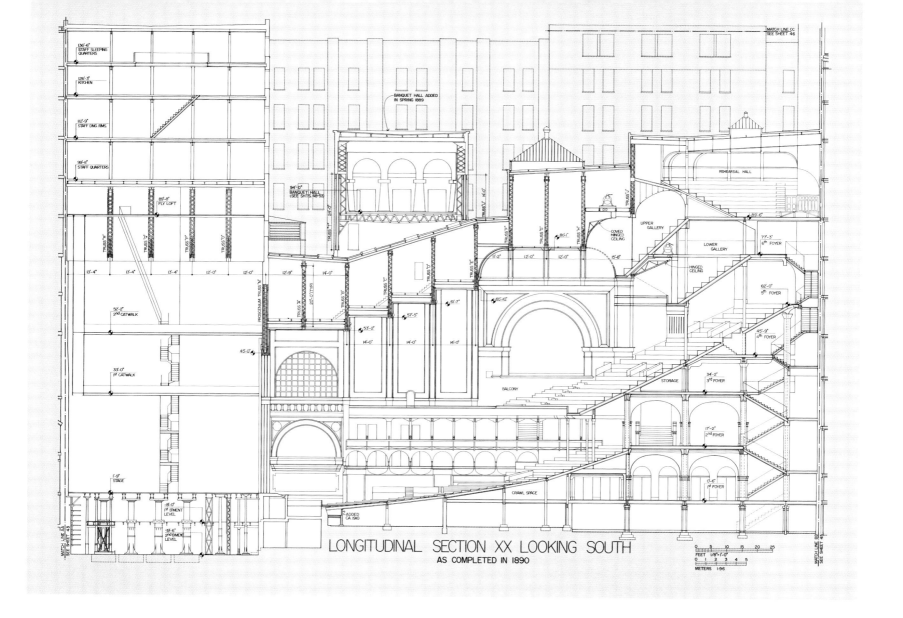

136'-6"
STAFF SLEEPING QUARTERS

126'-3"
KITCHEN

112'-9"
STAFF DNG. RMS.

99'-4"
STAFF QUARTERS

89'-8"
FLY LOFT

TRUSS "V" TRUSS "T" TRUSS "S" TRUSS "Q"

13'-4" 13'-4" 13'-4" 12'-0" 12'-0"

52'-2"
2nd CATWALK

33'-0"
1st CATWALK

45'-0"

1'-9"
STAGE

-8'-0"
1st B'MENT LEVEL

-19'-6"
2nd B'MENT LEVEL

PROSCENIUM TRUSS "N"

TRUSS "M"

20'-0" (TYP)

TRUSS "B"

TRUSS "A"

TRUSS "O"

TRUSS "P"

TRUSS "D"

TRUSS "E"

TRUSS "F" 46'-0"

12'-9" 14'-0"

53'-2"

57'-5"

14'-0" 14'-0" 14'-0"

61'-7"

60'-10"

BALCONY

ADDED CA. 1910

CRAWL SPACE

BANQUET HALL ADDED IN SPRING 1889

94'-0"
BANQUET HALL (SEE SHTS. 48-55)

24'-0"

11'-2" 12'-0" 12'-0"

15'-8"

COVED HINGED CEILING

HINGED CEILING

UPPER GALLERY

LOWER GALLERY

STORAGE

MATCH LINE CC
SEE SHEET 46

REHEARSAL HALL

89'-6"

77'-3"
6th FOYER

62'-0"
5th FOYER

45'-9"
4th FOYER

34'-2"
3rd FOYER

17'-2"
2nd FOYER

0'-6"
1st FOYER

MATCH LINE BB
SEE SHEET 45

MATCH LINE AA
SEE SHEET 43

LONGITUDINAL SECTION XX LOOKING SOUTH
AS COMPLETED IN 1890

FEET 1/8"=1'-0"
0 5 10 15 20 25
METERS 1:96
0 1 2 3 4 5

Structural Systems

In modern terms, the Auditorium Building was built on a fast track, as its design was not complete when construction started. Moreover, the actual program for the building changed while it was under construction. The decision to add a banquet hall above the theater roof and four floors of service space above the stage house was made when the building was already at the fifth floor level. This was only one of many major changes made during construction.

Because of these modifications, historic drawings to which the recording team had access had to be verified against the building itself. In fact, some of what appeared in original drawings may not ever have been built, since the design changed as construction progressed. The HABS team made two versions of the longitudinal section to compare the structure as designed in 1886 to the structure as completed in 1890 (see figs. 7.6 and 7.7).

A complication in documenting structural and mechanical systems is that HABS/HAER is nondestructive in its investigations. The team members do not open up walls or remove fireproofing from steel beams to determine construction details. The Auditorium Building documentation relied on earlier documentary sources for information on hidden features. Where possible, the information was visually verified. Structural information was delineated by isometric drawings of each floor so that the columns, beams, and bearing walls could be located (see fig. 7.8). Structural details were recorded through reference to documentary sources supplemented by construction photographs where possible. Exposed structural members, chiefly the major roof trusses, were photographed (see fig. 7.9).

Mechanical Systems

Several of the original Auditorium Building mechanical systems have nearly vanished. Heat has been supplied to the building from off-site boilers since 1893. The foundations for the direct-current dynamos are all that remain of the original electrical power plant under the Wabash Avenue sidewalk. Information on the plumbing comes primarily from published specifications, with two still-operating sewage ejector pumps among the only remaining original equipment (see fig. 7.10). The hydraulic stage equipment was substantially intact, although the stage was immobilized and the water tanks that supplied the necessary head had been removed from the tower (see fig. 7.11). The hydraulic elevator equipment, which utilized the same water supply as the stage equipment, had been replaced. Despite these limitations, a reasonably complete history and description of the systems was compiled from the remaining physical evidence and documentary sources. Significant remaining equipment was photographed. Only the ventilation systems of the theater and banquet hall were recorded in measured drawings (see fig. 7.12).

Aesthetics

The basic scheme of a theater wrapped with a hotel and office building is recognizable throughout the evolution of the design for the Auditorium Building, as evinced in records for seven different designs for the facades. Citations for the drawings of the unbuilt designs were included in the written history. In the 1963 measured drawings of the completed building, HABS recorded the Michigan Avenue facade using stereophotogrammetry (see fig. 7.3). The massing of the building was recorded in an aerial axonometric drawing that shows the Congress Street and Wabash Avenue facades and the roof configuration (see fig. 7.1). The north elevations of the tower and the Congress Street wing of the hotel were recorded in the longitudinal section of the theater.

The designs of the interior spaces were recorded with both historic and contemporary large-format photographs and written documentation, but not with measured drawings, as they were outside the scope of the project. The overall design for the interior of the theater was recorded in longitudinal and cross-sectional drawings of the building, but with little detail. The majority of the graphic records for the interior decorative elements consist of copies of historic photographs (see fig. 7.13). The stage and stage equipment were recorded photographically.

The banquet hall was the one interior space recorded in some detail, as it was undergoing restoration and thus was easily accessible for measuring. A HABS team produced hand-mea-

Figure 7.8

The complex structural system of the basement of the Auditorium Building is best revealed in a cutaway aerial isometric. This isometric drawing portrays the depth as well as the plan of the basement and illustrates the size and massing of the footings, as well as the placement, size, and configuration of the bearing walls and columns. The annotations further explain features in the basement, such as the hydraulic stage equipment and the vaults under the sidewalk. Similar isometric drawings of each floor portray structural information in three dimensions. Nonbearing partitions were not included, providing Roosevelt University, which now owns the building, with information on how to combine the small hotel rooms into larger spaces.

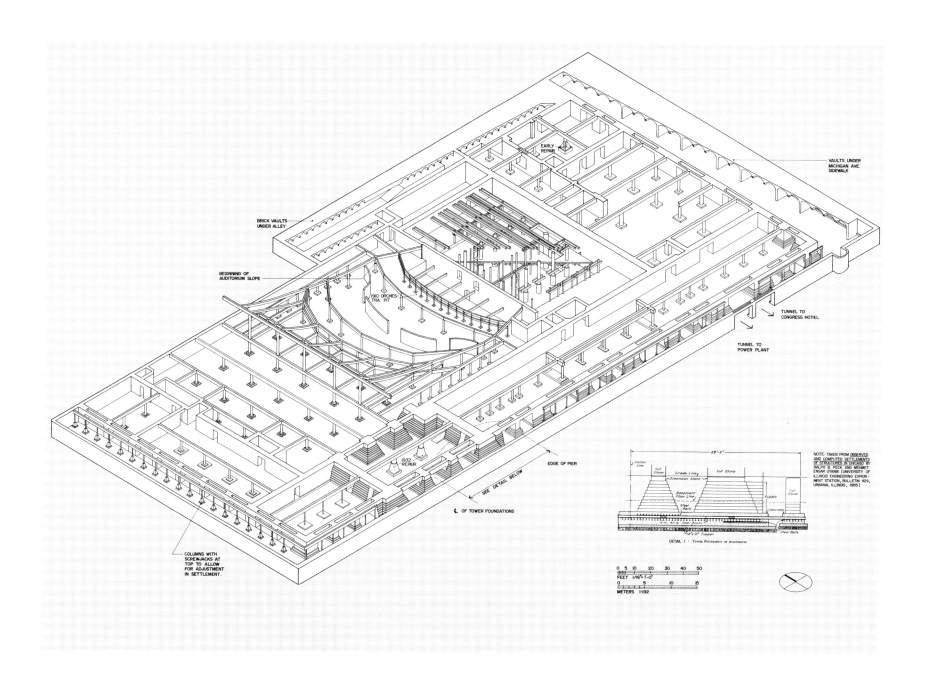

VAULTS UNDER
MICHIGAN AVE.
SIDEWALK

EARLY
REPAIR

BRICK VAULTS
UNDER ALLEY

BEGINNING OF
AUDITORIUM SLOPE

1910 ORCHES-
TRA PIT

TUNNEL TO
CONGRESS HOTEL

TUNNEL TO
POWER PLANT

1932
REPAIR

EDGE OF PIER

SEE DETAIL BELOW

℄ OF TOWER FOUNDATIONS

COLUMNS WITH
SCREWJACKS AT
TOP TO ALLOW
FOR ADJUSTMENT
IN SETTLEMENT.

NOTE: TAKEN FROM OBSERVED
AND COMPUTED SETTLEMENTS
OF STRUCTURES IN CHICAGO BY
RALPH B. PECK AND MEHMET
ENSAR UYANIK (UNIVERSITY OF
ILLINOIS ENGINEERING EXPERI-
MENT STATION, BULLETIN 429,
URBANA, ILLINOIS, 1955.)

58'-5"

Center
Line

Cut
Stone

Grade Line

Dimension Stone

Cut Stone

Basement
Floor Line

Cut
Stone

Rubble

Steel
Rails

Concrete

15-in. 40-lb Steel Beams

12"x12" Timber

Steel Rails

DETAIL 1 : TOWER FOUNDATION OF AUDITORIUM

0 5 10   20   30   40   50
FEET 1/16"=1'-0"

0   5   10   15
METERS 1:192

Figure 7.9
Fire protection for the trusses in the theater attic of the Auditorium Building is provided by the heavy plaster ceiling of the theater and the terra-cotta deck over the trusses, which support the roof surface. While not ideal from a fire safety standpoint, this method made the trusses easy to record in large-format photographs.

Figure 7.10
Among the only remaining original plumbing equipment in the Auditorium Building are these two sewage ejector pumps, which still pump sewage up to the level of the street sewer from the stage basement.

Figure 7.11
The hydraulic rams in the Auditorium Building have been fixed in position at stage level, making them inoperable. A new floor was built at the level the stage would have been when lowered.

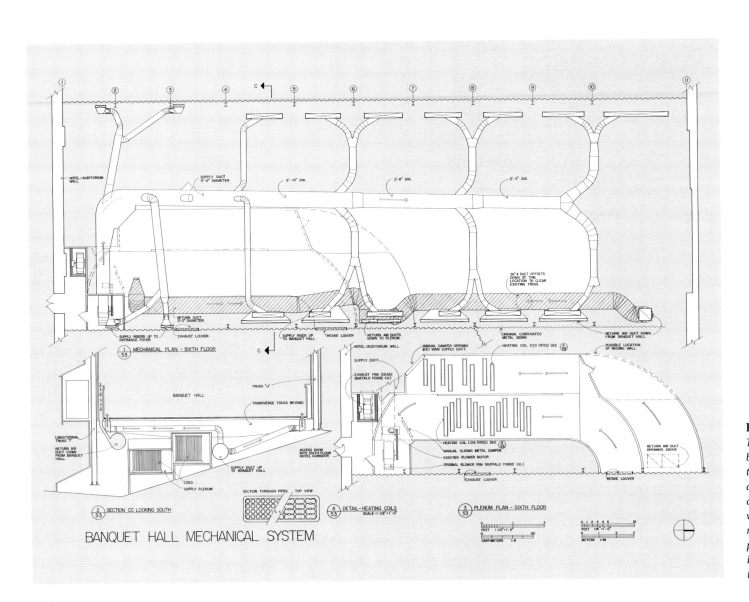

Figure 7.12
The restoration of the banquet hall in the Auditorium Building allowed access to the self-contained heating and ventilating system of the room. The system is independent of the main building, as it sits above the theater roof.

Figure 7.13

Photocopies of promotional photographs made of the Auditorium Building shortly after completion form the basis for the HABS photographs of the building's decorative features, saving the contemporary photographer a great deal of on-site time. Copying historic photographs may not always be possible if their owners are not willing to let them enter the public domain.

Figure 7.14

Contemporary photogrammetric plotting, combined with photogrammetric analysis of historic photographs of the Auditorium Building, allowed the delineation of the original musicians' gallery in the banquet hall and the re-creation of lighting fixtures that had been removed. Dimensions for the missing elements were determined photogrammetrically from the dimensions of objects in the historic photographs. This technique is called reverse perspective analysis.

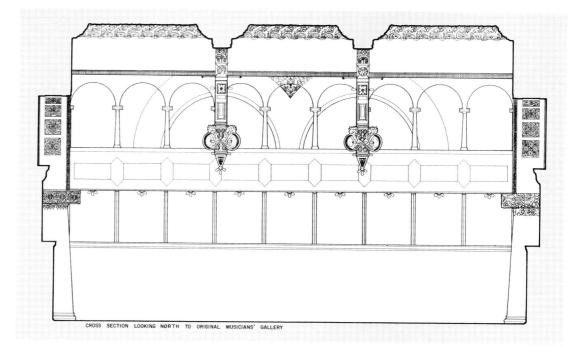

CROSS SECTION LOOKING NORTH TO ORIGINAL MUSICIANS' GALLERY

Figure 7.15

This historic photograph of the lowest level of the under-stage area shows the base of the hydraulic rams for moving stage floor sections. The pit is for the center rear ram, which could lower that section of the floor to this level. The other floor sections could be lowered only to the mezzanine level.

sured drawings of the plans and structural and mechanical systems. These drawings were supplemented by a photogrammetric drawing of both extant and missing decorative features produced from historic and contemporary photographs (*see fig. 7.14*) previously commissioned for the restoration of the musicians' gallery and lighting fixtures in 1979.

In 2001 the Auditorium Theatre Council began planning a long-needed expansion of the green room and other support spaces by renovating the space under the stage floor. The proposed work would require the demolition of the remaining Aesphaelia hydraulic stage equipment (*see fig. 7.15*). After consultation with the Chicago Landmarks Commission and the Illinois Historic Preservation Office, the Auditorium Theatre Council agreed to mitigate the removal of the stage equipment by producing measured and interpretive drawings, a description of its operation, and photographs of the dismantling, as well as leaving representative elements of the hydraulic system in place. This documentation was meant to be an addendum to the 1980 HABS documentation, and it was carefully planned by the interested parties, including HABS/HAER. The goal was to balance intellectual and historical interests with the practical limitations of time and funding. As a result, an integrated amalgam of different techniques and technologies was used for the project. Recording technologies included laser scanning and hand measuring, computer-aided drafting, a video of a theater consultant walking among and explaining various features, digital snapshots, large-format photographs, and written data. The measured drawings were the first in the HABS collection to be derived from laser scans.

The Auditorium Theatre Council retained McClier to produce the documentation. The architects were confronted with the difficult challenge of measuring and drawing a two-story space beneath a stage, with a later interstitial floor. The area was densely packed with large hydraulic rams for raising and lowering sections of the stage floor and horizontal rams with sheaves for raising and lowering the stage curtain, a fire curtain, and a painting frame for producing sets. The space also contained piping and mechanical controls that dated both from the original construction and from later building upgrades.

Laser scanning, a technology commonly used to record piping in refineries, was selected to gather the dimensional information necessary to produce the drawings. Quantapoint, a laser-scanning service, was retained for the work. The company's laser scanner, with a rotating head and 60° vertical angle of view, was positioned to make ninety-seven overlapping scans, called point clouds, which were stitched together to produce a digital 3-D model of the space and equipment (*see fig. 7.16*). The field-of-view characteristics of this particular scanner were ideal for the confined and poorly lighted spaces under the stage. Using proprietary CAD software, the digital 3-D model was cut horizontally to produce floor plan and reflected ceiling plan drawings and vertically to produce section drawings. The data extraction process was semiautomated, requiring some user intervention by the laser scanning service to produce base CAD drawings to architectural conventions; like conventional drawings, it required somewhat greater attention to detail to meet HABS/HAER standards.

The AutoCAD drawings produced by Quantapoint were organized with separate layers for walls, piping, and other building elements. All line work was of a single line weight. McClier modified the drawings to meet the graphic

requirements of HABS/HAER standards as well as to interpret previously removed original piping and equipment and later additions that were not part of the original stage hydraulic system. Quantapoint also provided what they call "Qviews" of the ninety-seven scans, which are near-photographic conversions of the laser scans into 360° JPEG images with a 6-to-1 aspect ratio (*see fig. 7.17*). Qviews can be viewed in any image-editing software and are extremely useful for verifying conditions shown in the CAD drawings.

Laser scanning relies on light rays to gather measurable data, and thus has limitations similar to those of photogrammetry. One such limitation is that any laser scanner, like a camera, records only what it can see. Obscured areas are left unrecorded. McClier hand-measured features out of the scanner's field of view and entered the additional information into the base CAD drawings produced from the laser scans. Some features could not be completely measured until they had been partially dismantled. Thus, as with other measuring techniques, supplemental trips to the job site for additional measurements were a necessary and expected part of the process. However, laser scanning and photogrammetry are both ungeneralized, which means they produce dimensional data that may not have been desired initially but can be extracted later without returning to the job site. These processes reduce return visits, unlike hand measuring, which records only data from actual measurements.

The stage equipment drawings are densely packed with information and include three floor plans, two reflected ceiling plans, two sections, a sheet of details, and a sheet of operational schematics. Complex enough to require extensive annotations, they are most easily understood in consultation with the associated

Figure 7.16
The Quantapoint laser scanner used at the Auditorium Building produces a 360° × 60° field of view called a Qview, which is downloaded to a laptop computer.

Figure 7.17

The near-photographic quality of this Qview is readily apparent. The scan, made as demolition was under way, recorded the view from the upstage center floor section to the basement level and was centered facing downstage (west). The mezzanine floor opening is visible in the upper left and right of the view. Racks for holding rolled screens along the back wall of the mezzanine level are visible at the extreme left and right. Bases of the two rows of rams for the movable floor sections are left and right of center. In the distance, against the wall of the orchestra pit, are specialty rams, the small vertical rams for the star lifts downstage left and downstage right (partially obscured), and a horizontal jigger ram with sheaves for operating the stage curtain downstage right (partially obscured). A pressurized water tank was used to operate the rams following the removal of the original gravity-feed water tank in the tower.

photographs and written data. The three types of HABS documentation are always intended to complement one another, as all three are essential to fully understand a resource. The floor plans focus on the mechanical features and include minimal architectural details (*see fig. 7.18*). The annotations identify and describe components and locate the camera station and direction of view of the formal HABS photographs. The reflected ceiling plans are the most complex, depicting the intricate system of structural support and movable elements of the stage floor (*see fig. 7.19 and fig. 7.20*). The section drawings show the range of movement of the movable sections of the stage floor (*see fig. 7.21 and fig. 7.22*).

The formal HABS documentation for the Auditorium Building includes 70 measured drawings, 119 large-format photographs, and more than 90 pages of written data, plus field records consisting of 8 photogrammetric glass plates, a CD with the Qviews, a CD with the vector CAD drawings, a video, and several folders of field measurements and paper records. These items make the Auditorium Building one of the most thoroughly documented structures in the collection. Ideally, though, HABS will return to the building. Despite all the work that was done, the most significant interior space, the theater, was not documented as extensively as the rest of the building because the 1980 documentation concentrated on areas of the building occupied by Roosevelt University. In addition, the roof trusses over the stage house and theater have not been measured and drawn. Nonetheless, within the HABS/HAER collections, the documentation of the Auditorium Building was a pioneering effort at recording the multiple areas of significance typically found in a large commercial building.

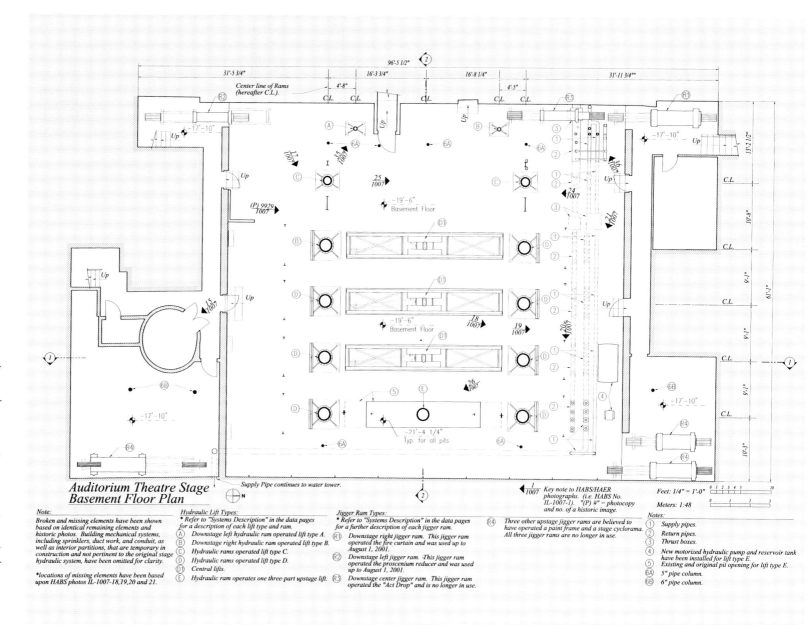

Figure 7.18

This measured drawing of the basement level, emphasizing the mechanical equipment, is annotated to identify features and camera stations and the direction of the formal HABS photographs. Missing features that could be verified and located from documentary sources were graphically restored in dashed lines. Recent intrusive features such as sprinklers, ductwork, electrical conduits, and temporary partitions were omitted from the drawing.

Auditorium Theatre Stage
Basement Floor Plan

Supply Pipe continues to water tower.

Note:
Broken and missing elements have been shown based on identical remaining elements and historic photos. Building mechanical systems, including sprinklers, duct work, and conduit, as well as interior partitions, that are temporary in construction and not pertinent to the original stage hydraulic system, have been omitted for clarity.

*locations of missing elements have been based upon HABS photos IL-1007-18,19,20 and 21.

Hydraulic Lift Types:
* Refer to "Systems Description" in the data pages for a description of each lift type and ram.
Ⓐ Downstage left hydraulic ram operated lift type A.
Ⓑ Downstage right hydraulic ram operated lift type B.
Ⓒ Hydraulic rams operated lift type C.
Ⓓ Hydraulic rams operated lift type D.
Ⓓ¹ Central lifts.
Ⓔ Hydraulic ram operates one three-part upstage lift.

Jigger Ram Types:
* Refer to "Systems Description" in the data pages for a further description of each jigger ram.
Ⓡ¹ Downstage right jigger ram. This jigger ram operated the fire curtain and was used up to August 1, 2001.
Ⓡ² Downstage left jigger ram. This jigger ram operated the proscenium reducer and was used up to August 1, 2001.
Ⓡ³ Downstage center jigger ram. This jigger ram operated the "Act Drop" and is no longer in use.

Ⓡ⁴ Three other upstage jigger rams are believed to have operated a paint frame and a stage cyclorama. All three jigger rams are no longer in use.

↙ 1/1007 Key note to HABS/HAER photographs. (i.e. HABS No. IL-1007-1). "(P) #" = photocopy and no. of a historic image.

Feet: 1/4" = 1'-0"
Meters: 1:48

Notes:
① Supply pipes.
② Return pipes.
③ Thrust boxes.
④ New motorized hydraulic pump and reservoir tank have been installed for lift type E.
⑤ Existing and original pit opening for lift type E.
6A 5" pipe column.
6B 6" pipe column.

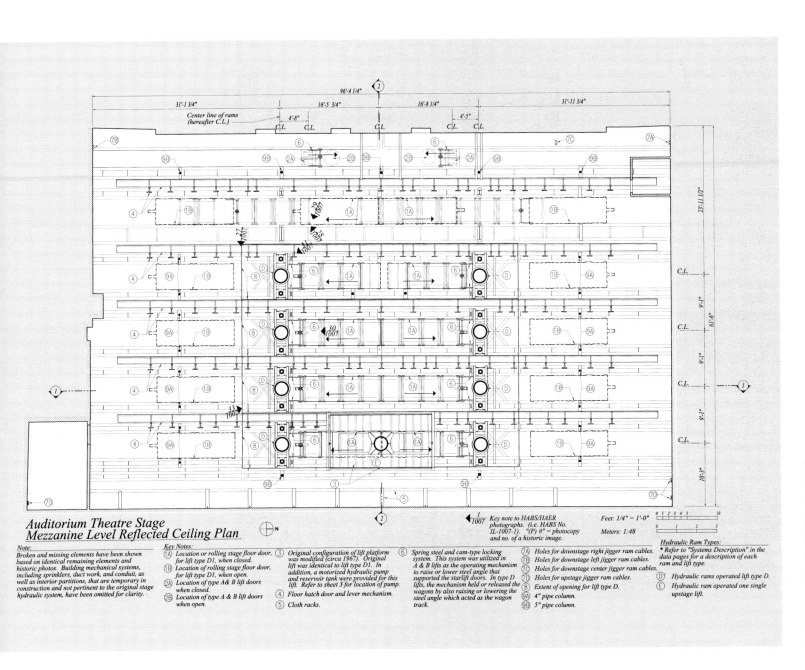

Auditorium Theatre Stage
Mezzanine Level Reflected Ceiling Plan

Note:
Broken and missing elements have been shown based on identical remaining elements and historic photos. Building mechanical systems, including sprinklers, duct work, and conduit, as well as interior partitions, that are temporary in construction and not pertinent to the original stage hydraulic system, have been omitted for clarity.

Key Notes:
1A Location or rolling stage floor door, for lift type D1, when closed.
1B Location of rolling stage floor door, for lift type D1, when open.
2A Location of type A& B lift doors when closed.
2B Location of type A & B lift doors when open.
3 Original configuration of lift platform was modified (circa 1967). Original lift was identical to lift type D1. In addition, a motorized hydraulic pump and reservoir tank were provided for this lift. Refer to sheet 3 for location of pump.
4 Floor hatch door and lever mechanism.
5 Cloth racks.
6 Spring steel and cam-type locking system. This system was utilized in A & B lifts as the operating mechanism to raise or lower steel angle that supported the starlift doors. In type D lifts, the mechanism held or released the wagons by also raising or lowering the steel angle which acted as the wagon track.
7A Holes for downstage right jigger ram cables.
7B Holes for downstage left jigger ram cables.
7C Holes for downstage center jigger ram cables.
7D Holes for upstage jigger ram cables.
8 Extent of opening for lift type D.
9A 4" pipe column.
9B 5" pipe column.

Hydraulic Ram Types:
* Refer to "Systems Description" in the data pages for a description of each ram and lift type.
D Hydraulic rams operated lift type D.
E Hydraulic ram operated one single upstage lift.

$\frac{1}{1007}$ Key note to HABS/HAER photographs. (i.e. HABS No. IL-1007-1). "(P) #" = photocopy and no. of a historic image.

Feet: 1/4" = 1'-0"
Meters: 1:48

Figure 7.19
The highly complex features in this measured reflected ceiling plan of the mezzanine level of the stage are difficult to understand, so the drawing is heavily annotated. The notes include camera stations and the direction of the formal HABS photographs. Recent intrusive features were omitted.

Figure 7.20
After layers were removed during demolition, it was possible to photograph a number of the stage floor features that previously were not visible.

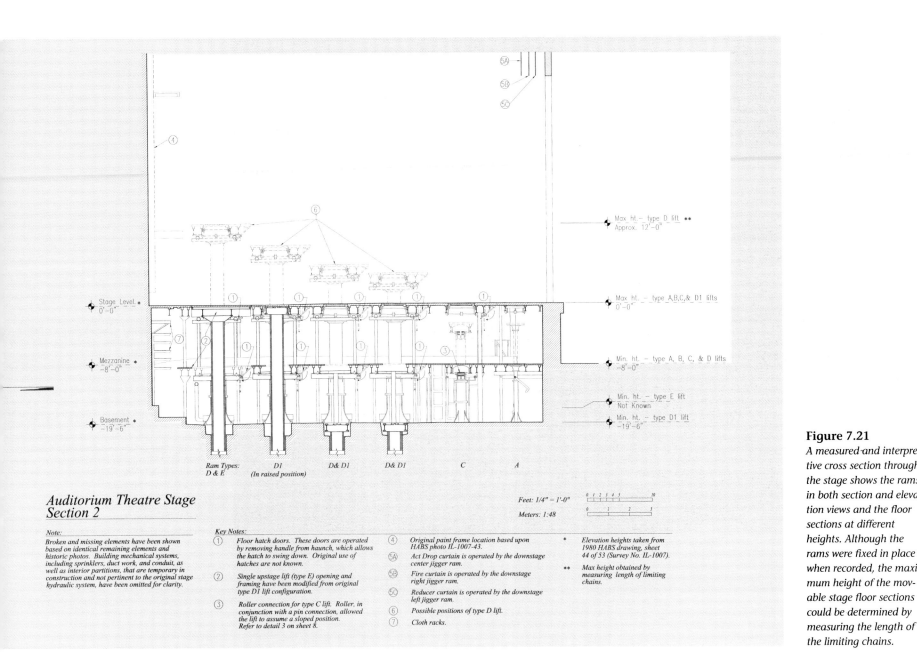

Max. ht. — type D lift **
Approx. 12'-0"

Max. ht. — type A,B,C,& D1 lifts
0'-0"

Stage Level *
0'-0"

Min. ht. — type A, B, C, & D lifts
-8'-0"

Mezzanine *
-8'-0"

Min. ht. — type E lift
Not Known

Min. ht. — type D1 lift
-19'-6"

Basement *
-19'-6"

Ram Types:
D & E   D1   D & D1   D & D1   C   A
           (In raised position)

Auditorium Theatre Stage
Section 2

Feet: 1/4" = 1'-0"

Meters: 1:48

0 1 2 3 4 5   10

0   1   2   3

Note:

Broken and missing elements have been shown based on identical remaining elements and historic photos. Building mechanical systems, including sprinklers, duct work, and conduit, as well as interior partitions, that are temporary in construction and not pertinent to the original stage hydraulic system, have been omitted for clarity.

Key Notes:

① Floor hatch doors. These doors are operated by removing handle from haunch, which allows the hatch to swing down. Original use of hatches are not known.

② Single upstage lift (type E) opening and framing have been modified from original type D1 lift configuration.

③ Roller connection for type C lift. Roller, in conjunction with a pin connection, allowed the lift to assume a sloped position. Refer to detail 3 on sheet 8.

④ Original paint frame location based upon HABS photo IL-1007-43.

⑤A Act Drop curtain is operated by the downstage center jigger ram.

⑤B Fire curtain is operated by the downstage right jigger ram.

⑤C Reducer curtain is operated by the downstage left jigger ram.

⑥ Possible positions of type D lift.

⑦ Cloth racks.

* Elevation heights taken from 1980 HABS drawing, sheet 44 of 53 (Survey No. IL-1007).

** Max height obtained by measuring length of limiting chains.

Figure 7.21
A measured and interpretive cross section through the stage shows the rams in both section and elevation views and the floor sections at different heights. Although the rams were fixed in place when recorded, the maximum height of the movable stage floor sections could be determined by measuring the length of the limiting chains.

Figure 7.22
This historic photograph shows how different sections of the stage floor could be raised and inclined.

CHAPTER 8

RECORDING HISTORIC SHIPS

Richard K. Anderson, Jr.

*T**he unique character and environment of historic ships require specialized recording techniques and technologies. In concept, the three media most commonly used to document land-based structures—written reports, photography, and measured drawings—are easily adapted to the documentation of vessels. The preparation of reports and photographs for a ship usually requires the same research methods, skills, and equipment as for a stationary structure. Creating measured drawings of ships, on the other hand, introduces some unique challenges. In contrast to land-based structures, most vessels contain very few straight lines or flat surfaces. A firm grasp of geometry and measurement techniques is necessary to properly handle the measurement complications introduced by a vessel's orientation and the compound curves of the hull, decks, and other features. Methods for obtaining the lines and recording structural features of a vessel may depend on the vessel's size, location (floating or in a dry dock), condition (intact or deteriorated), and attitude (upright, listing, or upside down).*

A full set of measured drawings of a ship commonly contains a least a starboard profile (right side elevation), deck plans, an inboard profile (longitudinal section), and sections (cross sections). Further sheets may show a port profile (left side elevation), sail and rigging plans, engine room and propulsion machinery, significant hull structure, interior features, and details of fittings and hardware. Conceptually, these views are analogous to the types of drawings produced for buildings. The principal information about the shape of a vessel's hull, however, is recorded in lines drawings. These are essentially a series of topographic maps of the hull viewed from the three Cartesian coordinate axes—water lines (seen from above), buttock lines (seen from the side), and sections (seen from the ends). One to three diagonal sections may also be taken. Ordinarily, only the port or starboard half of the hull is diagrammed this way, since symmetry is assumed. However, documentation of both sides of a hull may be warranted if information is sought on nonsymmetrical changes of shape.

The two case studies that follow focus on some of the field techniques used to measure and draw ships, since approaches to written and photographic coverage of ships do not require specialized changes analogous to those needed for measured drawings.

Recording the Schooner *Alabama*

The scope of the *Alabama* recording project included both lines drawings and construction drawings, as well as a written history and large-format photographs. The *Alabama* is a wooden-

Digital Technologies for Recording Historic Ships
Todd A. Croteau

HABS/HAER/HALS routinely investigates innovative technologies for documentation projects. In recent years, survey techniques for historic vessels have expanded greatly with advancements in digital technologies. In particular, numerous "black box" devices have been developed that record measurements with laser, infrared, or photographic equipment. This equipment basically captures xyz coordinates from remote stations to model the complex curvilinear geometry of a ship's surface. To prepare a surface model or lines drawing, most of these systems require postprocessing procedures in naval architecture or other three-dimensional software packages.

Remote surveying equipment should be used with some caution, however, because subtle details can be missed without the careful eye of educated field staff studying the resource at close range. In addition, remote measuring techniques require unobstructed sight of an object's surface. If the device cannot "see" part of an object that is hidden from view, another technique must be employed to fill in the gaps. These technologies are just one tool in the surveyor's box, and choosing the right tool for the job is crucial to the success of any project.

To test these new technologies for recording historic vessels and determine the most efficient ways to use them in documenting these complex resources, HAER partnered with Mystic Seaport Museum and several other maritime institutions. A grant from the National Center for Preservation Technology and Training (NCPTT) provided for the purchase of several measuring systems and the development of technical bulletins on the capabilities and operation of each. Markham Starr, ships documentation manager for Mystic Seaport, managed the project and developed the guidelines. The equipment and instructions are available to museums and other research programs interested in recording historic vessels with measured drawings. The following technologies for recording historic ships were studied under NCPTT grants.

Electronic Distance Measuring (EDM) Device

Referred to by many as a "total station," an EDM device emits a single laser or infrared beam toward the object of study. This beam is reflected back to the machine, and time, distance, angle, and relation to other points are recorded in a series of xyz coordinates. When multiple points are taken, a "point cloud" represents the shape of the object. These points can be downloaded into a variety of computer modeling and drawing programs for processing. HABS/HAER/HALS uses an EDM device to establish and verify wireframe models of sites, with details filled in with a variety of other recording techniques.

Coordinate Measuring Machine (CMM)

A CMM, designed to record existing information from a small, complex three-dimensional object, consists of an articulated arm with a pressure-sensitive ball at its tip. When the arm touches the surface of an object, it records an xyz coordinate relative to other points on the surface. A point cloud is developed that represents the surface of the object. This device has been used to quickly and accurately record half-hull models for the purpose of creating lines drawings. An assembly-line approach can be taken to maximize the efficiency of the equipment and staff.

3-D Laser Scanners

One of the more promising techniques for achieving fast, highly accurate recording of complex three-dimensional shapes such as ship hulls is 3-D laser scanning. Laser scanners can capture more than 1,000 points—or measurements—per second, with an accuracy of +/- 4 mm. Laser scanners can measure a large ship's hull in a half day, work that would take a week using traditional hand methods. This equipment was used to study the Statue of Liberty (see the monuments case study) and the Bodie Island Lighthouse in Cape Hatteras National Seashore prior to its renovation.

Virtual Documentation/Interpretation

Another study grant provided by NCPTT utilized CAD drawings to develop virtual re-creations of historic vessels, including the USS *Monitor*, the Civil War ironclad that sank off Cape Hatteras. Using the CAD data, designers at the Computer Sciences Corporation Center for Advanced Marine Engineering developed a software program to re-create the *Monitor* in a computer environment that operates under the laws of physics. The vessel can be placed in different sea states, weather conditions, harbors, and other characteristics to see how it might have maneuvered under real situations. Water can be seen splashing over the bow as it breaks through a wave, and the turret rotates toward its target. Stresses and other factors can be calculated from the computer model. Many of the great vessels lost to the sea could be relaunched in these virtual waters for research and interpretation.

Figure 8.1
The condition of the pilot schooner Alabama *at the time of the HABS recording project was documented with large-format photography. The original sailing rig was removed in the 1950s and replaced with what is shown in this photograph.*

hulled, sail-assisted pilot schooner built in 1926 for the Mobile Bay Pilots Association of Mobile, Alabama. It was built in Pensacola, Florida, to the designs of Thomas F. McManus, a noted designer of fishing schooners from the northeastern United States. The lines of several of McManus's vessels were recorded for the Historic American Merchant Marine Survey (HAMMS) in the 1930s, but no construction drawings were included.

The *Alabama* was recorded afloat, since there were no funds or opportunities to haul the ship and perform fieldwork out of the water. Since the lines had already been lifted by the owner, HAER replotted them from the owner's notes and focused most fieldwork on construction drawings. In addition to lines, the drawing schedule called for plans of the main deck and the 'tween deck (the first full-length deck between the main deck and the hold), inboard and outboard profiles, sections, and details. Since the ship lacked masts and rigging at the time of recording, the team searched for historic photographs that could be relied upon in "restoring" these features in a drawing (*see figs. 8.1, 8.2, and 8.3*).

Because the decks and features of the *Alabama* were a combination of compound curves and inclined surfaces, horizontal measurements alone were not enough to produce accurate drawings. Vertical measurements had to be made to some datum plane, in this case an arbitrary plane locked to and moving with the ship, since the ship was afloat. This plane was created by setting up a transit midships (halfway between sides and ends) on top of a deckhouse, and "leveling" it first athwartships (side to side) with respect to the ship and then fore and aft with respect to the earth's horizon.

Leveling athwartships was performed by setting the telescope to 0° vertical inclination and then adjusting the instrument's leveling screws until the scope sighted equal measure-

Figure 8.2
This is a print of a circa 1926 photograph copied by HAER with the vessel owner's permission. The photograph can be dated by the name Alabama *on the starboard bow (research of the ship registry showed this was the ship's name from 1926 to 1928). This photograph was one of many historic photographs used to reconstruct the* Alabama's *original sailing rig on the first sheet of the measured drawings (see fig. 8.3).*

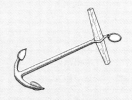

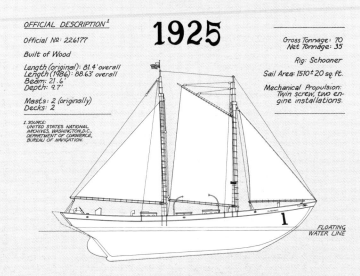

Figure 8.3
The original profile of the Alabama shown on the HAER title sheet was derived from several historic photographs as well as HAER field data; notes below the graphic scale record the sources and describe the limitations of the effort. This sheet includes the official description of the ship, a brief history, and details of the recording project.

ments above the extreme edges of the deck at points directly to port and starboard of the transit station. Leveling fore and aft was achieved by adjusting the leveling screws (not the scope) until the scope approximately sighted the horizon (water) over the stern, taking into account the up-and-down motion caused by waves. (Unlike leveling athwartships, leveling of the transit fore and aft is not particularly critical.) The distance to the tip of the bow beneath this plane was then recorded as one means to recover the plane in case the scope was accidentally upset. From this stage, all vertical measurements were taken by setting the zero end of a tape to the point whose height was needed, then following readings through the scope until a minimum reading was found as the tape was inclined in various directions. These readings were recorded in the field notes. (Geometrically, the minimum distance from a point to a plane is the true distance between them; it also lies on a line normal or square to the plane).

The plan of the main deck was recorded with a combination of horizontal and vertical measurements. To begin, a copper nail (to prevent rust marks) was set in the rail at the ship's centerline, and the location recorded. The end of a 100-foot tape was then secured to the nail, and a series of other copper nails was set in the centerlines of the port and starboard rails, going aft to the stern of the ship. Each pair of nails (one port, one starboard) was set equidistant from the bow nail. The distance of each pair of nails from the bow nail and from each other were recorded, as were their distances beneath the datum plane. An error estimate of +/- ¼ inch for vertical measurements was allowed for any movement of the transit caused by the deflection of the deckhouse roof under the transit operator's shifting weight. Less was allowed for the horizontal dimensions. Later on, these

dimensions made it possible for the team to draw a plan of the rail projected into a horizontal plane with the aid of trigonometry.

Though the ship was assumed to be symmetrical, a centerline check was performed by setting the transit scope approximately parallel to the ship's centerline and sighting measurements on a tape drawn athwartships between each pair of rail tacks. These points were plotted after the rail plan was drawn to see if they lay in a straight line. Similar check measurements were made to the deck edges.

Measurements of deckhouses, planking, anchor winch, steering box, and other features were made along the deck. Error introduced by the deck camber (upward curve or crown of deck) was judged to be negligible when dimensions taken athwartships were projected into a plan view. Profiles (elevations) were made of deckhouses and other features for which diagonal measurements (in planes parallel to the ship's vertical centerline plane) and the distances of corners and roof peaks beneath the transit datum plane were carefully recorded. Materials were noted as well.

Once the main deck was completed, vertical measurements were made through the fore and aft ventilators to spots carefully marked on the 'tween deck centerline below. The transit was then moved belowdecks for use on the 'tween deck. A datum plane was set parallel to the one above by procedures similar to those used on the main deck—sightings were made up to the underside of the main deck when leveling the instrument athwartships, and fore and aft alignment was made using the spots marked earlier on the 'tween deck. Measurements above these spots were subtracted from the ones made from the first datum plane and the leveling screws adjusted until the same result was obtained at both spots. Then the distance

between the two planes was recorded. Vertical measurements of 'tween deck features were taken in the same way as on the main deck.

Belowdecks, the team was careful to record all structures such as deck beams, clamps, frames, deck stanchions, carlins, mast partners, knees, ceiling planking, and so forth (*see figs. 8.4, 8.5, and 8.6*). Expert ship carpenters from a museum inspected the vessel with the team to help identify materials and point out matters of significance or interest. Features on deck were recorded by offsets from a centerline (marked on deck with a chalk line) and by triangulations among features. Bunks, galley and cabin stoves, appliances, engines, and auxiliaries were recorded, as were certain pieces of hardware. As much information as possible regarding equipment was collected from builders' plates. Even so, much of the *Alabama*'s structure was inaccessible, principally frames behind the ceiling planking and keelsons in the bottom. Field photographs were taken liberally to supplement the field notes.

After the ship's lines were plotted and faired, a profile and plan of the main deck and rails were made. (The team was gratified to see that the sheer line they had measured agreed almost exactly with the owner's twenty-year-old lines information.) All drawings were executed at a scale of ½" = 1'-0" to preserve detail (*see figs. 8.4, 8.5, 8.7, 8.8, and 8.9*). Since the drawings are projected views of a nonrectilinear object, considerable use of trigonometry, triangulation, and cross-references between plan and profile views was necessary to construct accurate drawings. Frequently, fore-and-aft measurements had to be plotted on the profile before they could be projected onto the deck plan, and vice versa.

The *Alabama*'s owner possessed a valuable collection of photographs that had been made

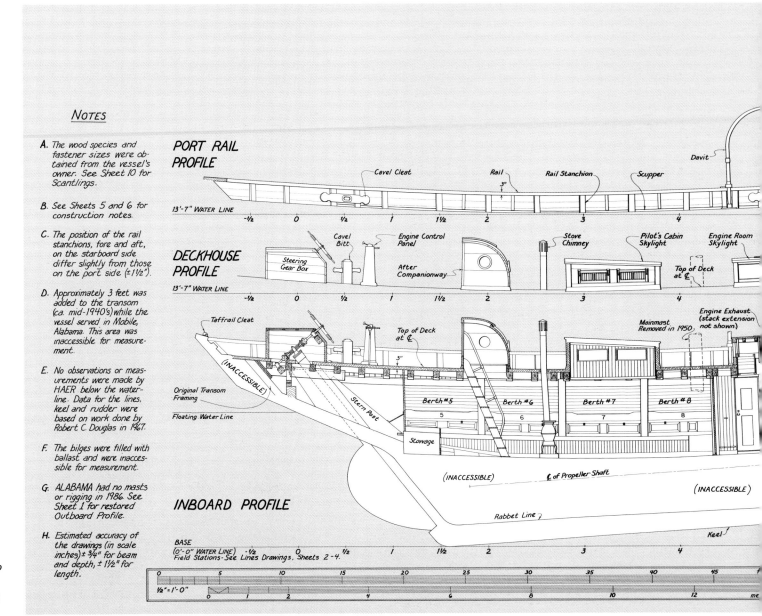

Figures 8.4 and 8.5
This section through the Alabama was carefully drawn from field data at ½" scale. Inaccessible areas are noted, as are other observations pertinent to the vessel's structure and the team's recording procedures. A long graphic scale is included to enable users to scale from enlargements, reductions, or the drawing itself.

NOTES

A. The wood species and fastener sizes were obtained from the vessel's owner. See Sheet 10 for Scantlings.

B. See Sheets 5 and 6 for construction notes.

C. The position of the rail stanchions, fore and aft, on the starboard side differ slightly from those on the port side (±1½").

D. Approximately 3 feet was added to the transom (ca. mid-1940's) while the vessel served in Mobile, Alabama. This area was inaccessible for measurement.

E. No observations or measurements were made by HAER below the waterline. Data for the lines, keel and rudder were based on work done by Robert C. Douglas in 1967.

F. The bilges were filled with ballast and were inaccessible for measurement.

G. ALABAMA had no masts or rigging in 1986. See Sheet 1 for restored Outboard Profile.

H. Estimated accuracy of the drawings (in scale inches) ± ¾" for beam and depth, ± 1½" for length.

PORT RAIL PROFILE

DECKHOUSE PROFILE

INBOARD PROFILE

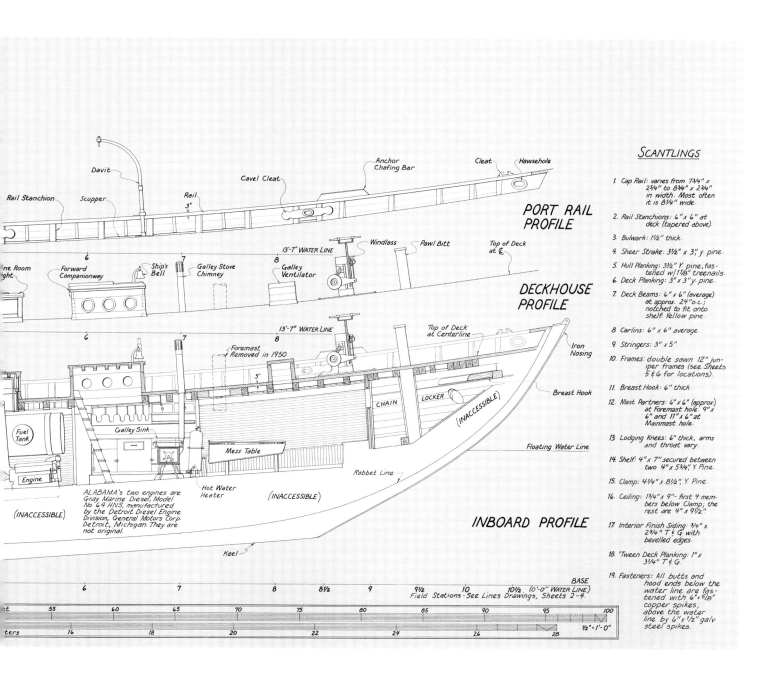

Davit

Anchor
Chafing Bar

Cleat   Hawsehole

Rail Stanchion   Scupper   Rail   Cavel Cleat

3"

**PORT RAIL
PROFILE**

ne Room
ght

6   6   7

Forward
Companionway   Ship's
Bell   Galley Stove
Chimney

13'-7" WATER LINE   Windlass   Pawl Bitt

8   Galley
Ventilator

Top of Deck
at ℄

**DECKHOUSE
PROFILE**

6   6   7

Foremast
Removed in 1950

13'-7" WATER LINE

3"   8

Top of Deck
at Centerline

Iron
Nosing

Fuel
Tank

Galley Sink

CHAIN   LOCKER

(INACCESSIBLE)

Breast Hook

Engine

Mess Table

Floating Water Line

(INACCESSIBLE)

Hot Water
Heater   (INACCESSIBLE)

Rabbet Line

ALABAMA's two engines are
Gray Marine Diesel, Model
No. 64 HN9, manufactured
by the Detroit Diesel Engine
Division, General Motors Corp.
Detroit, Michigan. They are
not original.

INBOARD PROFILE

Keel

SCANTLINGS

1. Cap Rail: varies from 7¾" x
   2¾" to 8¾" x 2¾"
   in width. Most often
   it is 8¼" wide.

2. Rail Stanchions: 6" x 6" at
   deck (tapered above).

3. Bulwark: 1½" thick.

4. Sheer Strake: 3½" x 3", y. pine.

5. Hull Planking: 3½" Y. pine, fastened w/1⅛" treenails.

6. Deck Planking: 3" x 3" y. pine.

7. Deck Beams: 6" x 6" (average)
   at approx. 24" o.c.;
   notched to fit onto
   shelf. Yellow pine.

8. Carlins: 6" x 6" average.

9. Stringers: 3" x 5".

10. Frames: double sawn 12" jun-
    iper frames (see Sheets
    5 & 6 for locations).

11. Breast Hook: 6" thick.

12. Mast Partners: 6" x 6" (approx.)
    at Foremast hole. 9" x
    6" and 11" x 6" at
    Mainmast hole.

13. Lodging Knees: 6" thick, arms
    and throat vary.

14. Shelf: 4" x 7" secured between
    two 4" x 5¾", Y. Pine.

15. Clamp: 4¼" x 8½", Y. Pine.

16. Ceiling: 13¾" x 9"- first 4 mem-
    bers below Clamp; the
    rest are 4" x 9½".

17. Interior Finish Siding: ¾" x
    2¾" T & G with
    bevelled edges.

18. 'Tween Deck Planking: 1" x
    3¼" T & G.

19. Fasteners: All butts and
    hood ends below the
    water line are fas-
    tened with 6" x ⅝"
    copper spikes;
    above the water
    line by 6" x ½" galv.
    steel spikes.

BASE

6   7   8   8½   9   9½   10   10½ (0'-0" WATER LINE)
Field Stations-See Lines Drawings, Sheets 2-4.

55   60   65   70   75   80   85   90   95   100

16   18   20   22   24   26   28   ½"=1'-0"

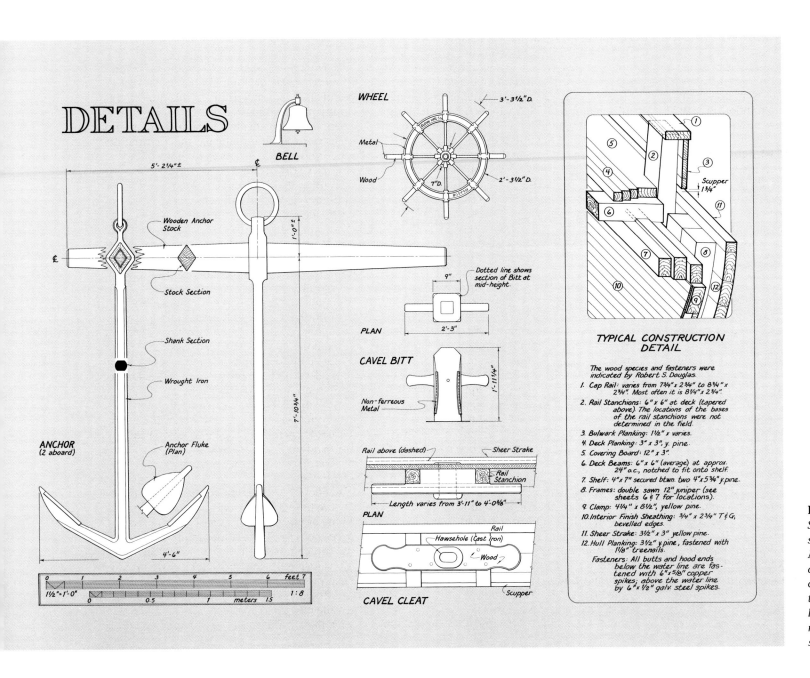

DETAILS

BELL

WHEEL

3'-3½" D.

Metal

Wood

7" D.

2'-3½" D.

5'-2¼"±

Wooden Anchor Stock

Stock Section

Shank Section

Wrought Iron

ANCHOR
(2 aboard)

Anchor Fluke (Plan)

4'-6"

1'-0"±

7'-10¾"

0 1 2 3 4 5 6 feet 7
1½"=1'-0"
0 0.5 1 meters 1.5
1:8

9"

Dotted line shows section of Bitt at mid-height.

PLAN

2'-3"

CAVEL BITT

1'-11¼"

Non-ferreous Metal

Rail above (dashed)

Sheer Strake

Rail Stanchion

Length varies from 3'-11" to 4'-0⅜"

PLAN

Rail

Hawsehole (Cast Iron)

Wood

Scupper

CAVEL CLEAT

Scupper
1¾"

TYPICAL CONSTRUCTION DETAIL

The wood species and fasteners were indicated by Robert S. Douglas.

1. Cap Rail: varies from 7¾" x 2¾" to 8¾" x 2¾". Most often it is 8¼" x 2¾".
2. Rail Stanchions: 6" x 6" at deck (tapered above). The locations of the bases of the rail stanchions were not determined in the field.
3. Bulwark Planking: 1½" x varies.
4. Deck Planking: 3" x 3", y. pine.
5. Covering Board: 12" x 3".
6. Deck Beams: 6" x 6" (average) at approx. 24" o.c., notched to fit onto shelf.
7. Shelf: 4" x 7" secured btwn. two 4" x 5⅜" y. pine.
8. Frames: double sawn 12" juniper (see sheets 6 & 7 for locations).
9. Clamp: 4¼" x 8½", yellow pine.
10. Interior Finish Sheathing: ¾" x 2¾" T & G, bevelled edges.
11. Sheer Strake: 3½" x 3" yellow pine.
12. Hull Planking: 3½" y. pine, fastened with 1⅛" treenails.
   Fasteners: All butts and hood ends below the water line are fastened with 6" x ⅝" copper spikes; above the water line by 6" x ½" galv. steel spikes.

Figure 8.6

Some surviving details of significance from the Alabama appear on this drawing, as well as typical construction details and the ship's scantlings—a list of dimensions and materials of the principal structural members.

shortly after the ship was built. Reverse perspective analysis of these was used to arrive at approximate measurements of the rig for inclusion in an outboard profile on the title sheet of the drawing set. All drawings were accompanied by scales and liberal notes relating to field procedures, materials, names of parts, and sources of information. The historic photographs were photocopied with the owner's permission and included with the large-format photographs. (In addition to their historical value, the older photographs were used to verify the drawings of the *Alabama*'s rig.) Using primary and secondary sources, a history was written to preserve information about the *Alabama*'s design and construction, designer, builder, owners, service, and significance in U.S. maritime history and engineering.

When recording ships, a full set of drawings should be annotated and highly detailed, covering every significant aspect of the project fieldwork and of the ship's appearance, design, construction, propulsion, interior features, and auxiliary equipment. The amount of effort required depends on the size of the vessel and the significant features that require the most concentrated attention, as well as available funds, personnel, and expertise.

Lifting the Lines of the *Wawona*

The *Wawona* lines-lifting project was a documentation effort of limited scope aimed primarily at recording the contours of this 1897 sailing ship's wooden hull. No attempt was made to gather enough data to produce a full set of construction drawings covering the ship's profiles, plans, sections, and details. The taking of lines, however, is a task of high priority when the designed hull shape of the vessel being recorded

is an important factor in its historical significance or if the data are needed for repairs or other preservation measures. If extensive drawings of a ship's hull structure include numerous cross sections, the lifting of lines will be essential, even if the hull's shape is not particularly significant. Usually the lines are taken on only one side, since the hull is assumed to be symmetrical. In the case of the *Wawona*, however, both sides were measured in order to detect any distortions caused by age or deterioration.

Lifting the lines of a ship can be accomplished in many ways. The method chosen depends on the size of the vessel, its location, its condition, and its historically significant features. Ultimately, some sort of convenient reference system must be devised that suits the field conditions of a vessel and permits measurements of its hull to be made accurately and efficiently.

In order to measure the *Wawona*, the ship was first lined up in a floating dry dock within a predetermined reference system set up with a surveying transit (*see figs. 8.10 and 8.11*). A very large horizontal wooden straightedge with two large vertical scales (or squares) was then set up repeatedly around the hull at thirteen different predetermined points along the ship's length. Measurements were made on both sides of the ship's hull from the squares and straightedge after the instruments had been aligned with the dry dock reference system (*see fig. 8.12*). The field data were then reduced at each station to plots on a drawing board for verification (*see fig. 8.13*). Each of the plots constituted a section of the hull, and since these sections were located at known points along the ship's length, sufficient information was available to plot the ship's lines in plan and profile. The entire lines-lifting process took six days and consumed about 500 work hours, not including actual dry-

docking or refloating of the ship or the drafting time for finished line drawings.

Numerous problems in setting up the dry dock reference system and measuring instruments had to be overcome in this project, and many potential sources of error had to be monitored during the fieldwork. Many of these problems were peculiar to the use of a floating dry dock and are not factors in all lines-lifting efforts. Constant changes of attitude inherent in a floating dry dock made it impractical to use ordinary levels and surveying techniques except over small distances or in special cases where error was judged to be within acceptable limits. These problems could have been controlled far more consistently and to finer limits (+/- ¼ inch maximum error in all directions) if more time-consuming procedures had been used, or if the ship had been placed in a land-based facility so that no shifts in attitude would occur. During this project, whenever a surveying transit was used, it was set up in the dry dock and adjusted to the dry dock reference system, not to the leveling devices in the instrument. Any influences from the shifting attitude of the dry dock were thus avoided. Plumb bobs and spirit levels were used only over distances not exceeding 5 feet, except for plumbing the large squares in the fore-and-aft direction. In this latter case, a possible error of +/- 1½ inches at the tops of the squares was accepted, due to the excessive time and effort that would have been required to ensure that the tops were square to the base plane of the reference system within an accuracy of +/- ¼ inch. A maximum error of +/- ⅛ inch for dimensions up to 20 feet and +/- ¼ inch for those up to 100 feet would have been preferred.

Back in the office, the data were redrawn at a scale of ¼ inch to the foot. Two sets of lines were then drawn for the *Wawona*, one showing

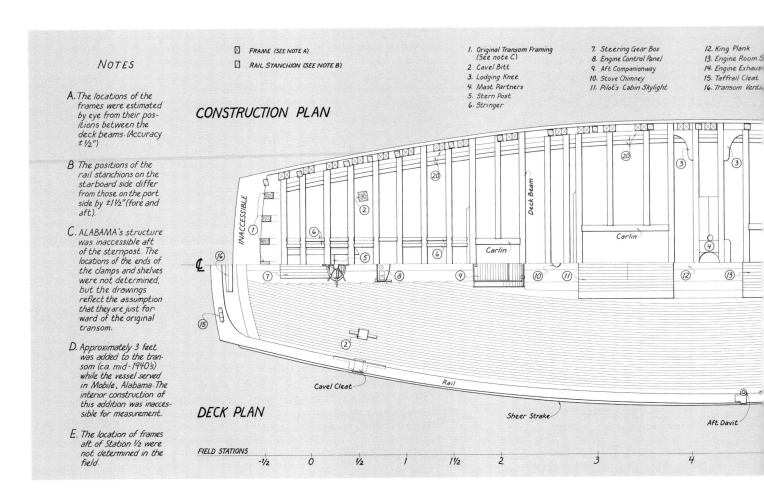

NOTES

☒ FRAME (SEE NOTE A)
☐ RAIL STANCHION (SEE NOTE B)

1. Original Transom Framing (See note C)
2. Cavel Bitt
3. Lodging Knee
4. Mast Partners
5. Stern Post
6. Stringer
7. Steering Gear Box
8. Engine Control Panel
9. Aft Companionway
10. Stove Chimney
11. Pilot's Cabin Skylight
12. King Plank
13. Engine Room S...
14. Engine Exhaus...
15. Taffrail Cleat
16. Transom Ventil...

A. The locations of the frames were estimated by eye from their positions between the deck beams. (Accuracy ±½")

B The positions of the rail stanchions on the starboard side differ from those on the port side by ±1½" (fore and aft).

C. ALABAMA's structure was inaccessible aft of the sternpost. The locations of the ends of the clamps and shelves were not determined, but the drawings reflect the assumption that they are just forward of the original transom.

D. Approximately 3 feet was added to the transom (ca. mid-1940's) while the vessel served in Mobile, Alabama. The interior construction of this addition was inaccessible for measurement.

E. The location of frames aft of Station ½ were not determined in the field.

CONSTRUCTION PLAN

DECK PLAN

FIELD STATIONS

-½   0   ½   1   1½   2   3   4

Figures 8.7 and 8.8

Taking advantage of symmetry, half the Alabama's deck plan is juxtaposed with the deck beam plan about the centerline. The names of various structural parts are keyed to the drawing, and important notes are included in the drawing sheet margins.

17. Mast Hole
18. Pawl Bitt
19. Chain Tube
20. Shelf

21. Breast Hook (Dashed)
22. Forward Companionway
23. Galley Stove Chimney
24. Galley Ventilator

25. Windlass
26. Anchor Chain
27. Fuel Tank Filling Port
28. Inscribed in aft
    face of deck beam:
    35 Tons · No. 226177

FRAME (SEE NOTE A) ⊠
RAIL STANCHION (SEE NOTE B) ⧄

(Notes continued from Sheet 5)

CONSTRUCTION PLAN

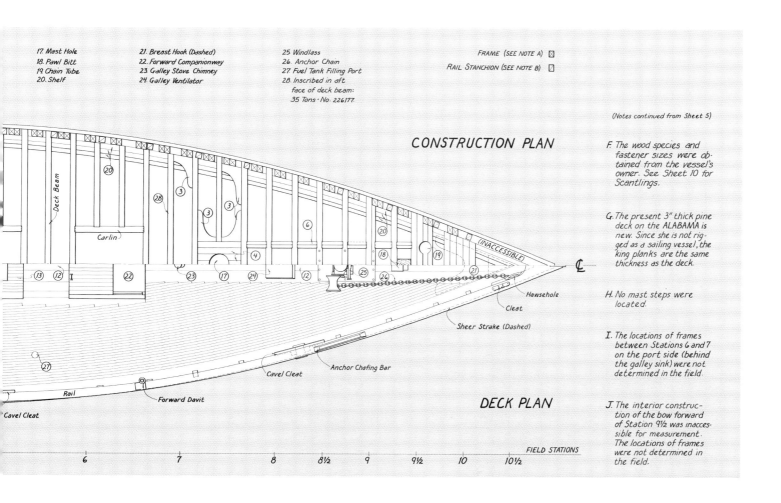

(INACCESSIBLE)

Deck Beam

Carlin

Hawsehole

Cleat

Sheer Strake (Dashed)

Anchor Chafing Bar

DECK PLAN

Cavel Cleat

Rail

Forward Davit

Cavel Cleat

F. The wood species and
   fastener sizes were obtained from the vessel's
   owner. See Sheet 10 for
   Scantlings.

G. The present 3" thick pine
   deck on the ALABAMA is
   new. Since she is not rigged as a sailing vessel, the
   king planks are the same
   thickness as the deck.

H. No mast steps were
   located.

I. The locations of frames
   between Stations 6 and 7
   on the port side (behind
   the galley sink) were not
   determined in the field.

J. The interior construc-
   tion of the bow forward
   of Station 9½ was inaccessible for measurement.
   The locations of frames
   were not determined in
   the field.

FIELD STATIONS

6   7   8   8½   9   9½   10   10½

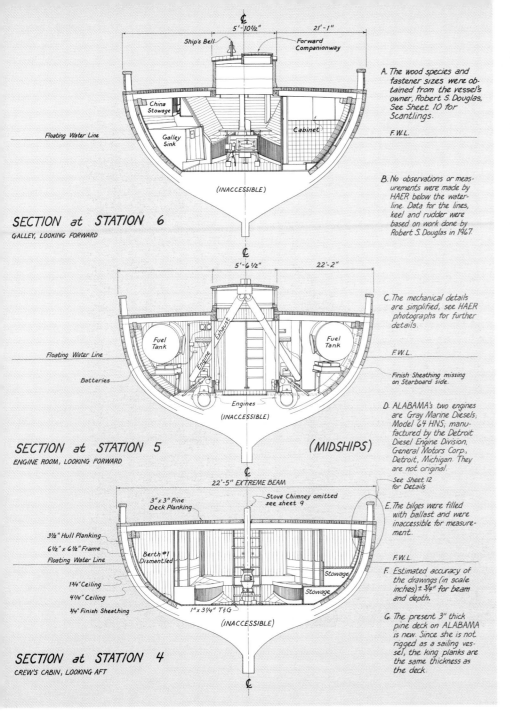

SECTION at STATION 6
GALLEY, LOOKING FORWARD

5'-10½" 21'-1"

Ship's Bell Forward Companionway

China Stowage

Galley Sink

Cabinet

Floating Water Line F.W.L.

(INACCESSIBLE)

SECTION at STATION 5
ENGINE ROOM, LOOKING FORWARD (MIDSHIPS)

5'-6½" 22'-2"

Fuel Tank

Fuel Tank

Floating Water Line F.W.L.

Batteries

Engine Exhaust

Engines
(INACCESSIBLE)

SECTION at STATION 4
CREW'S CABIN, LOOKING AFT

22'-5" EXTREME BEAM

3" x 3" Pine Deck Planking

Stove Chimney omitted see sheet 9

3½" Hull Planking
6½" x 6½" Frame
Floating Water Line

Berth #1 Dismantled

Stowage

Stowage

1¾" Ceiling
4¼" Ceiling
¾" Finish Sheathing F.W.L.

1" x 3¼" T&G

(INACCESSIBLE)

A. The wood species and fastener sizes were obtained from the vessel's owner, Robert S. Douglas. See Sheet 10 for Scantlings.

B. No observations or measurements were made by HAER below the waterline. Data for the lines, keel and rudder were based on work done by Robert S. Douglas in 1967.

C. The mechanical details are simplified, see HAER photographs for further details.

Finish Sheathing missing on Starboard side.

D. ALABAMA's two engines are Gray Marine Diesels, Model 64 HNS, manufactured by the Detroit Diesel Engine Division, General Motors Corp., Detroit, Michigan. They are not original.

See Sheet 12 for Details

E. The bilges were filled with ballast and were inaccessible for measurement.

F. Estimated accuracy of the drawings (in scale inches) ± ¾" for beam and depth.

G. The present 3" thick pine deck on ALABAMA is new. Since she is not rigged as a sailing vessel, the king planks are the same thickness as the deck.

Figure 8.10
Before the schooner Wawona was dry-docked, a rectangular coordinate system for lining up measuring frames was laid out in the dry dock using a surveying transit. Here a centerline has been set on the keel blocks, and lines-lifting stations are being set beneath it on the deck of the dry dock.

Figure 8.9
Cross sections of the Alabama further document the interior arrangements of structural members and spaces.

Figure 8.11
Tugs slowly move the Wawona *into a temporarily sub-merged dry dock, later raised for the lines-lifting project.*

the ship's actual condition, where the keel was hogged about 9½ inches amidships, and the second showing the probable condition of the ship when it was new (*see figs. 8.14, 8.15, and 8.16*). Extensive notes documenting field and drafting room procedures were added to the drawings, including error estimates, so that future users might follow the project's methodological development and have an adequate basis for judging its accuracy. Because of the project's limitations, no further drawings were made to show the ship's structural details except for a small-scale profile on the title sheet of the drawing set. Masts and rigging were drawn using existing drawings in the owners' possession, and these sources were noted in the title sheet profile (*see. fig. 8.17*).

Figure 8.12
Using two measuring tapes and a pole, the recording team measures points on the Wawona's hull from points on the horizontal and vertical scales of the lines-lifting frames. Another team member records dimensions. Points on the hull are taken only in the plane set by the frames (easily found by eye). Where the curves in the hull are more pronounced, more points are taken to ensure good documentation of the curve.

Figure 8.13

The shape of the Wawona's hull at each station is carefully plotted and faired on-site from field data before any measuring equipment is moved to the next station. Any serious errors in measurement or recording can easily be found and checked at this stage of operations.

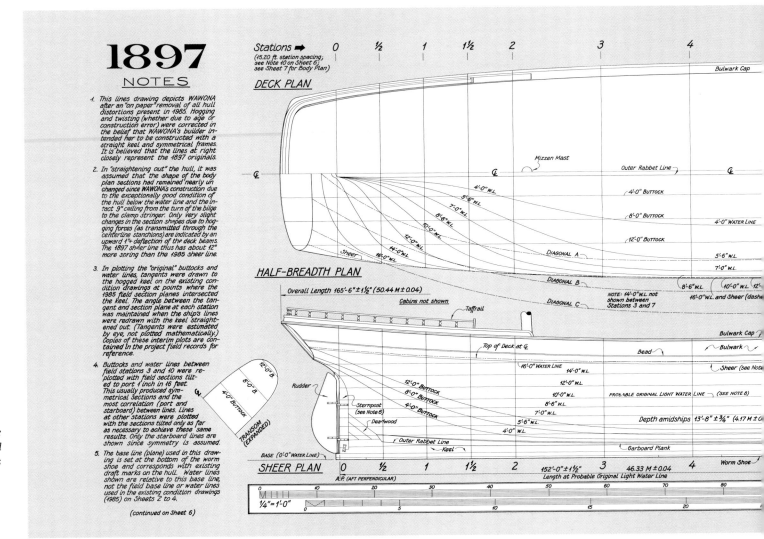

Figures 8.14 and 8.15

The probable original (1897) contours of the Wawona's hull were carefully derived from the 1985 fieldwork. Field and drafting-room procedures are outlined in notes on the drawings along with error estimations for these two phases of the documentation.

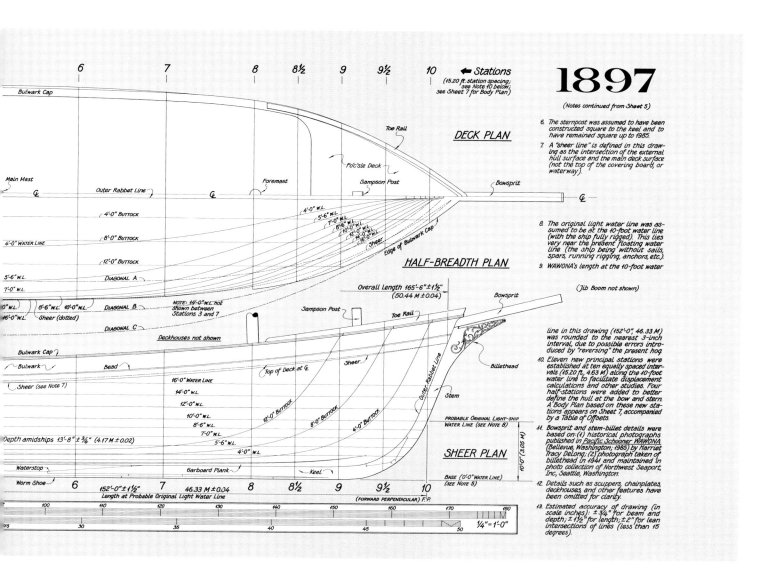

1897

6 7 8 8½ 9 9½ 10 ← Stations

(15.20 ft. station spacing; see Note 10 below; see Sheet 7 for Body Plan)

(Notes continued from Sheet 5)

Bulwark Cap

Toe Rail

DECK PLAN

Fo'c'sle Deck

Main Mast

Outer Rabbet Line

Foremast

Sampson Post

Bowsprit

4'-0" Buttock

4'-0" W.L.
5'-6" W.L.
7'-0" W.L.
8'-6" W.L.
10'-0" W.L.
12'-0" W.L.
14'-0" W.L.
16'-0" W.L.

4'-0" WATER LINE

8'-0" Buttock

12'-0" Buttock

Sheer

Edge of Bulwark Cap

HALF-BREADTH PLAN

5'-6" W.L.

DIAGONAL A

7'-0" W.L.

Overall Length 165'-6" ±1½"
(50.44 M ±0.04)

Bowsprit

(Jib Boom not shown)

8'-6" W.L. 10'-0" W.L.

DIAGONAL B

'-0" W.L.

16'-0" W.L. Sheer (dotted)

NOTE: 14'-0" W.L. not shown between Stations 3 and 7

Sampson Post

Toe Rail

DIAGONAL C

Deckhouses not shown

Bulwark Cap

Top of Deck at C̲L̲

Sheer

Bowsprit

Billethead

Bulwark

Bead

Sheer (see Note 7)

16'-0" WATER LINE

14'-0" W.L.

12'-0" W.L.

10'-0" W.L.

8'-6" W.L.

7'-0" W.L.

5'-6" W.L.

4'-0" W.L.

12'-0" Buttock

8'-0" Buttock

4'-0" Buttock

Outer Rabbet Line

Stem

Depth amidships 13'-8" ±¾" (4.17 M ±0.02)

PROBABLE ORIGINAL LIGHT-SHIP WATER LINE (SEE NOTE 8)

Waterstop

10'-0" (3.05 M)

Worm Shoe

Garboard Plank

Keel

BASE (0'-0" WATER LINE) (SEE NOTE 5)

SHEER PLAN

6 152'-0" ±1½" 7 46.33 M ±0.04 8 8½ 9 9½ 10

Length at Probable Original Light Water Line

(FORWARD PERPENDICULAR) F.P.

100 110 120 130 140 150 160 170 180

25 30 35 40 45 50 ¼"=1'-0"

6. The sternpost was assumed to have been constructed square to the keel and to have remained square up to 1985.

7. A "sheer line" is defined in this drawing as the intersection of the external hull surface and the main deck surface (not the top of the covering board, or waterway).

8. The original light water line was assumed to be at the 10-foot water line (with the ship fully rigged). This lies very near the present floating water line (the ship being without sails, spars, running rigging, anchors, etc.).

9. WAWONA's length at the 10-foot water line in this drawing (152'-0", 46.33 M) was rounded to the nearest 3-inch interval, due to possible errors introduced by "reversing" the present hog.

10. Eleven new principal stations were established at ten equally spaced intervals (15.20 ft., 4.63 M) along the 10-foot water line to facilitate displacement calculations and other studies. Four half-stations were added to better define the hull at the bow and stern. A Body Plan based on these new stations appears on Sheet 7, accompanied by a Table of Offsets.

11. Bowsprit and stem-billet details were based on:(1) historical photographs published in *Pacific Schooner WAWONA* (Bellevue, Washington; 1985) by Harriet Tracy DeLong; (2) photograph taken of billethead in 1941 and maintained in photo collection of Northwest Seaport, Inc., Seattle, Washington.

12. Details such as scuppers, chainplates, deckhouses, and other features have been omitted for clarity.

13. Estimated accuracy of drawing (in scale inches): ±¾" for beam and depth; ±1½" for length; ±2" for lean intersections of lines (less than 15 degrees).

TABLE OF OFFSETS

1897

ALL DIMENSIONS BELOW ARE GIVEN IN FEET, INCHES, AND EIGHTHS OF AN INCH
(See Notes 1 and 2)

		0	**½**	**1**	**1½**	**2**	**3**	**4**	**5**	**6**	**7**	**8**	**8½**	**9**	**9½**	**10**
HEIGHTS ABOVE BASE	UNDERSIDE BUL. CAP	22-0-4	24-4-6	20-10-6	20-5-6	20-1-0	19-7-0	19-5-0	19-7-2	20-2-4	21-2-6	22-5-6	23-3-4	24-2-6	25-4-2	26-6-6
	SHEER	18-2-4	17-6-2	16-11-4	16-6-6	16-2-2	15-8-2	15-6-4	15-8-4	16-5-2	17-3-6	18-7-4	19-5-2	20-4-0	21-5-4	22-8-0
	16' BUTT.			12-5-0	9-10-6	7-2-4	6-3-2	6-1-0	6-6-0	8-4-2						
	12' BUTT.	17-0-0	14-0-0	11-3-2	8-10-0	7-0-2	5-0-4	4-6-6	4-6-4	4-8-4	5-3-6	8-3-2	13-2-6	24-1-6		
	8' BUTT.	15-9-0	12-6-0	9-5-4	7-0-4	5-4-4	4-0-2	3-9-0	3-9-0	3-10-2	4-1-0	5-4-4	7-4-4	12-0-4	23-4-0	
	4' BUTT.	14-11-2	10-8-0	7-1-6	4-10-0	3-9-6	3-1-2	2-11-0	2-11-0	2-11-4	3-1-0	3-6-2	4-4-6	6-5-0	11-11-0	25-9-0
	RABBET	2-11-0	2-4-4	2-1-6	←————————→							2-1-6	2-2-0	2-2-2	3-11-6	14-9-4
HALF-BREADTHS	BUL. CAP	13-6-4	14-7-4	15-4-2	15-11-0	16-5-2	17-1-0	17-5-4	17-7-4	17-5-2	17-0-0	15-9-2	14-4-6	12-0-4	8-7-6	4-3-4
	SHEER	13-5-4	14-11-4	15-10-0	16-5-0	16-10-6	17-6-4	17-10-4	18-0-4	17-6-6	17-3-0	15-6-0	13-8-2	11-0-6	7-5-2	3-0-4
	26' W.L.															4-1-2
	24' W.L.													11-11-4	8-2-4	3-5-2
	22' W.L.	13-7-2										15-8-2	14-1-4	11-7-6	7-7-4	2-9-6
	20' W.L.	13-11-0	14-9-0	15-5-6	15-11-6	16-5-4				17-5-4	17-0-4	15-7-2	13-9-4	10-11-4	6-11-4	2-2-0
	18' W.L.	13-3-6	15-0-0	15-9-6	16-3-4	16-7-4	17-2-6	17-7-2	17-9-2	17-7-4	17-2-6	15-5-0	13-4-6	10-4-6	6-4-0	1-6-6
	16' W.L.	9-1-0	14-4-4	15-9-2	16-5-4	16-10-6	17-6-0	17-9-6	18-0-0	17-10-2	17-3-4	15-2-4	12-11-2	9-8-6	5-7-6	1-0-4
	14' W.L.	1-0-2	12-0-2	15-2-4	16-5-0	17-0-2	17-8-0	17-11-4	18-1-0	17-11-0	17-3-0	14-9-6	12-3-4	8-11-0	14-0-4	
	12' W.L.	0-6-4	6-7-0	13-2-4	15-9-2	16-10-4	17-8-4	18-0-0	18-1-6	17-11-0	17-1-0	14-2-4	11-5-4	7-11-4	4-0-2	
	10' W.L.	0-6-4	3-2-0	9-0-4	13-11-6	14-7-4	16-11-0	17-6-4	17-8-0	17-4-4	16-0-6	13-3-0	10-3-6	6-9-4	3-0-6	
	8'-6" W.L.	0-6-4	2-0-2	6-0-4	11-3-0	14-7-4	16-11-0	17-6-4	17-8-0	17-4-4	16-0-6	12-2-2	9-1-4	5-8-4	2-4-4	
	7' W.L.	0-6-4	1-5-0	3-9-4	7-11-0	12-0-0	15-9-0	16-8-4	16-10-6	16-6-0	14-10-2	10-7-0	7-6-4	4-6-0	1-8-2	
	5'-6" W.L.	0-6-4	1-0-4	2-5-4	5-0-2	8-3-0	13-3-4	14-8-6	14-10-6	14-4-2	12-5-0	8-2-0	5-7-0	3-2-4	1-1-6	
	4' W.L.	0-6-4	0-9-4	1-6-4	2-9-0	4-5-0	7-10-2	9-3-4	9-3-4	9-2-6	8-8-4	7-8-2	5-1-4	3-5-0	1-11-2	
	HALF-SIDING	0-6-4	0-8-0													0-8-0
DIAGONALS	A	2-2-2	6-8-0	9-7-0	11-9-0	13-3-0	14-8-6	15-0-4	15-0-4	14-11-2	14-7-4	13-3-2	11-9-0	9-5-4	6-0-6	1-3-0
	B	6-8-2	10-6-6	13-6-4	15-10-4	17-7-6	19-7-4	20-2-4	20-3-0	20-0-6	19-3-2	16-9-6	14-6-4	11-5-6	7-6-4	2-5-4
	C	11-6-4	14-11-4	17-7-0	19-9-0	21-4-2	23-1-6	23-10-0	23-11-6	23-8-2	22-5-4	19-2-0	16-6-2	13-1-4	8-10-4	3-8-6

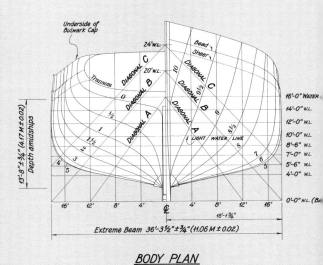

BODY PLAN

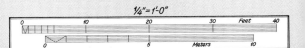

¼"=1'-0"

Figure 8.16

The table of offsets for the Wawona displays numerically what is shown in the body plan. The body plan is analogous to "slices" of the hull's shape and shows only half the hull from midships forward and the other half from midships aft, since the hull is symmetrical.

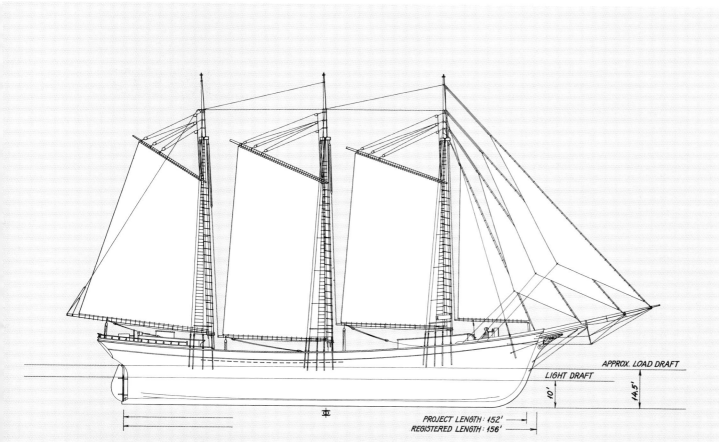

LIGHT DRAFT

APPROX. LOAD DRAFT

10'

14.5'

Φ

PROJECT LENGTH: 152'
REGISTERED LENGTH: 156'

Hull based on project field measurements; all other features based on HAER photos, historical photos, and profile by E. Harry Anderson of Seattle, Washington.

Figure 8.17
The title sheet for the lines drawings of the Wawona includes an outboard profile of the hull based on field measurements with rigging based on preexisting documentation. Sources are footnoted below the drawing.

CHAPTER 9

RECORDING MONUMENTS

Mark Schara

In 1991 HABS began a multiyear project for the National Capital Region of the National Park Service to document both the Lincoln and Jefferson memorials as one of the first phases of a comprehensive restoration project for both buildings. Early in the planning process, it was decided the two structures would be documented using computer-aided drafting (CAD). This was the first major comprehensive CAD project undertaken by the HABS/HAER office. In 1993, building on the success of the earlier projects, a similar project was begun to document the Washington Monument, the tallest structure ever recorded by HABS.

The National Capital Region required a complete, accurate, and up-to-date set of documents of the three monuments, showing current conditions with a high level of detail. Although a significant number of original construction drawings for the three structures survived, these were inadequate for the task at hand for a number of reasons. First, the drawings necessary for construction of the buildings were often not those needed for their restoration. Likewise, a number of essential drawings did not survive, and those that did usually did not show changes made to the buildings at the time of construction or subsequently. The relatively primitive level of scanning technology and raster-to-vector conversion software at the time precluded simply digitizing the construction documents. Thus it was decided to measure the buildings from scratch, although a number of the original construction documents proved useful as base drawings for the measurements, saving sketching time in the field.

The CAD software selected was AutoCAD, the National Park Service standard. The advantages of using CAD were apparent from the out-

set. For the project sponsor, electronic documents would facilitate distribution of base drawings to various contractors involved in the restoration work. Drawings in digital format could easily be updated as changes were made to the buildings. In addition, they could easily be linked to databases for maintenance and facility management purposes. On the HABS side, one of the great advantages of using CAD was that several delineators could work on different parts of the same drawing at the same time, and their individual drawings could be combined as each part was completed. The large size of the buildings dictated that the drawings would eventually be plotted on E-size sheets (34″ × 44″), a difficult size to work with using traditional hand drafting but easy to do in CAD. CAD also made it possible to apply a high level of detail to the base drawings, which could then be plotted at different scales to show different levels of detail. The use of "layers" that could be turned on and off meant that the same base drawing could be used for several different drawings. Likewise, the repetitive use of identical elements on the buildings (such as column capitals) could quickly be replicated using the "copy" and "array" commands (*see fig 9.1*).

The adaptation of traditional HABS measuring methods and techniques to the requirements of computer-aided drafting required a period of trial and error. For the most part, simple hand measuring was used to obtain dimensional information on the buildings. This process was abetted by an extensive system of scaffolding erected at each site, which allowed access to most of the surfaces the HABS team needed to document. However, because drawing in CAD involves essentially drawing at full scale, the measuring methodology had to be particularly accurate and precise. Nonetheless, we determined that the remarkable precision of the CAD software, up to $\frac{1}{64}$ of an inch, was well beyond our ability to achieve in measuring (as, in fact, it is well beyond the construction industry to achieve in building). Instead, we decided to measure to the nearest eighth of an inch, which was the smallest division on some of our tapes. Metal tapes were used exclusively because of the tendency of cloth (fiberglass) tapes to stretch when pulled over long distances.

The scale of CAD drawings created problems from the beginning because small discrepancies, which could be easily finessed in a traditional hand drawing executed at $\frac{1}{8}''$ or $\frac{1}{4}''$ scale, remained unresolved in a full-scale CAD drawing. This issue was complicated by the ease of drawing in CAD using orthogonal mode, which provided an incentive to use perfect right angles whenever possible. From the start, we found ourselves obsessing over dimensions that were off by a small amount. Finally, after a period of experimentation, we developed a drawing methodology with an allowable margin of error in the measurements, which was dependent on two factors. The first was the relative size of the buildings, with a larger margin of error allowed for larger buildings. The second

was the scale of the final plotted drawings (executed for the Library of Congress), with a larger margin of error allowed for drawings plotted at a smaller scale. The fact that both the Lincoln Memorial and the Jefferson Memorial were built to a remarkably high degree of precision certainly helped us come to terms with this issue.

The memorials did present two significant problems, however. The first was caused by the large size of some of the spaces, which made some of the surfaces inaccessible for hand measuring. The other was the high level of carved ornamental detail on the buildings, detail that would be particularly difficult to measure and draw using traditional methods. Both these problems were solved using digital photogrammetry. Traditional stereophotogrammetry is an awkward and expensive process involving a special stereocamera, glass plate negatives, and a photogrammetric technician to operate a large, cumbersome machine known as a stereoplotter. The advent of digital technology has transformed this process. Architects can now do their own photogrammetry with a 35 mm camera, off-the-shelf software, and a simple digitizing tablet, albeit with somewhat less precision.

For this project, the HABS/HAER office purchased two semimetric photogrammetric cameras, both Linhof Metrikas, one with a 90 mm lens and one with a 120 mm lens (*see fig. 9.2*). Although not off-the-shelf technology, these cameras were chosen for several reasons. The technology of the cameras involves the use of a vacuum applied to the film as it is rolled across a glass plate etched with an incised grid of crosshairs (known as a reseau grid), allowing an extremely high degree of precision during the digitizing process (*see fig. 9.3*). Despite this sophisticated technology, the cameras were easy to use for architects without the training of professional photographers. The cameras use 5"-wide roll film, resulting in 4" × 5" negatives,

which meet the minimum size requirement for HABS archival photography. The rolls of film can accommodate up to 60 images, an advantage when using the cameras in remote field situations. The 4" × 5" images can be enlarged substantially when printed (typically to 11" × 14") and still retain a high level of detail.

The photogrammetric software used was PhotoCAD, which was selected primarily because it was relatively inexpensive and works as an add-on inside AutoCAD. Two versions of the software are available. PhotoCAD-Single uses a single photograph to produce two-dimensional drawings. The photo is first mounted on a digitizing tablet. By inputting the coordinates of four known points in a plane, any shape in that plane can be traced with a digitizing mouse to produce an accurate, correctly scaled CAD drawing. The software automatically corrects for any perspective distortion in the photograph.

PhotoCAD-Multi, on the other hand, works in a slightly different manner. As the name implies, it employs multiple photographs, preferably at least three, taken from positions with convergent camera axes at least 10 degrees apart. The software requires at least seven common points in all the photographs and the known distance between two of the points. With this information, it can solve for any other point common to the photographs, locating it three-dimensionally. The obvious advantage of using PhotoCAD-Multi is that it enables the user to measure objects that can be seen in photographs but cannot be reached for hand measuring.

As with any technology, digital photogrammetry has both advantages and disadvantages. Although useful for vertical surfaces (elevations and sometimes sections) and relatively close-up, straight-on details, it is not useful for plans, which typically still need to be hand-measured.

Figure 9.2
HABS/HAER/HALS architects use a Linhof Metrika camera to produce 4" × 5" negatives with a superimposed reseau grid on 5" roll film. The resulting images are used to produce photogrammetric CAD measured drawings.

Figure 9.1
The "polar array" command in AutoCAD was used extensively at the Jefferson Memorial to simultaneously copy and rotate discrete, repetitive items. A drawing with this level of detail and accuracy would have been essentially impossible to execute by hand.

Figure 9.3
Note the reseau grid of small crosshairs in this enlargement of a photograph of the Lincoln Memorial frieze. On the negative, the crosshairs are precisely 10 mm apart at full scale.

And obviously, features need to be visible in order to be photographed. Thus, buildings encumbered with foliage or with features too high up for good photographic resolution are not the best candidates for photogrammetry.

Even with CAD and photogrammetry, we still faced certain logistical problems in documenting the memorials. Much of the ornament was too high up to be photographed from the ground. Scaffolding towers were erected to provide the HABS team and the restoration architects with access to most surfaces of the building for hand measuring. However, these towers were too close to the building for photography. This situation was resolved by mounting the photogrammetric camera on an 11-foot boom and then swinging it out into space for proper positioning. A 15-foot shutter release cable was used to take the pictures. The attic frieze, entablature cornice, and entablature frieze at the Lincoln Memorial were all systematically photographed using this method as the towers moved around the building. The pediment at the Jefferson Memorial was documented in a similar manner (*see figs. 9.4, 9.5, and 9.6*). At the Washington Monument, no exterior elevations showing stone joints had been drawn as part of the original construction documents. With scaffolding not an option, the solution was to photograph the monument in a series of vertical sequences from a helicopter. PhotoCAD was subsequently used to digitize elevation drawings from the photographs (*see fig. 9.7*).

In the decade after the commencement of the memorials project, HABS expanded its use of CAD and digital rectified photogrammetry to a wide variety of projects. The photogrammetric cameras have seen use at sites across the country, from Puerto Rico to Alaska. Single-photo photogrammetry has proven particularly useful for the documentation of buildings with relatively flat but highly irregular, nonorthogonal

Figure 9.4

The photogrammetric camera, mounted on a boom, is positioned to photograph the pediment sculpture at the Jefferson Memorial. This operation typically required someone stationed on the ground to aid in the positioning process. The scaffolding, erected in 1994 to facilitate documentation and restoration, provided the first access to the pediment sculpture since the building was completed in 1943.

surfaces. Three slave cabins, of log construction with mud chinking, at the Hermitage in Nashville, Tennessee, were documented in this manner. Likewise, the substantial adobe ruins at Fort Union National Monument in New Mexico were systematically recorded using this method (*see figs. 9.8 and 9.9*). Multiphoto photogrammetry has found frequent use as well. At the Mariscal Mine in Big Bend National Park, in the west Texas desert, extensive photography with the Metrika cameras was undertaken during a four-day field expedition. A similar method was used on a 13-day trip to the Kennecott Mine in Wrangell–St. Elias National Park in Alaska (*see figs. 9.10, 9.11, and 9.12*). In both cases, the data were brought back to the HABS office, where PhotoCAD was used to create substantial, detailed three-dimensional models of the structures at each site. This methodology has proven to be a cost-effective means of gathering a large amount of information over a short period of time in a remote location.

As HABS use of these technologies has become more extensive, the technologies themselves have been evolving. One disadvantage of the Metrika cameras is that they are heavy and cumbersome in the field, and another is that the film needs to be loaded and unloaded in complete darkness. As a result, HABS has investigated the use of other, smaller cameras with photogrammetric capabilities, although there is an inevitable trade-off in the resolution of the resulting images. The advent of digital photography has also transformed the documentation process. Good, straight-on digital photographs of small, two-dimensional details can now be inserted directly into AutoCAD, where they can be traced and scaled (*see fig. 9.13*). Full-scale field drawings of molding profiles can be similarly scanned and traced. The entire photogrammetric process has become digital with software such as PhotoModeler, in which multi-

Figure 9.5

In an attempt to capture each stone block as straight on as possible, a series of photographs was taken across the width of the pediment sculpture. The empty picture frame provided four points of known separation, which could be used in the digitizing process to determine scale and orientation. In this case, however, the outside corners of the individual stone blocks were ultimately used for this purpose.

Figure 9.6

The pediment sculpture, by Adolf Weinman, shows the five members of the committee selected by the Continental Congress to draft the Declaration of Independence, with Jefferson standing in the center. The relief of the sculpture was low enough that a photograph could be digitized using single-photo PhotoCAD as the source for an accu-rate two-dimensional drawing. Although documentation of a feature such as this invariably involves some subjective interpretation on the part of the delineator, with good photogrammetric images and careful attention to detail, a satisfactory and useful drawing is easily achieved.

Figure 9.7
At 555 feet, the Washington Monument is the tallest structure ever recorded by HABS. Extensive hand measuring on the interior of the monument enabled the HABS team to locate the horizontal stone joints above the 150-foot level. Exterior photographs were used primarily to locate the vertical joints. Above the 222-foot level some of the individual stone blocks are continuous through the walls, allowing measurements of the vertical joints taken from photographs to be correlated on the interior. Although two vastly different recording technologies were used (hand measuring on the interior, digital photogrammetry on the exterior), the measurements corresponded with a remarkable degree of accuracy.

ple digital images (either original digital photographs or scanned printed photographs) can be manipulated on the computer screen, as opposed to being traced manually on a digitizing table. Once again, however, a trade-off between resolution and file size must be taken into account.

The overwhelming majority of CAD drawings the HABS/HAER office has produced to date are two-dimensional. There are a number of reasons for this. In general, three-dimensional drawing requires a higher level of expertise, and the resulting files are typically much larger and more difficult to manipulate than two-dimensional files. The vast majority of buildings and structures documented by HABS/HAER are (more or less) orthogonal and readily lend themselves to traditional two-dimensional plans, elevations, and sections. These basic drawings are adequate for the needs of most project sponsors. Many HABS/HAER projects are undertaken with student teams during a short summer session, and often these students are not yet proficient in

Figure 9.8
The adobe walls at Fort Union are irregular in outline but relatively flat, which made them ideal candidates for documentation using two-dimensional digital photogrammetry. Targets were placed on the walls, and the distances between them (including diagonals) were measured to provide the control points necessary to digitize the photographs.

Figure 9.9
Each wall surface at Fort Union required a separate photograph. Seven photographs were necessary to produce this section drawing.

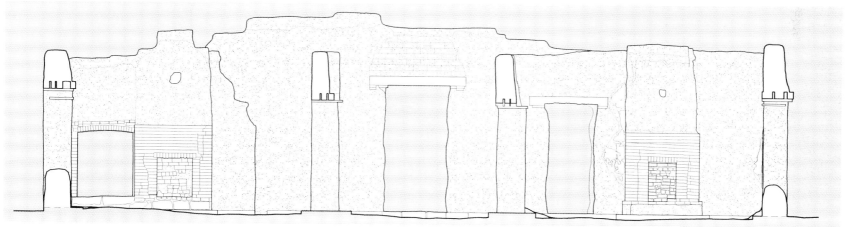

Figure 9.10
The Kennecott Copper Corporation facility in Kennicott, Alaska, was one of the largest copper production facilities in the United States at the time of its construction in 1905–11. The National Historic Landmark, shown from the northwest in this view, was the subject of a multipart HAER documentation project.

Figure 9.11
This view of the Kennecott Mill from the southwest and fig. 9.10 were part of a series of photos of the mill taken from different convergent angles in order to facilitate three-dimensional digital photogrammetry.

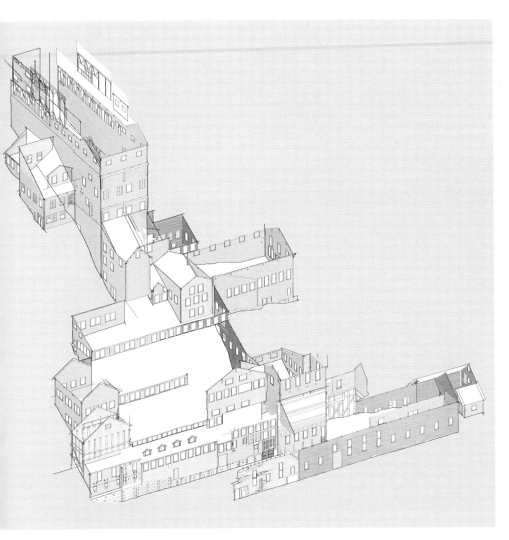

drawing three-dimensionally with CAD. Most
important, the final product of a HABS/HAER
project remains a set of hard copy two-dimensional plots on Mylar for the Library of Congress. Adept use of single-photo PhotoCAD has
enabled HABS architects to render even highly
sculptural objects in two dimensions with reasonable precision when three-dimensional drawings are not required (*see figs. 9.14 and 9.15*). On
the other hand, CAD has proven particularly
applicable to certain three-dimensional structures. Most notably, HAER architects have
become proficient in modeling ship hulls three-
dimensionally, which facilitates the production
of the standard line drawings (*see fig. 9.16*).
HAER has also found the three-dimensional
capabilities of CAD useful for interpretive draw-

Figure 9.12

*The scope of work for the
Kennecott Mill project
involved the documenta-
tion of 68 individual exterior walls of this complex,
many-storied structure.
Each wall was recorded
with a combination of
hand measuring and two-
dimensional digital pho-
togrammetry. In addition,
a series of overall exterior
photographs of the mill
was taken (see figs. 9.10
and 9.11). Back at the
HABS/HAER office (4,000
miles from the project
site), a three-dimensional
prototype model was
created with three-
dimensional digital photogrammetry, using the
dimensions taken for the
two-dimensional wall ele-
vations along with the
overall exterior photo-
graphs. The individual
wall elevations were placed
three-dimensionally in
space in relation to one
another. The model could
then be rotated to produce
overall elevations of the
entire structure.*

Figure 9.13

*The elaborate ornament on this doorway was documented
with digital photographs that were later traced in Auto-
CAD. The 6"-square piece of cardboard, handheld in the
same plane as the desired detail, provides scale.*

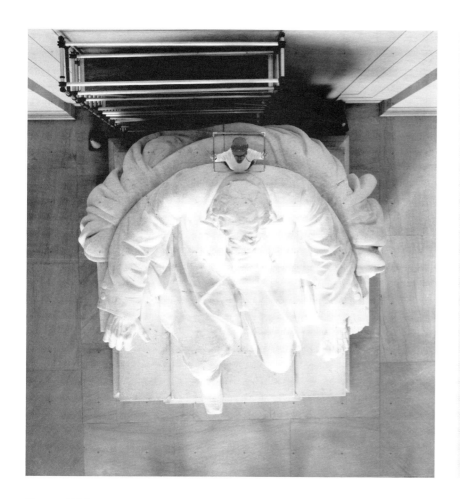

Figure 9.14
A series of photographs was taken of the statue of Lincoln at the Lincoln Memorial from above, as straight on as possible, with an empty picture frame held at different levels corresponding to the major features of the statue. The features were digitized individually and then combined into a single two-dimensional plan drawing. All four elevations of the statue were drawn in a similar manner.

Figure 9.15
This plan drawing, developed as described in figure 9.14, provides a unique view of the Lincoln Memorial statue.

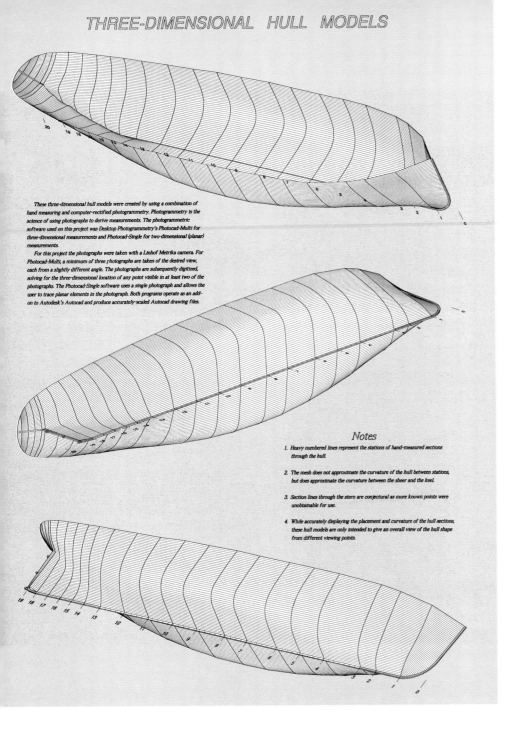

These three-dimensional hull models were created by using a combination of hand measuring and computer-rectified photogrammetry. Photogrammetry is the science of using photographs to derive measurements. The photogrammetric software used on this project was Desktop Photogrammetry's Photocad-Multi for three-dimensional measurements and Photocad-Single for two-dimensional (planar) measurements.

For this project the photographs were taken with a Linhof Metrika camera. For Photocad-Multi, a minimum of three photographs are taken of the desired view, each from a slightly different angle. The photographs are subsequently digitized, solving for the three-dimensional location of any point visible in at least two of the photographs. The Photocad-Single software uses a single photograph and allows the user to trace planar elements in the photograph. Both programs operate as an add-on to Autodesk's Autocad and produce accurately-scaled Autocad drawing files.

Notes

1. Heavy numbered lines represent the stations of hand-measured sections through the hull.

2. The mesh does not approximate the curvature of the hull between stations, but does approximate the curvature between the sheer and the keel.

3. Section lines through the stern are conjectural as more known points were unobtainable for use.

4. While accurately displaying the placement and curvature of the hull sections, these hull models are only intended to give an overall view of the hull shape from different viewing points.

ings, such as illustration of the structural systems of bridges (*see fig. 6.7*). Inevitably, as data collection technologies develop, resulting in more three-dimensional field data, more HABS/HAER drawings will be drawn three-dimensionally as well.

One such digital technology that has recently been integrated into the HABS/HAER documentation process is the use of an electronic total station, the Leica Geosystems TC(R)303. The total station, a surveying device, bounces a laser off either a smooth surface or a handheld reflective target to locate points three-dimensionally in space in relation to the station. The data points can be brought into AutoCAD and connected with lines and surfaces to create a three-dimensional CAD model. This process has proven especially appropriate for very large structures. In 1999 HABS began a multiyear project to document the historic city walls that surround the old city of San Juan, Puerto Rico. More than 2 miles in total length, and up to 65 feet tall in places, the walls consist of a series of straight sections interrupted by irregular, polygonal bastions. With its ability to shoot points over distances of hundreds of feet, the total station proved to be a highly efficient and cost-effective method for gathering the enormous amount of data necessary for this documentation project (*see figs. 9.17 and 9.18*). The total station data were combined with hand measuring of small-scale features and the selective use of photogrammetry to capture details to create a comprehensive set of documents. The total station has subsequently been used for a wide variety of applications, from typical HABS site plans to the aforementioned documentation of ship hulls by HAER and locating the plan outlines of the Oval Office in the White House.

Most recently, HABS/HAER has begun experimenting with the technology of three-dimensional laser scanning. This technique

Figure 9.16
This drawing shows a single ship hull model rotated in three different positions. HAER uses specialized CAD software, such as SurfaceWorks Marine, to document ship hulls.

Figure 9.17
A total of 91 "stations" (locations of the total station), each typically comprising several hundred points, was required to document the San Juan city walls. A HABS team member holds the target at a corner of one of the gun embrasures in the parapet wall, while a second team member shoots the point with the total station.

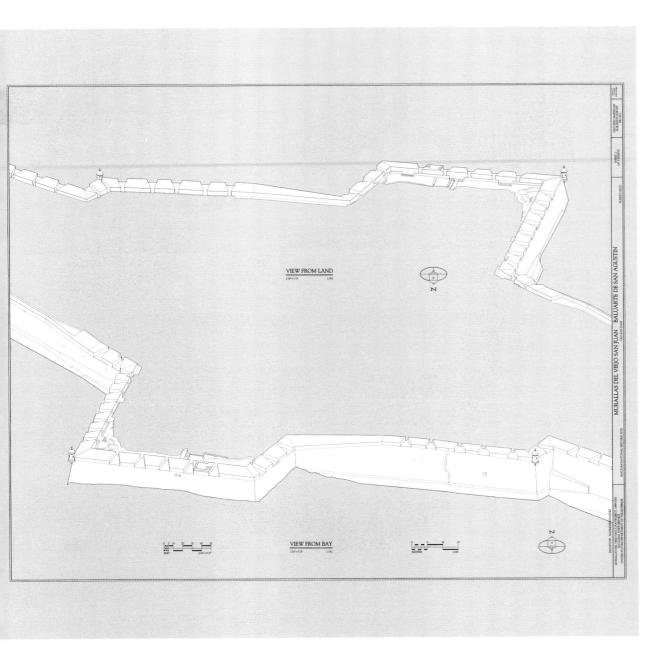

VIEW FROM LAND

VIEW FROM BAY

uses a device that shoots a laser at regular intervals across closely spaced rows, creating a three-dimensional "cloud" of points. Specialized software is then used to map a surface to the points, creating a three-dimensional model. Three-dimensional laser scanning is especially appropriate for large, highly sculptural objects and buildings. In 2001 HABS began a project, in cooperation with Texas Tech University, to document the Statue of Liberty using this technology. A Cyrax 2500 laser scanner was used to gather the data (*see figs. 9.19 and 9.20*). As with any technology, this technique has both advantages and disadvantages. As with photogrammetry, the surfaces to be documented must be visible. Thus, both horizontal surfaces and foliage that obscures vertical surfaces present problems. And unlike the photogrammetric cameras, which have been used in handheld situations on scaffolding and helicopters, the laser scanner requires a still platform from which to operate, typically the ground. In addition, the vast amount of data captured on the

Figure 9.18

The digital total station points gathered from the San Juan city walls, located three-dimensionally in space, were brought into AutoCAD and connected with lines to produce a wireframe model. Here the model of one of the bastions is shown in two different axonometric rotations, from opposite directions. The model was also rotated to show a plan view and straight-on elevations of the individual wall segments.

Figure 9.19
The Cyrax laser scanner gathers data at the Statue of Liberty.

Statue of Liberty project required an enormous amount of computer power for manipulation. The software required to create three-dimensional models is relatively specialized, and the translation of the models into the typical two-dimensional CAD drawings used by HABS remains unresolved (*see fig. 1.9*). Nonetheless, three-dimensional laser scanning presents exciting new possibilities for the documentation of historic structures and sites.

Figure 9.20
A point cloud of the face of the Statue of Liberty is the initial result of the data gathered by the laser scanner.

CHAPTER 10

RECORDING AN INDUSTRIAL PROCESS

Richard K. Anderson, Jr.

An interpretive drawing cross-references and integrates material by putting together details that may otherwise appear separately in accompanying written data, photographs, or standard measured drawings. Interpretive drawings help the user to see significant relationships and features impossible to present effectively with other documentary media. Characteristics that invite this treatment may be structural details, a manufacturing or materials-handling process, the organization of machinery or other elements within a building or site, or the operative principles behind a particular engineering device or system. Interpretive drawings should be made when no other type of presentation is as efficient in terms of content conveyed, cost to produce, or time required for a user to study.

Several types of drawings are effective, depending on what kind of information is to be presented. They may range from the purely schematic to the illustrative to carefully scaled views. Some drawings may combine all these approaches. Examples include sequential maps or plans showing progressive development of a site or building. These may be diagrammatic or highly detailed, depending on the scales and types of changes being shown. Schematic flow charts are excellent for showing the movement of materials and energy between components. Interconnections, flow direction, temperatures, quantities, types of materials, time, power, and other factors often cannot be efficiently presented together in any other way. Isometric or perspective views showing the relationship between components in space can often clarify physical connections, relative sizes, functioning parts, or other factors when surrounding obstructions are graphically stripped away.

Such drawings may also be used to carefully re-create a site from surviving documentary or on-site information, especially when no other representation of the site in its intact condition is known to exist. Isometric cutaways or exploded views are ideal ways to show how something is made internally or assembled from various parts. All such drawings should be copiously annotated but should not duplicate information more effectively left to a manuscript or to photography.

What distinguishes a good interpretive drawing from a bad one? Many of the technical rules governing typical measured drawings apply to interpretive drawings as well. The use of a variety of line weights and the skillful application of illustrating techniques, such as stippling and shadowing, help to convey form and detail, add interest, and provide a visual framework. Drawings done in only one line weight with one or two lettering sizes can be both boring and confusing because they do not "read" well. Clarity is paramount, but this does not necessarily mean simplicity. Several levels of detail or types of information can be presented simultaneously without confusion if each addresses a different aspect of the subject. The rules of good scholarship also apply. Don't insert baseless information or speculation. If you represent something in a manner different from the way it exists or appears in other parts of the project package (in photos, for example), add a note stating what you changed and why. Things omitted for clarity should always be noted. Always cite any preexisting sources on which you have based your work, such as other drawings, photographs, written or oral accounts, or published works. Cross-referencing features in a drawing to specific photographs, photocopied material, or parts of a written monograph about the site is strongly recommended. Labels, keys, descriptive and historical notes, and brief texts explaining your drawings are useful and informative. Scale may or may not be important, depending on its relevance to the information you are presenting. Finally, do not overlook the possibility of photocopying preexisting interpretive drawings. Many industries may permit the reproduction of nonproprietary schematics and flow diagrams once used for managing their historical operations.

Built in 1926, the 500 Area at Picatinny Arsenal was documented in 1983 because the buildings, contaminated by explosives, were slated for demolition as obsolete and unsafe for adaptive reuse. The chemical processes and facilities—state-of-the-art designs for their time—played a major role in developing the powder production facilities that supplied U.S. forces during World War II.

The top diagram on each of the three drawing sheets (*see figs. 10.1, 10.2, and 10.3*) focuses on the chemical process used to produce smokeless powder at this particular plant—not powder production in general, not the building architecture, not even specific production machinery. Coverage of these secondary aspects was left to photography, photocopied original engineering drawings, and the project monograph (*see figs. 10.4 and 10.5*). A highly detailed written description of the process was included on the diagram because the general nature of the monograph did not easily accommodate such concentrated material. Items of secondary significance were treated in the diagram only to help a reader key in other parts of the documentation package.

The perspective diagram was laid out and inked freehand. Liberties were taken with the scale and orientation of the buildings in order to clearly show their functional interrelationships. (Actual site conditions were recorded with a site plan and photographs; *see figs. 10.6, 10.7, and 10.8*.) The pictorial quality of the diagram was enhanced by zeroing in on specific details, such as escape chutes, railway equipment, and the joints in a vitreous tile fume line. Buildings themselves were ghosted in, showing only elements essential to their function and architectural character, such as fire walls, escape chutes, and roof overhangs (*see figs. 10.2 and 10.9*). Minor structures were omitted altogether. Functional elements (tanks, tubs, machines) were shaded to give them a firmer three-dimensional quality than the buildings. Flow arrows and building numbers were delineated boldly for prominence but often made to conform to the perspective planes of adjacent buildings to reinforce the pictorial quality of the drawing. Annotations were used profusely to refer readers to accompanying photographs, to identify buildings, to describe equipment, to indicate the materials and design of safety devices, and to point out speculative features. Care was taken to organize the notes in columns or blocks, defined partially by the buildings, to give the drawing an orderly appearance. Sources of information were clearly cited. As was done here, attention should be paid to the sizes of lettering, drawing details, and line weights in interpretive drawings, since they are often reduced in size, making legibility especially important.

The text for each sheet was composed with the intent of packing in as much relevant information as possible. With a chemical process, such factors as chemical formulas, weights, volumes, temperatures, pressures, times, reactants, products and by-products, purposes of procedures, and terminology must be recorded in detail in order for the drawings to be of maximum benefit to future researchers. Relevant historical notes, numbers of machines, equipment design, and construction features are also included. The language is kept free of unexplained jargon and is organized in a building-by-building, step-by-step fashion. Descriptions of buildings are omitted, since such information is covered elsewhere in the project record.

The schematic portion of the presentation boils down the process to its simplest elements and steps, as described in the text, and organizes them by building. The flow of the schematic is from left to right, the same direction as the pictorial diagram and the text. To help readers interpret the hierarchy of elements more clearly, larger blocks and major labels for buildings are delineated more boldly than those for process steps or smaller buildings. The drawing sheets are laid out parallel to one another in their major divisions so the three sheets may be combined into one with little trouble should any future user desire to do so.

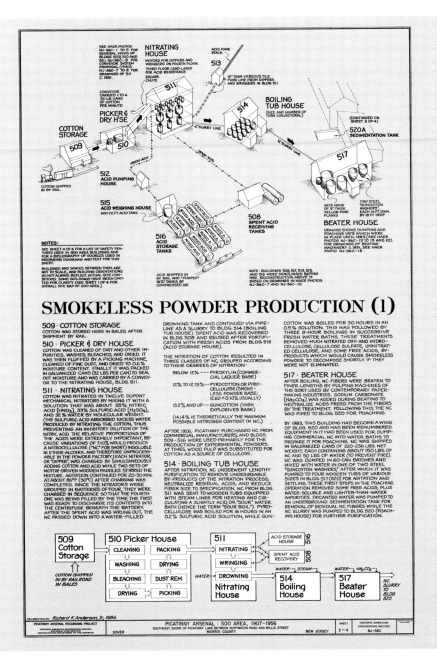

SMOKELESS POWDER PRODUCTION (1)

509 · COTTON STORAGE
COTTON WAS STORED HERE IN BALES AFTER SHIPMENT BY RAIL.

510 · PICKER & DRY HOUSE
COTTON WAS CLEANED OF DIRT AND OTHER IMPURITIES, WASHED, BLEACHED, AND DRIED. IT WAS THEN FLUFFED BY A PICKING MACHINE, CLEANED OF FINE DUST, AND DRIED TO 0.6% MOISTURE CONTENT. FINALLY IT WAS PACKED IN GALVANIZED CANS (32 LBS PER CAN) TO SEAL OUT MOISTURE AND WAS CARRIED BY A CONVEYOR TO THE NITRATING HOUSE, BLDG. 511.

511 · NITRATING HOUSE
COTTON WAS NITRATED IN TWELVE DUPONT MECHANICAL NITRATORS (OR MIXED IN WITH A SOLUTION THAT WAS ABOUT 35% NITRIC ACID [HNO₃], 33% SULFURIC ACID [H₂SO₄], AND 32% WATER BY MOLECULAR WEIGHT. (THE SULFURIC ACID ABSORBED EXCESS WATER PRODUCED BY NITRATING THE COTTON, THUS PREVENTING AN INHIBITORY DILUTION OF THE NITRIC ACID. THE RELATIVE PROPORTIONS OF THE ACIDS WERE EXTREMELY IMPORTANT, BECAUSE VARIATIONS OF ±10% WOULD PRODUCE A NITROCELLULOSE ("NC FOR SHORT) INSOLUBLE IN ETHER-ALCOHOL AND THEREFORE UNPROCESSABLE IN THE POWDER FACTORY.) EACH NITRATOR, OR "DIPPER", WAS CHARGED BY SIMULTANEOUSLY ADDING COTTON AND ACID WHILE TWO SETS OF MOTOR-DRIVEN WOODEN PADDLES STIRRED THE MIXTURE. AGITATION CONTINUED FOR 20-30 MIN, AT ABOUT 86°F (30°C) AFTER CHARGING WAS COMPLETED. SINCE THE NITRATORS WERE GROUPED IN BATTERIES OF FOUR, THEY WERE CHARGED IN SEQUENCE SO THAT THE FOURTH ONE WAS BEING FILLED BY THE TIME THE FIRST WAS READY TO DISCHARGE ITS CONTENTS INTO THE CENTRIFUGE BENEATH THE BATTERY. AFTER THE SPENT ACID WAS WRUNG OUT, THE NC PASSED DOWN INTO A WATER-FILLED

DROWNING TANK AND CONTINUED VIA PIPELINE AS A SLURRY TO BLDG. 514 (BOILING TUB HOUSE). SPENT ACID WAS RECOVERED IN BLDG. 508 AND REUSED AFTER FORTIFICATION WITH FRESH ACIDS FROM BLDG 516 (ACID STORAGE HOUSE).

THE NITRATION OF COTTON RESULTED IN THREE CLASSES OF NC, GROUPED ACCORDING TO THEIR DEGREES OF NITRATION:

BELOW 12% --- PYROXYLIN (COMMERCIAL LAQUER BASE)

12% TO 12.75%-- PYROCOTTON OR PYROCELLULOSE (SMOKELESS POWDER BASE; 12.60 ± 0.10% USUALLY)

13.2% AND UP-- GUNCOTTON (HIGH EXPLOSIVES BASE)

(14.14% IS THEORETICALLY THE MAXIMUM POSSIBLE NITROGEN CONTENT IN NC.)

AFTER 1926, PICATINNY PURCHASED NC FROM COMMERCIAL MANUFACTURERS AND BLDGS. 509-516 WERE USED PRIMARILY FOR THE PRODUCTION OF EXPERIMENTAL POWDERS. AT TIMES, WOOD PULP WAS SUBSTITUTED FOR COTTON AS A SOURCE OF CELLULOSE.

514 · BOILING TUB HOUSE
AFTER NITRATION, NC UNDERWENT LENGTHY PURIFICATION TO REMOVE UNDESIRABLE BY-PRODUCTS OF THE NITRATION PROCESS, NEUTRALIZE RESIDUAL ACIDS, AND REDUCE FIBER SIZE TO SPECIFICATION. NC FROM BLDG. 511 WAS SENT TO WOODEN TUBS EQUIPPED WITH STEAM LINES FOR HEATING AND CIRCULATING A SLIGHTLY ACID OR "SOUR" WATER BATH (HENCE THE TERM "SOUR BOIL"). PYROCELLULOSE WAS BOILED FOR 16 HOURS IN A 0.2% SULFURIC ACID SOLUTION, WHILE GUN-

COTTON WAS BOILED FOR 30 HOURS IN AN 0.5% SOLUTION. THIS WAS FOLLOWED BY THREE 8-HOUR BOILINGS IN SUCCESSIVE FRESH WATER BATHS. THESE TREATMENTS REMOVED MUCH NITRATED OXY- AND HYDROCELLULOSE, CELLULOSE SULFATE, UNNITRATED CELLULOSE, AND SOME FREE ACIDS, BY-PRODUCTS WHICH WOULD CAUSE SMOKELESS POWDER TO DECOMPOSE SHORTLY IF THEY WERE NOT ELIMINATED.

517 · BEATER HOUSE
AFTER BOILING, NC FIBERS WERE BEATEN TO FINER LENGTHS BY PULPING MACHINES OF THE SORT USED BY CONTEMPORARY PAPERMAKING INDUSTRIES. SODIUM CARBONATE [Na₂CO₃] WAS ADDED DURING BEATING TO NEUTRALIZE ACIDS FREED FROM THE FIBERS BY THE TREATMENT. FOLLOWING THIS, THE NC WAS PIPED TO BLDG. 520 FOR POACHING.

BY 1983, THIS BUILDING HAD BECOME A WING OF BLDG. 520 AND HAD BEEN RENUMBERED. EQUIPMENT IN IT HAD BEEN USED FOR DUMPING COMMERCIAL NC INTO WATER BATHS TO PREPARE IT FOR POACHING. NC WAS SHIPPED IN GALVANIZED CANS OF 220-236 LBS. NET WEIGHT, EACH CONTAINING ABOUT 150 LBS OF NC AND 50 LBS OF WATER (TO PREVENT FIRE). NC WAS DUMPED IN 60-CAN BATCHES AND MIXED WITH WATER IN ONE OF TWO STEEL "GUNCOTTON WASHERS," AFTER WHICH IT WAS PUMPED TO FOUR WOODEN TUBS OR VARIOUS SIZES IN BLDG. 517 (520) FOR AGITATION AND SETTLING. THESE FIRST STEPS IN THE POACHING OPERATION REMOVED SOME FREE ACIDS, PLUS WATER-SOLUBLE AND LIGHTER-THAN-WATER IMPURITIES. DECANTED WATER WAS PUMPED TO AN UNDERGROUND SEDIMENTATION TANK FOR REMOVAL OF RESIDUAL NC FIBERS WHILE THE NC SLURRY WAS PUMPED TO BLDG. 520 (POACHING HOUSE) FOR FURTHER PURIFICATION.

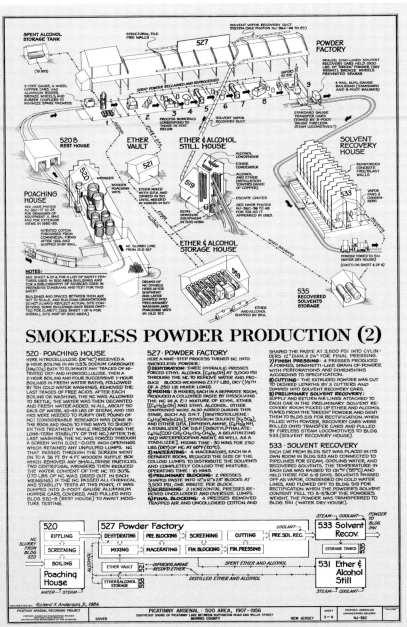

SMOKELESS POWDER PRODUCTION (2)

520 · POACHING HOUSE
HERE NITROCELLULOSE (OR "NC") RECEIVED A 6-HOUR BOILING IN AN 0.5% SODIUM CARBONATE [Na₂CO₃] BATH TO ELIMINATE ANY TRACES OF NITRATED OXY- AND HYDROCELLULOSE. THEN A 2-HOUR BOILING AND FOUR SUCCESSIVE 1-HOUR BOILINGS IN FRESH WATER BATHS, FOLLOWED BY TEN COLD WATER WASHINGS, REMOVED THE LAST TRACES OF FREE ACIDS. AFTER EACH BOILING OR WASHING, THE NC WAS ALLOWED TO SETTLE; THE WATER WAS THEN DECANTED AND FRESH WATER ADDED. IN ALL, ABOUT 150 GALS. OF WATER, 40-45 LBS. OF STEAM, AND 150 HRS WERE NEEDED TO PURIFY ONE POUND OF NC! (CONSIDERABLE RESEARCH WAS DONE IN THE 1930s AND 1940s TO FIND WAYS TO SHORTEN THIS TREATMENT WHILE PRESERVING THE LONG-TERM STABILITY OF THE NC.) AFTER THE LAST WASHING, THE NC WAS FORCED THROUGH A SCREEN WITH 0.012-0.025 INCH OPENINGS WHICH RETAINED ANY UNPULPED LUMPS. NC THAT PASSED THROUGH THE SCREEN WENT ON TO A 36 FT BY 4 FT WOODEN RIFFLE BOX WHICH REMOVED ANY SMALL, DENSE PARTICLES. TWO CENTRIFUGAL WRINGERS THEN REDUCED THE WATER CONTENT OF THE NC TO 30% (170 LBS. OF NC WAS DRIED OUT IN EACH WRINGING.) IF THE NC PASSED ALL CHEMICAL AND STABILITY TESTS AT THIS POINT, IT WAS DUMPED INTO 3-FOOT GAUGE ALUMINUM HOPPER CARS (COVERED, AND PULLED INTO BLDG. 520-B (REST HOUSE) TO AWAIT MOISTURE TESTING.

527 · POWDER FACTORY
HERE A NINE-STEP PROCESS TURNED NC INTO SMOKELESS POWDER:
1) DEHYDRATION: THREE HYDRAULIC PRESSES FORCED ETHYL ALCOHOL [C₂H₅OH] AT 3,000 PSI THROUGH THE NC TO REMOVE WATER AND PRODUCE BLOCKS WEIGHING 27.77 LBS, DRY (⅓TH OF A 250 LB. MIXER LOAD).
2) MIXING: 8 MIXERS, EACH IN A SEPARATE ROOM, PRODUCED A COLLOIDED PASTE BY DISSOLVING THE NC IN A 2:1 MIXTURE OF ETHYL ETHER [(C₂H₅)₂O] AND ETHYL ALCOHOL. OTHER COMPOUNDS WERE ALSO ADDED DURING THIS STAGE, SUCH AS: D.N.T. [DINITROTOLUENE: C₆H₃(NO₂)₂CH₃], POTASSIUM SULFATE [K₂SO₄], AND ETHER D.P.A. [DIPHENYLAMINE, (C₆H₅)₂NH], A STABILIZER] OR D.B.P. [DIBUTYLPHTALATE: C₆H₄(COO·CH₂·CH₂·CH₂·CH₃)₂, A GELATINIZING AND WATERPROOFING AGENT, AS WELL AS A STABILIZER]. MIXING TIME : 30 MINS. FOR 250 LBS (DRY) OF NC AT 68°F (20°C).
3) MACERATING: 4 MACERATORS, EACH IN A SEPARATE ROOM, REDUCED THE SIZE OF THE COLLOID LUMPS TO DISTRIBUTE THE SOLVENTS AND COMPLETELY COLLOID THE MIXTURE. MACERATION TIME : 10 MINS.
4) PRELIMINARY BLOCKING: 2 PRESSES SHAPED PASTE INTO 12"x12"x24" BLOCKS AT 3,500 PSI, ONE MINUTE PER BLOCK.
5) SCREENING: 2 HORIZONTAL PRESSES REMOVED UNCOLLOIDED AND OVERSIZE LUMPS.
6) FINAL BLOCKING: 4 PRESSES REMOVED TRAPPED AIR AND UNCOLLOIDED COTTON AND

SHAPED THE PASTE AT 3,500 PSI INTO CYLINDERS 12"DIAM X 24" FOR FINAL PRESSING.
7) FINISH PRESSING: 4 PRESSES PRODUCED A FORMED, SPAGHETTI-LIKE GRAIN OF POWDER WITH PERFORATIONS AND DIMENSIONS ACCORDING TO SPECIFICATION.
8) CUTTING : THE EXTRUDED POWDER WAS CUT TO DESIRED LENGTHS BY 3 CUTTERS AND DUMPED INTO SOLVENT RECOVERY CARS.
9) PRELIMINARY SOLVENT RECOVERY: SUPPLY AND RETURN AIR LINES ATTACHED TO EACH CAR IN THE PRELIMINARY SOLVENT RECOVERY ROOM PICKED UP ETHER AND ALCOHOL FUMES FROM THE "GREEN" POWDER AND SENT THEM TO BLDG. 519 FOR RECTIFICATION. WHEN FILLED WITH POWDER, RECOVERY CARS WERE ROLLED ONTO TRANSFER CARS AND PULLED BY FIRELESS STEAM LOCOMOTIVES TO BLDG. 533 (SOLVENT RECOVERY HOUSE).

533 · SOLVENT RECOVERY
EACH CAR FROM BLDG. 527 WAS PLACED IN ITS OWN ROOM IN BLDG. 533 AND CONNECTED TO PIPELINES FOR STEAM, COOLING WATER, AND RECOVERED SOLVENTS. THE TEMPERATURE IN THE WATER WAS RAISED TO 131°F (55°C) AND HELD THERE FOR 6-8 DAYS. SOLVENTS PASSED OFF AS VAPOR, CONDENSED ON COLD WATER LINES, AND FLOWED OFF TO BLDG. 519 FOR RECTIFICATION. WHEN THE POWDER'S SOLVENT CONTENT FELL TO 3-5% OF THE POWDER'S WEIGHT, THE POWDER WAS TRANSFERRED TO BLDG. 541 (WATER DRY HOUSE).

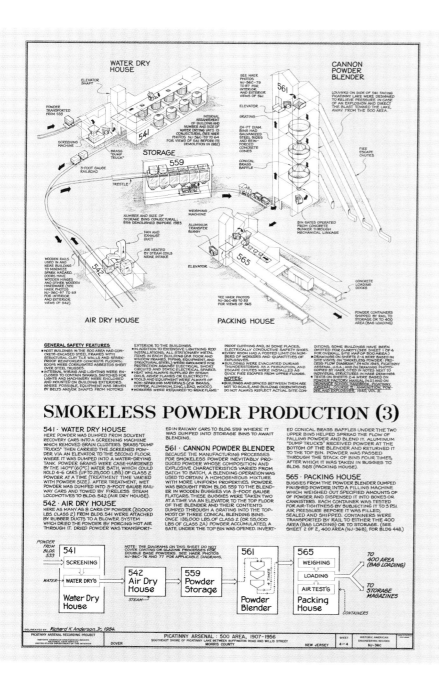

Picatinny Arsenal is one example of an interpretive presentation. The methods used in this case are not applicable to the documentation of all industrial processes. In some cases, sequential views should be used to show principal motions (as in the case of an elliptical picture frame lathe). Annotated sections of an object may suffice to present its operating features (as in the case of a blast furnace). Still others may benefit from a scaled isometric depiction of critical elements, with features such as the surrounding building stripped away for clarity. The possibilities are numerous, but the idea is to balance relevant information, appropriate analytical presentation, clarity, and visual appeal.

Figures 10.1, 10.2, and 10.3
Smokeless powder production at the Picatinny Arsenal is presented with three parallel descriptions spread over three sheets designed to supplement each other. A diagram at the top of each sheet realistically presents the forms of the buildings, examples of specific internal machinery, safety features, and major interconnections (pipes, ducts, railways). The text provides detailed, step-by-step chemical data, and the bottom diagram presents the whole process schematically. The information provided allows readers to study the 500 Area of the Picatinny Arsenal at several different levels: where one function takes place relative to others, how that function operates chemically, and how that function fits into the production concept.

Figure 10.4
This photograph of the distillation towers inside Building 519 at the Picatinny Arsenal picks up in mechanical detail where the process drawing leaves off.

Figure 10.5

These presses in Building 527 of the Picatinny Arsenal, drawn schematically in figure 10.2, removed water from pyrocotton slurry processed in Building 520.

Figure 10.6

This photograph of the cotton nitration line at the Picatinny Arsenal is one of many used instead of measured drawings to record the architectural appearance of Buildings 509, 510, and 511. Measured drawings were reserved for the more significant chemical processes taking place inside the structures.

Figure 10.7

Building 519 of the Picatinny Arsenal, shown in figure 10.2, recovered ether and alcohol vapors for reuse in the powder manufacturing process. Some of its exterior details, simplified in the process diagram, are made plain here.

Figure 10.8
This view of the cannon powder blender (Building 561 of the Picatinny Arsenal) from across Lake Picatinny shows a wall designed to relieve the forces of an explosion should any occur in the building. The isolation of the building further illustrates the potential danger of the operation it housed.

Figure 10.9
Building 519 of the Picatinny Arsenal was equipped with slides for quick escape by workers in the event of fire.

CHAPTER 11

RECORDING HISTORIC LANDSCAPES
Paul D. Dolinsky

One of the first broad attempts to document historic landscapes in the United States was organized by the Garden Club of America (GCA). The leaders of this established national club recognized the need to preserve early American gardens as a part of the collective heritage, if not as physical gardens, then in print and pictures. In response, the group initiated a general survey effort in the early 1930s. Local chapters documented historic landscapes, emphasizing settlement-era agriculture, subsistence gardening, and ornamental gardening. Most of the work took place in the twenty-seven states that had entered the Union by 1840.

There were no nationally defined standards for documenting historic gardens and landscapes, so the GCA survey work employed a wide array of documentation styles. Interestingly, the three typical forms of documentation paralleled those adopted around the same time by HABS and other similar documentation efforts: some type of written historical description of each site and hand drawings (ranging from sketches to professional measured drawings) and/or black-and-white photographs.

Early Federal Efforts at Landscape Documentation

From the founding of the Historic American Buildings Survey in 1933, the importance of landscape documentation was recognized, and documentation of historic landscapes, although not a priority, was routinely included in architectural projects when appropriate. This documentation usually took the form of a site plan or property plan associated with a historic structure and included botanical designations, though rarely any further analysis. Numerous examples exist throughout the HABS collection.

The Lindens, in Danvers, Massachusetts, was recorded beginning in January 1934, only two months after HABS was founded. Twenty-seven sheets of measured drawings were completed by July, including two site plans, a plan of the grounds, and a more detailed plan of the flower garden, making the property one of the more thoroughly documented houses in the early HABS collection. Accompanying the drawings were twenty-one photographs of the house, taken in January to minimize coverage by the foliage of deciduous trees. The only landscape features recorded in the photographs were in the foreground of the general views of the house.

The plan of grounds is a general site plan that defines major designed areas, including the axis that runs from the formal tree-lined front drive through the house to the informal rear lawn and terminates in the formal garden (see

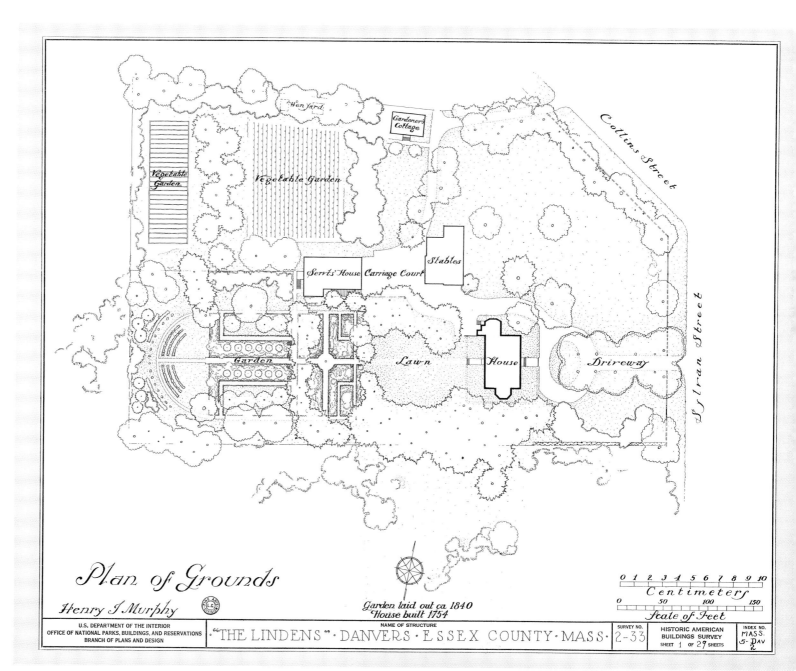

Figure 11.1

The 1934 HABS ground plan of The Lindens shows the overall site plan and the relationship of major architectural and landscape features. Landscape features were recorded in representational renderings, including the important spaces between the house and the support structures. Although the property line is clearly defined, no survey locations are indicated. The illustrative and schematic nature of this drawing reflects an architectural approach to documenting a landscape.

Plan of Grounds

Henry J Murphy

Garden laid out ca 1840
House built 1754

U.S. DEPARTMENT OF THE INTERIOR
OFFICE OF NATIONAL PARKS, BUILDINGS, AND RESERVATIONS
BRANCH OF PLANS AND DESIGN

NAME OF STRUCTURE
"THE LINDENS" · DANVERS · ESSEX COUNTY · MASS ·

SURVEY NO.
2-33

HISTORIC AMERICAN
BUILDINGS SURVEY
SHEET 1 OF 29 SHEETS

INDEX NO.
MASS.
5-DAV
2

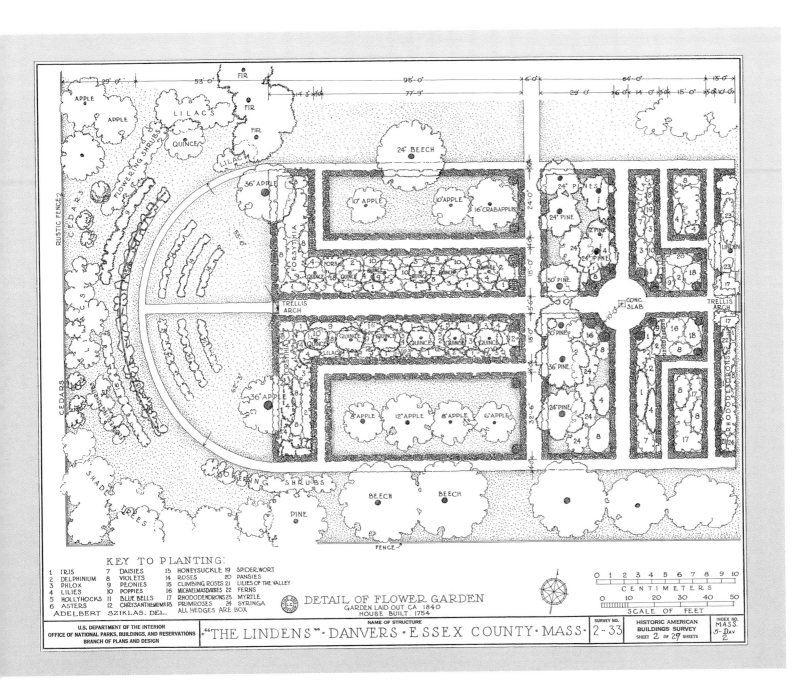

Figure 11.2
The 1934 flower garden plan of The Lindens was measured but not surveyed. The planting beds were made orthogonal in the drawing, and no topographic information was included. Selected specimen trees and planting areas were delineated and identified with common names. Compare this plan with that in the following illustration.

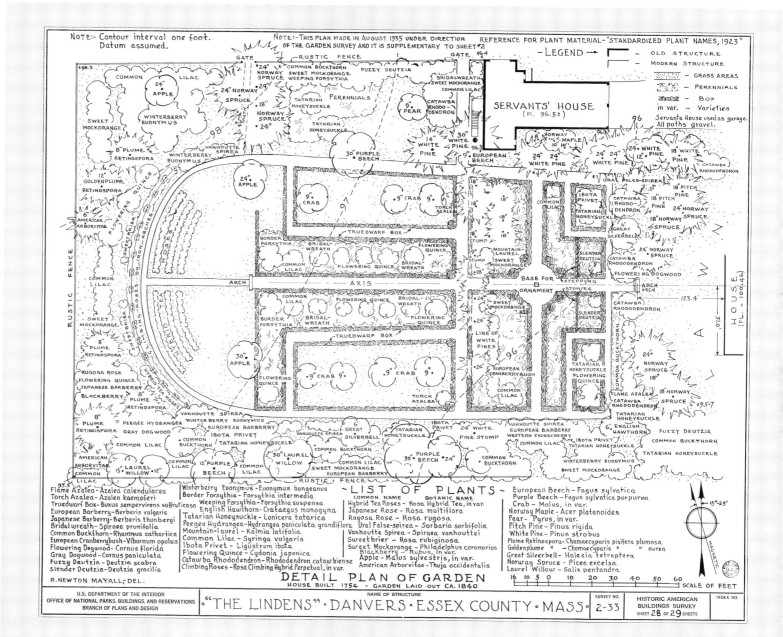

Figure 11.3

The 1935 detail plan of The Lindens garden, produced by HALGP, supplemented the 1934 HABS drawing of the same area. The garden was surveyed, as shown by the presence of contour lines and floor elevations in feet and decimal feet. Also note that the planting beds are not rectilinear. All plant materials are noted, sized, and identified by their scientific and common names, referenced to Standardized Plant Names (1923). Both magnetic and true north are identified. Compare this plan with the previous illustration.

fig. 11.1). Also noted on the grounds plan are support structures such as the servant's house, stables, and gardener's cottage and the important spaces between them, which include the vegetable gardens, carriage court, and informal surrounding landscape. Although the property line is clearly defined, no survey locations are indicated. The detail drawing of the flower garden shows various plantings, with specimen trees identified and sized. A numbered key is used to identify plant materials, which are labeled by their common names (*see fig. 11.2*).

Following the success of HABS, the Historic American Landscape and Garden Project (HALGP) was established in Massachusetts in 1935. This Works Progress Administration–funded documentation program was administered by the National Park Service field office in Massachusetts from 1935 to 1940. The HALGP team revisited the Lindens and supplemented the landscape plans completed the previous year by HABS with two additional drawings in HABS format.

Landscape architect R. Newton Mayall produced a detail plan of the garden, which includes detailed botanical designations, contour intervals, tree calipers, and spatial analysis (*see fig. 11.3*). The other HALGP sheet documents the evolution of the garden from 1754 to 1929 in a series of four similarly scaled plans that graphically analyze site development and are supported and interpreted with brief discussions of the plans (*see fig. 11.4*). Since the entire house was moved to Washington, D.C., little evidence other than the four HABS and HALGP measured drawings document the original site.

During its short existence, HALGP completed comprehensive documentation of forty-eight Massachusetts sites with historical landscape significance. Also similar to HABS was the requirement for historical perspective; HALGP focused on gardens established prior to 1840. The staff included seven landscape architects, a civil engineer, a surveyor, and an architect.

The HALGP documentation methodology and standards fundamentally mirrored those of HABS. However, the trained landscape architects were better able to capture the subtle, ephemeral nature of landscape and to add more layers of spatial and botanical analysis. The first measured drawing was typically an overall plan at a scale sufficient to capture boundaries, streets, foliage masses, significant trees, and buildings on one sheet, as well as the relationship of the garden to the house and its dependencies. Topographical lines were routinely included at either 1-foot or 5-foot intervals, and remains of old foundations or paths were drawn. Further drawings included important landscape features at a larger scale, including botanical and common designations for plant materials. Where significant garden structures or fencing survived, architectural drawings in a larger scale were prepared. Close observation reveals that the measured drawings produced under the auspices of HALGP are rich in informative annotations and graphic detail.

The Vale, in Waltham, Massachusetts, was one of the landscapes documented most extensively under the auspices of HALGP. The estate was the country seat of Theodore Lyman and included all the requirements of a country gentleman's seat, including a deer park, woodland, pleasure grounds, ponds, formal and informal gardens, and orchards (*see fig. 11.5*). A general plan of the entire property was drawn, followed by larger-scale detail plans. All the drawings are extensively annotated with botanical designations and construction details. Use of standardized botanical nomenclature was important to the HALGP advisory board, and *Standardized Plant Names* (1923), their accepted standard, was referenced on these drawings (*see fig. 11.6*).

It is unusual that the mansion at the Vale was not documented by HABS. Numerous reasons could account for this. The mansion may not have been accessible; the original measuring team may have hoped to return and never made it, or possibly the changes made to the mansion in 1882 reduced the building's perceived importance.

Although Massachusetts had the most defined effort, other HABS district offices undertook landscape documentation as well. A benefit of HABS landscape documentation is the vast number of measured drawings and photographs of early garden architecture that are included. Garden houses, well houses, greenhouses, sundials, fences, and summer houses were routinely recorded. The only documentation completed for the Ashhurst Estate in Mount Holly, New Jersey, were four sheets of measured drawings and one large-format photograph of the summer house (*see figs. 11.7 and 11.8*). The drawings include plans, elevations, details, and a perspective view of this unique Chinese pagoda.

An example of early documentation in the HABS collection that integrates architecture and landscape architecture and also communicates how the land was used is the Lobster Cove project in Massachusetts (*see fig. 11.9*). Through one general and four detail drawings, the vitality of an eighteenth- and early nineteenth-century fishing village was captured. The draftsman combined small plans and notes with rendered projections, including terrestrial views from the harbor, enlivened with ships, wharves, vegetation, and people (*see figs. 11.10 and 2.10*). Clearly, each element could have been documented individually as a fine architectural, maritime, or landscape example, but the intent was to recognize and document the significance of the interrelationships between these elements.

Figure 11.4

The HALGP team at The Lindens produced a drawing showing how the property evolved from 1754 to 1929. The series of plans depicting site development are supported and interpreted with a brief history and description of each. In addition to physical evidence on the site itself, the surveyors used documentary evidence from old engravings and diaries to learn of earlier site conditions. Sources for information about the historic features were cited on the drawing.

Slave Quarters & Burying Ground somewhere in the rear.

White Pines

Probable Garden

Farm Land

Cottage · Elms · Barn

Terrace

House

European Lindens

·OLD BAY, or IPSWICH ROAD·

·Before 1840·

1637–1644. Part of the 200 acre tract granted to John Endicott, first governor of Massachusetts Bay Colony.

1753–1765. Robert "King" Hooper of Marblehead bought parcels of land aggregating 40 acres, and built "The Great House." Of surviving planting it, it is believed that he was responsible for the double row of European Lindens leading from the front gate to the house; the English Elms and the row of White Pines behind the house.

1774. Property mortgaged to Hooper's London agents. Occupied by Gen. Gage, last Royal governor of Massachusetts, during the summer; his troops encamped across the road. There was, in this field, a large oak, called the King's whipping post, where soldiers were punished. When, years later, it was cut down to furnish timbers for the frigate ESSEX, an iron ring was found imbedded in its trunk.

1798. Property purchased by Judge Benajah Collins of Liverpool, Nova Scotia. He died in 1820, his wife in 1827, and the place was occupied by their daughter Deborah until 1832.

Work done with Mass. E.R.A. Funds.
R.E. Saunier, Del.

Orchard

Norway Spruces

White Pines Garden

Norway Spruces

Picket Fence · Elms · Barn

Terrace · House

Board Fence

Rail Fence

European Lindens

Picket Fence

·IPSWICH ROAD·

·1840–1860·

1832–1836. Property sold to Capt. Jeremiah Briggs of Salem, and divided into three parcels. Collins Street cut through, 1837.

1844. Rev. Petrus Stuyvesant Tenbroeck, grandson of the Revolutionary general of that name, bought the house and 7½ acres of land. He kept a private school for boys, and seems to have planted the rows of Spruce trees, and the orchard. He died in 1849.

1849–1860. The property changed hands a number of times, and suffered from lack of care.

~ REFERENCES ~
OLD ENGRAVINGS, DIARIES, & FEATURES EXISTING IN 1935.

~ GENERAL LEGEND ~

Trees, Deciduous. Grass. Trees, Coniferous.

Flowers.

ARBOR · Platform

Roses

Buckthorn Hedge

Sundial · Studio · Servants' House

Red Pines · Roses · Lodge

LAWN Elm

Stable

Statue

European Lindens

Urn · Urn

·SYLVAN STREET·

·1860–1914·

1860. Property bought by Francis Peabody, architect, and a descendant in the eighth generation from Gov. Endicott. During the fifty years that he and his wife lived here, the house and grounds were enriched and beautified. A new stable was built, partly incorporating the old barn; the Servants' House and Gardener's Lodge were built, and a great many trees were planted everywhere. The garden area was at first the children's play ground, with a railed platform in one of the apple trees of the old orchard. Behind the White Pines was a dump, from which relics were subsequently retrieved. Several acres of land were bought back.

1900. Martha Brooks, landscape architect, laid out a formal garden from lines already there. The walks were first edged with brick, later replaced with Box. An elaborate treillage arbor closed in the rear of the garden.

1910. Mr. Peabody died, and Mrs. Peabody the following year, leaving the place to their son.

Recorded 1935.

Roses

Vegetables (Lawn Later)

Studio · Servants' House

Elms · Lodge

Lilacs · Stable

Roses

House

European Lindens

·SYLVAN STREET·

·1914–1934·

1914. The place was bought by Mr. Ward Thoron of Washington, D.C.

1920. Fields at the rear were exchanged for the 40' strip at the south. Old rose bushes were collected and planted south of the house, surrounded with a circle of hybrid Lilacs supplied by Prof. Sargent, of the Arnold Arboretum. The arbor fell under a heavy weight of snow, and was replaced by the present semicircle of iron arches, brought from "Oak Hill" in Peabody. From "Oak Hill" also came the lattice arches at either end of the center path, and 4 urns, placed on posts along the front fence. These are all thought to have been the work of Samuel McIntire. The urns are now in the garden of the Endicott Farm in Danvers.

1933. Bought by Mr. Leon David of Boston.

1934. In August, the house was bought by Mr. George M. Morris, taken down and removed to Washington, D.C.

1934. In October, the land, now 5.275 acres, was bought by John J. Lynch, the present owner.

EVOLUTION OF THE GARDEN
HOUSE BUILT 1754 ~ GARDEN DEVELOPMENT ~ 1754 to 1929.

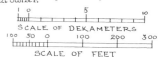

SCALE OF DEKAMETERS
SCALE OF FEET

| U.S. DEPARTMENT OF THE INTERIOR OFFICE OF NATIONAL PARKS, BUILDINGS, AND RESERVATIONS BRANCH OF PLANS AND DESIGN | NAME OF STRUCTURE "THE LINDENS" · DANVERS · ESSEX · CO · MASS· | SURVEY NO. 2-33 | HISTORIC AMERICAN BUILDINGS SURVEY SHEET 29 OF 29 SHEETS | INDEX NO. |

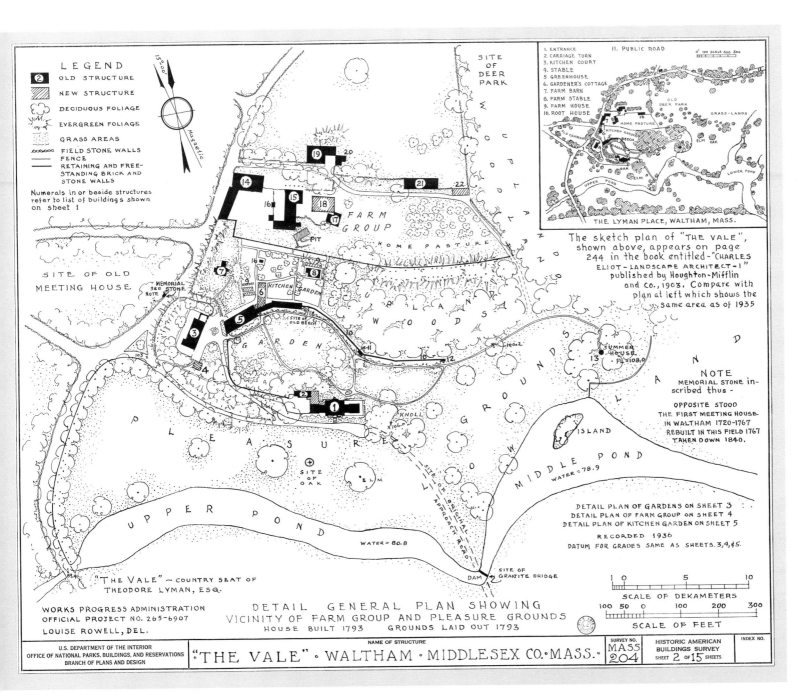

LEGEND
- **2** OLD STRUCTURE
- NEW STRUCTURE
- DECIDUOUS FOLIAGE
- EVERGREEN FOLIAGE
- GRASS AREAS
- FIELD STONE WALLS
- FENCE
- RETAINING AND FREE-STANDING BRICK AND STONE WALLS

Numerals in or beside structures refer to list of buildings shown on Sheet 1

15°00'
Magnetic

SITE OF DEER PARK

FARM GROUP

HOME PASTURE

SITE OF OLD MEETING HOUSE

MEMORIAL SEE STONE NOTE

KITCHEN GARDEN

SITE OF OLD BEECH

G A R D E N

P L E A S U R E   G R O U N D S

U P L A N D   W O O D S

The sketch plan of "THE VALE", shown above, appears on page 244 in the book entitled "CHARLES ELIOT-LANDSCAPE ARCHITECT-1" published by Houghton-Mifflin and Co., 1903. Compare with plan at left which shows the same area as of 1935.

NOTE
MEMORIAL STONE inscribed thus -

OPPOSITE STOOD THE FIRST MEETING HOUSE IN WALTHAM 1720-1767 REBUILT IN THIS FIELD 1767 TAKEN DOWN 1840.

SUMMER HOUSE FL=108.0
13

ISLAND

MIDDLE POND
WATER = 78.9

KNOLL

SITE OF OAK

SITE OF ORIGINAL APPROACH ROAD

U P P E R   P O N D

WATER = 80.8

DETAIL PLAN OF GARDENS ON SHEET 3
DETAIL PLAN OF FARM GROUP ON SHEET 4
DETAIL PLAN OF KITCHEN GARDEN ON SHEET 5

RECORDED 1936
DATUM FOR GRADES SAME AS SHEETS 3,4,&5.

SITE OF GRANITE BRIDGE
DAM

"THE VALE" - COUNTRY SEAT OF THEODORE LYMAN, ESQ.

WORKS PROGRESS ADMINISTRATION
OFFICIAL PROJECT NO. 265-6907
LOUISE ROWELL, DEL.

DETAIL GENERAL PLAN SHOWING VICINITY OF FARM GROUP AND PLEASURE GROUNDS
HOUSE BUILT 1793   GROUNDS LAID OUT 1793

SCALE OF DEKAMETERS
SCALE OF FEET

U.S. DEPARTMENT OF THE INTERIOR
OFFICE OF NATIONAL PARKS, BUILDINGS, AND RESERVATIONS
BRANCH OF PLANS AND DESIGN

NAME OF STRUCTURE
"THE VALE" · WALTHAM · MIDDLESEX CO. · MASS. ·

SURVEY NO. MASS 204

HISTORIC AMERICAN BUILDINGS SURVEY
SHEET 2 OF 15 SHEETS

INDEX NO.

Inset (upper right):

II. PUBLIC ROAD
1. ENTRANCE
2. CARRIAGE TURN
3. KITCHEN COURT
4. STABLE
5. GREENHOUSE
6. GARDENER'S COTTAGE
7. FARM BARN
8. FARM STABLE
9. FARM HOUSE
10. ROOT HOUSE

0' 100 SCALE 400 500

OLD DEER PARK

GRASS-LANDS

HOME PASTURE

KITCHEN GARDEN

OLD COMMON

BEECH

ELM   OAK

UPPER POND

OAK   ELM

LOWER POND

THE LYMAN PLACE, WALTHAM, MASS.

Figure 11.5
The Vale was the country seat of Theodore Lyman. The estate was laid out in 1793 with a variety of landscape features, including a deer park, woodland, pleasure grounds, ponds, formal and informal gardens, and orchards. This 1936 general plan of the central portion of the estate is accompanied by a 1903 sketch of the property to show changes over the intervening years. At this scale, area relationships are shown with little detail.

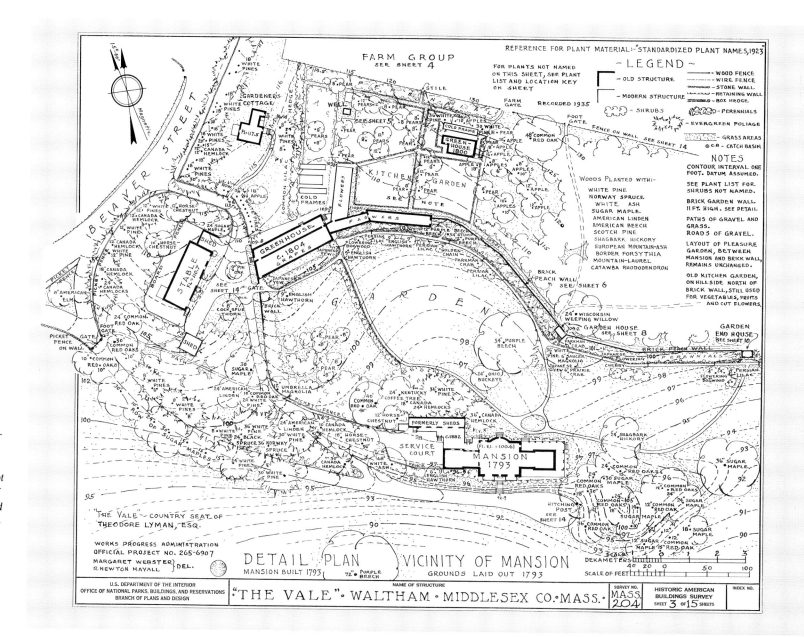

Figure 11.6

A detail plan of the immediate area around the mansion at The Vale includes contours at 1-foot intervals, identification of major plant materials and trees, and extensive annotations. A separate sheet with a plant list and location key provided even more detail. Numerous outbuildings were recorded, although the main house was not.

Figure 11.7
Compare this photograph of a summer house with the drawings in the next illustration. Each complements the other, offering unique information essential to understanding and interpreting the structure in its setting.

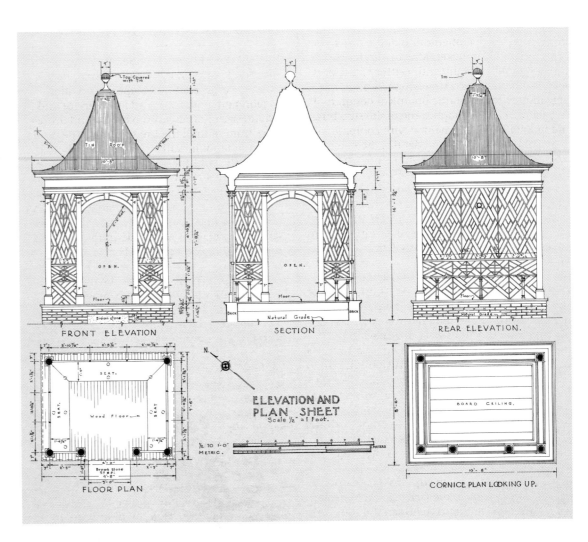

Figure 11.8
A series of measured drawings of the same summer house are detailed enough to allow its reconstruction, but offer little insight into its surrounding landscape.

An example of urban streetscape recording is found in the documentation of the India Street area of Nantucket, Massachusetts. A significant group of eighteenth-century structures was documented as a streetscape in plan and elevation with schematic botanical designations (*see fig. 11.11*). Although some of the structures are individually documented with comprehensive plans, elevations, and details, the neighborhood study analyzes the relationship between structures and the overall streetscape. Similarly, the streetscapes surrounding Lafayette Square in Washington, D.C., were recorded and three drawings were developed to depict the evolution of the square and streetscapes over time (*see fig. 11.12*). Again, some of the structures were individually recorded.

The 1970s HABS project to document the Missouri Botanical Garden in St. Louis, one of the oldest U.S. botanical institutions, renewed interest in landscape-only recording. HABS documentation guidelines were amended to address a more professional and methodical approach to documenting landscapes. *Hortus Third: A Concise Dictionary of Plants Cultivated in the United States and Canada* (1976) was adopted as the source for botanical designations.

The historic methodology of an overall site plan accompanied by detailed plans was maintained. However, because of the large size of the garden, a mosaic of detail sheets was developed to adequately capture the overall site at a reasonable scale (*see figs. 11.13 and 4.43*). A major difference between the Missouri Botanical Garden documentation and previous HABS landscape documentation was the conscious integration of all three forms of documentation. This comprehensive approach was more effective for recording and interpreting the unique character of landscape features (*see fig. 11.14*).

Modern Landscape Documentation

In 1984 the National Park Service convened a meeting to address the rapidly developing national interest in landscape preservation. Meeting attendees included Park Service and private sector landscape architects and academics from around the United States. The result was a series of initiatives or tasks distributed among the cultural resource programs of the National Park Service. HABS was tasked with developing pilot projects to serve as prototypes for investigating new and comprehensive methods for documenting sites of landscape significance. The first project in this effort was the documentation of Meridian Hill Park in Washington, D.C.

Meridian Hill Park, owned by the National Park Service, was one of the first public parks in the United States to be designed as a formal park based on French and Italian Renaissance traditions. A harmonious blend of architectural and horticultural elements sits on approximately 11 acres of steeply sloping land. Exposed aggregate concrete was used for the massive retaining walls and water cascade, as well as numerous decorative elements and paving patterns. The park suffered with the decline in inner city population and rise in crime beginning in the 1960s, but a general rejuvenation of the area in the 1980s encouraged the National Park Service to begin restoration plans (*see fig. 4.25*).

Original drawings of the park existed, but they reflected the design intent and not the existing conditions. Since numerous trees and shrubs had grown to maturity or been removed, the pilot project was to provide a complete set of existing-condition documents that could serve as the basis for the preservation planning and restoration process (*see figs. 11.15 and 11.16*).

The second pilot project undertaken by HABS was Dumbarton Oaks Park, also in Washington, D.C. This project explored a type of landscape far different from that at Meridian Hill Park. Dumbarton Oaks Park, also owned and maintained by the Park Service, is adjacent to the privately owned Dumbarton Oaks house and garden. The park was originally designed as the naturalistic component of the garden by Beatrix Ferrand, the famous landscape gardener of the overall estate. She designed the naturalistic park as a controlled watershed, with meadows, bridle path, and forest, in contrast to the formal spaces of the garden on the adjacent hillside.

When the documentation project began, Dumbarton Oaks Park was in poor physical condition. Years of management of the designed "natural" landscape had obliterated the more subtle design features, although significant remnants of the original design were evident to the trained eye. The challenge was to capture these ephemeral elements in the documentation (*see fig. 11.17*).

One of the innovations of the Dumbarton Oaks Park project was the use of comparative or repeat photography. Numerous photographs were taken of the park in the 1930s at the height of its private maintenance. The location and focal length of these images were analyzed and the views re-photographed. The results documented changes over fifty years and provided a good planning tool for landscape maintenance and restoration (*see fig. 11.18*).

HAER Landscape Documentation

Landscapes associated with engineering and industrial resources are distinguished by features far different from those of a historic garden, estate, or urban streetscape. Some sites are

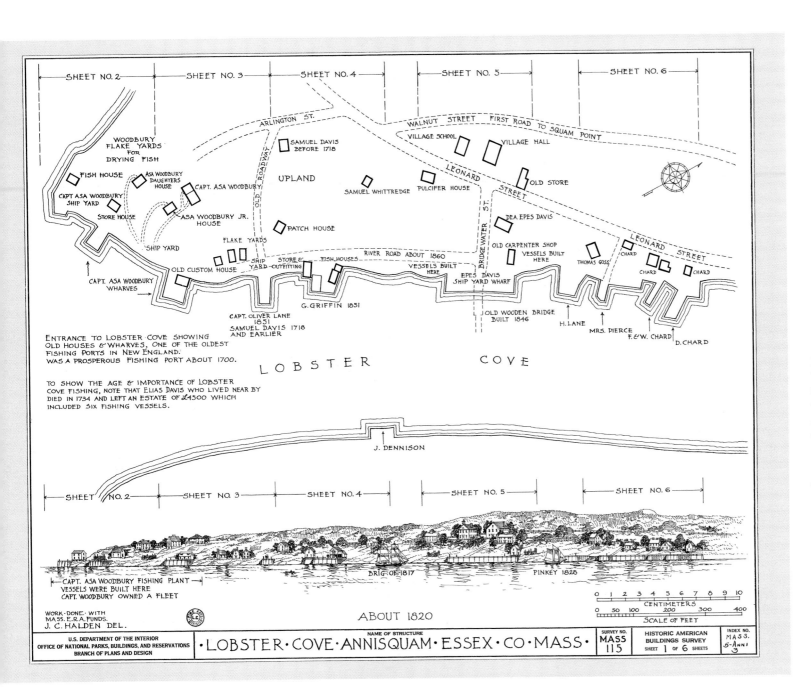

Figure 11.9
The fishing port of Lobster Cove in Massachusetts was documented in an unusual manner. The set comprises one drawing of the general setting and five detail sheets. The plans are highly schematic, with no indication of plant materials, topography, or property lines. The landscape is recorded in rendered elevation drawings, with no annotations. Despite the unconventional approach, the graphic analysis is effective in conveying the community's setting and landscape.

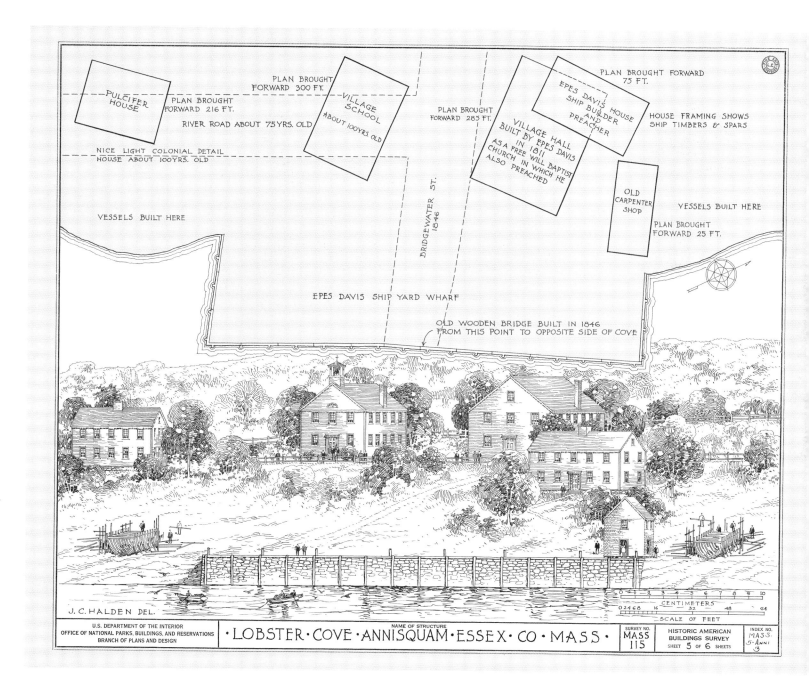

Figure 11.10
Each detail drawing of Lobster Cove is an enlarged and more detailed section of the general setting drawing. Note that the plans on the detail sheets are foreshortened to show the angular relationship between the buildings. Comparing this drawing with the historic photograph in figure 2.10 reveals that the delineator took some artistic license to more clearly depict various features.

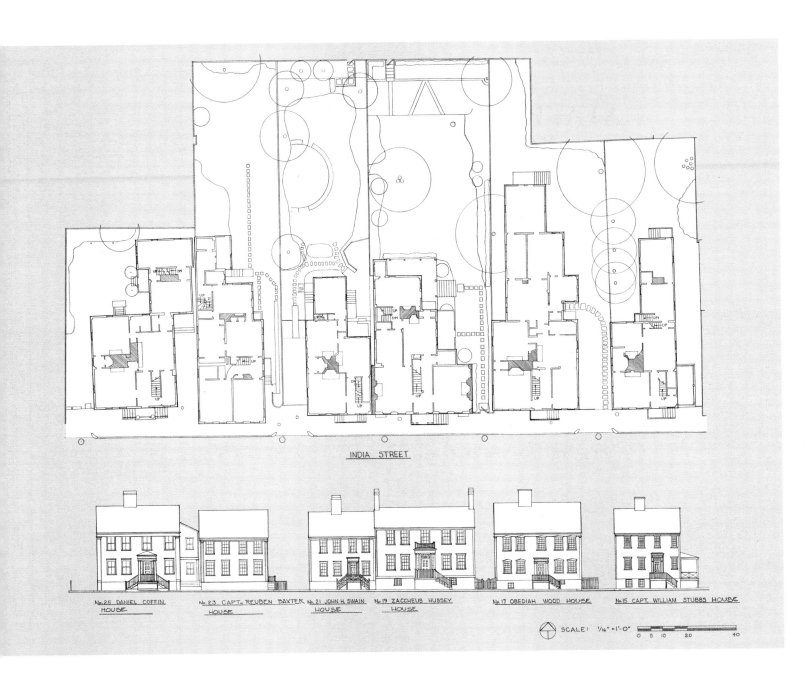

INDIA STREET

No. 25 DANIEL COFFIN HOUSE   No. 23 CAPT. REUBEN BAXTER HOUSE   No. 21 JOHN H. SWAIN HOUSE   No. 19 ZACCHEUS HUSSEY HOUSE   No. 17 OBEDIAH WOOD HOUSE   No. 15 CAPT. WILLIAM STUBBS HOUSE

SCALE: 1/16" = 1'-0"
0   5 10   20   40

Figure 11.11
A neighborhood study in Nantucket documents the plan, elevation, and lot plantings for each of six adjacent houses along India Street. Landscape features such as fences and shrubbery were omitted from the elevation drawing so that the lower portion of the individual facades would not be obscured. A number of the houses in the study were individually recorded.

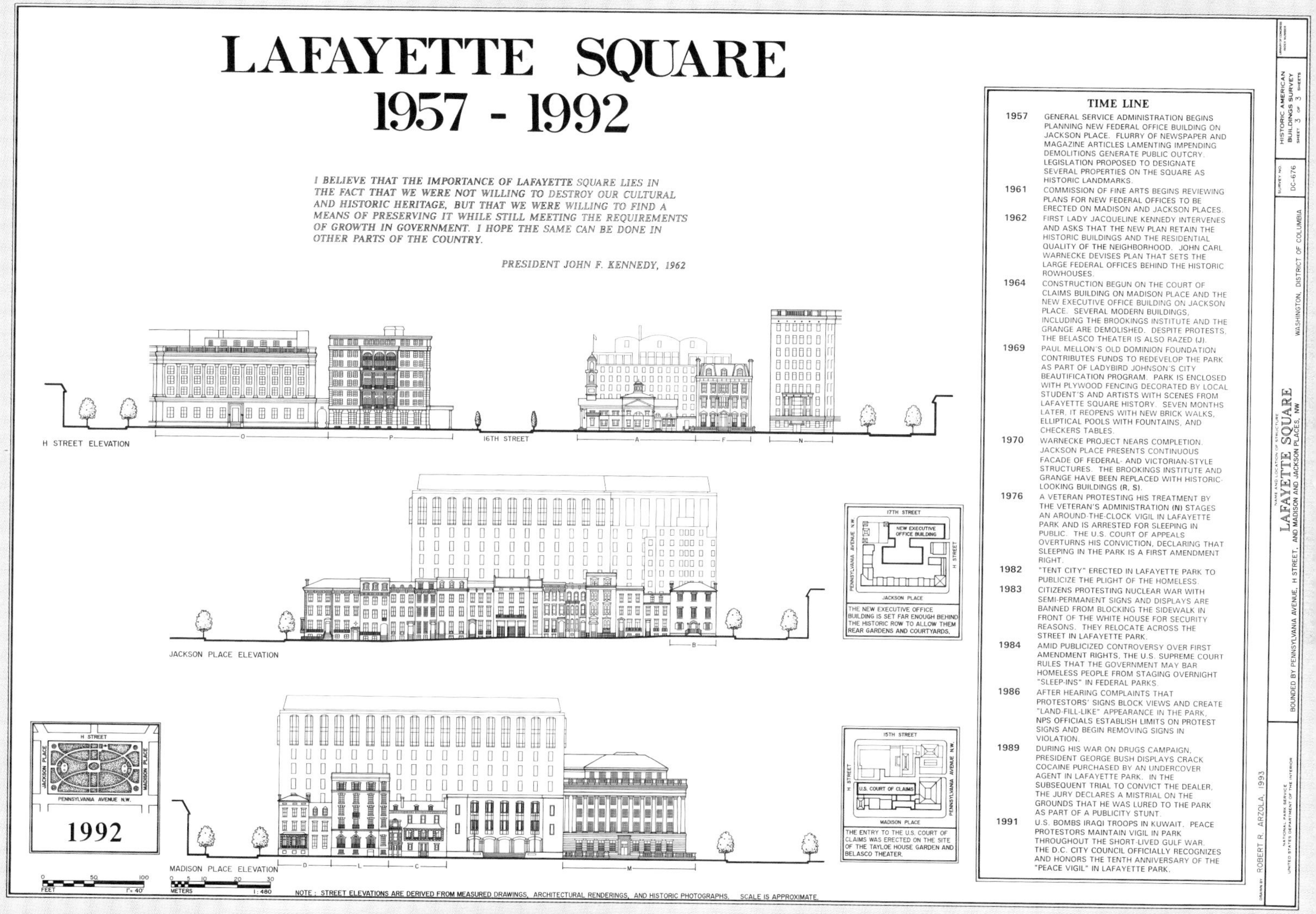
LAFAYETTE SQUARE
1957 - 1992
I BELIEVE THAT THE IMPORTANCE OF LAFAYETTE SQUARE LIES IN THE FACT THAT WE WERE NOT WILLING TO DESTROY OUR CULTURAL AND HISTORIC HERITAGE, BUT THAT WE WERE WILLING TO FIND A MEANS OF PRESERVING IT WHILE STILL MEETING THE REQUIREMENTS OF GROWTH IN GOVERNMENT. I HOPE THE SAME CAN BE DONE IN OTHER PARTS OF THE COUNTRY.
PRESIDENT JOHN F. KENNEDY, 1962
H STREET ELEVATION
16TH STREET
JACKSON PLACE ELEVATION
MADISON PLACE ELEVATION
1992
THE NEW EXECUTIVE OFFICE BUILDING IS SET FAR ENOUGH BEHIND THE HISTORIC ROW TO ALLOW THEM REAR GARDENS AND COURTYARDS.
THE ENTRY TO THE U.S. COURT OF CLAIMS WAS ERECTED ON THE SITE OF THE TAYLOE HOUSE GARDEN AND BELASCO THEATER.
NOTE: STREET ELEVATIONS ARE DERIVED FROM MEASURED DRAWINGS, ARCHITECTURAL RENDERINGS, AND HISTORIC PHOTOGRAPHS. SCALE IS APPROXIMATE.
TIME LINE
1957 GENERAL SERVICE ADMINISTRATION BEGINS PLANNING NEW FEDERAL OFFICE BUILDING ON JACKSON PLACE. FLURRY OF NEWSPAPER AND MAGAZINE ARTICLES LAMENTING IMPENDING DEMOLITIONS GENERATE PUBLIC OUTCRY. LEGISLATION PROPOSED TO DESIGNATE SEVERAL PROPERTIES ON THE SQUARE AS HISTORIC LANDMARKS.
1961 COMMISSION OF FINE ARTS BEGINS REVIEWING PLANS FOR NEW FEDERAL OFFICES TO BE ERECTED ON MADISON AND JACKSON PLACES.
1962 FIRST LADY JACQUELINE KENNEDY INTERVENES AND ASKS THAT THE NEW PLAN RETAIN THE HISTORIC BUILDINGS AND THE RESIDENTIAL QUALITY OF THE NEIGHBORHOOD. JOHN CARL WARNECKE DEVISES PLAN THAT SETS THE LARGE FEDERAL OFFICES BEHIND THE HISTORIC ROWHOUSES.
1964 CONSTRUCTION BEGUN ON THE COURT OF CLAIMS BUILDING ON MADISON PLACE AND THE NEW EXECUTIVE OFFICE BUILDING ON JACKSON PLACE. SEVERAL MODERN BUILDINGS, INCLUDING THE BROOKINGS INSTITUTE AND THE GRANGE ARE DEMOLISHED. DESPITE PROTESTS, THE BELASCO THEATER IS ALSO RAZED (J).
1969 PAUL MELLON'S OLD DOMINION FOUNDATION CONTRIBUTES FUNDS TO REDEVELOP THE PARK AS PART OF LADYBIRD JOHNSON'S CITY BEAUTIFICATION PROGRAM. PARK IS ENCLOSED WITH PLYWOOD FENCING DECORATED BY LOCAL STUDENT'S AND ARTISTS WITH SCENES FROM LAFAYETTE SQUARE HISTORY. SEVEN MONTHS LATER, IT REOPENS WITH NEW BRICK WALKS, ELLIPTICAL POOLS WITH FOUNTAINS, AND CHECKERS TABLES.
1970 WARNECKE PROJECT NEARS COMPLETION. JACKSON PLACE PRESENTS CONTINUOUS FACADE OF FEDERAL- AND VICTORIAN-STYLE STRUCTURES. THE BROOKINGS INSTITUTE AND GRANGE HAVE BEEN REPLACED WITH HISTORIC-LOOKING BUILDINGS (R, S).
1976 A VETERAN PROTESTING HIS TREATMENT BY THE VETERAN'S ADMINISTRATION (N) STAGES AN AROUND-THE-CLOCK VIGIL IN LAFAYETTE PARK AND IS ARRESTED FOR SLEEPING IN PUBLIC. THE U.S. COURT OF APPEALS OVERTURNS HIS CONVICTION, DECLARING THAT SLEEPING IN THE PARK IS A FIRST AMENDMENT RIGHT.
1982 "TENT CITY" ERECTED IN LAFAYETTE PARK TO PUBLICIZE THE PLIGHT OF THE HOMELESS.
1983 CITIZENS PROTESTING NUCLEAR WAR WITH SEMI-PERMANENT SIGNS AND DISPLAYS ARE BANNED FROM BLOCKING THE SIDEWALK IN FRONT OF THE WHITE HOUSE FOR SECURITY REASONS. THEY RELOCATE ACROSS THE STREET IN LAFAYETTE PARK.
1984 AMID PUBLICIZED CONTROVERSY OVER FIRST AMENDMENT RIGHTS, THE U.S. SUPREME COURT RULES THAT THE GOVERNMENT MAY BAR HOMELESS PEOPLE FROM STAGING OVERNIGHT "SLEEP-INS" IN FEDERAL PARKS.
1986 AFTER HEARING COMPLAINTS THAT PROTESTORS' SIGNS BLOCK VIEWS AND CREATE "LAND-FILL-LIKE" APPEARANCE IN THE PARK, NPS OFFICIALS ESTABLISH LIMITS ON PROTEST SIGNS AND BEGIN REMOVING SIGNS IN VIOLATION.
1989 DURING HIS WAR ON DRUGS CAMPAIGN, PRESIDENT GEORGE BUSH DISPLAYS CRACK COCAINE PURCHASED BY AN UNDERCOVER AGENT IN LAFAYETTE PARK. IN THE SUBSEQUENT TRIAL TO CONVICT THE DEALER, THE JURY DECLARES A MISTRIAL ON THE GROUNDS THAT HE WAS LURED TO THE PARK AS PART OF A PUBLICITY STUNT.
1991 U.S. BOMBS IRAQI TROOPS IN KUWAIT. PEACE PROTESTORS MAINTAIN VIGIL IN PARK THROUGHOUT THE SHORT-LIVED GULF WAR. THE D.C. CITY COUNCIL OFFICIALLY RECOGNIZES AND HONORS THE TENTH ANNIVERSARY OF THE "PEACE VIGIL" IN LAFAYETTE PARK.
ROBERT R. ARZOLA, 1993
LAFAYETTE SQUARE
WASHINGTON, DISTRICT OF COLUMBIA
DC-676

Figure 11.12
Lafayette Square in Washington, D.C., was the subject of a preservation battle in the early 1960s after the General Services Administration proposed tearing down the townhouses on the east and west sides of the square to construct government offices. This sheet, one of three chronicling the history of the square, illustrates the eventual solution, saving the houses and constructing the office buildings behind them. Many of the buildings surrounding the square have been individually recorded by HABS.

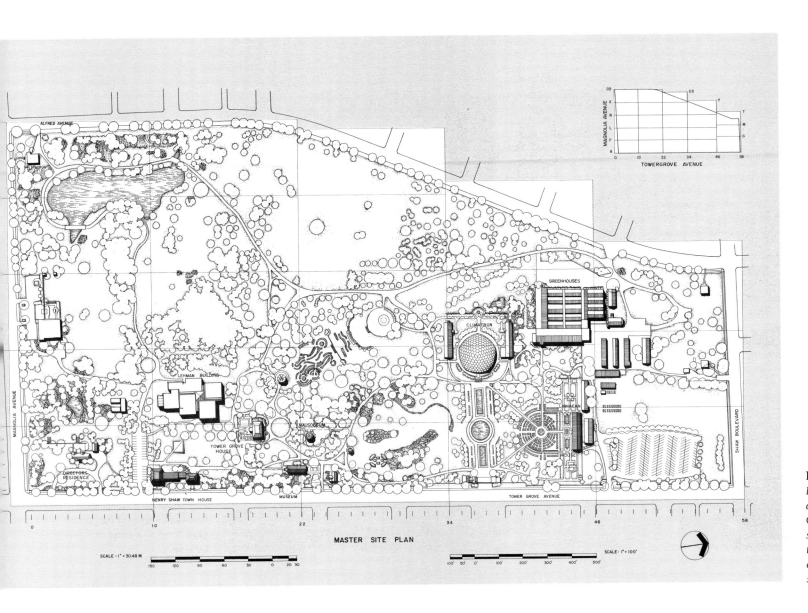

MASTER SITE PLAN

SCALE : 1" = 30.48 M

SCALE : 1" = 100'

Figure 11.13
Documentation of the 75-acre Missouri Botanical Garden required a master site plan to provide context for the overall site and a key for the 22 larger-scale planting plans.

Figure 11.14
Photographs convey different information than drawings do and were consciously integrated into the documentation scheme for the Missouri Botanical Garden. Tone and texture are readily apparent in the carefully raked stones in the Japanese garden. Even though the photograph is black-and-white, a sense of the colors is communicated in this view.

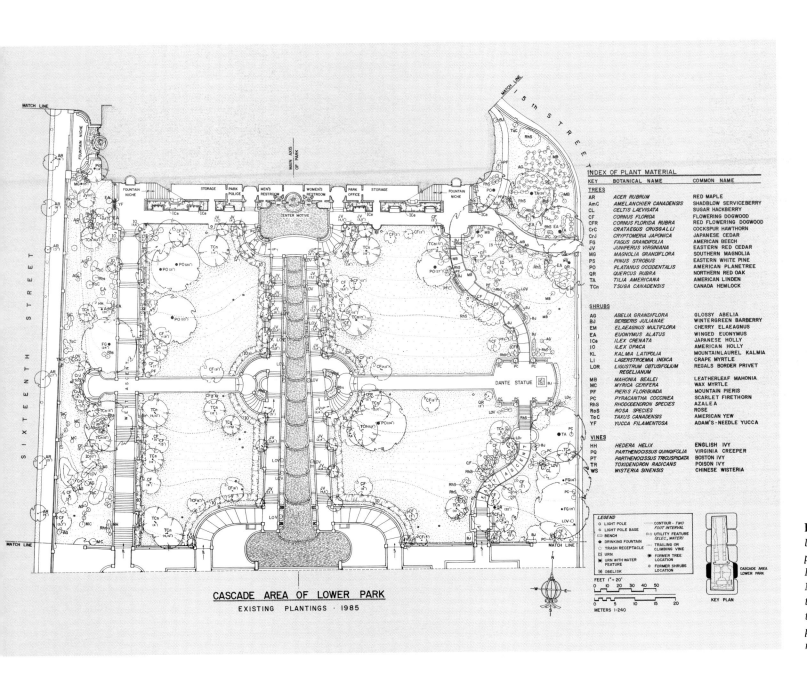

CASCADE AREA OF LOWER PARK
EXISTING PLANTINGS · 1985

INDEX OF PLANT MATERIAL

KEY	BOTANICAL NAME	COMMON NAME
TREES		
AR	ACER RUBRUM	RED MAPLE
AmC	AMELANCHIER CANADENSIS	SHADBLOW SERVICEBERRY
CL	CELTIS LAEVIGATA	SUGAR HACKBERRY
CF	CORNUS FLORIDA	FLOWERING DOGWOOD
CFR	CORNUS FLORIDA RUBRA	RED FLOWERING DOGWOOD
CrC	CRATAEGUS CRUSGALLI	COCKSPUR HAWTHORN
CrJ	CRYPTOMERIA JAPONICA	JAPANESE CEDAR
FG	FAGUS GRANDIFOLIA	AMERICAN BEECH
JV	JUNIPERUS VIRGINIANA	EASTERN RED CEDAR
MG	MAGNOLIA GRANDIFLORA	SOUTHERN MAGNOLIA
PS	PINUS STROBUS	EASTERN WHITE PINE
PO	PLATANUS OCCIDENTALIS	AMERICAN PLANETREE
QR	QUERCUS RUBRA	NORTHERN RED OAK
TA	TILIA AMERICANA	AMERICAN LINDEN
TCn	TSUGA CANADENSIS	CANADA HEMLOCK
SHRUBS		
AG	ABELIA GRANDIFLORA	GLOSSY ABELIA
BJ	BERBERIS JULIANAE	WINTERGREEN BARBERRY
EM	ELAEAGNUS MULTIFLORA	CHERRY ELAEAGNUS
EA	EUONYMUS ALATUS	WINGED EUONYMUS
ICe	ILEX CRENATA	JAPANESE HOLLY
IO	ILEX OPACA	AMERICAN HOLLY
KL	KALMIA LATIFOLIA	MOUNTAINLAUREL KALMIA
LI	LAGERSTROEMIA INDICA	CRAPE MYRTLE
LOR	LIGUSTRUM OBTUSIFOLIUM REGELIANUM	REGALS BORDER PRIVET
MB	MAHONIA BEALEI	LEATHERLEAF MAHONIA
MC	MYRICA CERIFERA	WAX MYRTLE
PF	PIERIS FLORIBUNDA	MOUNTAIN PIERIS
PC	PYRACANTHA COCCINEA	SCARLET FIRETHORN
RhS	RHODODENDRON SPECIES	AZALEA
RoS	ROSA SPECIES	ROSE
TaC	TAXUS CANADENSIS	AMERICAN YEW
YF	YUCCA FILAMENTOSA	ADAM'S-NEEDLE YUCCA
VINES		
HH	HEDERA HELIX	ENGLISH IVY
PQ	PARTHENOCISSUS QUINQIFOLIA	VIRGINIA CREEPER
PT	PARTHENOCISSUS TRICUSPIDATA	BOSTON IVY
TR	TOXIDENDRON RADICANS	POISON IVY
WS	WISTERIA SINENSIS	CHINESE WISTERIA

LEGEND

○	LIGHT POLE
○	LIGHT POLE BASE
⊟	BENCH
△	DRINKING FOUNTAIN
◇	TRASH RECEPTACLE
⊠	URN
▣	URN WITH WATER FEATURE
⊞	OBELISK
----	CONTOUR - TWO FOOT INTERVAL
□	UTILITY FEATURE (ELEC., WATER)
	TRAILING OR CLIMBING VINE
○	FORMER TREE LOCATION
○	FORMER SHRUBS LOCATION

FEET 1" = 20'
0 10 20 30 40 50

METERS 1:240
0 5 10 15 20

KEY PLAN

CASCADE AREA
LOWER PARK

Figure 11.15
Detailed plans of the plantings at Meridian Hill Park provided the National Park Service with the baseline data needed to manage the park and plan for its eventual restoration.

Figure 11.16
Photographs were used to capture the visual appearance of Meridian Hill Park and as a complement to the plantings plans.

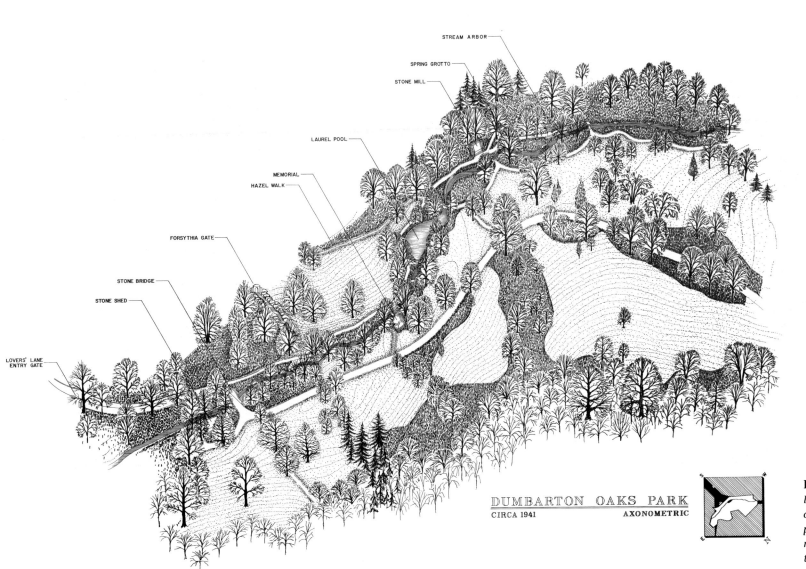

STREAM ARBOR

SPRING GROTTO

STONE MILL

LAUREL POOL

MEMORIAL

HAZEL WALK

FORSYTHIA GATE

STONE BRIDGE

STONE SHED

LOVERS' LANE
ENTRY GATE

DUMBARTON OAKS PARK

CIRCA 1941   AXONOMETRIC

Figure 11.17
*Extensive notes from the
original designer made
possible a 1989 graphic
reconstruction of Dumbar-
ton Oaks Park c. 1941,
when it was a fully mature
landscape representing the
original design intent.*

Figures 11.18

Repeat photography is an effective tool for showing the evolution of a landscape over time or through the seasons. Note how the designed natural features visible in the 1930 photograph on the left had deteriorated by the time the photograph on the right was taken in 1988.

inherently related to landscape, such as a mill sited next to a fast-moving creek or a dam with an engineered hydrological location. Other sites may dominate a vast level landscape near important mineral and transportation resources, such as an iron furnace that is located near coal mines and a river or railroad (*see fig. 4.39*). These relationships between technological process and landscape form the basis for much HAER documentation. The documentation for the Mount Pleasant Grist Mill in St. Peters, Pennsylvania, depicts and analyzes the operations of a water-powered mill (*see fig. 2.14*). A site plan defines in general terms the topography, building location relationships, and plant material. The significance of the surrounding landscape to this industrial resource is interpreted with annotations regarding the water supply necessary to generate the power to operate the mill, including the dam, head race, tail race, and overflow (*see fig. 11.19*). Documentation of the area surrounding the Mabry Mill along the Blue Ridge Parkway in western North Carolina includes the immediate area and water supply flume and explains how the Park Service designed a landscape to both preserve and protect the mill setting and features and provide access and interpretation for visitors (*see fig. 11.20*).

One of the major landscape documentation initiatives of the Historic American Engineering Record was the Park Roads and Parkways Program, a ten-year project to document national park roads. The program was a natural outgrowth of HAER's emphasis on documenting engineering structures. In many instances, these road systems represent remarkable feats of both engineering and landscape architecture. Capturing this symbiosis required a unique approach of blending conventional measured drawings of existing conditions with interpretive and illustrative images. Numerous park roads and parkways were documented through the program, including Going to the Sun Road in Glacier National Park, roads and carriage roads in Acadia National Park, the Blue Ridge Parkway linking Virginia to North Carolina and Shenandoah and Great Smoky Mountains National Parks, and Colonial Parkway from Yorktown to Jamestown Island, Virginia (*see figs. 11.21 and 11.22*). Park roads and parkways were conceived as linear parks unto themselves, providing the traveler with a series of recreational and inspirational stops, rather than as simple links from site to site. These designed landscape experiences were captured in measured drawings, which begin with an overall site plan at extremely large scale complemented by vignettes of significant landscape or architectural features. These views are always keyed to a plan location with the overall system and augmented with photographs and histories.

Similar in methodology to projects completed under the National Park Service Roads and Parkways program are a series of landscape documentation project of other parkways, including the Merritt Parkway in Connecticut, Bronx River Parkway in New York, and Arroyo Secco Parkway in California (*see fig. 1.7*).

Creation of HALS

In September 1999 interested professionals from the Historic American Buildings Survey, the American Society of Landscape Architects (ASLA), the ASLA Historic Preservation Professional Interest Group, and the Landscape Architecture Foundation met to discuss the possibility of creating the Historic American Landscapes Survey (HALS). The organizations believed that a generation of success and development in landscape preservation merited the creation of a landscape documentation program. In October 2000 Robert Stanton, director of the National Park Service, established HALS as a permanent federal program. An agreement formalized the relationships between the National Park Service, the Library of Congress, and the American Society of Landscape Architects, similar to those that support HABS and HAER. Subsequent meetings and workshops have led to the development of guidelines for landscape documentation and recommendations for pilot projects to further develop and refine documentation methodologies.

The Marsh-Billing-Rockefeller National Historical Park in Woodstock, Vermont, the only national park to focus on conservation history, was the site for the first HALS project. A significant amount of research had been completed at the site since its creation as a national park in 1993. A field team of landscape architects spent three months at the site during the summer of 2002. The substantial site plan and existing condition documentation already prepared allowed the HALS team to focus on capturing the more subtle and elusive nature of the park's landscape features. The 550-acre site and surrounding terrain were divided into four interrelated areas: the mansion and grounds, the forest, the farm, and the town of Woodstock. Site sections were used to document the interrelationship of these components, and detail sheets capture their more subtle aspects, such as the various ferns and upper-story trees that define the hillside gardens and lily pond (*see fig. 1.6*). Other drawings include a watershed analysis, soils and constructed water systems, renewed ecology forest analysis, and plantation analysis of the forest (*see fig. 11.23*).

The establishment of HALS as a program separate from HABS and HAER recognizes the unique characteristics of historic landscapes and will add to the Park Service legacy of rich documentation of the historic built environment.

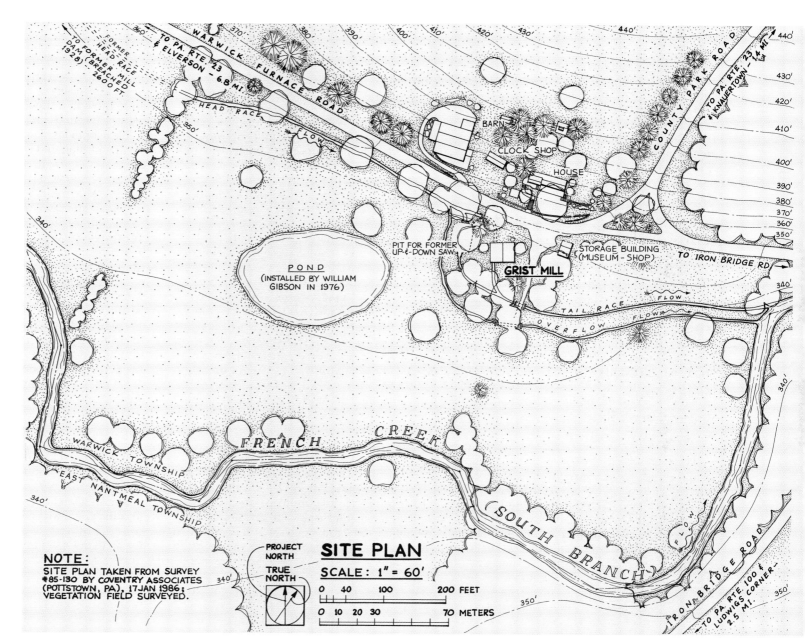

Figure 11.19
Mills are sited to take advantage of landscape features that can provide raw materials, water power, and transportation. This gristmill is sited next to a road and adjacent to a stream with a drop in elevation sufficient to provide the head to turn the water wheel. Head races and tail races and the miller's house and associated structures all are part of the landscape recorded in this site plan.

POND
(INSTALLED BY WILLIAM GIBSON IN 1976)

PIT FOR FORMER UP-& DOWN SAW

GRIST MILL

STORAGE BUILDING
(MUSEUM - SHOP)

TO IRON BRIDGE RD

BARN

CLOCK SHOP

HOUSE

HEAD RACE

FLOW

TO PA. RTE 23 & ELVERSON - 6.8 MI.

WARWICK FURNACE ROAD

COUNTY PARK ROAD

TO PA. RTE. 23 - 1.4 MI. & KNAUERTOWN

TO FORMER MILL DAM (BREACHED 1928) (BREACHED 2600 FT)
FORMER MILL HEAD RACE

TAIL RACE

OVERFLOW FLOW

FRENCH CREEK

SOUTH BRANCH

FLOW

WARWICK TOWNSHIP

EAST NANTMEAL TOWNSHIP

IRON BRIDGE ROAD

TO PA. RTE 100 & LUDWIGS CORNER - 2.5 MI.

NOTE:
SITE PLAN TAKEN FROM SURVEY #85-130 BY COVENTRY ASSOCIATES (POTTSTOWN, PA), 17 JAN 1986; VEGETATION FIELD SURVEYED.

PROJECT NORTH
TRUE NORTH

SITE PLAN
SCALE: 1" = 60'

0   40   100   200 FEET

0 10 20 30   70 METERS

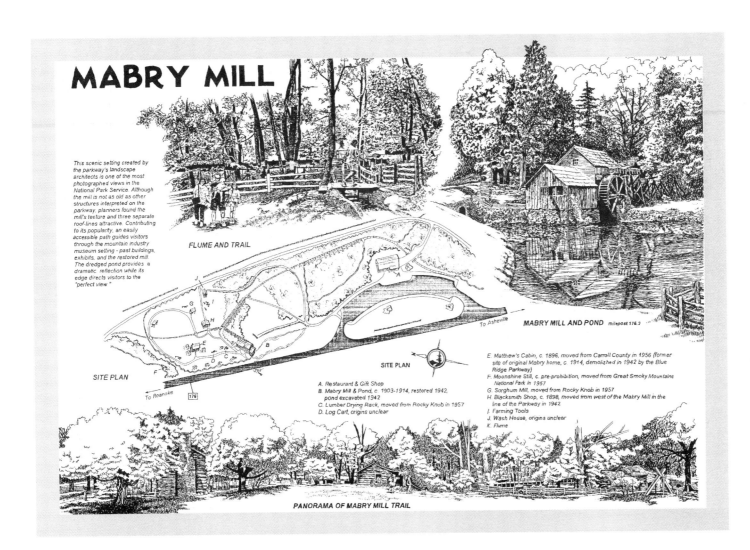

MABRY MILL

This scenic setting created by the parkway's landscape architects is one of the most photographed views in the National Park Service. Although the mill is not as old as other structures interpreted on the parkway, planners found the mill's texture and three separate roof-lines attractive. Contributing to its popularity, an easily accessible path guides visitors through the mountain industry museum setting - past buildings, exhibits, and the restored mill. The dredged pond provides a dramatic reflection while its edge directs visitors to the "perfect view."

FLUME AND TRAIL

SITE PLAN

To Roanoke

176

SITE PLAN

To Asheville

MABRY MILL AND POND milepost 176.2

A. Restaurant & Gift Shop
B. Mabry Mill & Pond, c. 1903-1914, restored 1942, pond excavated 1942
C. Lumber Drying Rack, moved from Rocky Knob in 1957
D. Log Cart, origins unclear

E. Matthew's Cabin, c. 1896, moved from Carroll County in 1956 (former site of original Mabry home, c. 1914, demolished in 1942 by the Blue Ridge Parkway)
F. Moonshine Still, c. pre-prohibition, moved from Great Smoky Mountains National Park in 1957
G. Sorghum Mill, moved from Rocky Knob in 1957
H. Blacksmith Shop, c. 1898, moved from west of the Mabry Mill in the line of the Parkway in 1942
I. Farming Tools
J. Wash House, origins unclear
K. Flume

PANORAMA OF MABRY MILL TRAIL

Figure 11.20
This drawing, part documentary and part interpretive, locates the Mabry Mill, flume, pond, and other nearby buildings alongside the Blue Ridge Parkway in a keyed plan. Sketches surrounding the plan show the landscape as it is experienced by park visitors.

Figure 11.21

Roads are essential for bringing park visitors to important sites but cannot be designed in a way that compromises preservation of the park. This sheet explains the challenge of planning a road through an ecologically sensitive area in Acadia National Park. Depicted are the various alignments considered and the alignment of the road eventually constructed.

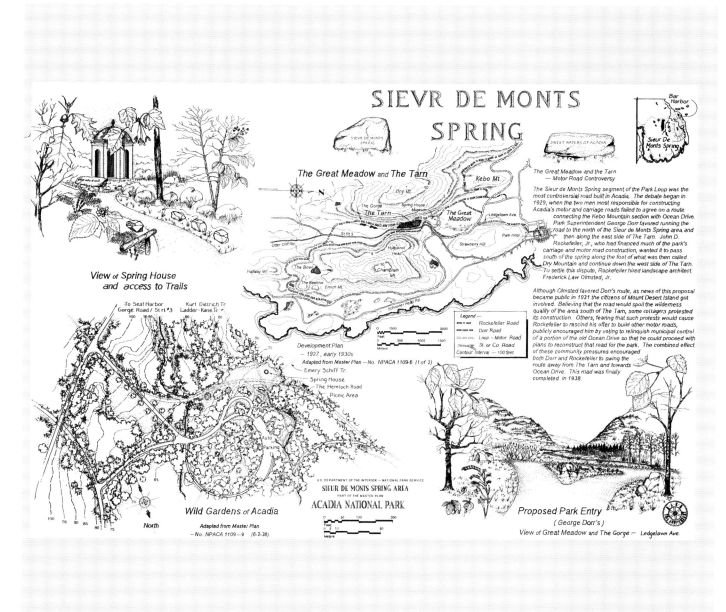

SIEVR DE MONTS SPRING

View of Spring House and access to Trails

The Great Meadow and The Tarn

The Great Meadow and the Tarn — Motor Road Controversy

The Sieur de Monts Spring segment of the Park Loop was the most controversial road built in Acadia. The debate began in 1929, when the two men most responsible for constructing Acadia's motor and carriage roads failed to agree on a route connecting the Kebo Mountain section with Ocean Drive. Park Superintendent George Dorr favored running the road to the north of the Sieur de Monts Spring area, and then along the east side of The Tarn. John D. Rockefeller, Jr., who had financed much of the park's carriage and motor road construction, wanted it to pass south of the spring along the foot of what was then called Dry Mountain and continue down the west side of The Tarn. To settle this dispute, Rockefeller hired landscape architect Frederick Law Olmsted, Jr.

Although Olmsted favored Dorr's route, as news of this proposal became public in 1931 the citizens of Mount Desert Island got involved. Believing that the road would spoil the wilderness quality of the area south of The Tarn, some cottagers protested its construction. Others, fearing that such protests would cause Rockefeller to rescind his offer to build other motor roads, publicly encouraged him by voting to relinquish municipal control of a portion of the old Ocean Drive so that he could proceed with plans to reconstruct that road for the park. The combined effect of these community pressures encouraged both Dorr and Rockefeller to swing the route away from The Tarn and towards Ocean Drive. This road was finally completed in 1938.

Development Plan
— 1927, early 1930s
Adapted from Master Plan — No. NPACA 1109-6 (1 of 2)
Emery Schiff Tr.
Spring House
The Hemlock Road
Picnic Area

Legend
Rockefeller Road
Dorr Road
Loop — Motor Road
St or Co. Road
Contour Interval — 100 feet

To Seal Harbor Gorge Road / St rt #3   Kurt Dietrich Tr. Ladder-Kane Tr.

Wild Gardens of Acadia
Adapted from Master Plan
—No. NPACA 1109—9   (6-2-38)

North

U.S. DEPARTMENT OF THE INTERIOR — NATIONAL PARK SERVICE
SIEUR DE MONTS SPRING AREA
PART OF THE MASTER PLAN
ACADIA NATIONAL PARK

Proposed Park Entry
(George Dorr's)
View of Great Meadow and The Gorge — Ledgelawn Ave.

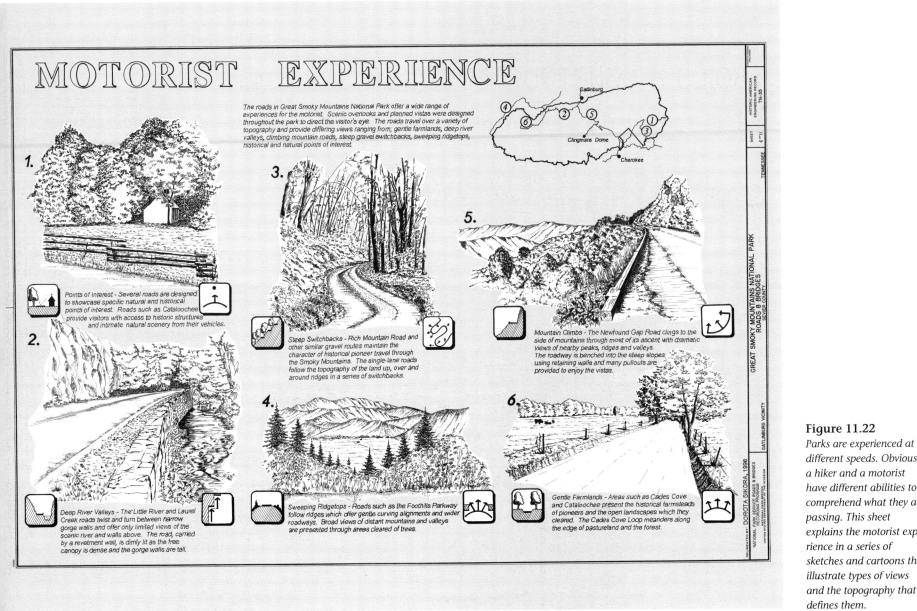

MOTORIST EXPERIENCE

The roads in Great Smoky Mountains National Park offer a wide range of experiences for the motorist. Scenic overlooks and planned vistas were designed throughout the park to direct the visitor's eye. The roads travel over a variety of topography and provide differing views ranging from; gentle farmlands, deep river valleys, climbing mountain roads, steep gravel switchbacks, sweeping ridgetops, historical and natural points of interest.

1. Points of Interest - Several roads are designed to showcase specific natural and historical points of interest. Roads such as Cataloochee provide visitors with access to historic structures and intimate natural scenery from their vehicles.

2. Deep River Valleys - The Little River and Laurel Creek roads twist and turn between narrow gorge walls and offer only limited views of the scenic river and walls above. The road, carried by a revetment wall, is dimly lit as the tree canopy is dense and the gorge walls are tall.

3. Steep Switchbacks - Rich Mountain Road and other similar gravel routes maintain the character of historical pioneer travel through the Smoky Mountains. The single-lane roads follow the topography of the land up, over and around ridges in a series of switchbacks.

4. Sweeping Ridgetops - Roads such as the Foothills Parkway follow ridges which offer gentle curving alignments and wider roadways. Broad views of distant mountains and valleys are presented through areas cleared of trees.

5. Mountain Climbs - The Newfound Gap Road clings to the side of mountains through most of its ascent with dramatic views of nearby peaks, ridges and valleys. The roadway is benched into the steep slopes using retaining walls and many pullouts are provided to enjoy the vistas.

6. Gentle Farmlands - Areas such as Cades Cove and Cataloochee present the historical farmsteads of pioneers and the open landscapes which they cleared. The Cades Cove Loop meanders along the edge of pastureland and the forest.

DELINEATED BY: DOROTA SIKORA, 1996
NATIONAL PARK SERVICE ROADS & BRIDGES RECORDING PROGRAM
GREAT SMOKY MOUNTAINS NATIONAL PARK
ROADS & BRIDGES
SEVIER COUNTY
GATLINBURG VICINITY
HISTORIC AMERICAN ENGINEERING RECORD TN-35
TENNESSEE

Figure 11.22
Parks are experienced at different speeds. Obviously a hiker and a motorist have different abilities to comprehend what they are passing. This sheet explains the motorist experience in a series of sketches and cartoons that illustrate types of views and the topography that defines them.

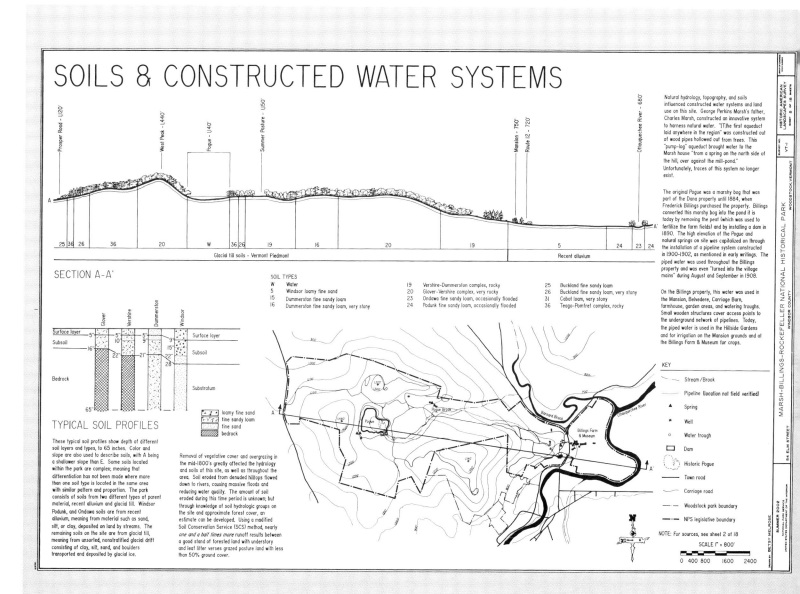

Figure 11.23
The first HALS project broadened the focus of previous landscape documentation to include such topics as regional context, geology and soils, and the hidden infrastructure necessary to sustain a designed landscape. Explained here are the soils and topography within Marsh-Billings-Rockefeller National Historical Park and how they were manipulated over time to create the current landscape.

List of Illustrations

Chapter 3: Photography

Chapter 4: Measured Drawings

Chapter 5: Recording Vernacular Building Forms

Chapter 6: Recording Bridges

Chapter 8: Recording Ships

BIBLIOGRAPHY

Chapter 1: Overview

The National Park Service has issued dozens of instructive publications on the techniques of recording, starting with the HABS bulletins and circulars of the 1930s through the HABS and HAER field instructions and procedures manuals of the 1980s. For that reason they are not all listed here. The most current versions of this supplementary material are available from the HABS/HAER office in Washington, D.C. (see Appendix B).

In addition to the book *Historic America*, cited below, there were several earlier national catalogs of both the HABS and HAER collections. Many state, local, and topical catalogs of the HABS and HAER collections have also been published. An up-to-date list of these catalogs is available from HABS/HAER in Washington, D.C. (see Appendix B).

America Preserved: A Checklist of Historic Buildings, Structures, and Sites Recorded by the Historic American Buildings Survey/Historic American Engineering Record. 60th anniversary edition. Washington, D.C.: Library of Congress, Cataloging Distribution Service, 1995. (National catalog of the HABS and HAER collections as of March 31, 1994.)

McKee, Harley J., comp. *Recording Historic Buildings.* Washington, D.C.: Government Printing Office, 1970.

Peterson, Charles E. "The Historic American Buildings Survey Continued," *Journal of the Society of Architectural Historians.* Vol. XVI, No. 3 (October 1957), pp. 29–31. (Contains the text of Peterson's 1933 memorandum proposing the establishment of HABS.)

Smith, Carol C. *Fifty Years of the Historic American Buildings Survey, 1933–1983.* Alexandria, VA: The Historic American Buildings Survey Foundation, 1983.

Stamm, Alicia, and C. Ford Peatross, eds. *Historic America: Buildings, Structures, and Sites.* Washington, D.C.: Library of Congress, 1983. (Published for the fiftieth anniversary of HABS, the book includes sixteen essays and a checklist of the HABS and HAER collections as of January 1, 1982.)

U.S. Department of the Interior, National Park Service. "Secretary of the Interior's Standards and Guidelines for Architectural and Engineering Documentation." *Federal Register.* Vol. 48, No. 190 (Thursday, 29 September 1983), Notices, pp. 44730–44734 (see Appendix A).

Chapter 2: History

Included here are reference works cited in the chapter, such as where to find architectural drawings or information on specific architects. It does not include basic texts in architectural history or American history. The scholarship in these fields is extensive and ongoing. Rather, this list includes bibliographies on American architecture, which will point the reader in the direction of some basic works.

This bibliography has been divided according to area of interest to help the reader locate specific references, although most begin with a list of general sources. Further references can be found in newsletters published by both the Society of Architectural Historians and the Vernacular Architecture Forum in their newsletters.

American Association of Architectural Bibliographers. *Papers*, Vols. I–XXIII. The first eleven volumes were published by The University Press of Virginia between 1965 and 1975, Volume XI being the cumulative index. Volumes XII and XIII were published by Garland Publishing Inc., 1977–1979.

Cuthbert, John A., Barry Ward, and Maggie Keeler. *Vernacular Architecture in America: A Selected Bibliography.* Boston: G. K. Hall & Co., 1985.

HABS/HAER: An Annotated Bibliography. Compiled by James C. Massey, Nancy B. Schwartz, and Shirley Maxwell. Washington: HABS/HAER, National Park Service, U.S. Department of the Interior, 1992. (A brief description of every known publication produced by HABS and HAER, from inception through 1992. This bibliography is the definitive work on publications issued by HABS/HAER.)

Hitchcock, Henry-Russell. *American Architectural Books: A List of Books, Portfolios, and Pamphlets on Architecture and Related Subjects Published in America Before 1895.* New York: Da Capo Press, 1976.

PCI [computer file]: Periodicals Contents Index. [Ann Arbor]: ProQuest Information and Learning Co., 2001. (Commercial bibliography available at subscribing libraries, includes *Architectural Forum, Architectural Record*, and other journals back to the late nineteenth century.)

Roos, Frank J., Jr. *Bibliography of Early American Architecture: Writings on Architecture Constructed Before 1860 in Eastern and Central United States.* Urbana: University of Illinois Press, 1968.

Schlereth, Thomas J., ed. *Material Culture: A Research Guide.* Lawrence, Kansas: University Press of Kansas, 1985.

Society of Architectural Historians. *Journal of the Society of Architectural Historians, Index to Volumes I-XX 1941–1961.* Compiled by Shirley Prager Branner. Chicago: SAH, 1974.

———. *Articles in the Journal of the Society of Architectural Historians, 1962–2001: A List.* http://www.sah.org/jsah/articles.html

Vernacular Architecture Forum. *Vernacular Architecture Bibliography.* 1979 to present. http://departments.mwc.edu/hipr/www/vafbib.htm

Wodehouse, Lawrence. *American Architects from the Civil War to the First World War: A Guide to Information Sources.* Detroit: Gale Research Co., 1976.

———. *American Architects from the First World War to the Present: A Guide to Information Sources.* Detroit: Gale Research Co., 1977.

Architects

For biographical information on specific architects, these three sources are indispensable. Note also the Wodehouse bibliographies, cited above:

Columbia University. *Avery Obituary Index of Architects and Artists.* Boston: G. K. Hall & Co., 1963.

Placzek, Adolf K., ed. *Macmillan Encyclopedia of Architects.* New York: The Free Press, 1982.

Withey, Henry F., and Elise Rathburn Withey. *Biographical Dictionary of American Architects, Deceased.* Detroit: Omnigraphics, 1996.

Architectural Drawings

Original architectural drawings are difficult to locate, and are most likely found in the building itself or in the architect's office. For drawings that have been published, the *Avery Index* is a good source. The *National Union Index*, begun as the *Cooperative Preservation of Architectural Records (COPAR)*, is a guide to architects' drawings in various repositories.

Columbia University. *Avery Index to Architectural Periodicals.* 2nd ed., rev. and enl. Boston: G. K. Hall & Co., 1973.

National Union Index to Architectural Records, at Prints and Photographs Division, Library of Congress, Washington, D.C.

Architectural Terms

These reference works contain the standard definitions and uses of architectural terms:

Harris, Cyril M., ed. *Dictionary of Architecture and Construction.* 3rd ed. New York: McGraw-Hill, 2000.

Harris, Cyril M., ed. *Historic Architecture Sourcebook.* New York: McGraw-Hill, 1977.

Jester, Thomas C., ed. *Twentieth-Century Building Materials: History and Conservation.* New York: McGraw-Hill Company, 1995.

Lounsbury, Carl R., ed. *An Illustrated Glossary of Early Southern Architecture and Landscape.* New York: Oxford University Press, 1994.

Saylor, Henry H. *Dictionary of Architecture.* New York: Wiley, 1952.

Sturgis, Russell. *A Dictionary of Architecture and Building: Biographical, Historical, and Descriptive,* 3 vols. New York: The Macmillan Company, 1902; republished by the Gale Research Company, 1966.

Styles

Blumenson, John J. G. *Identifying American Architecture: A Pictorial Guide to Styles and Terms, 1600–1945.* 2nd ed., rev. and enl. Walnut Creek, CA: AltaMira Press, 1995.

Gottfried, Herbert, and Jan Jennings. *American Vernacular Design 1870–1940: An Illustrated Glossary.* New York: Van Nostrand Reinhold, 1985.

McAlester, Virginia, and Lee McAlester. *A Field Guide to American Houses.* New York: Alfred A. Knopf, 1984.

Poppeliers, John C., S. Allen Chambers Jr., and Nancy B. Schwartz. *What Style Is It?* Rev. ed. New York: John Wiley, 2003.

Rifkind, Carole. *A Field Guide to American Architecture.* New York: Bonanza Books, 1984.

Whiffen, Marcus. *American Architecture Since 1780: A Guide to the Styles.* Rev. ed. Cambridge, MA: MIT Press, 1992.

Technological History

Armstrong, Ellis L., ed. American Public Works Association. *History of Public Works in the United States, 1776–1976.* Chicago: American Public Works Association, 1976.

Ferguson, Eugene S. *Bibliography of the History of Technology.* Cambridge, MA: Society for the History of Technology, 1968.

Kemp, Emory, and Theodore Sande, eds. *Historic Preservation of Engineering Works: Proceedings of the Engineering Foundation Conference, Franklin Pierce College, Rindge, New Hampshire, June 1978.* New York: American Society of Civil Engineers, 1981.

Koch, Jean E. *Industrial Archeology: An Introductory Bibliography.* Monticello, Illinois: Vance Bibliographies, 1979.

Kranzberg, Melvin, and Carroll W. Pursell Jr., eds. *Technology in Western Civilization.* 2 vols. New York: Oxford University Press, 1967.

Rothenberg, Marc. *The History of Science and Technology in the United States: A Critical and Selective Bibliography.* New York: Garland Publishing, Inc., 1982.

Starbuck, David, ed. *An Introductory Bibliography in Industrial Archeology.* Society for Industrial Archeology, 1983.

Grammar

HABS/HAER and many other institutions follow the grammar rules set forth by the University of Chicago Press. Turabian's book is a condensation of the *Manual of Style*, geared toward unpublished works.

The Chicago Manual of Style. Chicago: University of Chicago Press, 2003. 15th ed.

Turabian, Kate L. *A Manual for Writers.* Chicago: University of Chicago Press, 1996. 6th ed.

Chapter 3: Photography

The American National Standards Institute, New York City, publishes industry standards for the photography and conservation industries. Its list of publications should be consulted for specific discussions on various aspects of permanence of films. The Society of American Archivists, Chicago, has publications on conservation. They should be consulted for specific discussion on this issue.

Ansel Adams was the author of numerous how-to photographic books and television shows. In the early 1980s (he died in 1984), he revised his series on photography and it has been republished as *The New Ansel Adams Photography Series* (4 vols.) by New York Graphic Society, New York. Another excellent volume by Adams is *Examples: The Making of 40 Photographs*, published for the New York Graphic Society by Little, Brown of Boston, 1983.

Abraben, E. *Point of View: The Art of Architectural Photography.* New York: Van Nostrand Reinhold, c. 1994.

Borchers, Perry E. *Photogrammetric Recording of Cultural Resources.* Washington, D.C.: National Park Service, 1977.

Boucher, Jack E. "Suggestions for Producing Publishable Photographs." Washington, D.C.: National Trust for Historic Preservation, no date.

———. *A Record in Detail: The Architectural Photographs of Jack E. Boucher.* Columbia, MO: University of Missouri Press, 1988.

Buchanan, Terry. *Photographing Historic Buildings.* London: Royal Commission on Historic Monuments, Her Majesty's Stationery Office, 1983.

Chambers, J. Henry, AIA. "Rectified Photography and Photo Drawing for Historic Preservation." Washington, D.C.: National Park Service, 1973.

Dean, Jeff. *Architectural Photography, Techniques for Architects, Preservationists, Historians, Photographers, and Urban Planners.* Nashville, TN: American Association of State and Local History, 1981.

Harris, Michael G. *Professional Architectural Photography.* 2nd ed. Oxford; Boston: Focal Press, 1998

———. *Professional Interior Photography.* Oxford; Boston: Focal Press, 1998.

Hart, David M., AIA. *X-Ray Examination of Historic Structures* ("Draft"). Washington, D.C.: National Park Service, 1975.

Hedgecoe, John. *Photographing Landscapes.* London : Collins & Brown; New York : Distributed in the U.S. by Sterling Pub., 2000.

Hockey, William B. "Scaled-Rectified Photography on Site." *APT Bulletin,* Vol. VII, No. 3, 1975, pp. 36–77.

Hope, Terry. *Landscapes: Developing Style in Creative Photography.* Rochester, NY : Silver Pixel Press, 2000.

Jones, Harvie P. "Enhancement of Historic Photographs." *APT Bulletin*, Vol. XI, No. 1, 1979, pp. 4–15.

Kopelow, Gerry. *How to Photograph Buildings and Interiors.* 3rd updated and expanded ed. New York: Princeton Architectural Press, 2003.

Lowe, Jet, *Industrial Eye.* Washington, D.C.: Preservation Press, 1986.

Lyons, Thomas R., and Thomas Eugene Avery. *Remote Sensing. A Handbook for Archeologists and Cultural Resource Managers.* Washington, D.C.: National Park Service, 1977.

McGrath, Norman. *Photographing Buildings Inside and Out.* Rev. and expanded 2nd ed. New York, Whitney Library of Design, 1993.

National Park Service Preservation Assistance Division, U.S. Department of the Interior. "Using Photogrammetry to Monitor Materials Deterioration and Structural Problems on Historic Buildings: The Dorchester Heights Monument; Case Study." Washington, D.C.: National Park Service, 1985.

Pare, Richard, ed. *Photography and Architecture: 1839–1939.* Montreal: Canadian Centre for Architecture, 1982.

Robinson, Cervin, and Joel Herschman. *Architecture Transformed: A History of the Photography of Buildings from 1839 to Present.* Cambridge, MA: MIT Press, 1987.

Rokach, Allen, and Anne Millman. *Field Guide to Photographing Landscapes.* New York: Amphoto, 1995.

Saunders, William S. *Modern Architecture: Photographs by Ezra Stoller.* New York: Abrams, 1990.

Shulman, Julius. *Photographing Architecture and Interiors.* Glendale, CA: Balcony Press, 2000. (Update of Shulman's 1962 book of the same title. Introduction by Richard Neutra.)

———. *The Photography of Architecture and Design: Photographing Buildings, Interiors, and the Visual Arts.* New York: Whitney Library of Design, 1977.

Smith, G. E. Kidder. *Looking at Architecture.* New York: Abrams, 1990.

Sobieszek, Robert A., ed. *The Architectural Photography of Hedrich-Blessing.* New York: Holt, Rinehart and Winston, 1984.

Waite, Charlie. *The Making of Landscape Photographs.* London: Collins & Brown, 1992.

Chapter 4: Measured Drawings

American Institute of Architects. *Architectural Graphic Standards,* 10th ed. New York: John Wiley & Sons, Inc., 2000. (The standard reference for architectural information, the eighth edition and subsequent editions include a chapter on historic preservation, including four pages on HABS. Earlier editions have some material now considered historic, such as glass block details. A compendium of the first four editions was published as *Traditional Details: For Building Restoration, Renovation, and Rehabilitation.* Charles George Ramsey and Harold Reeve Sleeper. New York: John Wiley & Sons, Inc., 1991.)

Bodey, Hugh, and Michael Halls. *Elementary Surveying for Industrial Archeologists.* Aylesbury, England: Shire Publications Ltd., 1978. Excellent for surveying all types of historic structures, not just industrial sites.

Brunskill, R. W. *Illustrated Handbook of Vernacular Architecture.* 3rd ed., rev. and expanded. Boston: Faber and Faber, 1987. (A standard work. Bibliography.)

Bullock, Orin M. *The Restoration Manual: An Illustrated Guide to the Preservation and Restoration of Old Buildings.* New York: Van Nostrand Reinhold, 1983. (A standard reference. Glossary and bibliography.)

Chitham, Robert. *Measured Drawing for Architects.* London: The Architectural Press Ltd., 1980. (Good reference, but mostly English subject matter.)

Cramer, Johannes. *Handbuch der Bauaufnahme.* Stuttgart: Deutsche Verlags-Anstalt, 1984. (Excellent, if you read German.)

Kissim, Philip. *Surveying for Civil Engineers.* 2nd ed. New York: McGraw-Hill Book Company, Inc., 1981. (Good reference on surveying.)

Monticello in Measured Drawings. Drawings by the Historic American Buildings Survey/Historic American Engineering Record, National Park Service. Architectural commentary by William L. Beiswanger; foreword by Daniel P. Jordan. Chapel Hill: University of North Carolina Press, 2002.

Pannel, John Percival Masterman, and J. Kenneth Major. *The Techniques of Industrial Archeology.* 2nd ed. Newton Abbot, England: David & Charles, 1974. (Excellent for documenting all types of historic structures, not merely industrial sites. Bibliography.)

Patterson, Robert M. *Manual for the Preparation of "As Found" Drawings.* Victoria, Canada: British Columbia Heritage Trust, 1982. (Short booklet on recording historic buildings. Bibliography.)

Van der Putten, H. M. *Interim Guide for Measuring, Recording and Drawing of Historic Structures.* Ottawa: National Parks Canada, 1968. (Canadian equivalent of *Recording Historic Buildings.*)

Interpretive Drawings

Historic American Engineering Record, National Park Service, U.S. Department of the Interior. "HAER Field Instructions." Washington, D.C.: National Park Service, 1981.

Tufte, Edward R. *The Visual Display of Quantitative Information.* 2nd ed. Cheshire, CT: Graphics Press, 2001.

Multiple Areas of Significance

The books listed below concentrate on historic construction technologies. For information on architectural history, consult the bibliography for the history chapter.

Condit, Carl W. *American Building Art: The Nineteenth Century.* New York: Oxford University Press, 1960.

———. *American Building Art: The Twentieth Century.* New York: Oxford University Press, 1961.

Cowan, Henry J. *An Historical Outline of Architectural Science.* 2nd ed. London: Applied Science Publishers, 1977. (Bibliography on the history of building science.)

———. *The Master Builders: A History of Structural and Environmental Design from Ancient Egypt to the Nineteenth Century.* New York: John Wiley & Sons, Inc., 1977.

———. *Science and Building: Structural and Environmental Design in the Nineteenth and Twentieth Centuries.* New York: John Wiley & Sons, Inc., 1978.

Guedes, Pedro, ed. *Encyclopedia of Architectural Technology.* New York: McGraw-Hill Book Company, 1979.

Jandl, H. Ward, ed. *The Technology of Historic American Buildings: Studies of the Materials, Craft Processes, and the Mechanization of Building Construction.* Washington, D.C.: Foundation for Preservation Technology, 1983.

Peterson, Charles E., ed. *Building Early America: Contributions Toward the History of a Great Industry/The Carpenters' Company of the City and County of Philadelphia.* Radnor, PA : Chilton Book Company, 1976.

Maritime Documentation

Albion, Robert G. *Naval and Maritime History: An Annotated Bibliography.* 4th ed., rev. and exp. Mystic, CT: Munson Institute of American Maritime History, 1972.

Anderson, Richard K., Jr. *Guidelines for Recording Historic Ships.* Washington, D.C.: National Park Service, 1988. (Includes bibliography.)

Brouwer, Norman J. *International Register of Historic Ships.* 3rd ed. Peekskill, NY: Sea History Press, National Maritime Historical Society, 1999.

Jackson, Melvin H., ed. *The Historic American Merchant Marine Survey: Works Progress Administration, Federal Project No. 6.* Salem, NH: Ayer Company, Inc., 1983. (Available from the Ayer Company, Inc., P.O. Box 958, Salem, NH 03079. Copies of individual drawings may be obtained by writing the Division of Transportation, Room 5010, National Museum of American History, Smithsonian Institution, Washington, D.C. 20560.)

Kinnell, Susan K., and Suzanne R. Ontiveros, eds. *American Maritime History: A Bibliography.* Santa Barbara, CA: ABC-Clio, Inc., 1986.

Labaree, Benjamin W. *A Supplement (1971–1986) to Robert G. Albion's Naval and Maritime History: An Annotated Bibliography.* 4th ed. Mystic, CT: Mystic Seaport Museum, Inc., 1988.

National Museum of American History. *Ship Plan List: Maritime Collection.* Washington, D.C.: Smithsonian Institution, 1984. (This catalog contains ordering information and a complete list of all available merchant ship plans from a dozen collections maintained by the Smithsonian. There is a separate catalog covering warships, *The Smithsonian Collection of Warship Plans.* Write to Ship Plans, Division of Transportation, Room 5010, National Museum of American History, Smithsonian Institution, Washington, D.C. 20560.)

National Trust for Historic Preservation. *Guidelines for Maritime Documentation.* Washington, D.C.: National Trust, 1988. (This publication contains guidelines for the documentation of artifacts, folklore, and other maritime-related subjects in addition to ships and folklore, and other maritime-related subjects in addition to ships and buildings. Contact the Maritime Department, National Trust for Historic Preservation, 1785 Massachusetts Avenue, N.W., Washington, D.C. 20036.)

Bridge Documentation

DeLony, Eric N. "HAER and the Recording of Technological Heritage: Reflections on 30 Years' Work," *IA: The Journal of the Society for Industrial Archeology*, Vol. 25, No. 1, 1999, p. 29–55. (Highlights and an overview of HAER's first three decades.)

————. "HAER's Historic Bridge Program," *IA: The Journal of the Society for Industrial Archeology,* Vol. 15, No. 2, 1989, p. 57–71.

————. *Landmark American Bridges.* New York: American Society of Civil Engineers, and Boston: Little, Brown, and Company, 1993. (Includes ninety-one of the bridges in the HAER collection.)

Jackson, Donald C. *Great American Bridges and Dams.* Foreword by David McCullough. New York: John Wiley, 1996.

Plowden, David. *Bridges: The Spans of North America.* New York: W. W. Norton & Company, 1974, rev. edition 2002.

Vogel, Robert M., ed. *A Report of the Mohawk-Hudson Area Survey: A Selective Recording Study of the Industrial Archeology of the Mohawk and Hudson River Valleys in the Vicinity of Troy, New York, June-September 1969.* Washington, D.C.: Smithsonian Institution Press, 1973. An extensive report on the first HAER project.

Vogel, Robert M. *Roebling's Delaware and Hudson Canal Aqueducts,* Smithsonian Studies in History and Technology, Number 10. Washington, D.C.: Smithsonian Institution Press, 1971.

Landscape Documentation

American Joint Committee on Horticultural Nomenclature. *Standardized Plant Names.* 2nd ed. Harrisburg, PA: J. Horace McFarland Company for the American Joint Committee on Horticultural Nomenclature, 1942.

Burnap, George. *Parks: Their Design, Equipment and Use.* Philadelphia: J. B. Lippincott Company, 1916. (An excellent source book.)

Davis, Tim, and Todd Croteau, editors. Introduction by Tim Davis. *America's Park Roads and Parkways: Documentation by the Historic American Engineering Record.* Baltimore, MD: Johns Hopkins University Press, 2003.

Good, Albert H. *Park and Recreation Structures.* Boulder, CO: Graybooks, 1990.

Landscape Architecture. Vol. 77, No. 4 (July/August 1987) and Vol. 77, No. 5 (September/October 1987). (Both issues contain articles on the documentation and preservation of historic landscapes.)

Liberty Hyde Bailey Hortorium (Cornell University). *Hortus Third: A Concise Dictionary of Plants Cultivated in the United States and Canada.* New York: Macmillan Publishing Co., Inc., 1976. (A standard reference on plant materials.)

Nabokov, Peter. *Architecture of Acoma Pueblo: The 1934 Historic American Buildings Survey Project.* Santa Fe, New Mexico: Ancient City Press, 1986.

Newton, Norman T. *Design on the Land: The Development of Landscape Architecture.* Cambridge, MA: The Belknap Press of Harvard University Press, 1971. (A history of landscape architecture.)

APPENDIX A

SECRETARY OF THE INTERIOR'S STANDARDS FOR ARCHITECTURAL AND ENGINEERING DOCUMENTATION

These standards concern the development of documentation for historic buildings, sites, structures and objects. This documentation, which usually consists of measured drawings, photographs and written data, provides important information on a property's significance for use by scholars, researchers, preservationists, architects, engineers, and others interested in preserving and understanding historic properties. Documentation permits accurate repair or reconstruction of parts of a property that is to be demolished.

These Standards are intended for use in developing documentation to be included in the Historic American Building Survey (HABS) and the Historic American Engineering Record (HAER) Collections in the Library of Congress. HABS/HAER, in the National Park Service, have defined specific requirements for meeting these Standards for their collections. The HABS/HAER requirements include information important to development of documentation for other purposes such as State or local archives.

STANDARD I. *Documentation shall adequately explicate and illustrate what is significant or valuable about the historic building, site, structure or object being documented.*

The historic significance of the building, site, structure or object identified in the evaluation process should be conveyed by the drawings, photographs and other materials that comprise documentation. The historical, architectural, engineering or cultural values of the property together with the purpose of the documentation activity determine the level and methods of documentation. Documentation prepared for submission to the Library of Congress must meet the HABS/HAER Guidelines.

STANDARD II. *Documentation shall be prepared accurately from reliable sources with limitations clearly stated to permit independent verification of the information.*

The purpose of documentation is to preserve an accurate record of historic properties that can be used in research and other preservation activities. To serve these purposes, the documentation must include information that permits assessment of its reliability.

STANDARD III. *Documentation shall be prepared on materials that are readily reproducible, durable and in standard sizes.*

The size and quality of documentation materials are important factors in the preservation of information for future use. Selection of materials should be based on the length of time expected for storage, the anticipated frequency of use and size convenient for storage.

STANDARD IV. *Documentation shall be clearly and concisely produced.*

In order for documentation to be useful for future research, written materials must be legible and graphic materials must contain scale information and location references.

SECRETARY OF THE INTERIOR'S GUIDELINES FOR ARCHITECTURAL AND ENGINEERING DOCUMENTATION

Introduction

The following guidelines provide more specific procedural and technical information on how to produce architectural and engineering documentation and outline one approach to meeting the Secretary of the Interior's Standards. Agencies, organizations or individuals proposing to approach documentation differently may wish to review their plans with the National Park Service.

The Guidelines are organized as follows:

- Definitions
- Goal of documentation
- Content
- Quality
- Materials
- Presentation
- Architectural and engineering documentation prepared for other purposes

Definitions

The following definitions are used in conjunction with these guidelines:

Documentation—measured drawings, photographs, histories, or other media that depict historic buildings, sites, structures, objects or landscapes.

Field Photography—photography other than large-format photography (usually 35 mm), intended for the purposes of producing documentation.

Field Records—notes of measurements taken, field photographs and other recorded information intended for the purpose of producing documentation.

Large-Format Photographs—photographs taken of historic buildings, sites, structures, objects, or landscapes where the dimensions of the negatives are either 4″ × 5″, 5″ × 7″ or 8″ × 10″ and where the photographs are taken with appropriate means to correct perspective distortion.

Measured Drawings—drawings produced according to HABS/HAER/HALS guidelines depicting existing conditions or other relevant features of historic buildings, sites, structures, objects or landscapes. Measured drawings are usually produced in ink on an archival material, such as Mylar.

Written Data—inventory forms, data sheets, historical reports, or other original, written works of varying lengths that describe a building, site, structure, object, or landscape and highlight its historical, architectural, technological, or cultural significance.

Photocopy—a photograph, with large-format negative, of a photograph or drawings.

Select Existing Drawings—drawings of historic buildings, sites, structures, objects or landscapes, whether original construction or later alteration drawings that portray or depict the historic value or significance.

Sketch Plan—a floor or site plan, usually not to exact scale although often drawn from measurements, where the features are shown in proper relation and proportion to one another.

Goal of Documentation

The Historic American Buildings Survey (HABS), the Historic American Engineering Record (HAER), and the Historic American Landscapes Survey (HALS) are the national historical architectural, engineering and landscape documentation programs of the National Park Service. The goal of HABS/HAER/HALS documentation is to provide architects, engineers, scholars, preservationists, and interested members of the public with comprehensive information on the historical, architectural, technological, or cultural significance of a building, site, structure, object or landscape. Placed on permanent deposit at the Library of Congress, HABS/HAER/HALS documentation serves as a permanent record of the growth and development of the nation's built environment.

HABS/HAER/HALS documentation usually consists of measured drawings, large-format photographs and written data that highlight the significance of a building, site, structure, object or landscape. This documentation acts as a form of insurance against fires and natural disasters by permitting the repair and, if necessary, reconstruction of historic resources damaged by such disasters. It is also used for scholarly research, interpretation, and education, and it often provides the basis for enforcing preservation easement. HABS/HAER/HALS documentation is often the last means of preservation of a property: when a property is to be demolished, documentation provides future researchers access to valuable information that otherwise would be lost.

HABS/HAER/HALS documentation is developed in a number of ways. The National Park Service regularly employs summer teams of student architects, engineers, and historians to develop HABS/HAER/HALS documentation under the supervision of National Park Service professionals. The National Park Service also produces HABS/HAER/HALS documentation in conjunction with restoration or other preservation treatment of historic buildings managed by the National Park Service. Federal agencies, pursuant to Section 110(b) of the National Historic Preservation Act, as amended, record those historic properties to be demolished or substantially altered as a result of agency action or assisted action (referred to as mitigation projects). Finally, individuals and organizations prepare documentation to HABS/HAER/HALS standards and donate the documentation to the programs.

The Secretary of the Interior's Standards describe in general terms the fundamental principals of HABS/HAER/HALS documentation. They are supplemented by other material describing more specific guidelines, preferred techniques for architectural photography, and formats for written historical reports. This technical information is found in the procedure manuals for the individual programs.

These guidelines contain useful information on how to produce documentation for other archives, such as state or local archives. The State Historic Preservation Officer (SHPO) or the state library should be consulted regarding archival requirements if the documentation is to become part of its collection. In establishing archives, the important questions of durability and reproducibility should be considered in relation to the purposes of the collection.

Documentation prepared for the HABS/HAER/HALS collections must meet the requirements below. The HABS/HAER/HALS office of the National Park Service reserves the right to refuse documentation that does not meet these requirements.

Content

Standard: *Documentation shall adequately explicate and illustrate what is significant or valuable about the historic building, site, structure, object or landscape being documented.*

Guideline: *Documentation shall meet one of the following requirements for content:*

A. Level I

  1. Drawings: a full set of measured drawings depicting existing or historic conditions

  2. Photographs: photographs with large-format negatives of exterior and interior views; photocopies with large-format negatives of select, existing drawings or historic views that are produced in accordance with the U.S. Copyright Act (as amended)

  3. Written data: history and description

B. Level II

  1. Drawings: select existing drawings, where available, may be photographed with large-format negatives or photographically reproduced on Mylar in accordance with the U.S. Copyright Act, as amended

  2. Photographs: photographs with large-format negatives of exterior and interior views, or historic views where available and produced in accordance with the U.S. Copyright Act, as amended

  3. Written data: history and description

C. Level III

  1. Drawings: sketch plan

  2. Photographs: photographs with large-format negatives of exterior and interior views

  3. Written data: short form for historical reports

COMMENTARY

The kind and amount of documentation should be appropriate to the nature and significance of the subject. For example, Level I would be inappropriate for a building that is a minor element of an historic district, notable only for context and scale. A full set of measured drawings for such a minor building would be expensive and would likely add little new insight into the growth and development of the built environment at either the local, regional, or national level. Large-format photography (Level III) would be the more appropriate choice for documenting this type of building.

Similarly, the aspect of the building, site, structure, object or landscape being documented should reflect the subject's overall significance. For example, measured drawings of Dankmar Adler and Louis Sullivan's Auditorium Building in Chicago should indicate not only facades, floor plans and sections, but also the innovative structural and mechanical systems that were incorporated into that building. Large-format photography of Gunston Hall in Fairfax County, Virginia, to take another example, should clearly show William Buckland's hand-carved moldings in the Palladian Room, as well as other views, since Buckland's role in the creation of the building is one of the reasons why Gunston Hall is considered architecturally significant.

HABS/HAER/HALS documentation is usually in the form of measured drawings, photographs, and written data. While the criteria in this section have addressed only these media, documentation need not be limited to them. Other media, such as films of industrial processes, can be—and have been—used to document historic buildings, sites, structures, objects and landscapes. If other media are to be used, the HABS/HAER/HALS office should be contacted before recording.

The selection of the appropriate documentation level will vary from one project to the next. For mitigation documentation projects, this level will be selected by the National Park Service Regional Office and communicated to the agency responsible for completing the documentation. Generally, Level I documentation is required for nationally significant buildings and structures, defined as National Historic Landmarks and the primary historic units of the National Park Service.

On occasion, factors other than significance will dictate the selection of another level of documentation. For example, if a rehabilitation of a property is planned, the owner may wish to have a full set of as-built drawings, even though the property may not merit Level I documentation.

HABS Level I measured drawings usually depict existing conditions through the use of a site plan, floor plans, elevations, sections and construction details. HAER Level I measured drawings will frequently depict original conditions where adequate historical material exists, so as to illustrate manufacturing or engineering processes.

Level II documentation differs from Level I by substituting copies of existing drawings, either original or alteration drawings, for recently executed measured drawings. If this is done, the drawings must meet HABS/HAER/HALS requirements outlined below and be free of copyrights. While existing drawings are rarely as suitable as as-built drawings, they are adequate in many cases for documentation purposes. Only when the desirability of having as-built drawings is clear are Level I measured drawings required in addition to existing drawings. If existing drawings are housed and preserved in an accessible archival collection, their reproduction for HABS/HAER/HALS may not be necessary. In other cases, Level I measured drawings are required in the absence of existing drawings.

Level III documentation requires a sketch plan if it helps to explain the structure, site, or landscape. A short historical report should supplement the photographs by explaining what is not readily visible.

The HABS/HAER/HALS office reserves the right to refuse documentation that does not meet these requirements for content.

Quality

Standard: *Documentation shall be prepared accurately from reliable sources with limitations clearly stated to permit independent verification of the information.*

Guideline: *Documentation shall meet the following requirements for quality:*

A. Measured drawings: Measured drawings shall be produced from recorded, accurate measurements. Portions of the building that were not accessible for measurement should not be drawn on the measured drawings but clearly labeled as not accessible or drawn from available construction drawings and other sources. No part of the measured drawings shall be produced from hypothesis or non-measurement related activities. Level I measured drawings shall be accompanied by a set of field notebooks in which the measurements were first recorded. Other drawings prepared for Levels II and III shall include a statement describing where the original drawings are located.

B. Large-format photographs: Large-format photographs shall clearly depict the appearance of the property and areas of significance of the recorded building, site, structure, object or landscape. Each view shall be perspective-corrected and fully captioned.

C. Written data: Written history and description for Levels I and II shall be based on primary sources to the greatest extent possible. For Level III, secondary sources may provide adequate information; if not, primary research will be necessary. A frank assessment of the reliability and limitations of the sources shall be included. Within the written history, statements shall be footnoted as to their sources, where appropriate. The written data shall include a methodology section specifying the name of the researcher, date of research, sources consulted, and the limitations of the project.

COMMENTARY

The quality of architectural documentation cannot be easily prescribed or quantified, but it derives from a process in which thoroughness of research and factual accuracy play a large part, and it acts, for better or worse, as a measure of the integrity and reliability of the information. HABS/HAER/HALS promotes documentation of the highest quality and the principle of independent verification of all factual information.

The HABS/HAER/HALS office reserves the right to refuse documentation that does not meet these requirements for quality.

Materials

Standard: *Documentation shall be prepared on materials that are readily reproducible, durable and in standard sizes.*

Guideline: *The following material requirements shall be met for all levels of documentation:*

A. Measured drawings

Readily Reproducible: Ink on translucent material, such as Mylar

Durable: Ink on archival media

Standard Sizes: Three sizes: 19″ ×24″, 24″ × 36″ or 34″ × 44″

B. Large-Format Black & White Photographs

Readily Reproducible: One print per negative

Durable: Photography processed and stored according to archival standards; negatives on safety film only; prints on fiber paper, such as AZO paper; no resin-coated paper

Standard Sizes: Three sizes: 4″ × 5″, 5″ × 7″ or 8″ × 10″

C. Large-Format Color Transparencies

Readily Reproducible: One identical black & white negative and print per color transparency; one duplicate transparency and electrostatic or laser copy per color transparency

Durable: Photography processed and stored according to archival standards

Standard Sizes: Three sizes: 4″ × 5″, 5″ × 7″ or 8″ × 10″

D. Written History and Description

Readily Reproducible: Clean copy for photocopying

Durable: Archival bond

Standard Sizes: 8½″ × 11″

E. Field Records

Readily Reproducible: Field notebooks may be photocopied. Photo identification sheet shall accompany 35 mm negatives and contact sheets.

Durable: No requirements.

Standard Sizes: Only requirement is that materials can be made to fit into a 9½″ × 12″ archival file folder.

COMMENTARY

All HABS/HAER/HALS materials are intended for reproduction. Some 20,000 records are reproduced each year by the Library of Congress. Although field records are not generally reproduced, they are intended to serve as supplements to the formal documentation. The basic durability performance standard (that is to say, life expectancy) for HABS/HAER/HALS materials is 500 years. Ink on Mylar is believed to meet this standard, while color photography does not (although color transparencies are acceptable, their life expectancy is considerably shorter—50 years or less). Field records do not meet this standard but are maintained in the HABS/HAER/HALS collections as a courtesy to collections patrons.

The HABS/HAER/HALS office reserves the right to refuse documentation that does not meet these requirements for materials.

Presentation

Standard: *Documentation shall be clearly and concisely produced.*

Guideline: The following requirements for presentation shall be met for all levels of documentation:

A. Measured Drawings: Level I measured drawings shall be lettered mechanically (i.e., CAD, Leroy or similar) or in a hand-printed equivalent style. Adequate dimensions shall be included on all sheets. Level III sketch plans should be neat and orderly.

B. Large-format photographs: Level I photographs shall include duplicate photographs that include a scale. Level II and III photographs shall include, at a minimum, at least one photograph with a scale, usually of the principal facade.

C. Written history and description: Data shall be typewritten or laser printed on bond, following accepted rules of grammar.

COMMENTARY

The HABS/HAER/HALS office reserves the right to refuse documentation that does not meet these requirements for presentation.

ARCHITECTURAL AND ENGINEERING DOCUMENTATION PREPARED FOR OTHER PURPOSES

Where a preservation planning process is initiated, architectural and engineering documentation, like other treatment activities, is undertaken to achieve the goals identified by that process. Documentation is deliberately selected as a treatment for properties evaluated as significant, and the development of the documentation program for a property follows from the planning objectives. Documentation efforts focus on the significant characteristics of the historic subject, as defined in the previously completed evaluation. The selection of a level of documentation techniques (measured drawings, photography, etc.) is based on the significance of the subject and the management needs for which the documentation is being performed. For example, the kind and level of documentation required to record a historic property for easement purposes may be less detailed than the kind and level required as mitigation prior to destruction of the property. In the former case, essential documentation might be limited to portions of the property controlled by the easement (exterior facades, for example), while in the latter case, significant interior architectural features and non-visible structural details would also be documented.

HABS/HAER/HALS encourages other archives to use the Secretary of the Interior's Standards and related HABS/HAER/HALS guidelines as a basis for their own documentation guidelines. Levels of documentation and the durability and sizes of the items may vary depending on the intended use of the materials and various storage and preservation considerations. Review of documentary sources and the periodic verification of factual information in the documentation are among the best means of assuring quality. The reliability of the documentation is only strengthened by an accounting of the limitations of the research and physical examination of the property, and by retaining the primary data (field measurements and notebooks) from which the archival record was produced. The long-term usefulness of the documentation is directly related the quality and durability of the materials (ink, paper, film, etc.) used to record the historic resource.

APPENDIX B

Addresses of HABS/HAER/HALS and Related Organizations

Historic American Buildings Survey/Historic American Engineering
    Record/Historic American Landscapes Survey
U.S. Department of the Interior
National Park Service
1849 C Street NW (2270)
Washington, DC 20240-0001
202-354-2159
http://www.cr.nps.gov/habshaer/

National Historic Landmarks Program (2280)
    202-354-2216
    http://www.cr.nps.gov/nhl/
National Register of Historic Places (2280)
    202-354-2213 or 202-354-2210
    http://www.cr.nps.gov/nr/
    (same address as HABS/HAER/HALS)

The American Institute of Architects
    1735 New York Avenue, NW
    Washington, DC 20006
    800-AIA-3837
    202-626-7300
    http://www.aia.org

American Society of Civil Engineers
    1801 Alexander Bell Drive
    Reston, VA 20191
    800-548-2723
    703-295-6200
    http://www.asce.org

The American Society of Mechanical Engineers
    3 Park Avenue
    New York, NY 10016-5990
    800-843-2763
    212-591-7722
    http://www.asme.org

Institute of Electrical and Electronics Engineers
    3 Park Avenue, 17th Floor
    New York, New York 10016-5997
    212-419-7900
    http://www.ieee.org

American Society of Landscape Architects
    636 I Street, NW
    Washington, DC 20001-3736
    202-898-2444
    http://www.asla.org

Society of Architectural Historians
    1365 North Astor Street
    Chicago, Illinois 60610
    312-573-1365
    http://www.sah.org

Society for Industrial Archeology
    Department of Social Sciences
    Michigan Technological University
    1400 Townsend Drive
    Houghton, MI 49931-1295
    http://www.sia-web.org

HABS/HAER/HALS Collections
    Prints and Photographs Division
    Library of Congress
    101 Independence Ave, SE
    Washington, DC 20540
    202-707-6394
    http://memory.loc.gov/ammem/hhhtml/hhhome.html

INDEX

References to illustrations are in italics.

A

Academic study, as reason for documentation, 6
Acadia National Park, *273*
Accuracy, in HABS/HAER/HALS measured drawings, 118
Adirondack Iron and Steel Company, *137*
Adler, Dankmar, 184
Aerial photogrammetry, 115, *116*
Aerial views, *185*, *193*
   infrared, 86
   as research sources, 32, *38*
Aesthetics
   of Auditorium Building, 192–200
   in photography, 66–68, *68–70*
Agricultural structures
   Eisenhower Farm Two, *123*
   grain elevator, *10*
   Walker Family Farm, *15*
Air conditioning systems. *See* Mechanical systems
Alabama, 206–215, *208–209*, *210*, *212–214*, *216–218*
Alaska
   Kennecott Mine, 230, *234–236*
   through-truss bridge, *71*
Alteration drawings, 92
Alterations, structural clues to, 33, *40*
American Brass Company, *7*
American Institute of Architects (AIA), 19
American Institute of Mining, Metallurgical, and Petroleum Engineers, 19
American Memory—Historical Collections for the National Digital Library, 25
American Society of Civil Engineers (ASCE), 19
American Society of Landscape Architects (ASLA), 19, 270

American Society of Mechanical Engineers, 19
Analytical photogrammetry, 115, *116*
Appleton's Cyclopaedia of Applied Mechanics, 42
Aqueducts. *See* Delaware Aqueduct
Architectural documentation, definition of, 2
Architectural drawings. *See* Drawings
Architectural photogrammetry, 109–115
   See also Photogrammetry
Architectural photography, principles of, 59–68
Architectural records, 32
Architectural scales, 119
Architectural style, categorization of, 42
Archival stability
   of color photographs, 55–57
   of copies, 33
   digital technologies and, 20
   of measured drawings, 89
   of photographs, 55, 75
Archiving
   of large-format color transparencies, 12
   of negatives, 12, 82, *83*
   of photographs, 12, 75, 82, *83*
   of written records, 13
Arkansas, Maurice Bathhouse, *53*
Armory, Eli Whitney, *35*
Army barracks, 94, *95*
Arney's Mount, *148*
As-built drawings, 88, 92
Ashhurst, 254, *258*
Attics
   of Auditorium Building, *194*
   plans of, 122, *128*
   as structural information sources, 33
Auditorium Building, 184–205, *185–191*, *193–198*, *200–205*
AutoCAD, 199, 226
   polar array command, *228*
Avery Index to Architectural Periodicals, 32

Axonometric drawings, *46–47*, *126*, *268*
   bridge, *12*
   house, *89*
   state capitol, *138*

B

Babson, Seth, *36–37*
Balloon frame house, drawings of, 89, *89*
Balustrade, *65*
Banquet camera, 74
Banquet hall, 192–198, *197*
Bascules, 173–182, *177–183*
Basements
   of Auditorium Building, *193*, *201*
   plans of, 122
   as structural information sources, 33
Battle Creek hydroelectric project, powerhouse generator, *76*
Beauregard House, *128*
Ben Thresher's Mill, *91*, *131*
Bethlehem Steel press, *7*
Biallas, Randall J., 18
Bird's-eye views. *See* Aerial views
Black-and-white photography, 55
   lighting for, 60
   selection of, 70–72
Bollman Bridge, 163, 167–168, *169–171*
Borough House, *62–63*
Botanical nomenclature, *253*
   standardized, 254, 259
Boucher, Jack E., *57*, 66–68, 75
   equipment, *71*
   shooting log, *81*
Bowstring truss bridge, *45*, 159, *159–160*
Bridges, *39*, 158–183
   Bollman Bridge, 163, 167–168, *169–171*
   Delaware Aqueduct, *12*, *124*, 158, *161*, 170–171, *173*
   documentation of, 164–182
   Eldean Bridge, 166–167, *167*
   McKee Street Bridge, 171, *174–176*
   photographing, 59

   pin connections, *132*
   reading, 163
   Reading-Halls Station Bridge, *79*
   resources on, *41*, 42
   selection of, for recording, 164, 166
   through-truss, *71*
   types of, 163
   Whipple's, *45*, 159, *159–160*
   Willamette River bridges, 173–182, *177–183*
Broadway Bridge, 177–179, *181–183*
Bronx River Parkway, *9*
Buckingham Meeting House, *149–150*
Buckland, William, *90*
Builder's mini rod, *107*
Building permits, 29–30
Built in America Web site, 25
Bungalows, photographing, 59, *60*

C

CAD/photogrammetry, 21, 115, 227–233
Caleb Pusey House, *24*
California
   Battle Creek hydroelectric project, powerhouse generator, *76*
   City of Paris Dry Goods Company, *16*
   Leland Stanford House, *36–37*
   Scotty's Castle, *33*
Caln Meeting House, *144*
Cambria Iron Works, *38*
Cameras
   monorail, large-format, *57*, 57–59
   photogrammetric, 227–229, *228–229*
   types of, 57–59, 74
Capitols
   Maryland, *138*
   Texas, *6*
Caption list, 82
Cast-iron bridges, 163
Ceiling plan, *202*
Chain of title, 29
Charles E. Peterson Prize, 15, *22–23*
Chicago Stock Exchange, *61*
Chichester Meeting House, *145*, *152*
City directories, as research sources, 30, *32*